HAMISH'S GROATS END WALK

BY THE SAME AUTHOR:

HAMISH'S MOUNTAIN WALK
The First Traverse of all the Scottish
Munros in One Journey

HAMISH'S
GROATS END WALK

One man and his dog on a hill route through
Britain & Ireland

by

HAMISH M. BROWN

LONDON
VICTOR GOLLANCZ LTD
1981

ISBN 0 575 03029 1

Printed in Great Britain at
The Camelot Press Ltd, Southampton

For the friends of the storm
and for Storm, the best
of friends

O happy draught of solitude! Free from the pub-babel of life, from its smoky pokeyness and its bottled hours of toil, I am suddenly drunk with joy, skipping down a pavement of moss, under lit lines of stars, deafened by the heart-rhythm of silence. No one bids me this or that. I can toast the world so easily – when out of it. Cheers! And a hill road tomorrow.

Stand ye in the ways, and see, and ask for the old paths, where is the good way, and walk therein, and ye shall find rest for your souls.

Jeremiah 6:16

"That's Hamish Brown, he's just spent the last six months walking from John o' Groats to Land's End."

"Eh, he can't be much of a walker if he's taken all that time about it."

Overheard in Sheffield

The
Groats
End
Walk

Route
&
Chapter
Outline

CONTENTS

LIST OF ILLUSTRATIONS

The bleak summit of Britain: Hamish, Ray and Storm on top of Ben Nevis

Looking back along the old military road to Fort William while walking the Lairig Mor to Kinlochleven

The Blackmount Hills on the west of Rannoch Moor: Ray and Hamish walked round the far side on the old military road

Bog-wood: a common sight on decaying peat bog like Rannoch Moor

The octagonal church at Dalmally

On Loch Ard at the start of the canoe trip

following page 110

Camp by the Forth somewhere in Flanders Moss

The Forth bridges (*photo Aerofilms Ltd*)

Abbotsford: home of Sir Walter Scott by the River Tweed (*photo D. C. Thompson & Co. Ltd*)

The Tweed Valley: Hamish, with Lee Pen above

Cessford Castle, an old border keep now stark and ruinous

The Waterloo Monument on Peniel Hill – like a lost lighthouse

On the Eildon Hills above Melrose

A Cheviot shelter: Storm looking out from the railway waggon that gave us a good howff

Hadrian's Wall on Walltown Crags, Northumberland (*photo Janet & Colin Bord*)

Greg's Hut on Cross Fell

Lunch above Horton-in-Ribblesdale

Pennine Way crosses Motorway (the M62)!

Pennine bog: the slats put down are vanishing, and overhead a TV mast

High Force: the finest waterfall encountered on the Pennine Way

The iron fountain in Middleton-in-Teesdale

Skiddaw

Lingmell, Scafell Pike and Scafell – below is the head of Wastwater (*photo John Cleare*)

following page 142

Dufton: peaceful, despite being on the Pennine Way

Whernside from Old Ing

Horton Church and Penyghent

LIST OF MAPS

MAP SYMBOLS

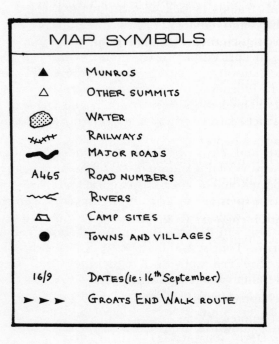

▲	Munros
△	Other summits
	Water
✗✗✗	Railways
～	Major roads
A465	Road numbers
～～	Rivers
⌂	Camp sites
●	Towns and villages
16/9	Dates (ie: 16th September)
▶ ▶ ▶	Groats End Walk route

ACKNOWLEDGEMENTS

As with any long solitary venture much help came from other people; perhaps most from my mother at home. My brother David delivered the canoe and helped behind the scenes; Charles Knowles, Ann Roberts and Margaret Griffith made their homes available for the hectic interludes and Ray Swinburn cheered many miles of the way. Braes o' Fife Mountaineering Club friends helped with the main packing, and various hotels, post offices and remote homes like the Duncans' on Loch Monar looked after parcels en route. Ultimate Equipment, Blacks of Greenock and Nevisport of Fort William made major equipment contributions, while Pedigree Petfoods Ltd ensured Storm enjoyed his daily *Frolic*. My log-books of the journey were reworked in several countries and quite a gang of typists helped to piece it together, and Debu Bose, Graham Elson and Michael Teal ferried proofs to and from Morocco – my thanks to them all.

Roger Smith and *The Great Outdoors* provided photographic help which eased the work of illustration. Kodak film was used exclusively and the cover is from a Kodachrome transparency. I received much help with the checking or provision of facts and figures and with tracing other illustrations from Gordon Adam, Aerofilms Ltd, The Alpine Club, John Bartholomew Ltd, Jim Barton, Dennis Beard, Bord Fáilte, Janet and Colin Bord, British Tourist Authority, R. W. Clark, John Cleare/Mountain Camera, The Fell and Rock Climbing Club, George Fisher (Keswick), Alec Gillespie, Jack Goff, Dennis Gray, Harry Griffin, Joss Lynam, Ronnie McOwen, Dr Mirrey, Charmian and Bill Pollok, E. C. Pyatt, Roger Smith, N. Shuttleworth, The Scottish Mountaineering Club, Snowdon Mountain Railway Ltd, Showell Styles, the Superintendent of the Edinburgh Meteorological Office, D. C. Thompson & Co and Walt Unsworth. I am grateful to the following for longer quotations: Dervla Murphy and John Murray Ltd for use of *Full Tilt*; J. H. B. Peel and David and Charles Ltd for *Along the Pennine Way*; Joseph Jacobs and Dover Publications Inc. for *Celtic Fairy Tales* and Roy Ferguson for his evocative poem. Lastly I would like to thank Livia Gollancz who has chased this book along and, knowing the mountains herself, has patiently borne with my wanderings.

H. B.

I

PICKING UP THE THREADS

"Life seems to me to consist of three parts: the absorbing and usually enjoyable present which rushes on from minute to minute with fatal speed; the future, dim and uncertain, for which one can make any number of interesting plans, the wilder and more improbable the better, since – as nothing will turn out as you expect it to – you might as well have the fun of planning anyway; and thirdly, the past, the memories and realities that are the bedrock of one's present life. . . ."

AGATHA CHRISTIE: *Autobiography*

MY STUDY-BEDROOM walls have slowly vanished under the spread of books, maps, pictures, postcards and souvenirs from many lands (an effective aid in drifting off to pleasant dreams), but the map-board by the door can prove stimulating. It was looking at the many potential ploys marked on it which one night suddenly gave me the idea of linking some of them together. From this conception the *Groats End Walk* was to be born.

I have had a life-long addiction to heading off into the wilds, which was well-satisfied with Braehead School expeditions for over a decade, with concurrent ploys in the Alps, Scandinavia and Morocco. In historic Alpine terms I was never a *centrist* nor could there ever be a *last* blue mountain. When Braehead closed and I grew chill in the shades of a bureaucratic prison house, the vision impelled me out and on for the continuous walk over the Munros. That story was told and my motives analysed in *Hamish's Mountain Walk* but now, some years on, I am simply grateful I put feet to the dream then. I could probably not do it now. Pooh-sticks are not retrievable but the game can be continued, with different twigs perhaps, off different bridges, into waters which by their very nature are new each second before they pass for ever. Since the Munro trip I have wandered from the Arctic to the Atlas and even to the Himalayan sanctuary of Nanda Devi. I have tasted sweet success and bitter failure. The dreamer has no illusions as to his mediocre status, but the sweet sugaring of new adventures still cannot be resisted.

Perhaps the Munro trip gave me my ultimate challenge, with

everything, *Dei gratia*, combining into joyous success. I was not trying to 'prove' anything then or, if I was, it was unconsciously to myself. Once as a youngster I set off to walk until I collapsed, out of curiosity and to find the measure of myself, so there was nothing to prove, just a naturally fine challenge to tackle. The word 'challenge' sounds rather presumptuous for something done for pleasure. The *Groats End Walk* would more truly answer to the term 'provocation'! It was T. E. Lawrence who pointed out the danger of those who dream by day. My map-board has much to answer for.

Circumstances ensured I did not over-plan this Walk, for which I am thankful. It is all too easy to destroy essential spontaneity and if a plan is rigid then it risks being broken when the waves of circumstance smash on to it. One grafts a philosophical detachment on to a hard head, to mix the metaphors! Being greedy for mountain and outdoor experiences of all kinds no doubt ensures I do not excel at any one. To walk and walk and walk, exclusively, would strike me as being a squandering of precious time. A Walk, on the scale to earn a capital W, is an extravagance I can afford only occasionally. What a glorious self-indulgence it is then! Any expedition plan must be flexible. It can only give the outline at best, a sort of laying out of arteries, the setting of chess men on their squares. Once battle begins who knows which veins will be wounded, or where the king's bishop's pawn will be after thirty moves? Plans must be made firmly and carefully, but never finally. There must always be room to manoeuvre. Swift, efficient change is the real test of any plan. Luke's Gospel has Christ telling related parables about 'counting the cost': if you build a tower you first sit down and prepare an estimate in case you end with a folly; if you go to war you calculate your chances of victory and deal with the enemy accordingly. The same thought goes into any journey, or any demanding activity (Christ was talking about the toughness of following him). For the hike over all the Munros I perhaps overdid the preparation, but I was still aware of its need for the *Groats End Walk*. It was rather a rush, and done piecemeal, sometimes along the way, but it was done. There has to be a safe balance between simplicity and spontaneity and the constrictions of over-organising. The happy medium is seldom a clear straight route and its signs are often overgrown in the hedgerows, not blazed in blue along some motorway.

Walking is not absolutely vital to me. I have shocked friends before now by saying I could happily do without it if I had to. I sometimes do for several weeks as it is. I never train for any ploy. Some reaches of this trip I expected to be duller than usual, which they were. If not resented, they were *tholled*, because of the whole which was, after all, a once-only venture, a 'special case' to use the political cliché. The end of the trip will illustrate this when you come to read it. In the Smiddy hut-book there is one entry I rather like. It says something like: 'I am not going to climb all 280 dull Munros, I am just going to climb superlative An Teallach 280 times.' Youth may squander jewelled time, middle age sees it ticking away faster and faster and therefore wants to experience only the best. We all die empty-handed. It is the soul's store that matters.

Often people say I am lucky to live the life I do – as if it were one long holiday – but the only luck, possibly, was in having the parents I had. A child accepts so much, trusts so much and as a result can be so easily broken. My parents were marvellously, wondrously matched and in a world of decaying morals and standards showed the virtues to be the rocks they are. As an erratic teenager such steadfastness could be annoying but, again and again, they kept their cool, gave me freedom, welcomed me back, encouraged, waited. . . . Yes, I reckon I am lucky, for this background blessing was none of my doing or choosing. The luck others see, and even envy, in my way of life, is a different matter. It does not exist, or only a blind fool would give it any credence. Luck is only a word used by someone who carries a rabbit's foot in his pocket!

Climbing big mountains or enduring a long expedition is nothing special or magical. I despair when I see youngsters (with almost mystical zeal) set to become 'Instructors'. The reality is often a shock. Life is not all cloud-walking. There is a great deal of bog to slog through in any profession (the aspiring general may begin his army career investigating a fiddle in the cookhouse). I hope this book gives a true, rounded picture of what is entailed in any venture, without too much repetition. Life *is* mostly repetitive. The renewal we gain from escaping to the hills does not rely purely on novelty. Anything repeated is no longer novel yet all the happiest hill-men I know are old men who have enjoyed a lifetime of hills. Bach, the baker and the budding Bonington are all equal in God's eyes, their work equally valid and valued. God has given us 'all things richly to enjoy', we in turn are asked to 'do all to the glory of God.'

In a story like this there has to be some of the childish essay-repetition of 'we got up – we got up – we got up' because that is just what happens. Romance is probably most absent at five o'clock on a wet morning, but a surfeit of spectacular sunrises would be as nasty as a diet of nothing but gorgonzola and champagne. A walk like this has only an illusion of freedom. It was a hard discipline but its modified independence was the price, the sacrifice, one pays for any desirable objective. We can never be free (whatever that means). We can enjoy reasonable freedom.

I am often in hot water because I will not take this game of ours seriously. The most obviously facetious comments will be taken literally by someone. But I believe we must take it in fun, for fun; it has no other justification, even for our guilded outdoor writers and all the hangers-on who make their pennies out of it. It should be fun, too, *at the time*, and that is another reason older folk are choosy about their hill-doings: the investment must have a high yield in fun and enrichment. At times I can be thoroughly depressed – usually by nasty rain – but will plod on dourly, simply because it cannot last long and even the best of plans cannot always run smoothly. One must be as tenacious as rowan roots among the rocks.

An ability to enjoy the ridiculous is an asset, again, at the time if possible, though sometimes equilibrium has to be regained first. Nature is quite as capable as man in springing surprises. Sometimes, perhaps, it would do all of us no harm to analyse our hill methods purposely, with the intention of breaking our ingrained traditions. When did *you* last do something personally unconventional? 'Unorthodoxy nearly always brings rewards out of all proportion to the effort involved' (Campbell Steven). I remember once, after a lecture on the Munro trip, an old man stood up and questioned my having done the expedition basically solo: "In forty years of going on the hills I have never gone alone" he admonished. I hadn't the heart to voice my reaction: "What marvels you must have missed, sir!"

The only justification for such a journey is in its clean, clear joy. We go to the hills for fun; whatever other personal reasons may underlie that enveloping word, and one of my concerns from the Walk is that I see some of the fun being taken out of our hill game – by interfering busybodies, however well-meaning, by the planners and bureaucrats who believe we are all incapable of doing anything unless it is organised for us, by commercial interests and rapacious gear manufacturers and retailers who will yet price us off the hill, by the educationists offering their synthetic lollipops. It is an alarming picture. We may yet be protected out of our own. Nor do I find some of our protectionist bodies encouraging. Extreme conservationists are as blind as all others who lash out in excess. Truth seldom lies in extremes, which is not to say it lies in acquiescence or indifference. The best has to be worked for, perhaps fought for; it is not the gift of a benevolent welfare state which merely, by some quirk of social mathematics, yields the lowest common denominator. We look for more than that when we sling a rucksack on our back.

I would not do this trip again, much as I enjoyed it as a celebration of the advent of middle age. Too much had to be done *en passant* as miles and time fought it out. It was too indiscriminatory a route, binding one to a narrow line when so many willy-wispy interests lay close but unattainable to one on foot. The hilly parts were all joy, but there was too much plain rural. Put it this way: why walk the fields of settled Somerset when one could walk the singing solitudes round Suilven?

Happily it is a far road and rough to Suilven, but even in England or Wales, as soon as I left the beaten track, I hardly met anyone. There is a deal of magnificent wild country in Wales, no matter how lapped it is by the millions of England. Basically ninety per cent of tourists never go more than half a mile from a car. This Walk quite consciously was a breaking-out from that encapsuled existence.

Collie, the great pioneer climber and chemist, in an address to the Cairngorm Club when he was eighty, said, "There is an enchantment hidden away amongst the lonely expanses of the wilds." The wilderness is so fragile however and can be damaged both physically and by our insensitive vision. Dervla Murphy, in *Full Tilt*, her tale of cycling to the Himalayas, flew with her cycle from Rawalpindi to Gilgit. She wrote, "When we passed 26,000 foot Nanga Parbat I suddenly became acutely aware that this was the wrong approach to a noble range. One should *win* the privilege of such a scene, and because I had done nothing to earn these beauties I felt that I was cheating and that this nasty, noisy little impertinence, mechanically transporting me, was an insult to the mountains. The more I see of unmechanised places and people the more convinced I become that machines have done incalculable damage by unbalancing the relationship between Man and Nature. The mere fact that we think and talk as we do about Nature is symptomatic . . . we've removed ourselves from it."

It was the Scot, John Muir, who began the fight to preserve the contact with nature in America. "When we try to pick out anything by itself, we find it hitched to everything else in the universe," he warned. I feel we are now rushing into what we do not fully understand, blatantly willing an inheritance of unknown dangers and desolation to our children. By chance, and only occasionally feeling some regret, I am a bachelor. (Someone once suggested a bachelor was 'a man who had not thought about marriage' only to receive the retort: 'No, a bachelor is someone who *has* thought about marriage.') With the way the world bends I am now rather thinking I have the best of it. I do not have to look at children of my own and ask what I am passing on to them. . . . Sometimes I grow weary. Why should I fight when those who have such responsibilities seem to sleep?

It feels as if we have sailed spacecraft Earth too near some mental and spiritual *Black Hole* and unlike *Star Trek* and *Dr Who* there may not be a way out – which is why it is alarming. The arrogance of fallible man is appalling. It is no longer bows and arrows where a mistake may kill a man, or cannons where a score may suffer, Hiroshima set a scale which in itself is now only trifling compared to present possibilities. We are talking about the survival of a world. The pattern is akin to the almost comic board-room joke about a million-dollar business being dealt with in seconds and then two hours going in arguing whether to raise the price of canteen coffee by a few cents. We cannot grasp the scale of potential disaster, so we dismiss it from our minds. Scientists are morally and in other ways as errant and silly as the rest of us, yet we leave them to their games, whether they understand the consequences or not. The world busies itself with trifles while the big business slips through almost unnoticed. In the week following the end of the *Groats End Walk* this was brought home to me – and I hope to many others. Call it alarmist if you dare.

Firstly, there was near disaster from a nuclear power-station leak, the radio-active material just stopping short of a major river; secondly, a train was derailed and in the fire that followed there was a risk of a tanker of chlorine exploding, so 250,000 people (that's the population of say Dundee or Newcastle) were evacuated; thirdly, a computer error gave a nuclear attack warning and bombers were made airborne and so on before the mistake was discovered. All that in one week, in the country which is supposedly the most technologically advanced and safe.

Much travelling and much reading gives one a healthy scepticism for the bland promises of the future. The scientists predict a better world. On what evidence? The human heart does not change and be it basically evil or good, it constantly fails. Man has always lived on the edge of a precipice. Our only progress is that we now have ability not only to knock one another over the edge but to blow up the precipice as well.

Faith and scepticism are like two sides of a coin: they can never meet, but are never far apart. We cannot release goodness – like some fragrance from garden grown flowers – by cultivation. Experience surely shows the fallacy of believing we can outgrow our deficiencies by wishing it so. The Gulags, the Bamboo Curtains, the Ayatollahs and the Amins have tortured, enslaved and murdered more people in our world, at peace, than perished in the bombed cities and concentration camps of the last war. So if we take to the hills in a growing escapism, this is itself a sad reflection of the civilization we build. Among the first 281 members of the Alpine Club only ten perhaps could be called countrymen, so even in those days they were urban slaves seeking escape and, though social and economic changes have occurred since, mountains have basically remained escapism. This is nothing to be ashamed of, or to apologise for. Thank God for it rather – and that it is so freely and easily available in this green land.

If a porcelain is old enough and rare enough a slight flaw will hardly alter its value, far less its beauty. Our landscape is like that. It is usually flawed. We simply turn the chip on the vase to the wall and forget the imperfection. But if the vase teeters on its pedestal and looks like falling, to ignore it is culpable. My walk through these islands makes me very pessimistic about our future. What indeed 'if this present were the world's last night?' (Donne).

If this is pessimistic, then so be it; better have it all out in this chapter, for the day to day doings generally delighted. How could they not? We still have so much. An aspect of continuing pleasure I once mentioned in an article in the 1975 Scottish Mountaineering Club Journal. It is only available on a big trip: "Marvellous peace to lie at dawn listening to a deer browsing, or the sandpiper call, to sup breakfast in bed and be off in the gold of day. The sweep of days nested in the sweep of the seasons. Snow fell and snows vanished away. Purple saxifrage flowered at the start and purple heather at the end. The arrivals of April. The clarion chorus of May. The speckled calves of June. The last calling cuckoos of July. What is time? What is truth? Can we know reality recrudescent?"

In this book I have tried to keep the form of its predecessor, *Hamish's Mountain Walk*, a day to day diary, but the material has had to be drastically pruned, for I covered twice the time and distance. It is bound to be uneven, but this in itself reflects the trip: there were ups and downs, days of interest and days of plodding, days of sun and days of storm – a shifting scene, the variations of which cannot be forced into an even flow of narrative. I hope I give the feel of the walk in general as well as starting (and following) all manner of hares, for this is how it was. Much of my youth was spent in tiny Clackmannanshire which had the admonitory motto, 'Look Aboot Ye'. This book if you like is my continuing response to that irrepressible urge.

In reality my comments are more restrained than are those of most travellers for my view was always restricted to a narrow ribbon of country. Too much should not be judged from too little. I have perhaps expanded a bit on the 3,000ers, the 'Munros' *furth of Scotland*, so that these can supplement the Munros described in *Hamish's Mountain Walk*. As I have climbed all the Irish 3,000ers many more times than I have all the Scottish ones, I have a knowledge of them unusual for an outsider. It would be inappropriate, and impracticable, to attempt a similarly detailed look at Lakeland or Snowdonia. There are thousands of books on those areas.

I have given far fewer statistics in this book for there was, first, little novelty in walking from John o' Groats to Land's End and, second, I used so many differing maps it was not always easy to keep an accurate tally. The only maps I used throughout, for wider interest, were the Bartholomew 1:100,000. Much of the original planning was done on them. For many areas, where I envisaged no return, I had purchased One Inch O.S. maps before they vanished from the market. This was a mistake, for they were often inconveniently out-of-date. It is worth having the most recent 1:50,000 maps and for much of the wilder parts of Scotland it is essential. Something like 70 maps were used for the 2,500 miles that I covered (Storm, my dog, probably covered twice that distance!). Not counting the periods working at Kinghorn, Sheffield, Ruthin, Dublin and other halts such as Kintail, we walked for 146 days which makes a leisurely daily average of 17 miles. There were only 250,000 feet of ascent (1,700 a day) – about half of the Munro trip total in twice the time. This was a linear route basically. The only unit of measure that matters on a long walk is time: one plans on a day-to-day basis and the miles and feet must fit in with that. I like the system on the continent where times rather than kilometres are given on signs to huts and hills. I have kept to feet and miles though many of my maps were in metric form.

I have tried to be accurate with information, spellings, heights, etc. but often maps and the reference books themselves have differed. Bear with me if I use the 'wrong' variant! Generally I have followed Ordnance Survey usage, whatever its shortcomings, for their maps are what we all have in common and few countries anywhere have better maps than ours. You'll find that out if you travel the Irish Munros.

If a disproportionate allocation of this book seems given to Scotland, then that is fair: a third of my time was spent there and in simply walking it from end to end, on a modified programme, I climbed more 3,000ers than in the other three countries combined – and that was all of theirs. As nothing else could have done, this trip banged home the geographical qualities of the various parts of Britain. My heart's in the Highlands – with no apologies. Recently, when asked why I had never climbed at Harrison's I apparently replied, "Why should I, when I can climb in Torridon?" But, having seen Harrison's, and a great deal besides, all with enjoyment, I would still choose Torridon. This is not bias. It is my blessed inheritance, a combination of heredity, geography and other things leaving me within easier reach of Torridon than of Harrison's. Which would you choose after all?

Several times I will refer to Braehead doings. Braehead was a school in Fife where I spent many years taking the boys and girls ski-ing, climbing, canoe-ing, trekking and so on. It was the first such full-time appointment in a state school and, with hindsight, I wish I had written more then or immediately after, for I have many reservations about the way 'Outdoor Education' has developed. (At colleges of education and the like I am seldom asked to lecture *twice*!)

Above all theoretical and practical educational issues, we were dealing with people, individuals who mattered, who deserved respect, who deserved self-respect. Some freedoms they found on the hills. (Didn't our headmaster, R. F. Mackenzie, call one of his books *Escape from the Classroom?*) So the memories are of people and hills. Because they were young people with a young teacher on new adventures the memories have the freshness of all things new. Many of my Munros were first climbed with Braehead pupils. Braehead pupils climbed all the Munros in the end, climbed in the Alps, Norway and Morocco, climbed, not as led kids in identikit gangs, but as capable individuals. Naturally then, on any high hill, when remembering times past, the memories are of Braehead. You will do wrong if you sneer at such references – and people do – for in most cases, if I simply left out the word *Braehead*, you could not tell the age of the people involved in any anecdote. The only major fiascos we had on the hills were with adults, not pupils, fiascos caused by closed adult imagination and conceit. Perhaps that was one of the fundamental qualities of the school. We saw individuals. There was no 'simulated adventure' such as is served up all too often today.

Robert Louis Stevenson talked of "the bear's hug of custom squeezing the life out of a man's soul" – and took steps to escape the hazards of civilization and the disease of routine. Pete Boardman believes "it takes more endurance to work in a city than it does to climb a high mountain." The awful average! Just think of the poor cliché-burdened average man in the street, provided with all the benefits of conformity. He is an odd creature really. Whatever his height everyone else is taller, or smaller, whatever his wealth everyone else is richer, or poorer. He must be a complete nonentity. Everyone else is something or other (be it good or bad), he is nothing. Yet the world we live in is planned and operated to suit the average man. Wee Davy Livingstone worked from six in the morning till eight at night when he was ten. His first week's wages he blew on a Latin grammar. He became a doctor, set on becoming a missionary to China. I have a horrible feeling that had he lived today he would have been smothered by the system. Barry Sheene, talking to Michael Parkinson on TV declared: "When I left school I began to learn."

I did not regard the Walk as any self-denying ordnance. I made my peace long ago and do not believe in redemption from the hills anyway. That is Christ's prerogative. At the comfort of the flesh level I am not against hotel or bed and breakfast living. Such places are simply less efficient on a long walk. You are bound to their rules and convenience instead of your own. (Just try for an early breakfast or ask for some socks to be dried!) Electric lights, flush toilets, comfortable furniture and hot baths are all very well – but you pay a price for them. Sunshine is free on the other hand and rates are not charged on a tent. Comfort is an attitude of mind not an accumulation of goods. The more complex everyday living becomes the more easily it breaks down. Leisure is illusion if one slaves for it so hard that exhaustion prevents its enjoyment. How upside-down our values have become I realised from the most frequently asked questions on the Walk: "Were you not terribly lonely?" and "Were you not awfully bored?" Being *alone* seemed a terrifying idea. Conventional life is fear-dominated, which is atrophy to a questing spirit. Solitude is a singing glory and quite different from the cold pain of loneliness.

In a group someone is always last, keeping the rest waiting, wasting life's precious moments. With several lifetimes of group-activity and being responsible for others, I find these moments become increasingly frustrating. In odd ways I am too expert, too efficient. No one holds you back if you are alone. Going by yourself does away with a whole host of communal delays, decisions and annoyances. There is always one hundred per cent unanimity in a party of one.

I hope readers, be they walkers or not, can associate with our doings in a way impossible in books by superstars performing on super peaks – which are beyond the leg-dreams of all but a handful. This is a walk through *our* country, moreover, a splendid landscape, for all we have sinned against it, and I'm sure there will be agreements and disagreements a-plenty over what I write. By writing a book, too, we may preserve, rather like a fly in amber, this brief summer (which ranged from snow to snow), a record of how it was at the end of the trembling seventies, for God alone knows what the future holds out for us and the countryside we love.

It is high time we took to the trail.

"I could tell you my adventures – beginning from this morning," said Alice a little timidly: "but it's no use going back to yesterday, because I was a different person then."

"Explain all that," said the Mock Turtle.

"No, No! The adventures first," said the Gryphon in an important tone. . . .

II

THE NORTH COAST SNOWS

Still a child in a world of wonder,
Heir of the sky and the earth thereunder,
Colours and songs and seas and thunder.
                                W. K. HOLMES

Tuesday 1 May   NORTHWARDS AT LAST   *Map. p. 14*
There is an infinite relief in setting out for any major expedition. All the
pressures suddenly pop off, like the gas under the coffee pot. You just
pick up the rucksack and go – "free as the road, loose as the wind", as the
poet Herbert has it.

The train waits for no man, we believed, so we chased out the *Today*
television team and with the *Dundee Courier* reporter dashed to Kirkcaldy
station where the train was then twenty minutes late. As connections at
Perth and Inverness were only a quarter of an hour apart there was little
pause on travelling north, hardly time to allow the dog out to anoint the
nearest upright. (It is tempting to call this book *From Pillar to Post*.)
Vigorous snow showers splattered on the windows all the way north yet,
after Perth, the sun shone as well. The heating was full on to create the
peculiarly unpleasant British Rail atmosphere. In the Highlands one
feels they take the line that if they make travel sufficiently revolting
nobody will go by train and they can then shut down completely.

I busied myself with writing letters and, by Wick, had a pile of 38 to
post. I had brought ample food and drink. I was still only half free. It is a
long way to John o' Groats. The train from Inverness dawdled delightfully, as if its progress had to adjust to the quieter rhythms of the north.
It stole down to kiss the sea periodically, then scampered inland to hide
in the curtains of snow which blotted out valley and moor. The Strath of
Kildonan was full of deer, even beside the tiny stations, where perhaps
one person would climb down to join a Land Rover and vanish into the
gloaming. Odd how the lonelier the landscape the more pleasant the
train. Here everyone knows everyone, people are individuals not just
statistics on office files or scurrying ants in a city nest. During the
previous winter this line had caught some of the worst of the abnormal

blizzards and eventually the BBC news gave out the extraordinary information that British Rail had 'lost a train'.

The train had left one station and not arrived at the next: it had simply
been swallowed up by the snow on one of the great loops in the empty
Caithness hinterland – a picture of desolation and remoteness which the
urban millions simply could not envisage. An engine sent to investigate
was engulfed in turn. The nearest road was many miles away and nobody
could move for the storm, anyway. Several days later a man was dug out
of his car, alive, because he had cocooned himself in his sales' stock of
women's tights! They found their train. In one remote glen a wisp of
smoke was seen coming out of the snow and a helicopter landed to find a
house so completely buried that communication had to be by the
chimney. "Who's that out there?" the inmates called up. "This is the
Red Cross," they yelled down, only to be told, "Ach, go away! We gave
last week."

My letter-writing finished, I could sit and dream, watching the
landscape both whiten, with snow, and darken, with black-edged night,
yet it never quite turned fully dark: through the murk there was the
gentle feel of the lingering northern glow. The 'simmer dim' they call it
in Orkney. Wick is further north than Moscow after all.

The station was a great deserted barn with not even a sign to indicate
the exit, which proved to be a big sliding door. I fought it open and
stumbled out to the courtyard. The town lights glowed through what
G. W. Young called "scuddles" of sleet. It was more like Christmas than
May. The first week in May often gives a brief flurry of snow – 'the peewit
storms' – but this was ridiculous. A Volkswagen van, the same blue as my
own, drew up and offered me a lift up the A9 to Keiss. As that was nearer
John o' Groats than Wick, Storm and I jumped in. Keiss was a small
place, not a town, so we should be able just to pitch the tent somewhere
and perhaps start up the coast the next morning, free at last, even though
the landscape was a sort of crazy cross between Norfolk and the Arctic.

At Keiss however it was snowing hard. I stood in the road gasping in a
cut-throat wind and the bewildering swirl of large flakes, unable to see
more than a few yards. A yellow glow at least proclaimed a street lamp
and from it I could see the larger lights of a pub which, better still,
proved to be the Sinclair Bay Hotel where I was soon ensconced before
the fire with a pot of tea. I was smugly aware of the wild night of storm.
For the first of many times I had to explain my doings. Later, snug in
bed, I chuckled. Things were happening even before we reached the
starting line.

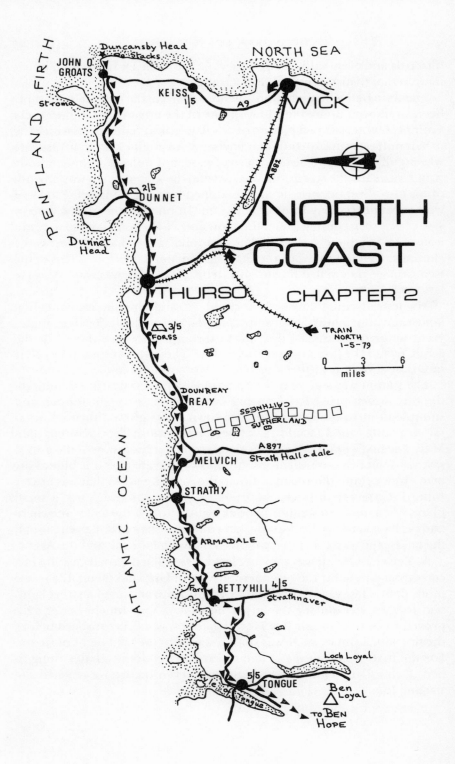

Wednesday 2 May   JOHN O' GROATS

The only other residents were an Australian couple who were as amazed by the snow as the locals were apologetic about it. 'Storm', the dog's name, was commented on, but it is what he came with. Later on in the trip there were times when I thought we might change it by deed poll to 'Monsoon'. Anything rather than his pedigree's 'Ellenlorn Spider's Web'.

I paced up and down the empty, snow-swept street, waiting for the local bus. Election notices on the wall I soon had by heart. Caithness regularly returns a Labour M.P., which one could almost gather from the varied messages being proclaimed. The bus stopped and started and slowly made northing. There was always a flurry of conversation whenever anyone entered or left, papers and parcels were delivered, children were taken to school. The landscape was undulating and still uncoloured by spring. The grey sea lay to the right with greyer curtains of cloud dimming the horizon. Freswick Bay appeared, site of a Viking settlement, then Warth Hill which has a large prehistoric burial cairn (*c.* 2,000 BC). We seemed to be pushing back into time itself.

Once over Warth Hill the Pentland Firth was suddenly visible – the north coast at last! Hoy and Stroma were laced with white as the Orkneys broke the rampaging sea. The Merry Men of Mey were dancing, spray shooting into the air and flying off over the shattered wave tops. It was a gloriously wild scene. I left the bus at John o' Groats post office and after a snack at the Sea View Hotel strode out with the wind for the Duncansby Stacks. The grass was combed flat by the wind but the brave larks were still singing their hearts out. The Stacks come in duplicate, tiered spikes of red sandstone verdigrised with vegetation and dotted with the white blossoms of nesting fulmars. The riven cliffs seem to be fending them off. The drop to the sea was over 200 vertical feet and the wind made the edge feel very unsafe. However I suddenly felt an un-trammelled freedom. My walkabout had begun. We went up to Duncansby Head lighthouse, this, geographically, being a truer end/beginning to the country than the touristy, rather trite John o' Groats. The light on the Skerries stood stark and the Boars of Duncansby churned grey seas into white spray. The last time I had passed that way had been by sea – charging out of the Pentland Firth on the topsail schooner *Captain Scott* after a wild run from Loch Eriboll. Furling sail a hundred feet above that sort of sea was no 'simulated adventure', especially with frozen sails and yards and shrouds covered in snow. The memory was bitter sweet for that ship of dreams no longer sails these waters.

The boats, with names like *Dora* and *Miranda*, were bobbing about in the harbour at John o' Groats and I had to wipe the sleet off to read the notice about the ferry to Orkney. Not today, thank you. West a bit, I snuggled down among the ribs of red rock that edged the white sands washed by the rush of impatient waves. We lunched, mainly on a tin of apricots and creamed rice, to lessen the load. I took to the road to see the old kirk at Canisbay. It goes back to the fifteenth century and several stones bearing the name of Groat have been discovered in it.

It is one of several along this coast which show a marked Scandinavian influence. I have pictures of Danish churches with the same squat, roofed towers and simple naves. Canisbay has jutting windows and porch but the white, clean lines are still marked and stand out well on that flat, treeless landscape. I walked with a bracing wind and a continuing fuss of waders: peewits, pied pipers and redshanks – which across the Firth, in Orkney, have the delightful name of 'watery pleeps'.

Dunnet Head was no place to camp (it was blurred in a mist of spray) so I kept inland on the road, feeling the brae up to East Mey, snoozing in a wood at one stage (as relief from the wind battering), passing the Queen Mother's Castle of Mey (a pre-Reformation fortified storehouse which by Victorian times had sham battlements and so on) and on by Scarfskerry. I read at intervals as I walked but hands could hold the book only for a few minutes before the cold became intolerable. Dunnet Kirk is starker than Canisbay and has interesting old gravestones. Timothy Pont was its minister from 1601 to 1608 and as well as being a famous cartographer he must have been the first real Scottish hiker, for most of his surveying was done on foot. Dunnet Bay echoed to the crash of surf. The lambs among the dunes were wearing plastic coats – but so was I. Storm romped on the sands and then we set up the tent behind a struggling, brown-seared planting where there was clean water. It was a raw night and I was just warm and no more: full marks for Black's 2 lb. Backpacker sleeping bag – this sort of survival camping had not been in the plan! The tent carried on a noisy argument with the wind and every now and then there would be the hiss of snow sliding off nylon.

Thursday 3 May   GENERAL ELECTION

An alarm call of commuting gulls woke us at 5.30. The tent was white with snow. Whoever loses the election, here anyway, has an unusual summer excuse, I thought, as I tramped off to make Thurso early, walking the miles of sand to Castletown, where we were almost glad to leave the continuous roar of the sea. The four miles of straight road were edged with white after a passing hail shower, and as I descended into

Thurso, *Thor's river*, it began to snow hard again. I wanted to see the Robert Dick House but nobody I asked knew of the museum. Dick was a local baker who became an expert naturalist last century. He spotted a local grass which is otherwise only known in Norway. There seemed to be more English accents about than local ones. The polling station was open and the rosette-garbed agents at its entrance seemed to have joined in the common cause of trying to keep warm. On the way out, I passed the house where Sir William Smith, founder of the Boys' Brigade, lived.

At Forss Mills my feet were feeling the effects of road-walking miles so I stopped by the bridge to bathe them. The sun shone briefly then the snow came on again – belting at us horizontally under the bridge. A wood nearby lured for an early camp. The dog rolled in something very dead so had to be washed – and then lived with. Sheep bleated nosily till they spotted a tractor and then charged off to be fed. A cloud of gulls followed a plough beyond. A blackbird was nesting in the rusty remains of an old harrow. The trees sounded like surf. It snowed again that night. These little incidents milestone the walk, but like so much else can only be touched on occasionally.

Friday 4 May   BETTYHILL BATTLE
My log-book entry began this day: "My, it will be pleasant to fester by a burn some day and even climb sunny hills." As soon as we reached the road we were caught in the mad commuter rush to Dounreay. Hundreds of cars and scores of buses barged past, one of the most dangerous spells I was to have the whole trip. The establishment had grown beyond all recognition, the original odd reactor-sphere was just a detail in a huge sacred sprawl; the lemming-like race of the worshippers was all too symptomatic of our world accelerating out of control. My views on many things were to change on this walk and perhaps the seeds of doubt were sown here. Civilisation's price has become too high for weak and fallible men to pay, and pay we must, for we have sold our freedom for a barrel of oil. This is being written a year later in Morocco (festering by a burn under sunny hills) and I wonder if only I have changed, or has the world staggered nearer to disaster? A thousand miles from here there is a war (for oil basically), Iran has gone to extremists, Afghanistan was simply taken over by the Russians, and at home we still have our Ulster problems and industrial bigotry. We seem suicidal. This walk was an experience, at many levels, but at the end of it I could sing little of good cheer. A great fear chills even more than snows can. Men are grown gods, self-congratulatory, smug, arrogant, selfish, supermen indeed,

with as much sense and responsibility as naughty children trying to cheat their way out of trouble. What Jimmy can fix it?

Dounreay is an extraordinary science-fiction spectacle in this stern, natural setting: a libertine gesture in a Calvanistic landscape. It was being swept by white hail showers as I passed; Reay itself was a ghost town with no public facilities and a desolate golf course. The church alone made me pause, its special feature being an outside stair to its tower. I jumped over a wall to escape the wild snow and brewed among smitten daffodils under the trees. If I keep mentioning trees it is not because of their abundance but rather the opposite. *Any* trees were so unusual that they were all made use of for shelter in this exposed northland.

We rose up to sweeping brown moors that welcomed to Sutherland, and enjoyed them in a pale sunny spell. There had been a claustrophobic feel to the flat fields further east with their Caithness flags for walling. The next blatter of snow caught me as I turned down into Strath Halladale by Bighouse Lodge and crossed the swaying river-mouth footbridge to Melvich. A shepherd was up to his elbow in a sheep – they had all been having desperate work with this endless snow and cold. Many lambs had died. Mackay's West End Store had a radio on, and I learnt that yesterday's poll had given us a change of government and our first female prime minister. I went into the Strathy Hotel and they produced a huge pot of coffee, oatcakes and cheese, cake and piles of biscuits, all for 55 pence! Perhaps they were celebrating the result. I simply felt sorry that Scotland had once more shown her yellow streak and turned back from possible exciting adventures.

Strathy Point was a tumultuous scene of cliffs and caves and wild seas, yet on a calm day when the sun shines the cliffs of this coast back idyllic sandy bays. A lighthouse on this prow, which points like a finger to the north, was completed only in 1958, the last major light to be built. *Primula Scotica* grows here (the emblem of the Scottish Wildlife Trust), the cliffs clamour with birds, the clouds sail high and free across the open seas.

On the moors by the Badigill turn-off I joined cows cowering behind a dyke but grew so chilled that I perforce went on into the storm. Some wicked hail among the snow was unpleasant on the poor dog's nose. We sheltered and brewed in a bus shelter at one point. The Armadale valleys were like wind tunnels. The road made endless annoying bends as it wound through the tortuous – and tortured – wilderness. Ben Loyal and Ben Hope showed briefly, plastered with snow. It was all quite crazy but we plodded on determined, in a thrawn way, to make Bettyhill, two days in one, for while this weather continued both hill and cliff-top walking were ruled out. A tractor collecting peat, a local bus, a car, all in turn, stopped and offered lifts. It was too uncomfy to explain and they went on no doubt thinking some folk were daft – an opinion I fully shared.

Bettyhill gave a weary toil up its slopes (the name does warn' one) so I was more than glad to ease my honest aches in the comfort of the Hotel. I had a parcel waiting there. In it was a pair of short trousers. A major and his wife from the Isle of Man were up to fish the Naver; they and a young couple, who had passed me three times that day, were the only other guests. We all trooped in to see the election results on the TV but whenever it snowed outside it did so on the television as well. We did not learn much.

Speculation turned to a local puzzle which was then several years old: the 'Skerray Beast', a secret, elusive killer of sheep which roamed from Lairg to Tongue to Melvich. Occasionally it had been glimpsed but its nocturnal habits had kept it safe. Lynx or puma were likely suggestions but the *hows* and *whys* were more speculative.

Bettyhill stands at the mouth of the River Naver and is supposedly named after the Countess of Sutherland (the Duke was an English industrialist) who helped perpetuate the brutal clearances when that Strath was emptied of people to make way for sheep. They were dumped here to found new fishing and agricultural industries but there was no suitable harbour and the soil was poor and thin. Whatever the pros and cons (and conditions were bad indeed with overpopulation and poverty) the Clearances were carried out with singular lack of charity. The burning of Strath Naver is well documented and makes sad, grim reading. It is extraordinary that whole peoples were uprooted from what was dearest to them and scattered to the ends of the earth. But they had stood by their chiefs and leaders. The betrayal was over before it was understood. They built their cairns and went weeping to the rocky coasts and the transport ships. Roy Ferguson, artist and painter, catches the sadness of those days in a poem he wrote on the Clearances in Arisaig, 'The Cairn of Sorrow'.

Cairn an' Dorin

And so they came on a far off evening up to the hilltop.
Child, and man, and woman.
Each with a stone wetted by their tears.
And every stone they placed and made themselves a cairn
    and called it Cairn an' Dorin.

Here was their hill, a hill of sorrow.
And they stood around in silence
For each stone held each their lives.
　　To be left here and to be seen from far upon this hill.
To be known to all the waters and the far islands.
To all the winds, the calm and the storm.
To the great cast shadows of the clouds.
The rain and the salt-sweet mist.
The sun and shade of the seasons.
Until the time each stone should fall and drop away
　　as brittle lichen falls finding no life within the dying tree.
Silent they stood, looking around and round and then
　　went down the long dark pathways to the sea.

Arguments are often put forward that the evictions were lawful (the lamentable ministers of the period argued on those lines) but 'title deeds' were something not long created and were simply an excuse to claim right as well as might. It is easy to be lawful when you make the law. By ancient tradition the land was the clans', the peoples', and it was simply stolen and the theft made legal.

Saturday 5 May   GIVING TONGUE

Ben Loyal was abandoned and low-level routes chosen to Tongue and beyond for Ben Hope *had* to be climbed: it was needed for the sixth round of the Munros. The land was more knobbly now with the road periodically diving down to some small strath and up again. All along the north coast I had had whiffs of peat reek and even sat before the occasional glowing fire. Near Coldbackie I watched chemicals being spread on the fields, *by hand*. The post office was shut, but of course they could sell me some stamps. I meant to camp but tea was served so kindly that I had no will left to leave the Tongue Hotel. Dinner lived up to the Egon Ronay sign above the door and the vast old lodge was full of character.

An easier day was very welcome as 70 miles of road plodding had been quite enough. My legs felt it, but I suppose there was some gain in fitness. I found a dead wild cat on the road today, flattened by a car, but the tail fluffy and undamaged. Tongue is the only hamlet in the most sparsely populated region of Britain. For several days we would be wandering in Reay country – clan MacKay country – whose chiefs are buried in the 1724 church near the new roadway across the Kyle. Beyond the Kyle the road to Melness undulated over the brown landscape. The Rabbit Islands were visible, an odd modern English name. Originally these were Eilean na Gaeil *the island of strangers* from the Viking raiders. In 1745 a French sloop bringing gold ran aground here – and Prince Charlie was to see none of it. Material for a novel.

The road goes on to Durness, the most north-westerly village in Britain and a place well worth a visit. Limestone gives it a green, oasis look and the Smoo Cave is a result of limestone erosion. It is a series of caverns (the vast outer one can be entered on foot) into which a river falls down through a hole. It would be the Pennines before I'd see anything similar this trip. At Balnakiel the ruined 1619 church has a pre-Reformation font. There are some interesting tombstones including one to Rob Donn, the great Gaelic poet. I would eventually cross the road to the south of Durness, but first we had to seek out Ben Hope, the most northerly Munro, which I wanted to link eventually to Ben Lomond, the most southerly.

Sunday 6 May THE HEIGHTS OF BEN HOPE
The hotel produced breakfast at 7.30 and dog and rucksack were waiting in the hall while I ate so we were soon away. The village was swarming with redwings, making as much noise as a gang of starlings. There were secretive warblers too and the first, clear unmistakable cuckoo call. Castle Bharraich (Vurrich) perched above a *still* kyle to the right, and Ben Loyal on the left, was arrayed in a row of symmetrical peaks, white and impressive. With gorse, celandine and daffodils flowering, slow spring seemed to come only in one colour in Sutherland. A jogger passed me on the road, which I was all too glad to leave at Kinloch to follow a Land Rover track and then a stalkers' path up into the hills. I actually broke into the first sweat of the Walk, which was excuse enough to brew. Through a gap I could see Klibreck which I had thought surprisingly snowy ten days ago, now it was many times whiter. Storm knocked the dixi over so we had to brew again. He suffers from curiosity. Everything has to be investigated – a beetle crawling about under the base of the stove led to the mishap. When we set off I noticed a young couple coming up the path hand in hand – a somewhat wet and snowy Lovers' Lane! An eagle floated above, and twice landed on a rock pulpit to peer down at us like a short-sighted minister. I kept the dog close! The sun shimmered over the sweeping view, the clouds set spinnakers and swept across the blue ocean of sky – a pleasant change from the wrack and wrath that had been breaking on the mountain skerries for the last week. I was more or less following in the steps of Sir Hugh Munro himself for

he climbed Hope from Tongue in 1898 but I was not to endorse his comment: "I do not know any mountain of the height which can be climbed with less exertion."

Our route had taken us up on to a plateau-like area east of Ben Hope and it was exhausting walking in the deep poggy snow which was all too apt to drop one through into hidden pools and streams. Even the golden plovers' tracks sank deep. Rather than face miles more of it I went directly up the steep flank which was craggy but therefore clearer of snow. The wet snow was often on ice and I was left on this unreliable surface under an ice-draped crag not liking things at all. Any icicles knocked down slid a long, long way. Eventually a line went: traversing above a bank of snow, which I hoped would stay attached, and ending on some blessed rock. Storm is equipped with built-in crampons so was away ahead. A last barrier of old snow was sufficiently hard to require something like thirty steps to be cut in it, each one created by about twenty vigorous digs with a section of tent pole. It's amazing what sweat and adrenalin can do. It was a relief to go over the top – to find myself on the south-facing high basin of Hope. What a skiers' paradise! I could have done with skis and skins to stay on top of the snow. Further on I discovered human tracks and hoped to find summit foreground figures but it was empty so Storm had to perch on the trig point instead. By the end of the Walk he posed with practised aplomb, never moving till I clicked first for slides and then for black and white. No biped friend would have put up with it.

The view was one of my unforgettable "greats": the sea to the north, then Loyal and Klibreck over their lochan-landscapes; on the other side, Foinaven and Arkle, their screes completely covered in snow, the near Cranstackie hills, glimpses of Suilven, Quinag, and the whole south a bewildering array. I could see one hill, which will remain nameless, on which Mike Barnes and I had once made a route which we gave the name "Eyrie" for the climb led us over an eagle's eyrie. The nest was largely composed of fence posts, carried from a derelict fence on the slopes above. The birds were not in occupation when we called!

When we hit water and a bare patch at 2,000 feet we could not resist camping there and then. The tent was larger than the patch so some clearing had to be done, but it gave me a long laze, reading and brewing and every now and then looking round with an amused wonder: was it really the 6th of May? Was that mighty array really snow and not just the pale screes of Foinaven? Sadly, there was no brilliant sunset. It quietly bled away in sinking shades of grey.

Monday 7 May   GOLLY

The high camp was pleasant enough, though stockings were warmed over the stove so as to don them warm and wet rather than frozen. Gaiters were like boards. Tent pegs were frozen in, and the tent stiff, clinging to the snow in which it had set. A cold going we had of it. . . . The dog careered about happily on the new piecrust, his master floundered through it at every step. The early start at least kept my boots from being soaked. We went down, along, down the Allt na Caillich with its secretive falls, then cut over to Dun Dornadilla (Dornagil), a broch with its entrance still intact and one gaunt section of wall. "Dundornigil," a 1726 account relates, "is an old building made in the form of a sugar loaff and with a double wall and winding stairs in the middle of the wall round about, and little places for men to ly in as is thought and all built of dry stone without any mortar" – a description it would be hard to better. How old no one knows nor why. These enigmatic forts of the west and north can become an interest as absorbing as Irish Round Towers.

One of Gaeldom's greatest poets, Rob Donn, was born hereabouts. Our route took us up big Strath More and then off for Gobernuisgeach. This Lodge is twelve miles from any hamlet and thirty from a shop – a remoteness not uncommon in the Highlands. We cut a corner to gain Glen Golly. We had a brew-stop on Bucktooth's Meadow with the deer watching us warily across the river from the slopes of birch and aspen. At one time there must have been many more trees. The glen's name comes from *goll* meaning blind, in the sense of buried in trees. Rob Donn wrote a poem on "Glen Golly of the Trees". There were attractive falls and a good path until it rose to snow level again. Zigzags led up to a streaked and stippled landscape of rare isolation, then the path split with one branch going over the hills to Lone and Loch Stack, the other, mine, dropping down to Loch Dionard where I planned to camp.

After shots of Ben Hope's western cliffs I found I was out of black and white film, so missed Arkle and Foinaven flanking me, and the great crags of Creag Urbhard dropping to Strath Dionard. I had only just made myself comfortable when the rain came on and drowned the evening hours. Book ounces in the rucksack are seldom superfluous. It became too dark to read comfortably so I just retreated into the pleasures of day dreaming while relishing the utter remoteness. Though there are remoter, wilder places. Take the story of the Rev. Neil Mackenzie of St. Kilda who in 1837 found he had been making prayers for King William IV for several months after the king had died. He quickly changed to a more general prayer "for His Majesty the King" only to find the next year that in fact the country had a queen.

Tuesday 8 May STRATHS WESTWARD

Strath Dionard must be one of the wettest and boggiest, and would be a good testing ground for amphibian vehicles. After paddling the river I came on the caterpillar tracks of some vehicle but they simply collected water so were no help. Several miles later I came on a small bothy with fishing gear about it. The door seemed stuck. I shook it a bit only to have it opened by a long-haired youth. Seated at the back was a gentleman who greeted me with the warmth of a disgruntled walrus, I just said "Cheerie-bye" and went off. I was hoping for at least an offer of tea! A hundred yards away I realised I knew who the man was. We might have had an interesting chat about greenshanks! It was a well-known or-nithologist and his son.

My timing was perfect, for the shepherd of Gualin on the A838, Robert McLeod, was about to go off with his dogs. Sheep were all round the place and its height made it an even harsher environment than most. The lambs were tiny. He could never recall such long-lasting snow in May. His wife brought out my parcel, so the rucksack was suddenly heavy again for a long, almost level watershed, beyond which the Abhainn an t-Strathain runs down Strath Shinary to the western sea. I nearly stood on an adder which was very sluggish about moving aside. It had probably only just come above ground for the first time in 1979. Tourists have a bad habit of pinching peats from roadside stacks in the north and think the 'Beware of Adders' signs merely a psychological deterrent. I wonder what makes an area one adders use? There must be some common denominator but no one can tell me. Some areas have them, some don't.

There was a figure at the door of Strathan Bothy so I looked forward to a chat with someone. Conversation was to prove completely one-sided however, the lad had obviously been having a hard time, his nerves were in tatters – but a psychologist at least is paid to listen!

The bothy book had frequent entries about adders, and many of the dull or self-righteous entries of any other bothy book. Dave Goulder obviously thought this too, his entry read: "Immediately on arrival we burned all the wood, stole the matches, gave the fat in the frying pan to the dog, decorated the shelves with adders and mice, invited a cow in to share our fire and left promising not to close the door – our departure was delayed while I pissed in the kettle. However as we journeyed we were blinded by the light and a great voice boomed out 'Get thee back ye dirty sods and clean up'. Even since then we have followed the Gospel according to St. Bernard, ever hoping that we may be admitted to the chosen twelve." There was an entry from someone walking from Berwick to Gretna who mentioned a planned book about his trip . . .

My own first visit was long before the bothy book started, with a *Captain Scott* expedition. It was the trainees' third shore expedition so they were on their own. Their first trip had been Ben Nevis, the second had been in Arran, and from Loch Inchard to Loch Eriboll was to be their last. They had to check in at the bothy here and I had come a different way to be ready for their arrival. I saw the innocents coming and climbed on to the rafters above the door. Though big tough soldiers and police cadets they hesitated a bit before an objectionable big mouth volunteered to go in. I forgot, later, to ask what they expected, but as the door opened I let out a great *skreich*. The result was pandemonium and ended with several lads lying on the ground or scrabbling off as fast as they could after their mates. I went into fits of laughter which only exacerbated matters. It was like the pirates trying to summon up courage to tip Captain Flint the Black Spot. John Hinde also came from the schooner and accidentally left his camera there, which I found later, to his relief. The *Captain Scott* with just the Captain, Mate, Engineer, Bosun and Cook on board was sailed round Cape Wrath to Loch Eriboll – a good spur to the expeditioners who could, all too literally, miss the boat.

A surprising number of people have written to me about the *Captain Scott*, which was mentioned, and pictured, in the Mountain Walk book. Alas, she now sails the Persian Gulf, renamed *Youth of Oman*, for nobody in this country would pay the price of half a mile of motorway to buy her. I felt that that was a tragedy at the time, and I still do. The cost of running a schooner within the Forces' budget for instance would be negligible. (The price of building one fifth of a single jet fighter.) The loss is sad because so many individuals are still inspired by her and what she stood for: discipline, freedom, character, hard work, inspiration. God knows, we need these qualities, but our whole centralised system is geared to promote their opposites.

Wednesday 9 May CAPE WRATH
I turned in and rose early (in self defence) and wended down to Sandwood Loch as the weather really began to mend at last. I took an inland route and passed Strathchailleach, another bothy, which had been lived in by a recluse for many years. It was deserted however and reeked of decay. Lurid murals in oils had been painted over the walls,

some of strange Neptunes and maidens, some of life-like birds and
beasts. There must be something about the bothies in Sutherland to
attract the unstable. Mail from Grenoble and papers pleading for the
occupant to register on the electoral roll lay on the table, with an old
pre-decimal penny. . . .

Loch Keisgaig demanded a brew; the first time I had been able simply
to relax in warm sun in an idyllic spot. Our snooze was abruptly ended
with a loud whirr of noise as a diver bombed overhead and landed by its
mate in the loch. Their wild calling had the dog's ears standing on end. It
was to become a well-known sound, one so full of all the wildness of
empty places in the north. Long live the wilderness yet! On the moors
the dog went charging after a "wounded" golden plover while I, not
being fooled, soon found its four big eggs.

The cliffs of Clo Mor (900 ft) are the highest on the mainland but are
often spoilt by the presence of low-flying aircraft who use the area for
bombing practice. Last time at Cape Wrath we watched them bombing
an islet off Kervaig and it was quite a dramatic performance. Today all
was quiet – a blue perfection. I reached the trig point just as the local
minibus reached the lighthouse. The loud tourist voices jarred and I
realised just how attuned I was already to the softer sounds of the
wilderness. The keeper had never even walked up the hill so could tell
me nothing of a superbly built dry stane dyke I'd seen. The driver
confirmed my sighting of a long-eared owl. He often saw it as he drove
to and from the ferry for Durness at Keoldale. Salmon have been
marked in the sea off the north west coast here and found as far south as
Whitby and even in Norway. One fish marked off the east Sutherland
coast was recaptured out from the Forth only a week later, an average
travelling speed of 35 miles per day, assuming they were caught on
arrival.

The lighthouse, built in 1828, stands on 400 ft cliffs. Cape Wrath is a
real *point of turning*, the name meaning that in the original Norse, *hvarf*.
To turn left at Cape Wrath was the first objective of my pilgrimage, not
that there were options. Nothing lay between us and the North Pole.

We moved half a mile south of the lighthouse and perched the tent on
a ridiculously exposed spot but the weather was so obviously set fair, it
was no real risk. I wandered along in bare feet to see the rock stacks of
A' Chailleach and Am Bodach, then simply lay by the tent while the day
ebbed away, reading *Scots Magazines* and *Blackwood's Magazines* which
had accumulated while I'd been in Morocco. My pitch was by a peat-
black pool which reflected the tent's bright yellow colour. The sky was as
clear as an animal's conscience. The view was along Rhum-like sea cliffs,

all the way down to Sandwood Bay, the sands of which caught the low light, and beyond which rose the pinnacle of Am Buachaille. The dog got a well-deserved trim and I wondered which birds would gain this unexpected nest-lining material. Wheatears (from Morocco?) were about and pipits never stopped their pipping. I could just see the Orkney Islands but most of the view was of open sea, into which the glowing sun so appeared to plunge that I half expected a hissing explosion to follow! A big moon rose and I ate by its light, spinning out the last moments of a great day. "Oh, ye mountains, Oh, ye waters, Praise the Lord."

CAPE WRATH TO KINTAIL

"These long marches, day after day, are the surest, if not the only, way to avoid spiritual blindness. They provide the possibility, or rather the necessity, of uniting the active and contemplative components of one's nature. This is never more easily achieved than on a long trek. . . ."

REINHOLD MESSNER: *The Challenge*

Thursday 10 May   SANDWOOD BAY   *Maps, pp. 30 and 41*

I can think of fewer places where I would like to wake to sunshine glowing golden through the walls of a tent. Perhaps sunrise is more impressive than sunset because it is an older spectacle. It is not very much older but it stands shimmering on the brink of creation. This is earth's oldest wonder. Sunset is too often a Sunday school award for being good boys all day. Sunrise comes out of the pit, as we do, and is a fearsome, tingling marvel, before which we bow in awe. It takes a while for the rising sun to warm flesh and blood and soul. It is a great gesture of faith.

The walk back to Strathan fell into three parts: cliff-walking, sand-strolling and glen-floundering, each attractive in differing ways. What a varied number of birds we saw: bonxies, stonechats, kestrels, eiders, hoodies, wrens, gannets, fulmars, cormorants, wheatears, pipits, redwings, divers, golden plovers, sandpipers – birds of the ocean meeting birds of strath and moor.

The going was strenuous: lots of ups, lots of downs – Keisgaig Bay, Strath Cailleach – deep-cut *geodha*, then a rock scramble down to the first sands which linked with the miles of Sandwood Bay as the tide was out. Boots were kicked off to walk barefoot, I piled the sack with driftwood and played soccer with Storm when we found a ball. The sands ran southwards to end at a square-cut headland from which is detached the 200 ft needle of Am Buachaille, *the shepherd*, and a fine climb for those prepared to swim for their fun. "He that mounts the precipices . . . has a kind of turbulent pleasure, between fright and admiration" as Dr Johnson declared. Tom Patey, John Cleare and Ian Clough made the first ascent. A Tyrolean traverse is rigged and you have just four hours before the tide covers it.

We turned into a nook which was in the sun yet out of the steadily-growing wind. I had tea and ate every last bit of food, then set off up the glen past Sandwood Loch trying, for interest, to track our outwards route and making a poor job of it. We reached 'Home' just before two Londoners staggered in with massive packs. They greeted us with "we have just seen an adder!" The resident member was off to Balchrick and came back with the news that some female had fallen off Clo Mor that afternoon, news picked up in Kinlochbervie via the fishing boat radios and soon passed about the area. *The Scotsman*, at Rhiconich next day, carried details: she had been one of that day's mini-bus party from Keoldale – her body was picked up by the fishing boat *Golden Fleece*, after having fallen 500 ft into the sea off the cliffs near Kervaig.

It became a wild night and the snugness of the sleeping bag was relished. The rain rattled on the corrugated iron roof and the door rattled as the wind tried to bully its way inside. After listening to it for an hour I suddenly remembered I had left my boots up on the roof, to dry.

Friday 11 May   TO RHICONICH
"A real soaker which had us longing for the simplicity of snow" my logbook noted. We procrastinated but eventually set off into the driving rain, up the hill on a path and then over trackless moors of riven peat, navigating by compass in the featureless landscape and eventually dropping directly down to Kinlochbervie to relax for an hour in the cafe at the Fishermen's Mission. Lunch was eaten in a road workers' hut during another deluge as we walked along above the fjord-like Loch Inchard. It was five-cuckoos-per-mile country.

The Rhiconich Hotel – cum shop – cum petrol station stands just along from a Police Station in one direction and the Post Office in the other. That *is* Rhiconich. The barman was off ill and Mr McLeod, the elderly owner, and a Canadian lassie (on her third year of wandering) were quietly and efficiently dealing with everything, and still had time to chat over welcome tea. A parcel had been left, the most northerly one of my hectic delivery run, so there was the usual fussing about: parcelling up maps and film I'd finished with, making several phone calls, washing clothes, writing letters, feeding and walking the dog, taking a well-deserved shower, and collapsing into bed. Rest days were far more frantic than simply walking. The old body had fully adjusted by now. There is always some suffering in the beginning but it soon goes. A cuckoo in the garden struck every minute while on the quarters a cuckoo clock in the hall joined in: a sleep-inhibiting combination.

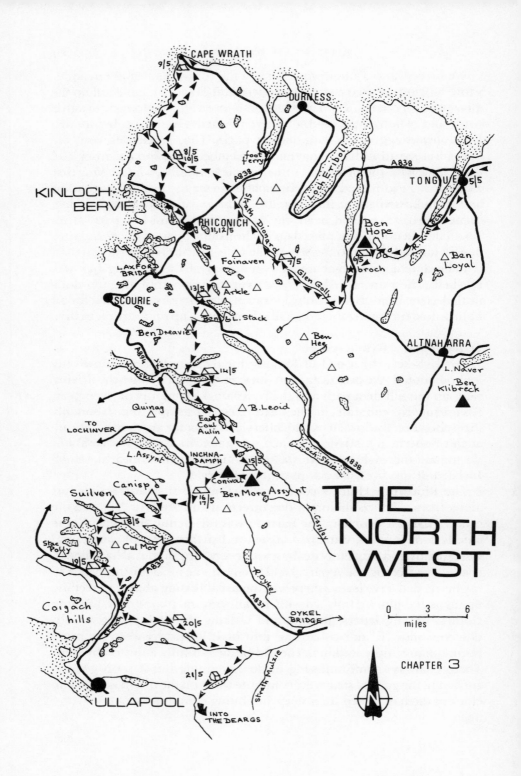

CAPE WRATH

9/5

DURNESS

8/5
10/5

foot
ferry

A838

TONGUE 5/5

KINLOCH-
BERVIE

RHICONICH
11,12/5

Ben
Hope

6/5

Ben
Loyal

Foinaven

7/5

Strath Dionard

Glen Golly

broch

13/5

Arkle

Ben

L. Stack

ALTNAHARRA

SCOURIE

Ben Dreavie

Ben Hee

L. Naver

A894

Kylesku

Yerry

14/5

B. Leoid

Loch Shin

A838

Ben
Klibreck

Quinag

TO
LOCHINVER

L. Assynt

East
Coul
Aulin

INCHNA-
DAMPH

15/5

Canisp

Conival

Suilven

16/5
17/5

Ben More Assynt

R. Cassley

18/5

THE
NORTH
WEST

Stac
Polly

Cul Mor

19/5

R. Oykel

Strath Canaird

A835

A837

OYKEL
BRIDGE

Coigach
hills

20/5

Strath Mulzie

0   3   6
miles

21/5

CHAPTER 3

ULLAPOOL

INTO
THE DEARGS

N

Saturday 12 May AT RHICONICH

I had half-planned to walk out and visit Ardmore, John Ridgeway's Adventure Centre, but it was a dreich sort of day and a long lie and laziness won over character building and so on. It was pleasant doing nothing and resting afterwards. The Gualin shepherd filled up with petrol but the Canadian lassie had no idea of prices so he simply said "Ach, I'll pay for it next time". By the bridge some kids left their cycles all day long; with lamps and pumps on them too. All six telephone boxes I had used in Caithness and Sutherland had been in working order. The bar that night was to close at eleven as the lassie wanted to go in to a dance at Kinloch. They would do breakfast for me the next day at six if I wanted it. No wonder Highland hospitality and atmosphere is renowned; what a sad commentary on elsewhere . . .

Gordon Adam and Alistair Hetherington arrived to subjugate me to an interview for a BBC 'Portrait' series. Gordon had been in Morocco with us just a few weeks before and had thus learnt of this escapade, Alistair was an SMC member (and head of Radio Highland) so it was all quite fun and we had a good tramp along Loch Inchard, racing back to not quite beat a deluge. Gordon had already interviewed Bob Aitken, with whom I'd climbed for many years in the Alps and who had also been on some Braehead School trips, Kirsty Adam, Director of Arts in Fife and an ex-Braehead teacher who came ski-ing with the girls and did trips to Ireland and Morocco, Stuart Thomson, a former Braehead pupil who still climbed regularly and had joined us in Norway and R. F. Mackenzie, our ex-Headmaster and well-known educationalist. As Bob wrote later it was "a grand excuse for character assassination". After dinner we all did a quick three minute piece as a sort of trailer – but we had to do it again as the first effort ended in noisy hilarity. For peace I had tied the dog to a chair, but at a crucial moment he caught sight of his food dish and made for it. The lead was not long enough and he was left doing a noisy, scrabbling breast stroke on the linoleum, having biffed his tin dish well out of reach. . . .

The cuckoo gave its usual evening serenade. I hate cuckoos!

Sunday 13 May LOCH STACK

The Rhiconich River was my route, leading to long narrow lochans, beyond which, framed by crags, lay Arkle, an oddly rounded shape from that angle. The scoured gneiss landscape is as much water as rock, and is as peculiar on the ground as it looks on the map. It can be tricky walking country, even my well-defined line gave one paddle which would have been impossible with the river in spate. I know of several near-drownings among my surviving mountaineering friends. People going on big backpacking trips like the *Ultimate Challenge* should plan with this in mind. It is quite possible to be marooned at the head of Loch Nevis, say, or have to climb 2,000 ft and many miles up streams before being able to cross them.

Storm and I had a delightful picnic under a rowan by one of the larger lochs, Loch a' Cham Altain. In the middle of the meal we were startled by the sound of wild waters. Over the calm loch came a rush of waves. The squall sent the spray flying over us, then all was calm again except for the cackle of laughter from a pair of loons. It was a warning and we camped early, in a wood, rather than up on Ben Stack, and the sounding surge of trees that night showed it had been a wise choice. A parcel, buried in the wood only about two weeks before, was already well nibbled by mice but I had learnt that danger during 'Hamish's Mountain Walk' so this time the contents were safe in a biscuit tin. The storm was one of warm and wet, and overnight an amazing amount of snow was washed off the peaks. It was probably fine midge-incubating weather. The larches in the wood were all sprouting their bright green mini shaving brushes and slowly, very slowly, the dead flats were taking on a sheen as the new grass sprouted.

Monday 14 May   BEN DREAVIE TO GLENDHU

At 5 a.m. it was blowing a great gale so I decided to sleep again. The dog was all for going. Whenever my alarm sounded he would jump up and start trying to dig me out of my sleeping bag, a very effective system when I really did want to rise but having disadvantages if only a false alarm.

We set off at nine by a path which goes over the north-west shoulder of Ben Stack and eventually joins the A894 some miles north of Kylesku. Ben Stack was in boiling cloud so would do some other day, but I was determined to keep in the wilds so we cut over for Ben Dreavie and a path beyond. It was rough going and once in the cloud wild enough to blow my balaclava off and make balance precarious on rocky steps. The lochans were flying up in sheets of spray again. The dog had chased after deer the day before, and had had a thrashing; today he knew better and instead tore round in tight circles and jumped on me after each circuit. The hint was not taken. The ban on deer, as on sheep, stood. Storm was very quick in learning anything and made the perfect hill companion. He was hard to live up to in fact: always cheerful, keen, never complaining – sometimes in contrast to his master. He had a delight in all living things, not to hurt them, but just out of curiosity. A chick held in the hand would be sniffed, not grabbed; and friendship would be offered to any and all dogs and cats, not always to his own good.

The summit of Ben Dreavie, over 1,600 ft, was a sandstone plateau, littered with the pebbles which had come from the crumbling rock. If this sandstone is among the oldest rock in the world, what of these pebbles which must have washed into the sea long before that? Most are round and smooth and, with a little tumbling, mount well to make homely jewellery.

I dropped down to pick up stalking paths through this desolation, one of the country's largest uninhabited areas. Miles on, I felt a new wooden hut was an intrusion but it made a welcome lunch spot. I crossed the inflow of a lochan and cut over the hill to angle down to Loch Glendhu, one of the two lochs that fork into this harsh country from Kylesku. I just made out a ferry on its crossing, a tiny beetle of blackness on the silver of the water away in the west. Among the tumbled red crags fragile wood sorrel was flowering. A path took me up to the head of the loch and I camped beyond the empty buildings and their two guardian leafless trees. A bonfire of driftwood was a doucer ending to a wild day, though the smoke pursued me round and round in circles. My clothes reeked of wood smoke for days.

Tuesday 15 May INTO ASSYNT

Rising from Loch Glendhu there is a path to the promontory that separates it from Loch Glencoul, though it is not on maps, and from the top of this neb I noticed a shaft of light striking my camp site. It was really green. Summer was winning – as it must. I lost the path and then climbed to find it again. It was Himalayan in style yet 1,000 ft below lay sea, backed by the barrelled buttresses of Quinag. Dropping dramatically down to Glencoul was like descending to a camp site somewhere in the Rishi Ganga. It was tempting to linger. We went on by Loch Beag where we had camped once before when exploring here. The tide goes well out, exposing sand and mud, and underneath it must be hollow for on the flow the surface bubbles and boils in extraordinary fashion as the air escapes again.

Up the glen I lunched opposite the Eas Coul-Aulin, the highest water-fall in Britain, which is four times the height of Niagara. Conditions were right for taking photographs. It is by no means the most splendid of falls for the vast, open setting gives no idea of scale. It drops in two steps and a slither before braiding away among the screes. The nearest path leads past the top so it cannot be seen well from there, nor is the descent easy. All in all, the fall retains a kingly distance from the casual gaper.

The Abhainn an Loch Bhig, which I was following, is attractive in its own right with many small, utterly charming falls but leading up into ever-rougher and remoter regions, debouching originally from a lost lochan through a black gorge. Beyond this is another of those forgotten uplands, shot with old snow and patched with a thousand pieces of water, edged with ermine-white ridges and muffed in cloud. This is Assynt. The very name has a stony ring to it for *ass* is the Norse for rocky.

We scrambled from loch to crag, to corrie, to settle by Loch Bealach a' Mhadaidh, *the loch of the pass of the fox*. It looked out over the tawny bowl to Beinn Leoid and Meallan a' Chuail, while shivering below the eastern rampart of Ben More Assynt. Beinn an Fhurain, immediately above, was a gigantic fossilised jam roll, the strata curling in massive convolutions. No site for the rest of the journey would so combine loneliness, emptiness, roughness and grandeur.

Wednesday 16 May   BEN MORE AND CONIVAL
We saw six dead deer within a quarter of a mile of the tent site: it was not only the sheep which had suffered in the late snows. Even with the violent thaw the ridge up Ben More was flanked with great depths of snow and *bergschrunds* gaped beside the crests. The blowing cloud gave the climb an Alpine feel. It was hard (as ever) to decide which was the higher of the bumps to call the summit of Ben More Assynt, *the Big Hill of Assynt*. Ten years before it had been my thousandth Munro. The chill of wind blowing off snow soon drove us on. A steep ski run could have been made right down into Coire a' Mhadaidh. The traverse to Conival was exhausting as I frequently plunged through the snow up to my thighs. Conival, *enchanted hill*, is the finer viewpoint of these two, looking north to Quinag, and then out to Canisp, Cul Mor and so on. Ben Hope and Klibreck looked oddly snowless.

We descended by the ridge I came up on the memorable day during the Munro trip; this time the fun was snow not wind for the patches often overlay slab and scree. Eventually I found a long clear slope and enjoyed a few hundred feet of standing glissade. The col leading to titillating Breabag is a corner crowded with effects: a gentle stream, red crags, tumbling falls and hanging gardens of starry saxifrage and green moss. We lunched there before descending a succession of quartz cliffs and heather shelves, till we came on an area of exposed limestone. This is part of the Moine Thrust and from just north of Ullapool right up to here this band of limestone creates a strip of flowery green among the barren wastes of rock. Our next descent took us to the Fuaran Allt nan Uamh, *the cold stream of the cave*, where a stream simply gushes out of the hillside. Caves, potholes, vanishing rivers all exist in the area, nothing perhaps compared to Pennine peculiarities, but so unexpected here. This cave water was chosen as the site for a recently-built salmon hatchery. We camped a bit upstream from it, after collecting some buried goodies from the nearby wood.

Food requirements would be set aside after pitching camp and putting a brew on, the rest packed for a pillow (boots were often wet), then over brew and biscuits the map would be studied, plans made and the log written up. Book and supper usually went together. Storm did his day on a packet of *Frolic* and a few dog biscuits. I did not starve, though the quality depended on the foot-poundage of the day's darg. Here it was Grant's haggis, spuds and carrots; fruit salad and cream, cake and coffee – mostly tins, being from a roadside cache, and with visitors expected to carry off my empties. The visitors never turned up and the rain poured down.

Thursday 17 May   DAMP INCHNADAMPH
At eight o'clock Roger Smith arrived: waterproofed from top to toe in skins and wellies. He had underestimated the drive up and stopped overnight in Ullapool. I sent him off to see the caves and springs while we had breakfast. It was in these caves the archaeologists dug out bones of bear, lynx, reindeer, lemmings and other tundra animals long extinct. It was still sheeting down when Roger returned.

"You have a car, Roger?"

"Yes."

"Would you like to go down the road a few miles to the comfort of the Inchnadamph Hotel? It would be a bit of a squeeze in here. We might as well be comfortable."

"Yes. Why not? I was afraid you'd be another John Merrill and want me to walk there!"

Roger is the editor of *The Great Outdoors*, the monthly magazine of the walking game. He had covered Merrill's round-the-coast trip the year before and was now assisting mine. For instance I'd phoned my sister-in-law from Rhiconich and she had phoned Roger who stopped off at Nevisport where Alex Gillespie gave him new waterproofs.

"It's a good day to try them," he suggested.

"I'm not going anywhere today thanks – except the hotel!"

So we passed a very pleasant, if busy, morning at Inchnadamph. Roger had brought a pile of mail and took off my black and white film which he then had developed and contact prints made. These went into my logbooks eventually: six bulging notebooks which went to Morocco to be turned into something slightly more presentable: this book. Roger drove off south again into the rain.

Friday 18 May   CANISP AND SUILVEN

A young lad arrived by motorbike at the hatchery where our river joined the A837. He took some mail to post that night. Once working fully the hatchery would require only two operators – fairly dull and repetitive work but, as he said, "any work is difficult to find here."

My route lay upwards round Canisp and eventually I left our gear at a clearly recognisable crag and headed off for the summit. It had a cover of new snow so, on the way down, having a visual check myself, I taught the dog to back track, which he did by nose alone. Kitchy never used his nose to the extent that Storm does, though a deer moving on a hillside miles away would be spotted by either while humans saw nothing.

Suilven came in sight as we edged up and round – an improbable fang of rock from this angle – so when we had climbed Canisp (in cloud) we headed over moors and round lochs to slot into the lie of the land through from the Cam Loch to Loch nan Rac where we camped, right under the tiered flanking wall of Suilven. The brew had to wait; the sun was out and we rushed madly about with cameras clicking: tent, with Suilven behind, tent with Cul Mor behind, tent and dog and Suilven, dog and reflections . . . the law up here is to take pictures while the sun shines – and forget it otherwise.

An hour later it was snowing so I had several brews while reading Galt's *The Entail*. A continuous keeking-sound eventually forced me to look out. I was camping just along from a crag where peregrines were nesting.

Saturday 19 May   DOIRE DUBH DAY

Frozen boots, ice-walled tent, and a landscape completely painted by winter again – that was the new day's start. It was dry so we moved fast, then rushed about taking all those pictures again, this time with the scenes under snow. It was a fantastic sight: Suilven, Cul Mor, even Stac Polly, all plastered. It was hard to know what to do: I wanted to be everywhere at once to marvel at it all. We continued along our natural line, passed Loch Gleannan a' Mhadaidh, then dropped into our slot again. Mhadaidh is *fox* – and we saw one! Storm put it up and looked at me. "No!" I warned so he sat trembling while the fox danced away, in turn setting off a dozen deer. Later we sat watching a hind and calf, from only twenty yards off, so the dog had learnt well.

We came to the Fionn Loch and followed its windings till we were able to paddle across where the Uidhe Fhearna flows into it. Fhearna is *alder* and a boulderfield beyond was covered with those trees. The poor primroses in the hollows had frozen snow on them. We wandered up several humps till we perched high above Loch Sionascaig. An old dyke, ruins, and various markings on the slopes showed past occupation, sad slabs of green in the brown furrows of history.

It took much up and down and in and out to wind round the loch. We ran into people and a filthy path, filthy as simply worn rather than made. This is a Reserve or something now – which is the surest way to attract people to any area. Stac Polly only produced a serious erosion problem after they built a handy car park on the road below it. When will they ever learn?

The National Trust for Scotland are great sinners in this way, developing and encouraging people to all their mountain properties – with sad wear and tear and destruction of the very things they are supposed to protect. Percy Unna must turn in his grave! Lawers, Glen Coe, Kintail, Torridon, these areas are all suffering; and the argument that by attracting mobs to them people keep off elsewhere is both fallacious and irrelevant: you do not sacrifice the superb for the sake of the mediocre.

Off the path or lochside I saw nobody else however and I enjoyed an afternoon and evening of ease in the Doire Dubh, *the black wood*, which was a riot of fresh green birch. A heron perched just offshore and the wood had its resident cuckoo and kestrel who passed and repassed in turn. A bold chaffinch came in to peck among the crumbs and risk a singeing on the stove. Loons woke the dog who then drooled for his supper. I had taken to throwing his *Frolic* on the ground outside so he took some time to find it; otherwise he demolished the whole packet in ten seconds. Not long after bedding down he shot up again on hearing yet another new sound: the bubble and squeak of a roding woodcock.

Sunday 20 May STRATHKANAIRD
I escaped from this empty quarter through between Cul Mor and Cul Beg; they and Stac Polly were cut-outs of dark colour against a grey, turbulent sky, yet once through towards Knockan the new shapes of Coigach could still startle. Is there any hill shape in Britain sharper than Sgurr an Fhidhleir? Walking down a crest parallel but away from the

road I looked south to the Deargs and Fannichs and An Teallach. They were still wintry enough. It looked as if some summer vandal had been spraying them with a tin of white paint.

I walked down the road to Strathkanaird hamlet. Mrs McLeod at the old post office had a parcel so I retreated to eat, pack things to post and pack things for going on. Every now and then the wind would whip away a poly bag and I'd chase after. Food had been a bit lacking in calories for the last few days and I scoffed a cake, a tin of spaghetti, a tin of apricots and a packet of Garibaldi biscuits – and felt much better. I telephoned home, this being a checkpoint, left a parcel with the McLeods to post, and went on up the glen which was fertile and quite the greenest landscape I'd seen since travelling north. At Langwell we were ambushed by a dozen noisy collies, then the road steepened and I sweated up it in the day's ration of sun. Near the end of Loch a' Chroisg we found a sheltered nook and camped. Scott's *Rob Roy* had been in my new parcel, an old copy which cost tenpence and could be abandoned page by page as read.

Monday 21 May KNOCKDAMPH

It rained most of the night and all day. Once along Loch a' Chroisg the going became a right *trauchle* – which hardly needs translating: a quivering bogland, full of lochans and deep-digging streams. Few of the paths existed and the buildings seemed to have been left to fall to ruin. In the scudding cloud and rain it was a scene of dreariness – but not boring – the senses are still receptive: I can smell it yet. I cut over the shoulder of Druim nam Fearnag and down to a proper track leading to Knockdamph, a bothy, which like so many good things could be seen a great way off. A deluge caught me 300 yards short of it.

In the previous year only about a score of parties had signed the bothy book and half of them were walking through rather than staying – there are no near Munros. An hour went busily: clearing out junk and litter, drying the dog with the pages of a pornographic magazine, washing muddy socks, hanging the tent to dry, brewing, of course, and startling all the deer for miles by blowing soulful notes on a big cow's horn. It was a kindly place in which to snib the day. The mind turned to other bothies, other days.

The locality of the following cannot be revealed, but if you take a rough track round a splendid Munro or two to a strath beyond you will find a bothy there beside a fine lochan. It was one I knew well enough and it was one which was popular with a certain Glasgow fraternity. We met now and then.

On one occasion one of their gang and I sat on a plank between two boulders yarning. I was off the hill and he was off the loch. I drank cup after cup of tea and he matched me, cup for cup, from a certain distinctively-shaped bottle. After a while I got a nice backhander. "Oh, you're yon Hamish Broon. Ach, I thocht you wis win o them, but you're jist ane o us".

He talked later of *Groome's Gazetteer* and all the quaint information it gave of Scottish places as they appeared 140 years ago. He had picked up a set at 'the barras'. (I made a mental note of the title and it must have been years later, in a London suburb, I found a set in a junk shop. It weighed all of ten pounds but was happily added to the returning-from-expedition clutter I already had to drag home by train.) The bothy conversation suddenly lapsed after discussing *Groome's Gazetteer* for following a dismal shake of the now empty bottle my mate fell off the end of the bench and lay unconscious.

This gang liked their bit fishing and one day they were caught by the authoritarian owner himself. There was quite a scene but the Glasgow lads came out victorious. One of them terminated the conversation by poking the redoubtable admiral in his midriff and saying: "See you, if you dinna let us have our wee bitty fushin, then *you'll* be in trouble; nae us. We're only here fir ane, mebbe twa weeks in the year. You can hae it the rest. Noo, if that disna satisfy you, next time we've been, we'll jist carry in a big jeely jar full o nice hungry wee pike."

Another friend was telling me of the time he was at the bothy when the gang was there. Somehow a touristy female reached it, quite a feat dressed as she was and wearing platform soles. Still, they gave her a cup of tea and chatted away. She was impressed by their air of command and enquired what they were doing.

"Us? Oh, we're frae the Department. Tourism an a that , ye ken. See yon affy road you came in, we're gonna mak that a richt motorway an this place isnae much noo, sae we'll hae a real five star hotel for the likes o you" – and with a proprietary sweep of the arm to the majesty of Suilven, he added the touch that sent my friend outside to giggle, "Aye, an we're gonna shift yon bing."

It was not Suilven, of course, but a hill equally fine and every time I see it now I think, "Aye, we're gonna shift yon bing!"

Tuesday 22 May
Twenty-two miles made this the longest day for a long time, and one of the few when I walked on into the darking of day. They were not easy road miles either, but over the roughest ground so far, rougher even

than Assynt. I had long wanted to stay at this bothy and also reach the Deargs up Glen Douchary, which everyone looks down into when collecting "awkward" Seana Bhraigh. It must be remote. Even the SMC Northern Highlands guidebook has no photographs of the group. Once beyond Loch an Daimh the terrain was deep heather, scattered Scots pines and far rims of snow, extraordinarily like the Cairngorms. The Douchary is a super-scenic river of astonishing clarity giving one water-fall after another, each by a tempting camp site. One fall had left a pillar of rock standing, and growing out of the top was a sturdy tree. The luxuriant growth on the sides of the gorge where sheep and fire have never reached gave a striking illustration of their long-term destructiveness.

A wide open Strath followed, the empty miles alive with deer. There seem to be far too many, everywhere, and I wonder if they are being culled as they should? There was a dismal number of corpses. Deer have to be shot or the numbers rapidly grow and then they over-graze and starve to death – a crueller fate than a quick shot. Originally they were forest animals, originally most of Scotland was forest, but man has destroyed the treescape and the deer are forced to live in the harsh uplands above cultivation level. Pleas to let deer live 'naturally' fail to take into account that *there is nothing natural* – man has misused the highland landscape for a thousand years. One bit of man's own sad history lies in the ruins of Douchary: among all the browns and yellows it had a flush of green about it, as if weeping "we were lived in once". Roy's map of 1755 shows this as the road from Loch Broom to Tain.

The upper glen is an immense peat bog, cut deep by the meandering river which has taken great strips of turf out its banks and strewn them downstream. The peat was six feet deep usually; lying on gravels, and here and there old tree roots waved long Tolkien arms as if trying to escape from their dead past. I had a brew beside a sink hole and then faced the hard slog up to the Cadha Dearg, *the red gap*, the col which links far Seana Bhraigh to the rest of the rough Deargs. The scrappy gully was a mass of purple saxifrage and a stream traced down the side walls instead of in the bed. (That, frozen, would be some climb!)

The sneck leads to a huge upland which was simply Arctic in quality. I have pictures from northern Norway which are exactly the same: a sour, scoured country with the hollows holding snow till late and the whole mass an ooze of melt water and bogs. On top of Seana Bhraigh I took virtually a complete panorama: everything I had done seemed to be in view from Coigach to Assynt to Caithness, the sea glittered in the west and beyond the Deargs other giants peered over. It is not often one can

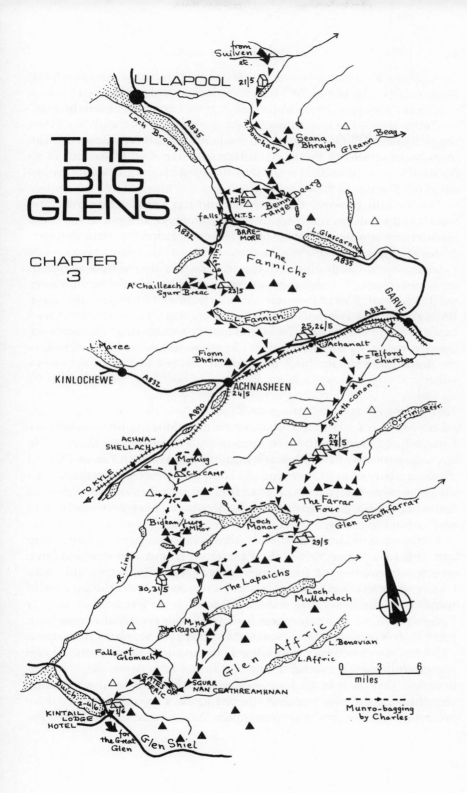

THE
BIG
GLENS

CHAPTER
3

from Suilven
etc.

ULLAPOOL 21|5

Loch Broom

A835

R. Douchary

Seana
Bhraigh   Gleann Beag

Beinn Dearg

22|5

falls N.T.S.

BRAE-
MORE

A832

L. Glascarnoch

A835

GARVE

The
Fannichs

A'Chailleach
Sgurr Breac   23|5

L. Fannich

A832

25,26|5

Achanalt

+ = Telford
churches

L. Maree

Fionn
Bheinn

KINLOCHEWE   A832

ACHNASHEEN
24|5

A890

Strath conon

Orrin Resr.

ACHNA-
SHELLACH

27
28|5

TO KYLE

Moruisg

C.K. CAMP

The Farrar
Four

Glen Strathfarrar

Bidean/Lurg Mhor

Loch Monar

29|5

R. Ling

30,31|5

The Lapaichs

Loch
Mullardoch

M.na
Dheiragain

Glen Affric

L. Benevian

Falls at
Glomach

L. Affric

0   3   6
miles

L. Duich

2-4|6

GATES OF
AFFRIC

1|6

SGURR
NAN CEATHREAMHNAN

KINTAIL
LODGE
HOTEL

for
the Great
Glen   Glen Shiel

N

Munro-bagging
by Charles

look from sea to sea across the British Isles. The colours were startlingly
blue. A fairy cave in the cliffs may have had something to do with it.

A heavy pack was cursed in the drifts. It was hard not to sink through
at times. Above Loch a' Chnapaich a rim of snow was still 30–40 feet
deep. Between Eididh nan Clach Geala and Meall nan Ceapraichean
(Munro mouthfuls!) I met a solitary lad. He had packed in from
Strathmulzie, whence he'd come over Breabag from Inchnadamph – the
start of a three week stravaig.

The lochans between Cona'mheall and big Beinn Dearg were still
frozen and what was not frozen was saturated, so we gathered strength
from a brew and climbed these Munros in succession. The wall going up
Beinn Dearg was completely covered in places. Six months later when
Charles, Donald and I came back, immediately after the walk, the drifts
were still about. The descent was nasty: over snow-covered boulders,
still by the wall. We cut through under Iorguill and down into the Allt a'
Bhraighe corrie to pitch the tent at 8.45 p.m., still 2,000 ft up. The sun set
beyond An Teallach, gently in pinks and greys and silver. I almost fell
asleep writing my log. And I slept like a log, last aware of the crying of
the golden plovers, the bird of the lonely places which gives the wind a
voice.

Wednesday 23 May   INTO THE FANNICHS
Strath More is a delightful, rich, green glen, leading up to Braemore
Junction and draining towards Loch Broom and Ullapool. Apart from
the well-known Falls of Measach in the Corrieshalloch Gorge (NTS) I
doubt if many tourists ever stop. As soon as I stepped onto the A835 a
car went careering past a line of heavy lorries as if driven by a suicidal
Corsican, then a jet roared down the Strath at zero feet. I was back to
civilization obviously.

The forest is old now and the Forestry have encouraged people to stop
and walk in it. Sgurr Mor of the Fannichs seen through the vivid larch
screen was my reward for being *à pied*. I also discovered old paths
leading to secret falls, going back to Victorian times no doubt, part of
some rich demesne. My own call was to a forestry cottage at
Fasagrianach, a fine house-name for a family who originally came from
Essex. Mrs Page had a parcel and their puppy gave Storm and me a great
welcome. We wandered up the river then, outside the walled garden and
shuttered house of another estate which had seen better days. On my
first visit here as a boy I had been given a huge glass of warm milk
straight from the cow, which made cycling back to camp on the Dirrie
More (after a day on the Deargs) much less of a strain. I followed the

gorse-bright banks to where the two rivers joined to form the River Broom: the Droma and the Cuileig. The map showed a bridge but it had gone. I was able to boulder hop across and by the Cuileig had a brew and dealt with the parcel. I was to follow the river right to its source in the Fannichs.

When we went on we found two ruined bridges and a pleasant fall and more overgrown paths. We kept to the waterside up a gorge, with the odd scramble above pools, but it eventually turned into a gorge of Corrieshalloch proportions so we had to scrabble out. High above we found another path which led, by some tremendous viewpoints, to a dramatic crossing of the gorge by an arched iron bridge. This decayed structure was only 20 feet long but the drop into the waist of gorge below made that quite enough. I sat on the bank below the Dundonnell road to recover and thought what a wasted asset there was hereabouts. The Forestry have attractive Inverlael, the N.T.S. have Corrieshalloch, and there were these remains from the heyday of the lodges, etc., all contained within motor roads. Could they not combine and open out a whole array of attractive walks?

Thoughts like these filled my mind as I wandered over the moors towards Loch a' Bhraoin, *loch of the showers*, and then up the lonely, peaty glen. The name was ominous for the scene was one drawn in the dark lines of a 4B pencil. The clouds however did no more than shake their umbrellas over us that night.

Thursday 24 May   FANNICH PEAKS AND STRATHBRAN RAIN
I was surprised to be off dry but it was desperately hot and muggy and I only traversed Sgurr Breac and A'Chailleach because they were wanted sixths. The North East Ridge up Breac was a fine curve of snow to guide through the damp murk. Inside skins I sweated so much I preferred just to tolerate the more natural wet. Tom a' Choinich, at last finding its place in Munro's Tables as a Top, was traversed going and returning from A'Chailleach, a perambulation of drift-dodging. The soggy snow soon wet my boots however and as I had a long bum slide off the northern arm of Breac I ended wetter than ever. That slide almost ended by shooting into a cavern carved out in the snow by a hidden stream. I packed up camp and we walked over the pass to Loch Fannich, which is artificially controlled by a dam at the east end. The tide was in.

We had an easy bog-flog round its head and even found the sometimes difficult Abhainn a' Chadh Bhuidhe had a girder over it for a bridge. The absence of "shore" made it rough going along the south side of the Loch, being very much peat-bog country. A foul, decaying deer was floating in the loch – we only discovered it after drinking from a few feet away. Yesterday we saw the remains of a prematurely born calf. Poor deer. Across the loch, in the trees behind Nest of Fannich, we once put up a deer which had broken a leg. It charged off along the hillside with one leg flailing. As it was dusk and deep snow covered the land there was little we could do. The hills can punish as well as bless and we do well to remember sometimes that nature is not tame. I set off several herds of deer after coming on them all unseen. What a reputation man has among the beasts that we can cause such panic among them by our mere presence.

There had been a continuous grumbling from the Deargs while I'd been on the western Fannichs which made me fly this way rather than traverse the main Fannichs and camp high. I have a distinct dislike of thunderstorms. Kitchy, my old dog, shared this fear and could give warning long before I noticed things like my hair standing on end. It was a lesson he taught me on Beinn Dearg. We traversed Cona'mheall and then he showed a distinct disinclination to climb Dearg and cringed his way up it. We were coming off the dome when a thunderstorm broke. I apologised to him for my blind stupidity – once we'd stopped our pell-mell flight downwards.

You cannot always run, though. With a friend, John Burslem, I was once caught in a spectacular storm not far down the Italian Ridge of the Matterhorn; it was quite the most unpleasant I have known. We sat it out miserably. John found that his cigarettes and matches were sodden. No comfort there. A blaze of light followed and he casually held out a cigarette saying, "Ach, missed again!" A guide on the summit had assured us the weather was set fair – which taught us several other lessons.

The Fannichs had vanished into inky clouds and it rather looked as if we were being overtaken, so I had a quick brew while still dry. The rain came on instantly and the bridge we had chosen for a shelter proved useless – it dripped along all its planks. The shower passed as we followed upstream over moors of black peat, passing Loch na Moine Mor and Loch na Moine Beag, joining a path and scurrying on frantically. The poltergeists above seemed to be all around us and the east was really grim. An old iron sign said "Cabuie Lodge 5 miles". It is now a pile of brick rubble at the head of Loch Fannich and the name has gone from the metric map.

Chuntering down to Dos Mhucarain we were finally caught and we walked along to Achnasheen in a downpour. Achanalt was my real destination but, as I'd won a couple of days ahead, a night in a hotel seemed a fair reward for wet and wildness. I knew there would be a warm welcome from Sid Abraham at Achnasheen, the pub being the nearest to Gerry's Hostel at Achnashellach where we had spent Christmas for over ten years in a row. Gerry came in later and did a superb double-take on seeing me. Bathed, and with wet things (even rucksack) taken off to the boiler room, I went down for a dram: my favourite Jura.

Ivan and Helen Waller were in the bar and as they had a copy of *Hamish's Mountain Walk* in their car I was recognised. We had corresponded about Morocco so the talk was soon of mountains all round the world. Ivan had done the Cuillin Ridge with 70-year-old Charles Warren a couple of years before. Ivan was one of that irresistible gang of mainly university climbers in the late twenties (Longland, Piggott, Hargreaves and others) and I'm sure is the only one of them still active on rock. He had recently added the sin of Munro-bagging to his septuagenarian crimes and had camped in Strathmulzie beside the lad I'd met on the Deargs. (He cuts weight down by the simple expedient of not carrying food.) An RAF gang on a big north-south trek had passed through the day before and Joe Brown and Mo Anthoine had been in the day before that. Achnasheen may take over from Llanberis yet.

A wholesome dinner and a bottle of wine rounded off the day.

Friday 25 May   ACHANALT
We wandered along Strathbran-of-the-curlews-calling to Achanalt, collected a parcel from a lad Kalinowski, and set up camp just across from the one-time church in which he helped make ice axes for Mo and Joe. A small industry such as an ice axe factory makes far more sense than your massive schemes like Kishorn.

The Spanish-Gaelic hybrid *Dos Mhucarain* had puzzled me yesterday. In the old graveyard here there was a mausoleum with the name "Bignold-de Cologan, Marquis de Torrehermosa of Strathbran 1890–1968" which explained the mystery. His widow still lives nearby.

Saturday 26 May   ACHANALT
As a fan of the Kyle line I took a trip on it to Dingwall and back in the morning, wrote letters all afternoon and in the evening greeted Charles Knowles who had come up from Sheffield via Dunoon to grab some Munros and was willing to share my route for a few days, as long, in fact, as we had mutual interests. The night before I had left Kinghorn we had fixed up a meeting at the telephone kiosk at Achanalt at 8 p.m., a rendezvous which rather puzzled his fellow workers in a city insurance office. Being Charles, he arrived at five to eight. I don't know how many

countries we have skied and climbed in together but he is a grand lad to have along being strong, diligent, organised – all the happy characteristics which most of us (especially mountaineers) usually lack.

Sunday 27 May   TO STRATH ORRIN

For convenience we each set up our own tent, and the site under a big beech tree looked cheerful with the blue and yellow combination. Storm found a slow worm burrowing through the accumulated litter of beech mast.

Our first joint Munro-appointment lay well south, what we often called 'the Farrar Four' as they stand above that glen. North of them was lonely Glen Orrin, the lower parts now flooded in a Hydro scheme, north again Strath Conon, a motorable glen but a dead end, and north again Strath Bran, the east-west road and rail link where we were camped.

We crossed to Strath Conon in a single push and stopped for a brew beside the Telford Church. Most people know of the famous engineer as being responsible for the Caledonian Canal and many miles of highland road, few realise he built 32 churches in places from Shetland to the Outer Isles, Mull, Islay and remote sites like this. They are unmistakable, being small and simple, with a tiny 'lantern' belfry on one end and always four windows on the sides. There is another near Lochluichart, the next hamlet east of Achanalt, so have a look at it next time you pass. Two windows have been changed to doors in Strath Conon but the pattern still holds. The stark similarity was needed to keep within the £1,500 allowed for each church and manse.

The daffodils and rhoddies were in flower in the lush gardens of a big house, a contrast to the empty landscape we reached as soon as we pulled up to break through to Glen Orrin by Gleann Chaorainn. We set up camp on the close-cropped grass under a remnant of Scots pine forest with, above us, Greag a' Ghlastail which had a long ribbon of fall tumbling down it. We looked over the grassy strath to the snowy northern corries of the Farrar Four. If the tones were subdued, the effect only gained by the softness. It was one of the remotest sites, but idyllic, not fearsome as many had been this trip.

Monday 28 May   THE FARRAR FOUR

This was a group for which I had especially wanted a sunny day. Five previous visits had provided no photographic record. We left with the hills steaming and blue sky appearing: classic good weather signs. A couple of hours later I sat brewing beside the Fhuar-thuill Loch, *cold hole*

Where it all begins – in the "office" at home overlooking the Forth

Canisbay Church

Duncansby Stacks

Camp on Ben Hope, 6 May!

. . . And on 9 May at Cape Wrath

Sandwood Bay: first of many fine bays in the Four Countries

Opposite: The remote Eas Coul-Aulin, t[highest falls ir Britain

Left: Life goes on – gull chic[hatching

Suilven: the view from the south

Conival from Ben More Assynt

Above: The Beinn Dearg Hills – the desolate country at the head of Glen Douchary

Right: A Telford Church in Strath Conon

Hamish and Storm in camp in lonely Glen Orrin

Storm on the trig point of An Socath – looking back to the
Sgurr na Lapaich hills

loch, one of the corrie-lochans that are a feature of the group. The loch was still frozen over, the tops more in cloud and the rain "kept coming in squirts and the wind in squalls, until one's heart grew weary of such fitful, scolding weather" (R.L.S.).

I had burned-up to this best of corries but Charles, collecting Tops rather than aesthetic routes, had gone on for an outlier. We met again as we groped our separate routes up Sgurr Fhuar-thuill. A couple of bumps later we had a brew, which was as well, as the weather became progressively wilder and wetter, with sleet and snow at times. On big Sgurr a' Choire Ghlais our hair was tingling so we did not linger. Navigation was easy as a mob had traversed the peaks recently and their tracks were visible on the old snow. They had also waymarked their route with empty sardine tins, paper, plasters and orange peel. Carn nan Gobhar has the mossy feel of a golf course and Sgurr na Ruaidh lies away off in the wrong direction for the club house in Glen Orrin. We had a long downward-circling off it to eventually splash through the river opposite camp. We saw a big badger sett. If you must walk through rain all day then there are worse places. The sun shone once we were back, of course.

Tuesday 29 May   STRATHFARRAR CAMP
We walked right up Glen Orrin, passing a grey Am Fiar-Loch and then a sparkling Loch na Caoidhe – the difference being the sun's return after a night of rain. An English family were camped by a ruin and we set them speculating with our animal noises as we crept past.

The upper parts are rather featureless and we were both so careful (and so busy talking) that we overshot a path that would have taken us over Druim Dubh for the Farrar side of the hills. A golden plover went flapping off to lead us away from her nest but Storm soon nosed out the nest when told to. We climbed steeply up on to Druim Dubh and looked down to Loch Monar, which we reached through a glen with a good path. We wended east to the Lodge and while Storm and I entertained the sheep and lambs (still being fed) Charles went off to collect parcels from Mrs Duncan. He came back with one of mine but not his own which he had posted a week before. This at once posed problems so we adjourned over the dam to a cosy spot to brew and plan again.

We decided we'd do the Lapaich group the next day and Charles could then check the Lodge again (the post came only every second day) and if still no food parcel had come, he could exit to Gerry's at Achnashellach over something on his 'wants list'. We had food enough for that and my own exit to Loch Duich. We camped by the rowdy Uisge

Misgeach, *water of intoxication*, a beautiful spot again, because of the trees and the sun. We paddled and chatted on the green sward. At 6 p.m. it rained hard and the poltergeists started banging around upstairs again, with a deal of flashing lights . . .

We had met three other English lads packing in to Glen Orrin so wondered how they fared. The holiday period had brought this invasion. Fancy meeting *two* other parties in one day! Glen Strathfarrar is barred to the public by a locked gate, despite having a reserve and a hydro road built at the public's expense. Limited day visits with cars can be made by applying to the cottage beside the gate but camping is not allowed. This is still the easiest approach for The Farrar Four. The glen is long and varied scenically. It abounds in deer, and free-ranging cattle pose beside white foxgloves with the Lapaichs filling the head of the glen. There were graphite mines here in the early nineteenth century. Marble outcrops at Inchvuilt, and Loch na Meine is *loch of the mine* – lead in this case.

Wednesday 30 May   THE LAPAICH HILLS
"A good month to have away" was a comment this May-month earned. It was one of the poorest I can remember, yet, with hindsight now, it was the best month of the whole trip for enjoyment. It had been so much my type of country – and no month ahead would be so wild or empty again. If not quite all downhill now, there was still a subtle lessening of quality once Kintail and the Great Glen were reached.

We were off at 5 a.m. for Charles had a great number of Tops to collect. We began, as the day before, by Charles dashing off for an outlier while I was able to go to the first col and up Carn nan Gobhar without the rucksack. Gobhar has two summits and each of us arrived on one simultaneously which was immaculate timing. Sgurr na Lapaich, 3,773 ft, is the highest hill north of Glen Affric. It was an important point in the Ordnance Survey work of 1846 and 1848. Charles, in red, with ice axe, seen on its steep summit cone, a plume of white blowing off the snow into the blue, made a very standard picture of Himalayan scenes. The blue at least was welcome. So were ice axes which he had brought. He charged off for more Tops and I ambled down to the An Riabhachan col. In the wettest of ground there was suddenly a great squeaking at my feet and on looking I found I had stood on a nest of naked baby mice. It was a puzzle how their cocoon of grass stayed dry in the melting surroundings.

On An Riabhachan there was a vast amount of snow still. You could have skied its corries. I found a good sheath knife on the peak; if the owner reads this and would like it back, please write! Below the South West Top I enjoyed some good trundles down on to the snow. At the col before An Socath I brewed and spread the tent to catch the attention of Charles when he came following after, so he could do the same. Storm fell off the trig point on An Socath when I said "okay" after I'd been photographing him. Wheatears and mountain blackbirds went chakking off as we skidded down to the col again. An eagle flapped off like a plaid blowing in the wind. We met Charles and drank a last brew together. (Charles I'm sure regards all this brewing as very degenerate – but drinks it with a Yorkshireman's zest for char if there is nothing better.)

I baled off from the col with several standing glissades and headed round and down the bulk of An Socath. Charles came down the North East Ridge after I'd crossed it, and made back along northern flanks of the range to his tent. He wrote later of his successive doings: "I got back to the tent about seven and walked up to the Lodge for 8.30. No parcel. The Duncans invited me in and we had a pot of tea and some sandwiches but about 10.30 I said I must leave so I could pitch in the remaining daylight, along the loch. Instead they offered me the assistant keeper's bothy which had a gas cooker and hot shower! They also sold me a couple of tins of meat, some cheese and teabags, which with your donations, lasted out till I got back to the car on Saturday evening.

"I left the bothy early Thursday and was soon in cloud, using compass and altimeter over all the peaks from Creag Toll a' Choin to the Bealach Bhearnais. It was windy and inhospitable, so I dropped to camp in the valley. Friday was a marvellous day. I did the circuit to Lurg Mhor, plus Feartaig, very enjoyable. Saturday I was off at 5.30 for Ceannaichean and Moruisg and back at the tent by ten for a rush down to Achnashellach to just miss the midday train. Spent a pleasant afternoon by Loch Dughaill and going up to the station had a lift instead, back to Achanalt, so this gave time to drive to Achnasheen to add Fionn Beinn. Sunday it was back to Dunoon and Sheffield. I hope you managed Bidean and Lurg Mhor under the circumstances. See you in two months when you've done the Pennine Way. . . ."

Once off An Socath I cut over by An Cruachan, where I exchanged a last yodel with Charles, before dropping into the Allt Coire nan Each glen. Ceathreamhnan showed at its head but the awkward pair of Bidean–Lurg Mhor first had to be visited. I hid the tent and other non-essentials before following downstream and round for Maol-Bhuidhe bothy which I reached at 5.15, the exact time of the estimate; not bad, as it had been made twelve hours before. You do not have short days on the Lapaichs.

Nobody had been in the bothy from October to April. Twice, long ago it feels, we had Hogmanay visits there, but lack of wood and other comforts did not make it a good choice. It is too well moated. An old newspaper told me the details of how one vote had toppled the government and led to the recent elections (news I'd missed being in the High Atlas). It also told of the *Loch Arkaig* sinking in Mallaig harbour (the boat on which we went to Rhum over many years) and that a minibus had crashed into the Cuileig River we had come up a week ago. Talk of 'connections'.

Thursday 31 May   LURG MHOR – BIDEAN
This pair gave quite a battle. The wind came from the east and had an icy spite in it. We crossed a bit below the outflow of Loch Cruoshie, a known spot, but much altered since last used. A freezing paddle, waist deep, is a cruel start to a climb, but the gentle river up from the loch is unfordable for miles in normal conditions. I crossed the path, and went on up the snow-edged slot into the fierce storm above for further sleet and snow batterings. I had wanted to go west-east along the ridge, but the weather ruled that out. At least the wind being so strong and definite helped in one respect: I could use it as a navigation aid, for somewhere, sometime – tell it not in Gath – I had lost my compass.

Lurg Mhor was simply a matter of going uphill till there was no hill left. That is the top. Ninety per cent of navigation (the practice rather than the theory) occurs in setting off *from* a summit. Any error there simply grows with the descent. I took one cast before finding the corrie edge and, trying not to get blown off it, followed it to the col and then up to Bidean a' Choire Sheasgaich. Of the two it is the finer, rockier hill, and it has helpful features; I also built tiny two-pebble cairns as I went so I could backtrack. The wind is an unreliable aid as it can change all unexpectedly, but it had to be trusted today. There was much less snow than on the Lapaichs, these being much smaller hills.

We backtracked for a while until I was sure we were heading correctly, then abandoned the line of cairns to cut straight down for Loch Calavie and its warmer climate. We had had our ration of cloud-clouting and punishing snow. Anyone seeing my line of mini-cairns, please knock them over, as I would have done. (Two pebbles on top of each other have a surprising survival facility: a mini-cairned route we abandoned in Skye, we were able to find again and follow, after five years.) Our mad rush down the hill set the deer spraying off over the grassy wetness. We floundered across the black and boggy moor. I abandoned intentions of seeking out other crossings: better the devil known. We came over the watery doorstep of the glen, back to the bothy, home and happy as only weather-worn hillmen can be.

Let me quote from my log: "I was in at 2 p.m. At 3 p.m. the wind died away. At 4 p.m. it came howling out of the west – so all the bloody weather of the last 24 hours comes back again! The clouds this morning were pouring along Beinn Dronaig. They are again now, but from the opposite direction."

Friday 1 June SGURR NAN CEATHREAMHNAN

The bold Deargs and the big Lapaichs had ambushed us with splendid conditions, now it happened again for another big, hard day of 21 miles over Ceathreamhnan. It could have been split into two days but food was low and Kintail comforts beckoned. We returned to the Allt Coire nan Each valley, picked up the tent, walked up to Loch Mhoicean and then broke through a low col above to descend to the glen west of Loch Mullardoch. The map showed Loch Mhoicean having a stream flowing out of both ends, but there was no exit at the north-east end. The name horse (*each*) commemorates a punitive expedition by General Monck in Commonwealth times. They had come through Lochiel country to Loch Quoich and Kintail and then wandered through for the head of Loch Monar and Glen Strathfarrar. Here, in the bogs, over a hundred baggage horses were left behind – their bones are still dug out of the peat – so one wonders who was punishing who.

The new metric map has given Munro's Tables a shock in all this part of the country. If you want to see just how big the changes are between the old One Inch and the Second Series 1:50,000 maps, look at the ridges of Sgurr nan Ceathreamhnan and in particular the one running out to that faraway Munro, Creag a' Choire Aird. It is no longer Creag a' Choire Aird for a start: it is now Mullach na Dheiragain and the mapping agrees with reality. I wonder how many times in the good old days we went astray because of map errors – the last thing one was trained to expect? (There are 1,000 ft rock climbs hidden away under the old 'rough pastures' symbol.) Up here, once you use the new metric map, you will never go back to the antique One Inch.

At the foot of Gleann Sithidh, *the fairy glen*, it was hot enough to change into short trousers for the first time. This is the glen to the west of Dheiragain, and its flanks are the two long ridges running out from Ceathreamhnan which so dominates the view. Mam Sodhail and Carn

Eighe (to the east) may be slightly bigger but they are shapeless lumps. Ceathreamhnan is a queen among mountains.

By making a very gentle rising line I landed on the ridge behind Dheiragain, so collected that bump of bumps, *sans sac*, but laden with cameras. Melt-water pools below the banks of snow reflected a landscape of rich browns, purples and blues. Only in the straths and valleys and by the warm western sea were the greens assertive, but there tree leaves are so green that one is afraid to touch in case they are still wet from spring painting. Up on the tops the grass still lay cobwebby and flattened round the snowfalls, edged here and there by brave purple saxifrage and unfurling Alpine mantle. There was still a whiff of deadness to it – like vegetables stored too long under the fridge. And yet there was life there too. I had seen eagles often enough. As I walked along for Ceathreamhnan two ravens casually stepped off the pavement (like city gents in tidy suits); there was an area furrowed with the channels of mice, and ptarmigan belched at us (invisible among the grey speckled rocks). These all belong there, as much as the rocks themselves, tenacious, awe-inspiring residents. We go up as puny, nervous day-trippers.

Had it been freezing my ice axe would have been essential for there were parts of the ridge up Ceathreamhnan (pronounced: Kerranan) which still were crested with snow. The traverse to the flat West Top presented no difficulty, but I made plenty by taking an exciting route off, on the shady side, so had to cut steps downhill and cross a crevasse and deal with one small rock climb. From the grassy slopes above Sgurr Gaorsaic I had an eagle's eye view over the sprawl of Ben Attow to Kintail and Sgriol and the far Cuillin, then chuntered down the brutal slopes to picnic by Loch a' Bhealaich, under the Bealach an Sgairne, the Gates of Affric. (Affric means *dappled* water.) We ate the last of our day's food so had every incentive to move on but I still grudged doing so. Since Achanalt we had covered 80 miles without walking half a mile on tarmac. We would not do that again. Ben Attow above us was shown in a 1910 geography book as 4,000 ft, but at that time Ingleborough and Whernside were over 5,000, and St. Kilda 5,400 ft. The taming of our hills by maps and Tables is not yet a hundred years old. Colonel Thornton managed to turn Crianlarich into *Cree in La Roche* and it must have been a Lancashire lad who made Loch Ba into *Loch Ball*. One old map even managed to have a place called *beg more*!

Grassy zig-zags took us up into the defile of the bealach, an 1,800 ft col which has been used from prehistoric times. Loch Duich is the *Loch of Duthac*, an Irish saint (died Armagh 1065) who used the pass which has a St. Duthac's Well on it. What raiders and drovers, pedlars and stravaigers must have used it since, for it was on the main route from Skye to Inverness. The minister of Kintail in 1793 wrote, describing it, "Within three miles of Kintail is a high ridge which environs this district and would render it inaccessible if nature had not left a small gap in the mountains, as if it had been sawn down the middle, which leaves room for three to go abreast. The ascent on the east is in a zig-zag direction. The western aspect is truly steep and vexatious." Two hundred years has not changed it.

The descent seemed long, walking into the glare of the westering sun and legs feeling the jarring of a hard path. The slopes are wooded: patterns of pines like unfinished tapestry-work, stitched on the frame of hills. An entrance to the wood had a notice: "Ponies please close gate". Some wag had added "Humans also please close gate". We swung down to the boggy flats at Innis a' Chrotha and the alder-lined riverbank camp site. There we stopped. The Morvich site was no longer run by the NTS. I had hoped for a shop but it was all rather characterless and sterile. There was not even a public telephone. I used the site, however, and oddly enjoyed the busy scene for its contrast to what had gone before. I had not long pitched when the sun moved behind the hill and a heavy dew came down. The cuckoo-in-residence had a cracked voice, a good sign, pointing to the species soon losing its voice altogether. Supper was rather dull: plenty of tea, but otherwise just a tin of pâté with dried beans and macaroni. Kintail is Ceann at t-soile, *the head of the salty water* – I was down to sea level again.

Saturday 2 June SOME SOUTH GLEN SHIEL HILLS

"A rather crazy day" was my night-time report on the day. I was up early, for a second day of good weather in succession was not to be left in the cupboard. I phoned Ray in Cleethorpes hoping he could come up tomorrow, but had to make do with the original Monday evening rendezvous. (I would keep going a day or two ahead!) At the Kintail Lodge Hotel I photographed a couple of walkers who had come through from Cannich by Glen Affric and were returning via the Cean-nacroc hills. They were cousins, one English (Mr Bedford), one Dutch (Mr Biegel), in their sixties and had been making annual rounds like this for several summers. We walked along to the Shiel Bridge shop, after I had left my pack at the hotel. The others had a lift at once up the glen so should have been back to Cannich no bother. I had tea and read a *Scots Magazine*, determined to enjoy a good fester in the sun, but when I came out from the cafe I was offered a lift up the glen as well. Being an opportunist, I took it.

Two of the peaks on the Cluanie Ridge were on the list of sixes and I
had intended doing them tomorrow or the next day, or even with Ray,
but given a perfect day and a lift, well, it was not to be refused. From a
familiar lay-by, two miles west of Cluanie, we set off, the dog as ever
simply carrying himself, I, in shorts, bearing a plastic carrier bag of
fairly useless shopping and the *Scotsman*. I had no waterproofs, no
compass and no maps. The last was rather missed as I could not
remember which peaks I *had* to climb – so had to do extras to "mak sic-
car". This was an off-route, off-day expedition, not really part of the
Groats End Walk. It was one on which to make very certain not to break
a leg!

The main risk, however, was heatstroke and we went up by ridges and
kept on crests to utilise the slightest breeze. I sat on Aonach air Chrith to
read my paper. It had an article of Bill Murray's recounting how he had
come to write his classic book *Mountaineering in Scotland* in POW camp. It
and its even better sequel *Undiscovered Scotland* had just been re-issued in
a single volume by Diadem Books. There was also a review of the
Hamish McInnes volumes of *West Highland Walks*.

There was a tempting ridge off Maol Chinn-dearg but I went on just in
case Sgurr an Doire Leathain was a sixer and from it of course Sgurr an
Lochain was irresistible. We came off down the northern corrie stream –
in which we paddled – and our only regret was not having the tea kit or
cameras (washing powder, a pot scourer, salt, midge cream and other
tinned foods were my odd burden). Storm was recognised by a family
who had been on the camp site the night before so we had a lift back as
well. (Why is it lifts are so easy on the fine sunny days of no urgency – and
impossible when desperately needed?) We were so busy talking we drove
past the hotel so had to walk back to it. Mrs Main soon produced tea, a
walker's-sized pot of it. I sorted our parcels later and then read *Peter
Duck* till all hours, having found it in the lounge bookcase. A rather crazy
day.

Sunday 3 and Monday 4 June
Some hours I lay in the old woods of Ratagan among scented hyacinths,
primroses and violets, some hours I lay above the loch where there was a
cairn inscribed "To the Rev. William John MacLeod 1898–1941 with
love from his children Katherine and Ann 1966". Ray found me in the
hotel garden drinking tea and writing to Roger, so unkindly gave me a
pile of mail he had brought. Kintail Lodge Hotel we knew well from

Hogmanay holiday visits, when a dinner there was always high on the list of activities. Even in busy summer we had a gourmet menu: iced gaspacho soup, piles of beef, and a trifle off a groaning sweet trolley. Comforts are doubly relished after stern abstinence.

WEST HIGHLAND WAYS

Most at ease among the mountains
For they tell of youth and mystery –
And all men would travel backwards:
The womb is warm!
                    Did you smell the sea?
Did you lie in heather with diamonds overhead?
Or see all secrets in a snowflake?
Did you weep for joy and, in the morning place,
All hungers fill and fearful thirst slake?
               Scottish Mountaineering Club Journal 1978

Tuesday 5 June   THROUGH GLEN SHIEL   *Maps, pp. 57 and 69*

Ray Swinburn comes from South Humberside where, living all of 300 feet above sea level, he calls his house Hill Crest. Several years ago, however, he saw the light and has become an irregular visitor to 3,000 feet. A confirmed long-distance 'backpacker' (horrible Americanism) he had run out of routes south of the border so now was making the most of Scottish through-routes. He was keen to do the West Highland Way before it became the designated, statutory, commissioned dirt-track that such routes are south of the border and he took little persuading to link on the miles through to the west, a sort of 'Road to the Isles', to be played backwards.

A few years before, we had set off on a Jubilee coast-to-coast trek from Skye to Montrose and ran into a heat wave which lasted for the two weeks of the crossing. Ray fell out in Knoydart and I only managed by taking such drastic measures as starting at four in the morning. An account of that crossing is given in the 1979 *Scottish Mountaineering Club Journal*. The following September Ray and I set off again and had a very non-sunny crossing. The route varied each time and it was from doing these trips that the idea came of the *Ultimate Challenge*, a non-organised organised 'event' with a vast area to choose from and not just a single fragile line. 'Ways' are a foreign intrusion of very doubtful benefit to Scotland, but the bureaucrats are giving them to us whether we like it or

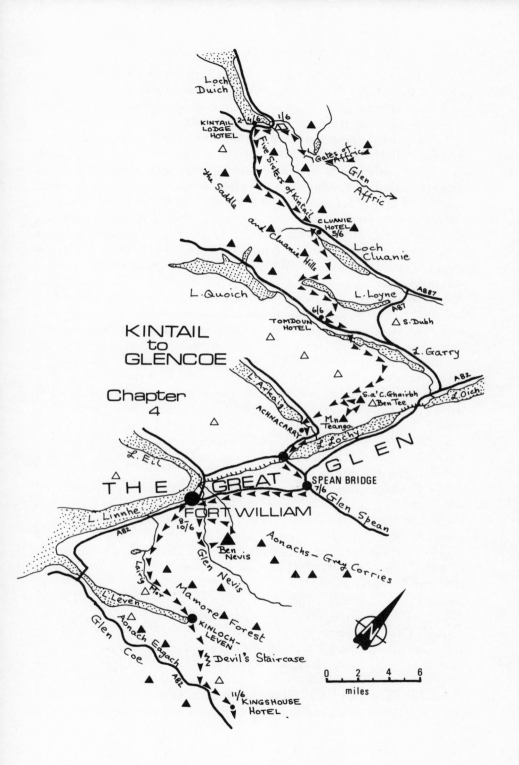

Loch
Duich

KINTAIL
LODGE
HOTEL
2·4/6   1/6

Gates of Affric

Five Sisters of Kintail

The Saddle

and Cluanie Hills

Glen
Affric

CLUANIE
HOTEL
5/6

Loch
Cluanie

L. Quoich

L. Loyne

A887

A87

KINTAIL
to
GLENCOE

TOMDOUN
HOTEL

6/6

S. Dubh

Chapter
4

L. Arkaig

L. Garry

A82

L. Oich

S. a' C. Ghairbh
Ben Tee

ACHNACARRY

M.n
Teanga

L. Lochy

L. Eil

GLEN

SPEAN BRIDGE

7/6

THE   GREAT

Glen Spean

L. Linnhe

FORT WILLIAM

8·
10/6

A82

Ben
Nevis

Aonachs - Grey Corries

Glen Nevis

Larig Mor

L. Leven

Mamore Forest

Glen Coe

Aonach Eagach

KINLOCH-
LEVEN

Devil's Staircase

A82

11/6

KINGSHOUSE
HOTEL.

N

0   2   4   6

miles

not. Democracy means being able to say what we like and the government doing what it likes. Bodies seem quite incapable of realising that *doing nothing* may be best of all in some circumstances, though that produces no congratulatory statistics or O.B.E.s.

The lack of imagination is frightening. We passed a classic case today in Glen Shiel where the road, a major tourist one, has to run right through the dust and noise of a quarry, which grows year by year in all its unscreened ugliness. When the power lines to Skye were a possible threat to Glen Shiel the NTS were loud in complaining yet when I wrote to them about this quarry there was not even a reply. The Mountaineering Council for Scotland did look into it and apparently the quarry only has a year to go – and will be tidied up. Could it not have been screened by trees 20 years ago, though? "Where there is no vision the people perish" still holds true.

A walk up Glen Shiel between its chiselled ridges might seem an odd line but by keeping to the side opposite the road it was remarkably pleasant. The river sounds made the road sounds inaudible and, quarry apart, there was little of man to be seen. Lousewort was in flower, as were the first butterwort which looked like stranded starfish along the boggy, myrtle-tangy riverbanks. The slopes were white with the nodding paws of bog cotton. A dipper, *the smith of the stream* in Gaelic, shot off ahead of us. We had one pause at the Telford Bridge, which only recently has been superseded by the main highway west. It is a solid structure of simple lines. When building it several old muskets were found wedged in the river, having been abandoned during the 1719 rebellion which came to a quick, inglorious end in a battle here.

The Jacobite risings of 1715 and 1745 have very much overshadowed the 1719 affair but it is worth remembering. Eilean Donan Castle was shelled by Hanoverian ships and largely destroyed, only being restored, added to and given its causeway bridge in this century – to become possibly the most photographed building in Scotland, the dream-image of a clan castle. The exiled James, the Old Pretender, managed to miss the boat, literally, and only a straggly, inefficient force arrived to set off east to raise the country. They were met by the government forces under General Wightman here, in the narrows of Glen Shiel, and completely routed. One feels some sympathy for a Spanish contingent, far from their sunny homeland, but this has given us a Top, Sgurr na Spainteach, *Spaniard's Peak*, overlooking the scene. Rob Roy somehow came to be involved, in what was his last battle, and the real leader of the rebels, excusably ill that day, was James Keith, brother of the Earl Marischal, who went on to serve the Empress of Russia and then became a Field

Marshal under Frederick the Great. For 200 years the armies of Europe were full of dispossessed Scots and Irish. In one period of 50 years the Austrian empire had sixteen Irish generals or higher ranking officers.

One outcome of the successive Jacobite risings was the need for maps of the Highlands, a need then gradually fading but brought into life again by the threat of the Napoleonic invasion. The Ordnance Survey was set up. (Their first map was of Kent.) The risings also brought the need for roads, and first Wade and then Caulfeild built hundreds of miles of road, many of which are still used today. Ironically the first person to use Wade's new Corrieyairack Pass road was Bonnie Prince Charlie on his triumphant march from Kilcumin (Fort Augustus) to Edinburgh. Later, as a hunted fugitive, he was to scrabble over the Cluanie ridge and up roadless Glen Shiel (as we did today) to find refuge in caves on Sgurr nan Conbhairean, guarded by the "Seven Men of Glenmoriston". The road through Glen Shiel was built by Caulfeild. It led to the Bernera Barracks at Glenelg, via Mam Ratagan.

It was the road taken by Dr Johnson and James Boswell in 1773 when they were on their 'Road to the Isles'. The Mam Ratagan pass was as steep, then, as it is today, and the weighty doctor had to ride two ponies turn about up its slopes. He had a somewhat jaundiced view of the hills of Glen Shiel; when Boswell called one of the prodigious hills immense Johnson told him it was merely "a considerable protuberance".

The Cluanie Inn, *inn of the meadows*, where we ended the day, was a military and coaching inn and is one of the oldest in Scotland. It just clings to something of its old character externally but is completely modernised inside, with standard lack of taste. We were well looked after. This is not a complaint!

Many years ago our Fife school bus stopped there when returning from a visit to Skye. The teacher driving was an Aberdonian and retained an unmistakable accent. The granite city was having a typhoid epidemic. As soon as the petrol pump attendant was addressed, he backed away vowing that there was no more petrol that day. The Highlanders' lingering terror of infectious diseases could not have been more evident. It was justified too.

One of the highest points on Mingulay is known as MacPhee's Hill. Many years ago, when the island was inhabited, it was noticed from the next island that there had been no smoking chimneys for a long time. A boat went over to investigate. MacPhee was put ashore and found the whole population had died, presumably of some infectious disease. When the others heard this they put to sea, simply leaving the poor man behind. For weeks he climbed nightly to the top of the hill and lit a fire till eventually everyone realised that if he had survived all that time, then the danger was over and he could be rescued.

Wednesday 6 June   THE OLD ROAD TO TOMDOUN
Caulfeild's road to Glen Shiel left the Great Glen at Invergarry and continued west to Tomdoun and then doubled up the hill, dropped west of Loch Loyne and crossed another hill to Cluanie. Recently Loch Loyne was much enlarged by a dam which flooded the old road, and the present road was built instead. Its steep pull up from Loch Garry has added a splendid roadside view into the hills of Glen Kingie and Knoydart, a view more than doubled for those prepared to climb Sgurr Dubh above the new road.

We followed the old road today and, because it is cut by Loch Loyne, had the entertaining addition of rounding the Loch. We descended to the Loch's western end by the Allt Guibhais, a stream which splits into several streamlets in the course of its descent – a rare feature. This is a forgotten corner now, giving glimpses up into the rough, seldom-climbed northern corries of Spidean Mialach. The going along Loch Loyne was of a similar nature to Loch Fannich, endless peat bog, but it was a paradise for waders and duck. Ospreys nested here till 1910. In a dry summer when the loch is low there is the odd spectacle of the old bridge sitting high and dry out in the middle of the water. We had the road again for a hill over and down to Tomdoun, a favourite hotel for walkers and fishermen. It has not altered in appearance over the years.

It had changed hands recently and the new owners were French. Their youngest still did not speak English and thought my French rather peculiar. A cuckoo came and perched on the fence. A silent cuckoo. An English couple had been speaking to a lad in Fort Augustus who had been months on the way from Land's End and was now pushing to John o' Groats. He had chucked a factory job to follow his dream. Some Scottish Mountaineering Club acquaintances came in for dinner, having walked out from Barrisdale along that superb Loch Hourn-side path. Hotel life makes camping life seem quite monastic.

Thursday 7 June   SUMMITS AND A SOAKING
This was to be a day of peaks, passes and puddles, beginning well enough and I suppose ending well enough too as we shifted from comfy hotel to comfy hotel. Madame produced breakfast at seven so we were given a good start. It rained as far as Greenfield, which Ray, with his gift of mis-naming, later produced as "Greenland".

Glen Garry suffered as badly as anywhere from the Clearances with the mother of the chief (then under age) driving out every crofter in the glen. It was intended to ship them to Australia but as no ships were available they were sent to America instead. Those who refused to move were simply burnt out. That was in 1772. Sheep ate men. And now trees and deer have largely eaten the sheep.

After walking through the forest for some miles we had what Ray called "a wee piece" beside some old sheds where the stalking gentry had carved their names in the woodwork; 1881 was the oldest we spotted. A path, messy with recent forestry working, led us out of the trees to the rather wet flanks of the Ben Tee hills. Ben Tee *the fairy hill* is a symmetrical cone and instantly recognisable though it is only 2,957 ft and sits beside two Munros in Glengarry's Bowling Green. The hills lie immediately west of Loch Lochy and add much to the scenery of the Great Glen. Coast-to-coast trips either have to round them to north or south or go over them. We were skirting to go south across their west flanks and I, perforce, had to pop them in the bag for the sixth time. Richard Wood, who lives conveniently below them, has sclimmed Sron a' Choire Ghairbh over 300 times. A year of his life to a mountain.

Ray left me to my peaks at Fedden (*chanter*) and went off down the Cia-aig Glen for Achnacarry and Spean Bridge. I could catch up. I crossed to the path that comes over the Cam Bhealach between the two Munros. I shot up the path and then the zig zags off it to gain the Sron. Few Munros have a path leading almost to the top. Meall na Teanga is less well served but a wending ascent of it can be made almost as easily.

My memories of peaks are often from their association with people rather than weather or anything else. These hills we first came to know with Braehead school parties. Charlie Gorrie and I had a gang of girls and boys up Teanga from Loch Lochy Youth Hostel and lingered on ourselves on the Sron to watch the sun set, which it did in glorious technicolour. Charlie's route down left much to be desired and we ended in the black forest crawling down backwards through the trees to avoid having our eyes poked out. He, then, was probably no older than I am now but, being an SMC member, the innocent young teacher regarded him as infallible, ancient and to be revered, like all SMC worthies. In the forest we kicked up patches of glittering soil, a phenomenon due to phosphorescence in the decaying pine needles.

I collected the rucker, then took a short cut off the path to follow the Allt Cam Bhealaich, racing to escape the rain which soon was lashing down. Having won the summits dry seemed a miracle, but on them I had had the best of the day. Forestry felling had generally messed up paths and I was wet and sweaty by the time the Cia-aig Falls were reached. This fall is another 'witch's cauldron'. It has its tale. A cattle sickness was traced to a hermit woman who was putting the evil eye on them. A party out to slay the *caillich* broke in to her hut only to find a vicious cat. They wounded it with their dirks as it broke out through the doorway and trailed it from the blood till they found it exhausted by the Cia-aig Falls. At their final assault the beast leapt, screaming over the falls – but it was the form of the old hag which splashed into the deep pool below. They stoned her till she drowned. As their cattle improved forthwith their analysis had no doubt been correct.

The Clunes-Loch Arkaig road here is 'The Dark Mile' of Broster novel fame: a gloomy passage with trees and rocks upholstered in decaying moss and lichen like some natural counterpart of Dickens' Miss Haversham. It was from an oak tree by Loch Arkaig that Cameron of Clunes waited to ambush an officer of Cumberland's army after Culloden, shooting his victim dead in the gloaming – only he shot the wrong man, for the officer had had word of an attempt on his life that day and ensured a fellow officer rode his all too recognisable white horse.

I left the road to go round a shorter route by Achnacarry, the clan seat of the Camerons. The house is relatively modern. Donald, 'Gentle Lochiel' of the Forty Five was forfeited and his house was burnt down. His grandson had the estate restored in 1784 and began building in 1802. London lights were more attractive however (as they were to so many chiefs) and he abandoned it. It was 1837 before the next chief, also Donald, finished it.

On the south bank of the Arkaig river is a fine avenue of beeches which from being evenly spaced suddenly become carelessly positioned. Story has it that Lochiel was engaged in planting this avenue when Prince Charlie landed. The remaining trees were just "shuggled" in, to be tidied when he returned – which was not to be.

This whole region became one of sorrow during the Clearances as thousands took ship from Loch Eil and Loch Linnhe. In 1801 alone eleven ships sailed off with 3,300 impoverished 'refugees'. Nearby, where Caol now stands on the edge of the Blar Mor, folk evicted from Glendessary and Loch Arkaig tried to carve a living from the bogs. The absentee Lochiel tried to say he did not know of the evictions when he met the people. No white-washing can exonerate this man or his like. To follow their London life they quite brutally sacrificed their people.

In 1843 'The Disruption' split the Church of Scotland. This was a fight for principles when conscience made a sacrifice which must be revered for all time. Ministers could be appointed by local landowners, a practice that was open to gross misuse. Congregations demanded the right to choose their ministers. The State had no right to take upon itself this spiritual authority. Eventually there was a 'walk out', though the secessionists outnumbered the 'rump' left as the Church of Scotland. Legally they had no claim to property, and land-owners often denied them all help: services were held in graveyards or between tide-lines, even in a floating ark – sometimes for years. Under threat of eviction nobody would accommodate secessionist ministers. It is all old history now; but to this day the Clearances and the Disruption have left the people bitter at their double betrayal by those who should have been their leaders.

Ray had also taken the Achnacarry road. He had had a snack in the church as the only place out of the monsoon. I was glad just to road-walk for once – instead of exploring the canal and old military roads as I'd suggested to Ray. We all crossed the Caledonian Canal at the Gairlochy Locks.

The construction of this canal was an early example of how government operations can escalate in cost. James Watt surveyed the 60 mile long route in 1773 and gave an estimate of £164,000. No action was taken. John Rennie in 1793 pushed the same scheme again to no avail. The Napoleonic War at last made for its start: privateers off the north coasts could be dodged – and there was a great pool of labour thanks to the Clearances. The Highlander was a prized soldier too. The government was actually becoming alarmed at the emigration rate. The canal was made big enough to take seagoing traffic (sailing ships for America or the Baltic). It is now the only canal link of its size from North Sea to Atlantic. Thirty-eight miles of it are through lochs.

In 1802 Telford put in an estimate for £350,000 over seven years. A year later Parliament authorised the scheme. Final surveys put this estimate up to £474,000. The canal was opened in 1822, after much difficult work. £645,000 had been spent. It was a considerable engineering feat and the basin at Corpach and the locks at Fort Augustus (Neptune's Staircase) are still impressive. By 1827 the expenditure was £973,000 and after increasing the depth later in 1847 the cost was £1,311,270. It was really a sort of nineteenth century Concorde.

A fishing boat was pushing along into dimmed reflection as I crossed the Gairlochy swing bridge. At the turn of the century hundreds of Zulus used it, now it carries mainly pleasure traffic. Roads have won. Even the 400 ton *Captain Scott*, carefully built to fit the canal, never used it.

The pull up from the canal was tiresome, the gutters were like rivers and a 27 mile day could have done without such a conclusion. The

Commandos on the memorial were facing into it with jaws set – no doubt they had had their fill of rain while training in these parts during the war. Rain like this does not simply wet you through to the clammy skin, it sneaks into the very marrow and heart and brain. It gives a hammering more psychological than physical. Depression is not just a meteorological term. My own defence is simply to turn inwards and think of other things, to set a rainbow in the mind, and plod on. Ray had been in for an hour and I had gained half an hour on my estimated time of arrival. The day took my mileage past 500. When conditions are utterly foul, they can only improve.

Friday 8 June   FORT WILLIAM

Last night the Spean Bridge Hotel had done Ray's steak as he ordered it – like iron. They did mine likewise, which was bad enough, but when I bit it a tooth disintegrated.

Today, by following the old military road, the golf course and other odd tracks we made it to Fort William without having to walk on the lethal A82. We met the first midges however – Scotland's far from extinct man-eaters. The summer hubbub of 'The Fort' had already begun. Such quantities of people! Over a bar lunch in the Imperial we parcelled off our ice axes to Charles, as I had borrowed one from him, and Ray could retrieve his from Sheffield easily. With the Ben to do next day, that was a sad comment on the conditions since Ceathreamhnan. I also sent off several unused films, a change from always running short. We booked in for Bed and Breakfast at Leesholme. The Lees were not long back from a family holiday in Snowdonia.

Saturday 9 June   BEN NEVIS – NUMBER ONE

We called in at Nevisport before heading for the Ben. Alex Gillespie there had arranged to keep me supplied with any gear needed during the trip and had also supplied much beforehand.

The tourist route up the Ben is one of my few dislikes among the hills so we went up the glen to the waterslide at the car park to make our own devious route up to the top of Britain. As the water was low I enjoyed going up the slabs of the Allt Coire Eoghainn itself. We met at the rowan tree before the corrie and then swung west for Carn Dearg. There is a fine view through the gorge to the Steall Fall from these slopes. Carn Dearg was in cloud but, if anything, the top of the Ben is best disguised. The dog and I could hear people on the path but managed to keep Ray off it and suddenly presented him with the Observatory ruins. We wended down to the old spring for water and back up to brew near the trig point. There was a constant stream of visitors. I recognised one voice through the mist and turned to Ray and said, "I'll introduce you to John Hinde in a few minutes." John duly arrived and Ray was left to work that one out. John had a 'clan' from the Lochiel Outward Bound Centre with him and naturally they had a stove and dixi. John directed one lad on a certain bearing for a certain number of paces to find the spring, and another was told to start the primus. Ray commented something about "two old foxes on the one summit".

The cloud began to break up and there were impressive views down the cliffs through the swirling clag. I was telling John that I had at last found a copy of Kilgour's book, *Twenty Years on Ben Nevis*, which gives the story of the old Observatory and, better still, is full of marvellous photographs. One shows the staff playing ping pong on a carved block of ice and many show dramatic winter conditions with everything covered in fog crystals – which once grew five feet in one week. After the first winter they added a 'conning tower' entrance – which was essential when there was 20 feet of snow on top.

An excellent article on the Observatory appeared in the *Climber and Rambler* of May 1978, and anyone interested could order a photo copy (see any issue for details). On a tour in Ireland I was praising this article to Jim and Harriet Barton only to find that Jim had written it! Thomas Stevenson (of lighthouse fame and father of R.L.S.) first suggested high-level weather observations but Government funds were not available. In 1880 and 1881 Clement E. Wragge climbed the hill daily (June – October) to take readings. The Government promised a £100 annual grant but the Observatory had to be built with money raised by public appeals, and a pony track constructed to the top. It opened in 1883 and was in use for 21 years. An estimated 4,000 visitors called in 1884, and later a hotel was built as well. There was a toll on the track up from Achintee. Lightning once started a fire in the kitchen, and winds could be strong enough to stop all observations outside. A weekly contact with Fort William in winter was all they could manage – unless climbers called. Rubbish was simply tipped down the nearest gully which climbers soon named Gardyloo Gully (the bucket-emptier was sometimes belayed for this job). Collie has an interesting description of the settlement in an early *Scottish Mountaineering Club Journal* (vol. III, p. 151; see also vol. I for Naismith's note). Some of Scott's polar team trained on the Ben and the *Scotia* expedition was led by one of the staff. A summer volunteer went on to win a physics Nobel Prize and in his speech pointed to the original stimulus coming from his stay on Nevis. On the verge of air travel and other vital scientific advances the Obser- vatory shut down in 1904 – owing to Government cut-backs.

The summit is long overdue a real clean-up to bury all the remains, cairns and vain monuments of man's visits. Not that this is a new state of affairs.

An English vicar in 1789 noted there were 30 cairns on Nevis and various names and initials in bottles, etc., etc. Nothing changes it seems. Keats was one of the many early visitors. He came up in 1818, just three years before he died in his mid-twenties. "I am heartily glad it is done – it is almost like a fly climbing up a wainscot." As he came up the tourist path this is no doubt poetic licence. Edward Burt, who was Wade's agent and surveyor, wrote fascinating *Letters from a Gentleman in the North of Scotland* which was published after the Forty Five. He tells of a band of officers out all day from five in the morning who came back beaten by bogs and perpendicular rocks, thankful for a break in the clouds: ". . . if those vapours had continued, there would have been no means left for them to find their way down, and they must have perished with cold, wet, and hunger." Who was first up we will never know. The Commissioners on the Forfeited Estates financed an ascent by the botanist James Roberston, one of the greatest hill wanderers of all time, in 1771, and in 1774 the Welsh geologist John Williams was likewise sent up. James Dickson was another early botanist visitor, climbing up with his brother-in-law Mungo Park. Professor Forbes made history by cutting steps on the mountain – with a tripod. Quite a few Coast-to-Coast or Groats End Walks take in the top of Britain. The Naylors in 1871 referred to Nevis as *the Ben* which I had always thought a recent ab- breviation. They failed because their guide became ill. This gentleman was "mortified to have failed, for he had been up the hill 1,200 times". Most of the popular hills such as Ben Lomond, Ben Nevis, Lochnagar, Ben Macdhui and the Skye summits had regular guides to assist the Vic- torian visitor. Let us leave the Ben to the words of Byron:

> Ben Nevis is monarch of mountains,
> They crowned him long ago,
> On a throne of rocks, in a robe of clouds,
> With a diadem of snow.

A party coming up from the Carn Mor Dearg Arete said it was clear of snow and possible to descend Coire Leis so Ray and I went that way. We were hoping the C.I.C. Hut might have been open. It was occupied but empty, if you see what I mean. The weekend we were at Rhiconich had seen the hut celebrating its Jubilee and quite a crowd assembled, including some Inglish Clark relatives. Robert Elton, the club president, who was the original custodian, was also present. Charlie Gorrie had arranged a dinner in Fort William afterwards. A hut of many memories. Being so handy for the cliffs it is frequently full in winter and this is often held as being the SMCs fault, as if it were some free-for-all Snowdon cafe. The poor owners themselves only manage ten per cent of the bed-nights.

We went on round to Lochan Meall an t-Suidhe, having traversed right under the cliffs, then crossed the Tourist Path and through to descend a line beside the soda-water Red Burn. We then walked down Glen Nevis back to Leesholme, for Storm and I were now committed to linking the Country Summits without mechanical aids. Ben Nevis was number one.

Sunday 10 June   FORT WILLIAM SABBATH
A Free Church service was a novel experience for Episcopalian Ray. I had briefed Ray that one stood to pray and sat to sing but he still was taken by surprise when 'Amazing Grace' turned out to be one of the psalm tunes. Storm was tied up outside and *would* bark at every passing dog. I found a paperback of Patrick Macgill's grim classic, *Children of the Dead End*, which was appropriate as we were to go by the Blackwater Dam the next day, the start of our walk down the official West Highland Way.

Monday 11 June   ON TO RANNOCH MOOR
The Lairig Mor pass from Fort William to Kinlochleven is one I always seem to cross on hot days. The sun, beating off the bare red or grey screes of the Mamores, can turn it into a micro oven in no time at all. We sweated through it. Even Ray tried to emulate my withdrawal into the pages of a book, which was all right on the switch-back tarred road but too risky on the rough track beyond. Gorse and broom were full out now, exploding along the hillside at times. Helicopters kept flying through the pass in noisy groups. The woods above Loch Leven were shady and welcome, their green coolness a contrast to the stuffy heat of Kinlochleven. But we must not grudge Kinloch the sun: for several months in the year the steep hills deny it any at all and the houses are painted bright colours to try to relieve the gloom. We bought drinks and ices and fled up the old military road for the Devil's Staircase which drops down the other side to Rannoch Moor at the mouth of Glen Coe.

The name was probably given by Caulfeild's soldiers who built it.

"Glencoe itself is perfectly *terrible*. The pass is an awful place. It is shut in on each side by enormous rocks from which great torrents come rushing down in all directions . . . there are scores of glens, high up, which form such haunts as you might imagine yourself wandering in, in the very light and madness of a fever. The very recollection makes one shudder. . . ." That was written by Charles Dickens who was by no means an early traveller. Turning the other way we walked on to Rannoch Moor for the Kingshouse Hotel. Perhaps Dickens was copying the style of Rev. John Lettice from Sussex who described the Moor in 1792 as "an immense vacuity, with nothing in it to contemplate, unless numberless mis-shapen blocks of stone rising hideously above the surface of the earth, would be said to contradict the inanity of our prospects."

The Kingshouse Hotel claims to be the oldest licensed inn in Scotland. Ray made a dive for beer, I made a dive for a bath with tea and a read of Borthwick's *Always a Little Further* which as well as telling more about the Devil's Staircase and the dam is one of the few really amusing hill books. A grouse was making a fine old chakker outside and a brat of a wren was scolding with the voice of six. It is not often one 'birds' in a bath.

We had a very good meal which ended with several sweets from the tempting selection. The girls serving were not averse to strawberries either. Talking, dealing with a parcel and so on, meant we did not go to bed till midnight. A couple of hours later I noticed Ray banging about, clawing at the window and then, grabbing his bedding, go storming out. I put his behaviour down to sunburn, assuming he felt as hot and sleepless as I did. It turned out however that a water pump was sited just through the wall near his head and the buzz of the pump on top of the sun, had driven him literally up the wall and out the door. A mobile bed, which he found, was wheeled into the bathroom and he slept there. You'd be surprised how many times the handle was tried . . .

Tuesday 12 June   RANNOCH MOOR HILLS

The old military road wends over Rannoch Moor on a higher line than the present one, giving wider views. The *new* road is now about 50 years old, which shows how well it was built, for it is as good as anything made in the last decade.

We wandered, haggis-fittit, up past Blackrock to the highest point on the road, above which there is a cairn inscribed "Peter Fleming. Author, Soldier and Traveller, 18 August 1971". I always find it fascinating to see how brothers, of such differing character and interests, sometimes have

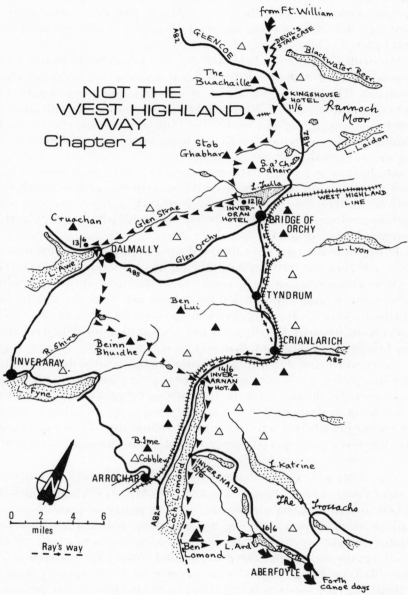

NOT THE
WEST HIGHLAND
WAY
Chapter 4

from Ft.William

GLENCOE

DEVIL'S
STAIRCASE

Blackwater Ress

The
Buachaille

KINGSHOUSE
HOTEL
11/6

Rannoch
Moor

L. Laidon

Stob
Ghabhar

S. a' Ch.
Odhair

L. Tulla

WEST HIGHLAND
LINE

Glen Strae

INVER-
ORAN
HOTEL
12/6

BRIDGE OF
ORCHY

Cruachan

13/6

DALMALLY

Glen Orchy

A85

L. Lyon

L. Awe

TYNDRUM

Ben
Lui

CRIANLARICH

A85

R. Shira

Beinn
Bhuidhe

INVERARAY

L. Fyne

14/6
INVER-
ARNAN
HOT.

B.Ime

Cobbler

Loch Lomond

INVERSNAID
15/6

L. Katrine

ARROCHAR

The
Trossachs

0   2   4   6
miles

Ray's way

Ben
Lomond

16/6
L. Ard

R. Forth

ABERFOYLE

Forth
canoe days

authorship in common, as Peter Fleming and Ian Fleming, or the Durrells or the Attenboroughs . . . . Peter Fleming died of a heart attack while out on his Blackmount moors, which is perhaps the way to go. The simple cairn looks over the moody Moor, this day a patchwork of chasing wind colours as the clouds spilled their shadows over its lochs and braes.

We twined again at Ba Bridge, Ray following the road to Inveroran, Storm and I following the River Ba up into one of the widest corries in Scotland. The huge bowl is almost level for miles and echoed to a concert of bird sound: dunlin reeling, shanks fluting, snipe drumming, oystercatchers piping and behind it all the larks setting an extravagant *continuo*. Have you noticed, with lark song, how we always look too high for the careless singer?

All the flowers seemed to be out now too: tormentil, lousewort (pink and white), wood anemone, trefoil, butterwort, cudweed, milkwort, violets, wintergreen, blaeberry and bearberry. Some areas were white with bog cotton or hare's tail, others were scented with bog myrtle. High summer had come at last.

Beyond the flat corrie we followed up a granite-lined burn into the hills. The rock was warm and rough, the water like quick-silver. From a loch we continued our rocky choice of route, up *en face* to a rib which gave some scrambling and landed us not far from the top of Stob Ghabhar *the goat's peak*. We had a huge view of a world of contrasting greys while towards Achallader it was black and grumbling. Obviously the hills had had more sun than was good for them.

We rimmed round the cliffs and slithered and trotted down to the col and on up Stob a' Choire Odhair *the peak of the brown corrie* only to have our *dwam* (day dream) shattered by reaching the cairn just as there was a great bang of thunder. It was probably still miles away but I stopped running only when down the zig zags towards the Allt Taoig. The dog thought this a game specially designed for his amusement and reacted by trying to trip me up every few yards.

The views west from Clashgour were of silken greys and silver, a watery sheen of rare beauty – but a meteorological warning. The black rolled in and we dived under the Victoria Bridge to perch on a precarious ledge while the rain and hail hissed and sizzled into the river. As soon as it let up we made a dash for Inveroran, another historic inn that produces the right atmosphere and a good table. Later on Angus Macdonald of the Bridge of Orchy Hotel came in. A bar was welcome, for outside the rain was tropical in intensity, the burn boiled brown under the bridge and the mists crept among the pines like ghostly rivers. I'm not a great one for hotels (I can't afford them) but I must say I was impressed by most I had met in Scotland. The old tradition of hospitality remains. In the Lakes and the South West it was sometimes different. No hotel in Scotland ever refused Storm entry (though one had the cheek to charge for him). South of the border he was often unwelcome. I am not being biased as these were also the opinions of Sassenach Ray who uses hotels extensively.

Wednesday 13 June   PASSES TO LOCH AWE
Ray continued more or less on the West Highland Way: to Bridge of Orchy, Tyndrum, Crianlarich and Glen Falloch while I went off on a diversion to add Argyll's Beinn Bhuidhe. Ray's chief note of interest was finding several fish lying on the old road from Auch up to Tyndrum. Perhaps they came from a passing train – the line was above – but who passes the time, even on the West Highland Line, flinging fish out of the window?

One of the joys of a big traverse is being able to go on and on without the usual need to return to a starting point. I had often looked on the map at the long line of Gleann Fuar and Glen Stae, which links Loch Tulla and Loch Awe, but it was only now it became for me the natural and practical through-route it probably was centuries ago.

Druimliart, at the start of the day, is where Duncan Ban Macintyre was born. There is a monument to him above Tyndrum but his birthplace is unmarked. Were he half as famous a Welsh poet, or an English, there would be some monument and the site proclaimed. We paused awhile to brew – and to remove a couple of minute ticks from my legs. These seem to have spread over the years. They are nasty things but one can only admire their tenacious lifestyle. They dangle on grass till a host comes along (sheep or Storm or human), gorge on blood, drop off, repeat several times and then have to find a mate in season to breed.

Gleann Fuar began as a tawny strath then, after some bogs, it produced a fine remnant of old forest which went well up towards the twisted cols over to deep-set Glen Strae. Glen Strae was full of ruins and sadly empty, even the falls were low and the summer sandpipers seemed to be playing laments.

The busy Oban road came as a shock. The dog went on a lead for once. One car crept in behind me and I was hailed by the Cosgroves, he being a Grampian Club ex-President. I could hardly fool him as to what I was up to. He has done the Munros twice.

I had a night in the Carraig-Thura Hotel, a Victorian mansion, which looks down on Kilchurn Castle on Loch Awe, a castle built by Sir Colin

Campbell of Glenorchy in the mid-fifteenth century, the family later growing in power as Earls, then Marquesses of Breadalbane with lands reaching to the east end of the Tay. Now it has all gone and their castles lie in ruins. Kilchurn was abandoned before the Forty Five and one of its towers was blown down by a great gale early in 1879 – the same storm that destroyed the Tay Bridge. A surprising amount remains to make it a romantic monument.

Thursday 14 June   BEINN BHUIDHE

I was overstocked with food from the parcel sent to the hotel, and the room had tea-making facilities, so I paid my bill in the evening and slipped off before anyone was up. The main road was not busy at 6 a.m., just wet. I tried to by-pass Dalmally but became thoroughly lost in scrub until I stumbled on the railway line. The moors above gave much simpler navigation. We passed a sheep fank, Barran, which had corpses of fox and hoodie hanging beside it. A succession of burns led to the Bealach nan Cabrach – and more rain. Looking back, I could see Loch Awe and the white-streaked slopes of Cruachan, the peak of peaks, above Loch Awe. It was mentioned by Barbour in his poem on Robert the Bruce (c. 1375) which makes it the first named Munro to come down to us. Not till Timothy Pont were things arranged in some order; the results of his work appeared in *Blaen's Atlas* in 1654, and included Ben Nevis. The hills had names of course, but they were not recorded. Even the most recent maps chop and change. (Recognise Learg Ghrumach? It is now Lairig Ghru.)

Forward, through the pass, was an empty, ochrous landscape, alive with deer, and calves, and an afterbirth on the grass. We were soon in cloud and the strongest wind for a long time. A burn led to the Shira dam where I cringed by its wall to make tea. We set off into a hail storm.

I was still adding to the summer flowers: bedstraw, least willow, star saxifrage, thyme, thrift, orchids, both lady's mantles, moss campion (clumps like pink birthday cakes) and, high on the wet slopes under the summit of Beinn Bhuidhe, half an acre of bright marsh mallow. The final crest was in cloud and the wind gave a mad battering over the humps and bumps to the stone trig point, which we simply slapped *en passant*, and dropped down the ridge beyond. We were not quite checkmated by the crags on the flank, but they concentrated the mind somewhat. It was steep all the way down to Inverchorachan in Glen Fyne, not much above sea level. We had dropped 3,000 feet in about a mile and a half. There is a fine waterfall above the lonely shepherd's house of Inverchorachan.

I cut corners again to join a road up to a reservoir (not on the map) which has now dammed the Allt na Lairig. It was a long, wet, trackless, almost level watershed and if the rain came on hard at times the wind soon dried things again. The Allt Arnan began fussily: endlessly wending about, like a sniffing dog, till we were nearly distracted, then changing into cheerful, tumbling falls as it plunged for Glen Falloch after all. The Beinn Ghlas Falls across the glen were visible too. Wind and water, these had very much been the sounds of a long day. Wordsworth described Glen Falloch as "the vale of awful sound". A train added its forlorn note as it left Ardlui and slowly caterpillared up the glen below us: a sight which can excite me every time – especially on the magical West Highland Line. Where a viaduct curves over the Dubh Eas the track is only seven feet lower than the Forth Bridge.

We were soon sprawled before a log fire in the historic Inverarnan Hotel, tucking into tea and scones and swopping experiences of the past two days with Ray. We had a room up many flights of stairs, a treetop's view, loud through the night with the calling of a barn owl, the *cailleach oidhche* (old woman of the night). If a stage coach had rolled up it would have been quite in keeping.

Friday 15 June   BY YON BONNIE BANKS

As we approached Beinnglas Farm we could see the farmer waiting – bristling – and sure enough he rudely asked where we were taking the dog. This was the only such reception in 600 miles. "A soft answer turneth away wrath." We were on a right-of-way and the dog was under control . . .

The army were out in force, building a bridge here, and others at Inversnaid, all part of creating the West Highland Way. The woods were full of them too, playing all manner of games. Storm rather betrayed some of their hiding places and at a debriefing later we overheard comments about problems created by dogs. The soldiers' camps were being violently attacked by midges – and the soldiers seemed to be losing.

This was lush country of hawthorn woods and oak and birch. The sun beamed wandering searchlights across it. Loch Lomond reached away south, to the lowlands; northwards, Glen Falloch was backed by the hills of Ben Lui. It was a *Swallows and Amazons* type of place: Inversnaid with its secretive harbour and bridges over waterfalls and rhododendron thickets made for dens. The *Maid of the Loch* paid a call – one of the few surviving paddle steamers which were once such a feature in the west. When we had a house at Carrick Castle before the war seven boats a day called. After the war there was just the wee *Comet*, till she was sold to the

Congo. Now you reach Carrick by bus over by the Rest and Be Thankful and Hell's Glen.

Ray had been trying to memorise the names of the hill flowers but when he started talking about a *cloud barley* he really had me puzzled. He pointed one out eventually – a cow wheat. There were still primroses and stitchwort, wild garlic, yellow pimpernel and masses of wild hyacinth which to Ray were bluebells, the 'Scots bluebell' being the Sassenach hare bell. The path was delightful, and you had to keep walking to avoid the midges. It wended up and down and in and out, giving sudden flashes of view as if at a slide show. As even Boswell's Johnson admitted to being "much pleased with the scene", we could be no less. Ray was being met that night at Rowardennan, so pushed on, and continued to Drymen the following day, to finish his West Highland Way.

I stayed in Rob Roy country, at the Inversnaid Hotel which was swamped by a Canadian Iron Works bus tour. All the male members were dressed in red blazers. Cameron McNeish looked in for an hour. Friends seemed to grow everywhere! Storm had his too: the hotel door said NO DOGS.

Saturday 16 June   BEN LOMOND: SIXTH ROUND
Two miles of fine oak forest led to Cailness where we struck up for the heights. A grey squirrel was a new excitement for the dog. There were two notices: "Haggis Conservation Area. Please fasten gate and keep dogs under control. Breeding season. Jan.–Dec." and "You are at Culness, a sheep farm. Camping is restricted. Enquire please. We do not bite!" Beinnglas Farm take note.

I brewed when we had climbed above the tree line but the midges drove us on – up through the corrie threatened by the Craigroystan hydro scheme. We were into cloud by then and navigation was far from easy as there were many bumps. I now had a compass so eventually the extra big bump of the summit cone was climbed and, all alone in the cloud, we celebrated our North-South tramp, Ben Hope to Ben Lomond – and the completion of a sixth round of the Munros.

We lingered for an hour hoping for a view, for a picture, for people to take a picture. Only one couple arrived which was strange for a mid-summer Saturday lunch time. Ben Lomond is one of the most climbed hills in Britain – and long has been. Recently I heard another old tale of it. In 1814, four years after Scott published *The Lady of the Lake*, a visitor on top of Ben Lomond was told by a savage-looking local, who had been a guide on the mountain for more than 40 years, that a Walter Scott had spoiled his trade. "I wish I had him in a ferry over Loch Lomond; I should be after sinking the boat . . . for ever since he wrote his *Lady of the Lake*, as they call it, everybody goes to see that filthy hole, Loch Katrine. The devil confound his ladies and his lakes!"

Five minutes along the tourist path we discovered why the summit was deserted. There were mobs gathered on a slight rise which someone had declared the summit and all had believed it so. As the summit has a trig point and the map shows a trig point the standard of navigation was rather frightening. We counted 70 people in the half mile of the tourist track we followed. We swung off it to descend east, away from Loch Lomond, down to Comer in Gleann Dubh. When we came out from under the cloud our view was of Loch Ard and the Trossachs and the far away Ochils. The waters of Loch Ard soon become the River Forth and our home is on the Forth Estuary. Charmian and Bill Pollok, who live 30 yards from Loch Ard, had my canoe in their garage. One stage was nearly over and I regretted having to leave the Highland fastness, no doubt as many a drover did, or poor follower of plundering armies. So I drank in the view: back up the craggy slopes into the silent, timeless mists which brushed the ridges soft as music, and on to the silver sequins in the purpled plains homewards. We went down through a scatter of deer and the jagged flights of snipe. In the woods the bird song came in a great chorus – an ill-disciplined Philharmonic. Canoeing would be very dull after this – or would it? for in the last few days I had produced a large, ripe boil on my sit-upon!

DOON THE WATER O' FORTH

" 'Slow and easy goes far in a day' as Moleskin Joe once said!"
PATRICK MACGILL: *Children of the Dead End*

Sunday 17 June   DOWN TO GARTRENICH MOSS   *Map, p. 77*

My physical disability was kept from my hosts, Bill being a doctor. Charmian and her sister Valerie (née Jones) had grown up in Dollar as had we Broon brothers. We had recently been in touch again and they had kindly been looking after my canoe which my brother David, still living in Dollar, had delivered. Bill and Charmian had had years in Germany and Brunei before settling by Loch Ard.

Storm was welcomed by Schwartz and Himmel (black retrievers) and Dusky and Carruthers (cats). I stole a frantic hour to pack, a vital one, for everything had to be sealed and made watertight. The tent and sleeping bag had come by yesterday's post. I'd sent them from Kintail as they were not needed for the soft Swinburn days. As Ray was setting off for Milngavie and the end of the West Highland Way, Bill and Charmian were seeing me launched in a placid Loch Ard. It was four miles to Aberfoyle and the book gave 37 miles from there to Stirling, several times the shortest road distance, for the Forth meanders as few other rivers. It has created rich farmland, and there is an old saying that "a crook in the Forth is worth an Earldom in the North".

Storm had never been in a canoe but before we had paddled a mile to the island castle he had fallen asleep in the shimmering sun, which is doubled in intensity by its reflection off water. There was next to nothing left of the castle but I was interested to see underwater stepping-stones between the islets.

There was a slight flow in the narrows of the loch, and beyond I had a spell battering through reeds. A swan landing by its nest woke the dog with a start. We landed beside the road. From there we looked back to Ben Lomond reflected in the reedy lochan like some instant postcard view. Even without Sir Walter Scott I think the Trossachs would have

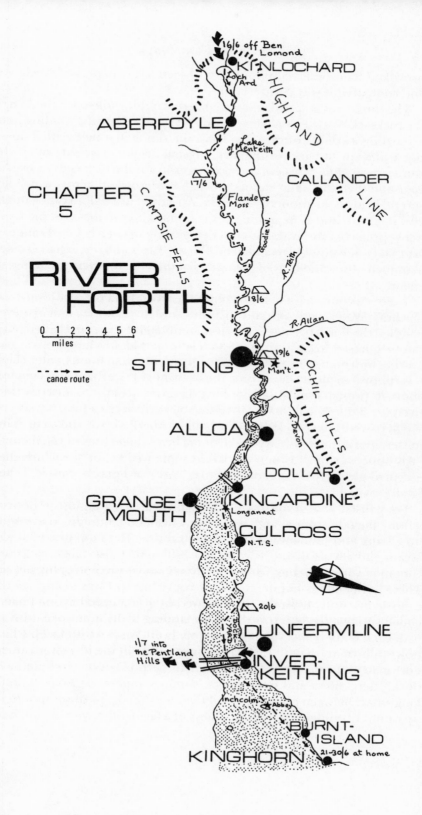

16/6 off Ben Lomond

KINLOCHARD

Loch Ard

HIGHLAND

ABERFOYLE

Lake of Menteith

17/6

CALLANDER

CHAPTER 5

Flanders Moss

LINE

CAMPSIE FELLS

Goodie W.

RIVER FORTH

R. Teith

0 1 2 3 4 5 6
miles

18/6

canoe route

R. Allan

STIRLING

19/6

Mon't.

OCHIL HILLS

ALLOA

R. Devon

DOLLAR

GRANGE-MOUTH

KINCARDINE

Longannat

CULROSS

N.T.S.

N

20/6

DUNFERMLINE

1/7 into the Pentland Hills

DOCK YARD

INVER-KEITHING

Inchcolm

Abbey

BURNT-ISLAND

KINGHORN

21-30/6 at home

provoked their deserved popularity. Queen Victoria praised Loch Ard
and compared it with Switzerland.

The canoe was emptied and somehow everything piled in or tied on to
the rucksack. We then staggered about 500 yards along the winding road
– startling a couple of cars – to leave the canoe in a field with a nosey
horse and sprint back for the sack, hoping the horse would not eat the
canoe meanwhile. This portage was necessary as the loch ends in a small
weir and then the water shoots through a narrow gut across which are
several bridges, at about chest height. An expert in a slalom canoe might
run it, Storm and I, in an old canvas home-kit craft that cost me £5 in
1963, preferred survival. I am not denigrating my much-loved canoe: it
had taken me down rivers like the Tweed, Tay and Spey, it had crossed
Rannoch Moor and braved the waters of the Minch. A very good investment.

There was quite a lot of lining down the Avondubh until we joined the
Duchray Water and officially became the River Forth. I had never
paddled the Forth because it is a river completely lacking in challenge, as
can be guessed from its drop of 80 feet in 37 miles. When in spate and
flowing into high tides and storms from the east it can flood badly. There
was rubbish in plenty decorating the branches of riverbank trees ten feet
above its present level. A sad-looking sheep hung in the fork of one tree.
Even the Bailie Nicol Jarvie Hotel in Aberfoyle keeps a boat handy.

There were Glasgow kids on the bank at Aberfoyle who begged, "Hey
mister, gies-a-hurrell". My shake of the head called forth a valedictory,
"Ah hope ya sink!" I found a ball in some wedged debris which they
accepted gleefully for a game of fitba. "Are yous playin' mister!" they
kindly invited.

We paused at a camp site – Cobleland – arriving almost unnoticed
among the rafts, canoes and swimmers. I felt it odd, though, to scramble
up a bank and suddenly be in a tented suburb. The shop provided ice-
cream and a *Sunday Post*. If you can't beat 'em! I also filled my gallon
container with tap water, for the Forth was not very tempting further on.
There were endless minute rapids or rocky bits so I was in and out the
canoe constantly. Even the map showed us going uphill at one stage. I
ended sitting *à cheval* across the canoe instead of dribbling water into it
with each entry. I was very aware of my boil! We ran into forest which
now spills on to the carse. What a strange shut-in world a river can be.
Fortunately there were snags enough to keep us awake and plenty of
duck, mergansers and goosanders, summer pipers, and one flashing
kingfisher. Between plantation and river we found a pleasant spot to set
up camp. I could just see the chimneys of a farm, otherwise I could have

Maol-Bhuidhe bothy

Ray in upper Glen Loyne

Bidean a' Choire Sheasgaich from Beinn Tharsuinn

Lurg Mhor from the south, showing the *long flank* of its name

The hills of Kintail from Sgurr nan Ceathreamhnan

The Great Glen – always an important landmark on long walks

Ben Tee across Loch Garry

The Ben Nevis Observatory under an incredible covering
of frost crystals

Ben Nevis: in summer with still a deal of snow on the
northern cliffs

The Ben Nevis Observatory
in its heyday

The bleak summit of Britain:
Hamish, Ray and Storm on top of Ben Nevis

Looking back along the old military road to Fort William while walking the Lairig Mor to Kinlochleven

The Blackmount Hills on the west of Rannoch Moor: Ray and Hamish walked round the far side on the old military road

Bog-wood: a common sight on decaying peat bogs like Rannoch Moor

The octagonal church
at Dalmally

On Loch Ard at the start of the canoe trip

been miles from man's presence. The farm had the name Offrins of Gartur. Close by was Nether Easter Offerance and we had passed Barbadoes on the Kelty Water feeder. We stopped early and relished the long day of sun right to its setting – it dipped behind Ben Venue. The dog stepped on a pheasant in the long grass. All three of us nearly had heart failure. Later Charmian wrote to say they had gone off for a day on Ben Vorlich. "As we passed the head of Loch Ard we saw you paddling through the reeds . . . We had a marvellous day on the hill – the best of the summer – one really sees how mountainous Scotland is when one is standing on the roof of it . . . I have been sitting out lazing in the sun this morning reading. I feel in this short life one must get priorities straight – so to hell with the dust inside."

Monday 18 June   BY FLANDERS MOSS
Flanders Moss was once a forest but it was destroyed many hundreds of years ago, partly to remove a rather efficient cover for raiders and thieves. It was virtually a 'debatable land' between Highlands and Lowlands, a great moss with secret fords and dangerous peat morasses. Much of the peat was removed (being thrown into the Forth to float out to sea) and the land is now mainly rich agricultural ground but with the risk of being flooded. The river banks are therefore kept high, and the canoe-ist sees very little of anything apart from the bend ahead. On the Forth it was possible to canoe several miles and end with only a hundred yards of gain eastwards. I'm sure time and effort could have been saved by carrying an unladen canoe across some of the necks. But canoeing is a bit like eating muesli: you cannot hurry it.

At dusk the wind had dropped and the midges came out. My last memory was watching them climbing through the mosquito netting ventilators of the Merrillite tent. There was just enough breeze at 5 a.m. to hold them off so we started out. We passed a place called Faraway. Two fishermen were the only humans seen on the river. We had a brew near South Flanders, to recover from having to perch on a tree trunk which completely barred the river, and over which the canoe had to be wrestled. Miles on we stopped for lunch by Frew Bridge. Fordhead Farm hinted at the historic Fords of Frew – across which James IV had battled, Rob Roy raided, and Montrose and the Young Pretender's armies crossed on their varied ploys. A Hydro store filled my water container. We phoned to arrange a rendezvous with Roger. It became too hot for pleasure so once past Culmore and Culbeg (I'm not making up the names), I took two hours off and lay reading and snoozing. Some of the other names hereabouts were Pendicles of Collymoon, Backside of

Garden, Stock o' Broom, Goodie Water, Drip Moss, Kerse-bonny, Blackdub and Deafleys. Trailing water crowfoot was attractive and there was a lot of bird life. Why do flies all hover in a precise band at a set distance above water? Our planned camp-spot was a bank of nettles and our eventual one gave a rather muddy landfall. The river was the colour of treacle toffee and it was often impossible to see rocks. We kept the canoe in one piece, however.

Tuesday 19 June   TO STIRLING
The day dazzled again – a morning kissed by the sun like a child asleep – so we were up early. Muesli soaked in drinking chocolate proved a failed brainwave that the ducks enjoyed. Canoe-ing became very unexciting for the river does not do very much, but takes a long time about it. We were heading north-west at times thanks to the loops and bends. Bird life alone caused stirs. There was a fine old bridge, and a plain utility modern one, both in reflecting duplicate. The Teith joined us and then, after passing below the M9, we came on the only bit of rough stuff: a jumbled mess of broken rock strata and white water. It was too low to shoot and gave intricate lining down on the starboard bank. The Wallace Monument and Stirling Castle had been landmarks for many miles (so, occasionally, but shrinking, were Ben Vorlich and Stuc a' Chroin north of the Highland Line) and it was good to be almost below them. The camp site proved not to be on the river but 200 yards away and I had to carry our gear over to it.

I put the tent up, then made an awning out of the fly-sheet and paddles. It was hotter than ever. I'd carefully kept covered, for sunburn is a common canoeing complaint. The only skin to suffer was the white band where normally I wore a watch. It was red.

Roger Smith arrived just after we'd eaten and then he kindly interviewed me on a run to and from Dollar so I could inspect a new nephew. Graeme had returned from Stirling Hospital just a few hours before. I took the chance of dumping boots and other non-canoeing items with David and Marina. Roger had contact prints of Ben Hope and the snowy start of the trip. In that beating sun they seemed to belong to some other incarnation.

Wednesday 20 June   TAKING THE TIDE
The alarm went at 1.30 a.m. and I stole off just after 2 a.m. The early start was dictated by the uncooperative nature of the tides. Estuary canoeing means using the tides and if the ebb starts at 3 a.m., you have to sacrifice

sleep for tide. It was hardly dark, even here, on these days of mid-summer. We had some tea and rather teuchie rolls.

The canoe had been left on the bank. I found it in the water – and full of water. It was a struggle to drain it and then haul it up the bank. Vandals had stuck a knife through it ten times, along the bottom, and then kicked a hole in it for good measure. My feelings were mainly of disbelief. (Mrs Thom at the camp site had warned me.) The Cornton housing estate had quite a reputation I learned later. It looked pretty grim. The houses across the river were enclosed by high wire-mesh fences, presumably to stop idiots falling into the Forth but the impression and atmosphere was prison-like. I'm sure if I lived there I'd feel like breaking out! (Vandalism is seldom irrational.) It was not even very efficient in this case: the frame was undamaged and after some patient work with scissors and tape, an hour later we were ready again. A test run produced no leaks. It had been held to the bank by the painter so I should think was thrown in at night when that attachment was not seen – or it would have been away up river. We shook the mud of the place from our feet and were soon zipping downstream through the quiet town, shooting the bridges, the old one which goes back to 1400 or so and which for long was the lowest bridging point on the Forth. It is splendidly proportioned. The new one is simply utilitarian. Upstream, invisible under the water are the foundations of the early wooden bridge which was the site of the battle of 1297 when Wallace defeated a vast English army sent by Edward I, that thirteenth-century Amin. The Wallace Monument looks down on the scene; indeed escape from it was not easy for the river loops its way through the steamy flatness until all sense of direction goes. Even when free of the built-up area we kept paddling towards the glow of its lights. The ebb bore one along at a great rate and for the first time I actually made progress when not even paddling. It is a smelly, filthy river for many miles, with banks of black gooey mud where landing was impossible.

At about six I was glad to pull into the old car-ferry landing slip at South Alloa. There I took the canoe out and gave it a thorough sponging, had a chittery bite and some sleep. The slip had seaweed clinging to it so I felt we really were in the estuary. Alloa was a grey Lowry-like industrial picture across the water. The folk in the only house on my side of the river spotted me and insisted I went in for tea. Later an old fisherman came out and chatted. He had one tale of a ship sunk near here which gave years of salvage problems. Someone at last bought the wreck and applied his secret technique: he filled her with barrels for buoyancy but the result was unexpected, for the pressure simply lifted the deck off the ship. I've heard of ping pong balls for buoyancy in canoes, which are excellent as any damage can only affect a percentage of the buoyancy. I was still finding sitting rather painful but had been able to pad a bit with the tent. Having it handy was later to prove fortunate. At least I could echo "pleasure's in a gowden tyke, an' respite frae the rumple-fyke". Blistered palms and a numb bum were even avoided for once.

When the *Leckie* started so did we but the wind forced us over to the north bank. Nearing the Kincardine power station the wind came hard out of the south, a dangerous flanker, so we had to cross into it back to the south bank. We landed below the Kincardine Bridge for a breather. My next leg-stretch was at Longannat power station. (It is coal-fired and the coal comes to it, underground, from a pit several miles away.) Pushing off I slightly buckled my paddles at the sleeve joint where they fitted together. Well out to sea, off Culross, a long pier-like arm, some skerries, wind and tide all combined to make a sea of utter chaos. The waves shot straight up! In the middle of this exciting bit of water my paddles broke.

I grabbed several sections of tent pole, cut off guy lines from the tent and made a bulky splint, effective enough to take us out of that nasty sea over the Craigmore Rocks. We went in to Crombie Pier and had a well-earned brew. The canoe stuck on the mud and there was no way I was going to move it to high-tide level ready for the next ebb. So we had to launch again, a very messy job. Not far on we found a big solid pier where we put in, carried all the gear up to a grassy spot outside a wired-off area, moved the canoe up above high-tide level and thankfully fell to brewing. We were in about six. After supper my eyes just refused to stay open and I went to sleep lying in the sun. The dew woke me at midnight; I just leant the paddles against the wire and threw the flysheet over it and went back to sleep in this shelter.

Thursday 21 June   HOME SWEET HOME
An hour later I was woken by flashing lights and found a policeman, with an alsatian, regarding my bivouac with a certain incredulity. He called up a patrol car which called up a sergeant. It was rapidly becoming a bit James Bondish but fortunately the sergeant recognised me – he had married the sister of one of my former pupils – so we had a right old blether instead of being arrested. I'd camped beside a high explosive depot. Apparently there were big notices to this effect all round the place, except facing the sea, for nobody was expected to come from that direction. There is something to be said for the British system

after all. Imagine the same sort of thing elsewhere: my implausible tale of walking from John o' Groats to Land's End and being found in a canoe on the Forth . . . I bet it gave them something to talk about.

It was hardly worth settling down to sleep again, the tide was splashing past a few yards away. My paddles looked like ungainly Roman *fasces*, but dipped and pushed us on our way.

There was the most glittering display of phosphorescence I have ever seen in British waters. Even the dog was fascinated by the cascading diamond drops when I splashed with the paddles. It lasted for several miles. I had to go well out because of the long pier on Kinniny Point, then passed a large floating dock and all the naval vessels at Rossyth Dockyard. At any moment I expected to be investigated again. If they had a radar watch for instance, what would they make of my craft? Should I have navigation lights I wondered – and how did you fix lights on a vessel all of two feet wide? I was quite glad when dawn arrived and I could slip in to North Queensferry for a quick brew and walk about.

My next call was to Inchcolm, a site I had always meant to visit, but being close to home had just never done so. We were escorted in by grunting, snoring, singing seals which seemed quite unafraid of the canoe and frolicked round it till we left the islands. Storm stood and wagged his tail at them. The Inchcolm Abbey was a surprise. Serendipity! I expected some pathetic pile of stones and found one of the best preserved ecclesiastical foundations in the land. It reminded me of the ruined Abbeys of Ireland. I read it up that night. Inchcolm is the Gaelic *Colum's Isle*, and has at times been known as 'the Iona of the East'. There is no doubt that in the twelfth century a Columban hermit inhabited the island and that Alexander I, being driven there for shelter in a storm, in gratitude endowed an Augustinian Abbey. It became a holy spot and the illustrious sought burial there, being an island 'close to heaven'. This is mentioned in Shakespeare's *Macbeth*. Despite savage depredations during the English Wars the abbey flourished until the Reformation, thereafter being used occasionally by the Earls of Moray. Its island site saved it from being pillaged for its stone so it is well preserved and carefully maintained today.

I did not have a conducted tour at 2.30 a.m.

We made Kinghorn in one long haul from there, keeping well out from Burntisland and using all the vague currents that showed on the surface of the water. At low tide (as it then was) there are several miles of sand between Kinghorn and Burntisland, a favourite walk of Storm's. Burntisland Church has a sailors' loft reached by an outside stair to allow them to come and go without disturbing the rest of the congregation. The sea is such a casual, tame acquaintance till one comes to live and work on it. It shares that domination of man with the mountains. "Two voices are there . . . each a mighty Voice" – Wordsworth knew it, man of the hills that he was.

I landed Storm at the Black Rock so he could romp along the shore, but he was not going to part from me and simply splashed out after the canoe so, for my own comfort, I lifted him on board again before he became completely saturated. My final landfall was at 6.40, on the gravelly patch just off the end of the Kinghorn *hynd*.

I took the canoe up to the glassworks' road and then staggered up to the house with the rucksack. Mother seemed unperturbed at being knocked up at that hour. I dug out the canoe's "wheels" and trailed it home. No sooner had mother looked at the much patched bottom (the canoe's, not mine) when the rain came lashing down and the wind steadily rose to gale force. You do miss the odd one. At lunchtime we had a polite telephone call from the Crombie police – "just checking" to see we had made it home all right.

Saturday 23 June – Saturday 30 June   INTERLUDE
This week at home was one of the busiest of my life, with a visit to the dentist and some urgent shopping – and sitting till all hours at my desk. It took a whole day just to open my accumulated mail and when we'd finished packing parcels for the Pennine Way, Sheffield and Ruthin the post office actually sent their van to pick them up: £28 in postages! There were some interesting books in: the numbers I needed to complete my set of *Scottish Mountaineering Club Journals* and a copy of the Naylor brothers' book of their walk from Land's End to John o'Groats in 1871. It weighed ten pounds and was as big as a family Bible. I had previously known no books specifically on this sort of long walking, but having become involved I keep finding them. This was the best by far as it is lavishly illustrated, and the Naylors really did wander and look at things along the way. It was privately printed and is a fairly rare book. Mine came from a dealer, Stansfield, who lives on the Black Isle near Inverness. How did it end there I wondered?

We eventually cleared the decks (i.e., postponing everything possible) so managed to Communion with mother at our own kirk, a couple of parties, had the Dollar family through and watched Wimbledon on TV. I did not grudge the interlude one little bit but we were glad to return to the restfulness of just walking. Storm too had had a pretty dull time. For the first time in weeks I went out without him and found myself peering under a bus seat looking for him. A widow with a two-year-old boy took that situation to extremes one day for, having a baby sitter for once, she escaped to town. Coming back on the bus a train thundered across the bridge overhead and she turned enthusiastically to the man sitting next to her saying encouragingly, "See the bonny choo-choo?"

VI

A BORDER RAID

"To my eye these grey hills and all this wild border country have beauties peculiar to themselves. I like the very nakedness of the land; it has something bold and stern and solitary about it. When I have been for some time in the rich scenery about Edinburgh – which is like an ornamental garden – I begin to wish myself back again among my own honest grey hills, and if I did not see heather at least once a year I think I should die."

Sir Walter Scott

Sunday 1 July   COMMUTING TO THE PENTLANDS   *Map, p. 87*

As Storm and I set off from Kinghorn by bus I felt almost like a commuter returning to work after a Whit Holiday break, but quite glad to 'gee ma ginger'. We picked up the GEW line again on the River Forth. We walked from Inverkeithing, past the Thomas Ward ship-breaking yard where so many fine ships have met their end, from warriors such as *Dreadnought, Rodney* and *Howe* to famous liners such as the *Mauretania*, and then on through the reddish blocks of the cutting to reach the Forth Road Bridge.

I had never walked across it before so sewed in another stitch of novelty to the comfortable garment of experience. Today was to be a sample of rural walking with which I was to become all too familiar in future: stitching which could sometimes tear the colourful patches of enjoyment. All expeditions are easy in retrospect. The 'future perfect' is a myth. Learning to sew involves pricking fingers . . .

Apparently the Forth Bridge and the Severn Bridge were 'swopped'. The planning go-ahead was ready for one and the design for the other: so they combined them – a curiously imaginative move on the part of the bureaucrats if true. The Forth Bridge (née Severn Bridge) was opened by the Queen in 1964. We crossed its gently swaying eastern walkway so as to have a clear view of the Forth Railway Bridge. One suspension bridge is rather like another but the old Forth Bridge was, and still is, a unique engineering structure. (I have met pictures of it in an Arabic manual and an Afrikaans encyclopaedia.)

Originally it had a different design, but work had progressed little

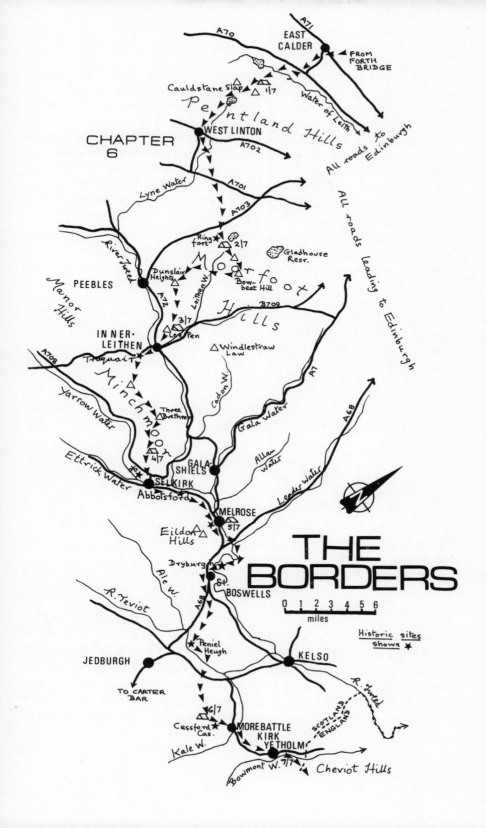

beyond a brick pier on Inchgarvie at the time of the Tay Bridge disaster (1879 – a hundred years ago) and, as the same designer had been used, there was rapid reconsideration, a new design was demanded and work began only in 1883. Today we still marvel at a unique piece of engineering. The bridge took seven years to build, eight million rivets and 250 tons of paint (to this day a team paints it non-stop, for when they finish at one end it is time to begin again at the other), the towers reach 358 feet, 50,000 tons of steel carry trains a mile and a half at 157 feet above high water, it cost £3½ m. and 57 lives. The figures are still impressive. The last rivet was driven home by the future Edward VII.

We had a coffee in the service place, once across, a cafe I would never have thought of visiting while motoring to Edinburgh. The road to Kirkliston was being remade and traffic lights were creating tails of up to 70 cars. We strolled by and I no longer felt a commuter.

Kirkliston had reverted to a sleepy little town. We left it to pass under the stilts of the M9 and followed the huge verges of the A89 (space had been left for a second lane) which led to the many-arched Almond railway viaduct and the landscape of red shale bings. We managed to keep out of towns and industry, and lunched quietly by the dead Union Canal. A farm had the name Lookaboutye – the motto of our once smallest county, Clackmannanshire, before it was devoured by regionalisation. The Almondell Country Park provided pleasant walking on footpaths to East Calder. My first desire there was for a bottle of lemonade. I said, "Don't bother charging for the bottle, I'm just going to pour it into my own water bottle" – indicating the rucksack outside – but no, I had to pay my deposit and two minutes later jangle the sour shopkeeper's doorbell to recall him to claim my pittance. Obviously I had reached civilization! We escaped through a large, impersonal housing scheme without going astray, but a line of pylons helped. Places like that are far harder to navigate through than the wildest of Nowheres.

There was a long haul up, which had my feet fretting, past Ainville (which looked as French as its name), and Little Vantage (a ruined inn near an old toll house of which only the chimney now stands). A Scottish Rights of Way Society signpost said "West Linton by Cauldstane Slap". I was truly back to the hills again, albeit the modest Pentlands, beloved of Edinburgh folk from genial Cockburn to R.L.S. and Allan Ramsay to Edwin Muir. Even Burns had a walk on the Pentlands, with the painter Nasmyth, setting out from a High Street tavern at three in the morning which I should think was a late rather than an early start. Lord Cockburn, author of *Memorials of His Time*, knew the Pentlands well. He was once seated with a shepherd, and, seeing a sheep lying on an exposed slope, remarked, "John, if I were a sheep, I would lie on the other side of the hill", to which the reply came: "Ay, my Lord, but if ye had been a sheep, ye wad hae had mair sense." Bartholomew have just re-issued a book full of associations of this sort: *Pentland Walks*, originally written in 1908 and now revised by Donald Moir, secretary of the Royal Scottish Geographical Society and editor of the invaluable booklets *Scottish Hill Tracks*. Bartholomew also publish a special 1½ inch to the mile *Pentland Hills* map – these capital wee mountains are well served.

We brewed on an island in a tiny burn in lee of a bridge. Gala Ford it was called on the map and, tracing the waters down, I discovered the stream was the Water of Leith. It cooled our feet, the dog splashing about and setting off dragonflies from the kingcups. We camped up in the quiet hills above where we could hear the wind in the grass again and the click-click of the sheep walking the paths across the gravels. It was crow-land on arrival (a school playground effect) but in the dusk the plaintive half-calls of the snipe gave it the tingling feel of the wilds again. I had not walked hills since Ben Lomond and if yesterday had been steak, strawberries and Wimbledon, tonight it was dried veg., macaroni and a tin of mince.

Monday 2 July MAKING THE MOORFOOTS

Storm was delighted to be on the long trail, the out trail, once more. Every time I turned over in the night he would start swishing the tent wall with his wagging tail or leap up to poke his cold nose in my eye. When the alarm went off at six so did he: wild circuits and bumps until he crash-landed over the front guy line and collapsed the tent on me.

The cloud was on the tops, a sort of maybe aye, maybe hooch aye day. The Forth Bridge could just be seen under its darkness – like a looper caterpillar on the underside of a dead leaf. Cauldstane Slap, now there was a real south-from-Edinburgh name. At one time it was the major drovers' road for the black cattle being driven to England, and later up to 30,000 sheep a year poured over it heading for the Highlands. The name appears as early as 1370; in 1490 James IV crossed it; in the killing times Covenanters were hunted by the infamous General Dalyell for holding a conventicle there and border freebooters (Armstrongs, Scotts etc.) thought little enough of its defences that they raided over it as late as 1600. The "four black brothers of Cauldstane Slap" appear in Stevenson's great unfinished novel *Weir of Hermiston*.

A *slap* is an opening in a dyke through which sheep or cattle can pass, so its figurative use for this route shows bright imaginations a long, long time ago. The pass, 1,435 ft, runs between the hills of East and West Cairn. (There are prehistoric cairns on top of these gateway hills.) Once through, the other side of the hills proved to be surprisingly heather-clad, big sweeps loud with *go-backing* grouse and wild waups' curdling cries. I crossed the Lyne Water below the Baddinsgill Reservoir to follow the old road, via legend-haunted Cairnmuir and Stonypath on the old Roman road, and was soon back to a green-painted landscape again, following a tree-lined avenue down the Loan into West Linton. There was no problem filling my bottle with lemonade. I bought an envelope to post home the *Pentland Walks* book and map. A fire, and coffee, in a small room of the Old Bakehouse was welcome. A gang of French *gamins* and Scots *keelies* from the nearby camp were enjoying the multi-murder of language and I had my share of Lothian accents from a fierce female at a farm. She relented however and let Storm and me wander off for several miles of long-abandoned railway track. As we righted a coupit sheep the kindness was repaid.

At Lamancha (a John Buchan name) we tried to take a short-cut and ended in a jungle of nettles and willow herb growing over felled pines, the sort of going Collie encountered in the Canadian west, but ridiculous half a mile from a busy road. A few hundred feet up, though, the country was strangely deserted and fast vanishing under forestry plantings. We brewed in the shelter of the trees, for the wind was snell. We passed a Royal Observatory 'outpost' which made me feel really at the back-of-beyond. By the Eddleston Water a house had collected some railway souvenirs about itself but rather spoiled their effect by super-imposing a TV aerial on an old signal tower.

Cool woods of deep leaves and dainty sorrel led up to the three-fold concentric rings of Northshield, a prehistoric hill-fort, more clearly seen than most as it is covered in a carpet-pile of heather. It was worth a diversion. The Pentlands were already hull down in the raw, sun-wounded west as we hove-to for the night, well up a stream under Dundreich of the Moorfoots.

Tuesday 3 July OVER THE MOORFOOTS
Surely this is an oddly-named group; how do *moorfoots* come to apply to hilltops? We found them misty from top to foot so lay late, then sensing that shivering, uncertain movement which often means the mists will break, we rushed up the burn to the draughty summits. As the mist just refused to clear, we abandoned the cold trig point of Dundreich for a route out to Jeffries Corse. There were acres of cloudberry which made

the going a bit like a cross between an abandoned strawberry patch and paddy fields. Gey dreich. And weird with the waups crying in the thick, silvering air. At last I had a glimpse into a valley. It should have had trees but there were none – consternation! – till I saw they were so tiny as to be hidden. Map, landscape, and we twa, still all agreed, as feathers the gether.

We dropped to leave the rucker by a stream, which would ensure I found it again, then edged our way and felt our way up Bowbeat Hill, the last of the 'wanted' Moorfoot Donalds, these being the list of *lowland* 2,000 ft summits, which appear after the Corbetts in Munro's Tables. Donalds are not to be scorned; on misty days they can provide navigational problems often absent from larger but more defined hills. Try crossing Garvald Punks in November. Storm backtracked efficiently again. I was able to check because I could see our swathe through the 'dew-dagged' grass. The grass of the strip between trees and fence was feet deep and lush; outside the fence the grass of the hillside was cropped like a lawn by the sheep. Overgrazing was not just a nineteenth-century phenomenon. I stepped on a mouse, caught a young pipit and Storm set up a hare. One area was snowing with white butterflies. Any hillside has this ability to suddenly startle with its varied wildlife, yet books constantly use terms like 'dull hill' or 'lifeless moor'.

We kept high, passing south and east of the ever-deepening valley of the Leithen (another John Buchan name), with the sun, as if working to rule, at last rousing itself to switch on full power and evaporate the clouds. It became almost too hot for our switchback walk. We were glad to use a new forestry track. A lorry was unloading fertiliser under Makeness Kipps and from the col beyond we went straight up to the radio relay mast of Dunslair Heights. The hillsides beyond were planted, and across the Leithen on the bold bums of hillside were stretched the corduroy of the ploughing. Long sheep and short sheep are giving way to trees. We had become desperate for water and after toiling up Black Law we just went down until we found some hidden among a hollow of altitude-loving nettles. We spent the rest of the afternoon there, reading and eating and simply dreaming until the beating strength of sun weakened, and we staggered on.

Looking down on the Tweed I really felt on the edge of 'the Borders' – and thrilled to it quite consciously. For a score of years I have tried to break any journey to England (which was usually itself only a step to the far corners of the world) with at least one day to explore the hills and history of this stirring land. The one day has often enough grown to a week or ten days, for in few places do hills and history spring to life as here. The Highlander regards 500 years as 50, admittedly, but it is all backward-looking; the Borderer, from any one of the cocky burghs or lonely uplands, has just as long a view of history, but still is out to make it.

The Borders were the anvil on which much of Scotland's history was hammered out: it all lies there between Bannockburn and Flodden, so to speak. Who owned the Outer Hebrides or Shetland hardly really worried the king sitting in Dunfermline toon, but what was happening on the Borders was of vital consequence. For the Borderer to survive the clashes of English-Scottish history, he had to be peculiarly resilient, resourceful, independent, exploiting every situation. They must have succeeded for they are still there, very self-aware, slightly cynical, and patriotic.

Looking down on Tweed I was also aware of the rich tapestry of the Border landscape. It is well varied, crowding seemingly endless miles of hills, rich woods, famous rivers, busy towns all into its small compass. It has a flashing, stabbing beauty which constantly catches the visitor unaware.

We looked over Cardrona Forest and hazy cushion-piles of hills beyond, which vanished in the muslin-haze of their own warmth. A big land. Beyond those tree-tapestried hills lay Ettrick Forest and St. Mary's Loch, Moffat, Hermitage Castle, the Debatable Land, Carlisle and all Galloway – none of which I would see this trip. More than anywhere else on the journey it was here I would have lingered instead of passing through.

> Three crests against the saffron sky
> Beyond the purple plain,
> The well remembered melody
> Of Tweed once more again.
> *Andrew Lang*

We broke out of our dwam and moved on. The glint of car windows catching the sun suddenly stopped: Tweed lay in shadow, while we walked in sunshine to Lee Pen where we camped in a nook within chuckie-stane reach of its cairn. When the lights of Innerleithen winked through the milky valley mists we still enjoyed a golden afterglow. No wonder our ancestors worshipped the sun.

Wednesday 4 July MINCHMOOR
The sun shining in the door woke us at five. The valley was glacier-deep

in cloud but cleared as we romped down off our summit. There were scores of rabbits careering about and Storm, regretfully, left them alone. All his desire to chase is due to good-natured fun. I have never known such a soft Sheltie, but on the hill a dog chasing can cause havoc and must be safe – and seen to be safe.

We entered friendly Innerleithen through cool woods, from the pre-historic fort (rather spoilt with twentieth century erections). Several shops were open, at 7.30 a.m., so I bought a paper and goodies and sat by the bridge while my tent was spread to dry off. It was saturated from overnight dew. "You make me jealous," one old man commented. Children passed going to school. The clock on the town hall jangled every quarter. At ·9.00 a.m. Roger Smith arrived. He was living in Peebles at the time, seven miles off, so, after coming with me for a while, Roger would "just run home" and then go in to his Glasgow *Great Outdoors* office as usual. Runners always fill me with awe. Walking is grand self-indulgence compared to running.

We looked back over the Tweed Valley to Lee Pen as we headed up for Minch Moor and, though I knew it not, that was an important moment on my way. When I stopped to finish off films for Roger to jog home with, we were covered with flies, an obnoxious cloud which seldom let Storm and me alone for the rest of the day. It turned what had been an idyllic morning into a high noon of horror. This was repeated on various days later and I can think of few things more loathsome. Clegs and midges are companionable by comparison. Both dog and man were reduced to rage and despair on that and other days – but I'll have it off now, for the Scottish dose, in case I'm later thought to have something against English flies.

Where we left the valley we looked down on Traquair House which may be the oldest inhabited building in Scotland. Legend has it that the main gates are permanently closed until a Stewart rules again. Fact cer-tainly shows the gates shut and they have been for unknown years. The Innerleithen school children have a much older superstition in their ceremony of *cleiking the deil* each July at the medieval St. Ronan's Well, made famous by Scott.

We had planned to brew at the Cheese Well but the fly millions made a stop there unbearable and the summit of Minchmoor was equally beyond endurance. They eased off a bit over Hare Law, Brown Knowe and Broomy Law but were back for the Three Brethren. I could have wept, for I had carefully chosen a crossing of Minchmoor to savour all sorts of historic and literary associations.

A chapter of Dr John Brown's *Horae Subsecivae* is entitled

"Minchmoor" for instance. If you tend to say "Dr Who?", then it is the author of *Rab and His Friends* – which many have thought the greatest dog story ever written. It turns up in every anthology of animal pieces. Brown was the Charles Lamb of Scottish writing. "The Bush Above Traquair" by Principal Shairp is a local poem still recited. Andrew Lang, J. B. Selkirk and others are among the Victorian minstrelsy. Volume I of the *Scottish Mountaineering Club Journal* even has an article on Minchmoor by W. Douglas, of Douglas Boulder fame.

It was on a journey up Minchmoor that Sir Walter Scott parted with his great doctor friend, Mungo Park, who came from Yarrow. The list of people of restless inspiration who came from the south of Scotland is a long one; offhand I can think of John Leyden, Joseph Thomson, Mungo Park, Lord Minto (Governor-General of India), even David Livingstone if we slip towards the Clyde. Perhaps anything was better than sheep and almost anything better than Edinburgh. Park was as 'driven' as any of them, preferring rather to return to Africa than practise again at Peebles. Park's horse stumbled as they went and Scott voiced fears of this being an ill-omen but Park only replied: "Freits (omens) follow them that fear them."

The road over Minchmoor is as old as travel itself. Often it has been a thieves' road and on a grim day in 1645 it saved a few of the fleeing Highlanders when the Great Marquis, Montrose, had his small force shattered and his followers butchered at Philiphaugh. One of the shames of our educational system is that, outwith early 'story' years, history taught and examined in Scottish Schools is blatantly Anglo-biased. Montrose is probably more admired in Europe than in Scotland. He was an ungrateful British monarch's Captain General in Scotland, a military genius, a glorious martyr, the stuff of hero-worship, the enslaving subject for historical writers such as C. V. Wedgwood and John Buchan and novelists such as Maurice Walsh, Neil Munro and Nigel Tranter. How much more worthy and substantial a figure he is than Bonnie Prince Charlie, for instance. In our local pub the other day I asked everyone I could what they knew about Montrose. The sum total is less than I've mentioned above, yet he was one of the greatest field leaders of all times. No Welshman could be so ignorant of his historical past, nor yet Irishman, nor Englishman. Scotland is by far the least nationalistic or patriotic of the countries set in these islands. She is noisy, yes, but noise is not nationalism; it is rather the unruly behaviour of the child whose school reports endlessly state, "Could do better if she tried".

The Three Brethren are three big 'stone men' on the most easterly top of this range that lies between Tweed and Yarrow. The Selkirk Common Riding sweep up here in wild array each summer. Horsemanship is still a Borders special love. I can still picture Storm leaning wearily against one of the cairns, on the shady side, panting and tongue lolling, and, surrounding him, a mad buzz of flies at which he now and then pawed feebly. Below Peat Law we lost the fuss of the flies for an hour and brewed thankfully. An irate grouse chased a kestrel off across the heather. We went round to the east side of the hill to camp with a splendid view of the haunting Eildons. They had been in sight much of the day but it was impossible to look at any view through shifting screens of irritating insects. Alas, even the tent was invaded, and each mouthful of braised kidneys had to be carefully inspected for undesirable additions. Only in Ethiopia have I seen flies to equal this plague. I was to see worse.

Thursday 5 July ABBOTSFORD AND THE EILDONS
The wind rose in the night making sleep impossible, then the wind fell at dawn and the midges came out. What an accursed site it had been. I could see the Cheviot on the horizon and the pencil stroke of the Waterloo Monument above Ancrum Moor. For once I wished myself elsewhere. We crackled down through the burnt and dusty heather to cross the Ettrick (which joins Yarrow only a mile or so upstream) on the outskirts of Selkirk, another of those tight little border towns which have kept their identity over centuries of pillage and modern sprawl. The small market place is dominated by a statue of the 'Shirra' (Scott was sheriff of Selkirkshire for 32 years), there is another of Mungo Park but the remembered one is the Memorial. It shows the legendary sole survivor of the eighty-strong contingent who followed James IV to Flodden, staggering home, wounded and weary and bearing tattered colours – which hangs in the museum yet. The inscription simply says "O Flodden Field". The floors o' mair than yin forest were a' weed awa.

We walked down the banks of the Ettrick to avoid the A7 and its mad motorists. After walking through the local sewage works (interesting) we still landed on the A7 (horrifying) but the verges were large so we survived. At Abbotsford we dried off a bit – even rucksack straps were sodden through with sweat. Storm and the rucksack were left behind the tearoom and both of us were made very welcome. I was so engrossed in the library that I missed Mrs Maxwell-Scott, who lives there and keeps up the family link. Scott had a large room full of books in several languages (he read French, Spanish, Italian, Latin and Greek) and his sheer professionalism and efficiency was astounding, yet it was equally as an interesting person that his contemporaries knew him; a large man, both physically and mentally, and a good man. The last preserved his memory as much as anything. A man honoured in his own country is rare. Scott in fact lived the life many of us would like to have lived if we had been alive in those days of Scottish renaissance. As "Author of Waverley", he managed to stay anonymous for many years. He had enormous influence in many different ways, such as stage-managing the 1822 visit of George IV to Edinburgh (a period when government troops were still garrisoned in the Highlands), or bringing Mons Meg back to Edinburgh Castle and rediscovering the Scottish regalia, and opening up whole areas of the Highlands and the Borders simply by the force of his poems and novels. It is amazing that he found time to write at all, but in the end he wrote desperately to clear off enormous debts of over £100,000 which had resulted from the collapse of Ballantyne, the printers whom he had unwisely backed over many years. The creditors left him Abbotsford and his pen and he virtually cleared the debt by his writing. What might he have written had he lived longer without this pressure. Abbotsford cost him dear.

Abbotsford was Scott's ridiculous, extravagant and very successful Wendy House. People are always surprised how small it is, having expected some baronial palace, but much of its charm is in its intimate compactness. Rooms could be designed to fit the trophies and souvenirs; the hall is panelled and full of armour and armorial crests, the library is a long room with a bay window facing the Tweed, off it is the compact study, lined with books and with a little stair to a gallery also lined with books. A door in the gallery led to Scott's sleeping quarters. He would slip down and be at work by six in the morning. He eventually wrote himself to death.

Scott is probably more admired than read, suffering, like Shakespeare and others, the discouraging scalpel study of one's young years. How either of those two would detest the thought of their works being dissected and set for examination papers. "Compare and contrast" too often has resulted in a follow-up of "and never touch again, thank goodness". I was lucky in never, ever, having an English teacher who leeched his subject. Scott wrote "rattling good yarns" I thought then, and still do, and on every trip to Morocco a Scott goes with me (I'd read *Rob Roy* this trip). A lot of comment is simply a parrot-like repetition of clever criticism in the past. You don't keep making operas, plays, or TV serials from dull books.

Stevenson and Buchan receive similar, untested, abuse. Both wrote some poor stuff, both had the flaws or prejudices of their period – which has nothing to do with the merits of overall enjoyment. Buchan of course was another Border chiel by adoption – hence his use of place names and the settings of many of his stories: *Witch Wood*, for instance, catches the local landscape as few books do – "here there is a long preparation and flowers steal very softly back to the world" – though I always feel it somehow fails as a story (he was to use his adopted Oxford landscape in the same way in *Midwinter*). Stevenson's unfinished *Weir of Hermiston* I consider the finest of all Border stories, an extraordinary bit of writing considering it was done by a dying exile in the far Pacific. Landscape is a priceless birthright and, seemingly, a last love; sad the country that sells it for a mess of concrete!

Walking on from Abbotsford to Darnick a Sheltie-owner stopped her car to say hello to Storm (something which we were to become quite used to) and I'm sure regarded my tale of walking from John o' Groats to Land's End as fantasy (something else which we had already become used to and which I never mentioned if I could help it). At Abbotsford they told me of someone walking from end to end, on roads, in bare feet, and his dog, because of the road battering, had been forced to wear boots. Someone else went by in shorts and brolly with Milk Marketing Board written across his chest. Roller skates, pushing a wheelbarrow – someone can always dream up a new stunt.

Melrose camp site was on the edge of playing fields and for us proved the most expensive in Britain: £2 for our one tiny tent. I bought a huge stock of fresh food and then rushed off on two planned extras: Melrose Abbey and the Eildon Hills.

The Abbey is the oldest (1136) and best preserved of the various abbey ruins in the Borders, its red sandstone giving it a warmth which grey stone always seems to lack. It does not have Dryburgh's arboretum setting but the Eildons are no bad backcloth for history. Bruce's heart is buried here – his body lies in Dunfermline Abbey – after it had been carried on a Crusade which cost the life of the faithful Sir James Douglas. Also buried here is Michael Scott, a sort of intellectual 'Wizard', even more awesome than Thomas of Ercildoune, whose rhyming prophecies still work like yeast. Scott came from Fife, studied later in Oxford, Paris, Padua and Toledo. He translated Aristotle from the Arabic, was Astrologer Royal to the Emperor Frederick, became a skilled doctor, was knighted by Edward I and, at over seventy, sailed to bring home the Maid of Norway, the heir of Alexander III who had ridden over a cliff at Kinghorn one stormy night. The maid died unfortunately and Scotland was plunged into the Wars of Independence, when the Borders were frequently ravaged by the scorched-earth policy as Bruce struggled with the English might under megalomaniac Edward and his ineffective son. Thomas of Ercildoune was forever set in legend by Scott, but was an historical figure in those troubled times. He seemed to have managed things well, taking seven years in Aberdeenshire rather than elfland and retreating to a monastery in Ayrshire rather than magically vanishing into the woods never to be seen again. On a lighter vein one of the few surviving carvings in the Abbey depicts a porker blowing the bagpipes. Perhaps even the destructive Reformers had a sense of humour.

We headed up, out of Melrose, to the triple-topped Eildons. A tearing wind made for fast crossings from top to top. It was bitter cold. Yet there had been a township of over 300 dwellings on the north summit in pre-Roman times. The Romans had a signal station there, King Arthur and his warriors sleep in "Eildon's caverns vast" – among other places. The Cobbler is also Ben Arthur and several other Scottish sites vie with Wales and England for association with this mysterious hero figure. We fled Eildon – to seek warmth in action.

Back at the camp site a transistor in the next tent brought me the news of Borg winning his unique fourth Wimbledon title and the next day Billie Jean King was to create her record of 20 Wimbledon titles. Elizabeth Ryan with whom she had shared the record died just two days before. That pins down the year of this trip in some minds! French, English and local kids were playing football which was noisy if not always understood. Scotland's misdeeds at this type of contest are by no means new. In 1457 the Scots Parliament banned both football and golf; the former because it created riots (shades of Wembley) and the latter because it wasted time which should be given to archery. I tied Storm to the tent before going off to have a shower. When I came out the dog was sitting patiently by the ablution block door and the tent and its contents had been trailed across from where I'd first left him. There are sometimes problems being owned by a dog. I noticed that the Episcopal Church's canon had the name of Dover: appropriate for one whose job is looking after souls.

Friday 6 July   SOUTH FROM TWEED

Yesterday had taken up a few pages of log book but that is often the way, for the peopled parts stir more varied experiences than do the empty summits. The hills relax the body, the valleys restore the mind.

Did you hear the one about the minister who always did his gardening after sunset – so he could watch over his phlox by night? Or the old wifie, looking at a bonny kirkyard, commenting "Aye, I'd like fine tae lie there one day, if I'm spared"?

A salvation wind made walking just bearable, for it was another hot day. An excellent one *not* to have been on Minchmoor. I think we'll save a return visit for ski-ing. We left Melrose by the Priors Walk to Newstead. Newstead was the site of the important Roman Fort of Trimontium (the Eildons), where Dere Street crossed the River Tweed. There is nothing much to be seen now but it is surprising what digging can discover, even if only among the rubbish dumps of history. Remains of the Soay sheep have been found in the middens of this fort, an odd link with St. Kilda. As a measure of protection Soay sheep are now kept in various places in Britain, as are other rare species which could be wiped out in an epidemic. How easily it can happen. How easily too man can be the cause of wiping out a species. The last great auk was killed (on St. Kilda in 1840) with its captors unaware of what they had done. The St. Kilda wren survived only because in 1904 parliament passed an act specifically to protect it. It is not only raw materials we burn up in our selfish greed. All through this trip wild life gave the deepest of pleasures but always with a consciousness of its vulnerability. Few birds sing in Avonmouth.

Beyond Newstead we came to the Three Bridges of Tweed: one, a tall, many-arched railway bridge which looked as if it had been made of Lego bricks, the second, a finely-proportioned road bridge and the third, a new steamlined sweep of concrete which carries the A68 that had not existed when a gang of us from Braehead canoed down the Tweed. We crossed the Tweed, then the River Leader, and pulled up to Scott's View, the spot where the author always reined-in his horse to admire the view of homely Tweed and its bonnet of the Eildons. When his funeral carriage passed this way his faithful horse stopped, as he had always done. . . .

Scott was buried at Dryburgh Abbey which we looked at. It has the unusual architectural feature of being built on several levels. It has a beautiful setting, surrounded by magnificent mature trees, including cedars. I had coffee in the wee post office before we crossed Tweed, for the last time, to follow properly-maintained paths along its banks through superb parkland. Last time I followed the Tweed was with the Braehead canoe party. We went on by Kelso to finish at Coldstream – after that there was no more white water fun. The Douglas-Home home, the Hirsel, lies outside Coldstream; the three brothers have achieved varied fame: Alec, who became Prime Minister, William, the playwright and Henry, the Birdman. All have recently written books: dull, gossiping and hilarious. *The Birdman* is a must for naturalists, full of splendid yarns. One tells of a cruise with a thousand ornithologists to St. Kilda when the captain took his ship through the narrows between Boreray and the Stacks. Experts on the bridge commentated on the cliffs and the blizzards of birds. Suddenly Chris Mylne's voice rang out over the speakers, "If you go quickly to the port side there is a rare sooty shearwater". Everyone charged across to the port side and the ship lurched dangerously by the cliffs. Later the culprit apologised to the captain, then added: "I never do get it right. I really meant starboard."

We left the Tweed at St. Boswells, which is named after an early prior of Melrose rather than the doctor's friend. It was George Borrow who challenged, "which of the world's streams can Tweed envy, with its beauty and renoun?" A Border Way would be far more enjoyable along it than over the grey heights. I shopped in neat, red-stoned, heat-shimmering St. Boswells, drank several cans of juice and left sooking Berwick Cockles. It was dripping hot. We lunched at Maxton in the shade of a bee-loud sycamore. A long slog, walking parallel to Dere Street, took us up the Peniel Heugh, 744 ft. A shady track led through trees with a thriving undergrowth of nettles, a Borders speciality, to land us at the Waterloo Monument. It is a tall tower, like a supernumerary lighthouse, and shrilled with the wind rushing up its hollow heart. It was locked and rather forlorn, a wasted tourist asset, for it is a great viewpoint over the whole Borderland. Ancrum and the Teviot lie to the south with the paps of Minto and Ruberslaw plain – country again of battles and legends. Jedburgh also lies to the south, perhaps the most historically interesting of all the Border towns, for it has been carefully and tastefully restored and has the most entire of the ruined Border Abbeys with tiered rows of arches and a sturdy tower.

Thinking of the scores who each year must tramp from John o' Groats to Land's End, it horrified me that so many simply walked the hard roads. Often there is no choice, and designated alternatives for pedestrians, at this valley level, would be welcomed. In the wide freedom of the hills set 'Ways' are quite unnecessary but in the complex rural parts they are sometimes the only hope, as old Rights-of-Way have become impractical through lack of use. In the north we are lucky to have the efficient watchdog of the Scottish Rights of Way Society. (Information, membership, etc., S.R.O.W. Society, 28 Rutland Square, Edinburgh, EH1, 2BW.) Our routes are not registered, and therefore restricted, as in England. They are safeguarded and, being fewer, more regularly walked, with little controversy between landowners and public. Long may these gentlemanly freedoms continue.

Groats End walking has always held popular appeal. I am not sure why for road-pounding is tough work. Perhaps the appeal lies in the personalities it attracts – like Dr Barbara Moore, the Russian-born imp of the outdoors, who in the drab fifties, aged fifty-six, made her tramp on a diet of grated vegetables, fruit and honey; or the Billy Butlin Walk of 1960 when 700 set off to race it (for the record 113 men and 25 women made it, the winner, Jim Musgrove, took 15 days 11 hours and 31 minutes). There is a readable account of this expedition by a Border farmer "A. Walker" called *The Big Walk*. He lashed out all of twelve shillings for a sleeper to Inverness at the start.

We dropped down into the sweltering Teviot valley. Crailing was only a hamlet, offering no chance of refreshment. We crawled up the brae from it and on top lay in the long grass of the verge to recover. The air felt brittle as old paper. It quivered with pollen dust, and a million insect wings spangled the sky.

An effort to reach a stream marked on the map failed – a cornfield barred the way – and it took more devious nettle-fighting before we at last stumbled into the gasping cool of a woody den. There we drank and drank, water first then tea, we made supper, and drank more tea and tea. The day's oven was switched off at about seven o'clock so we came out of the oak woods above Brownrigg (in a noisy scattering of pheasants) and wended over the Cessford Moor. In the end we camped in a surprisingly noisy plantation: down in the valley a bird-scaring cannon fired regularly, the trees creaked and groaned in the hot wind, pheasants, curlews, black-headed gulls, cushies, crows and a kestrel all kept up their calling and later a woodcock added its spooky sound. I was lying on the unpitched tent, and when a twig snapped I was able to discover and then watch, unobserved, a pair of roe deer. They passed just six feet away. Storm was equally fascinated. Periodic bumps puzzled both of us but were being made, we saw, by rabbits banging the ground.

Saturday, 7 July YETHOLM

I wrote up my log at 6 a.m. while dressed in shorts and shirt. It was thundery hot. The wind snarled in the tree-tops, a real *chien du ciel*. When we left the other end of the wood the roe deer went prancing off in front of us. Cessford proved a huge farm and house, and beyond even a *row* of houses. A farm toon almost. Our descent track to it had been beaten by passing horses – riding is another Borders speciality, from unforgotten reiving days. There is probably a higher horse population here than anywhere else in Scotland. Cessford Castle is a cloven ruin but still showing its strength. It was an old seat of the turbulent Kers, a clan which when not fighting others fought itself, the Kerrs of Ferniehurst (with endless male heirs) seeing no reason to honour the Kers (who with endless females inheriting could only hyphenate their name). However, the Kers ended with a Dukedom.

Cessford was once protected from the north by a loch four miles long, but a Teviot tributary cut back to capture the loch and the Kale Water that fed it. We followed its old route to Yetholm. We wandered through sleepy Morebattle, a wide, neat, village and by the crook of the Kale Water had a leisurely second breakfast. One half of the bridge had been repointed. Presumably the other half belonged to some other parish. We were drawing into hills again and the atmosphere became fresher. An erratic cuckoo went dashing by. A farm lad was out checking his cows by riding over the hills on a motorbike. We came to the tree-lined Bowmont Water, the river which moats the Cheviot so effectively before turning tail and joining with the Till to enter Tweed north of sad Flodden Field. We wandered into Town Yetholm: another trim village with a wedge of green square lined with flowery chestnut trees. I found The White Swan and two parcels and had a frantic repacking to make the post office before it shut at lunchtime. I had a tiny room over the front door so fell asleep to the playing of an accordion in the bar below. It was crowded with brosy locals. Most of the afternoon I lay by the Bowmont Water, drying the clothes I'd washed after lunch. Later, from my bedroom window, I looked down on a couple waiting for a bus. They were dressed in Rohan breeches, pile jackets (in that heat!), big boots and gaiters, obviously the uniform of the Pennine Way. With a shock I realised that tomorrow I would be on it, in England. Scotland had proved "a good land. Wide and high and far, yet it could be encompassed. A land that changed from bend to corner, from ridge to crest, yet had that in it from ancient time that did not change." (Neil Gunn.) The route through the Borders had gone in a walker's wink – and with a great variety of interest. I doubted then the wisdom of trying to write a book about the trip. I could only skim over our doings. Even that might have its place, however, pressing a seasonal bloom into the pages of experience which someone, someday, might open and read and see how it was to a gangrel going south at the end of the seventies.

VII

PENNINE WAY AND LAKELAND STRAY

A lover of the moorland bare
And honest country winds you were;
The silver-skimming rain you took,
And loved the flooding of the brook,
Dew, frost and mountains, fire and seas,
Tumultuary silences,
Winds that in darkness fifed a tune,
And the high-riding, virgin moon.

R. L. STEVENSON

Sunday 8 July ON TO THE BEATEN WAY *Maps, pp. 104 and 116*

As we left Kirk Yetholm a kindly local rushed over and said he hoped I'd
covering for my legs. It could be cold and wet up high. It *was* cold and
wet on high and we used all the covering we could find. The young eyes
of daybreak were to be the hooded eyes of dusk. In fact we were being
glared at almost as soon as we left. A promised coffee spot no longer
existed. Even the official route had been changed. I overestimated the
landscape and went too high above Burnhead Farm, but there were soon
acorn symbols and map boards to help the incompetent. It stopped
raining when we went through a gate into England and up The Schil. We
had thick cloud instead of rain.

We met various groups of people, most of whom looked weary and
muddy. They were generally splendidly garbed with heavy climbing
boots and Haston Alpiniste rucksacks: splendid examples of overkill. (I
wish I could afford such gear for climbing, never mind strolling along a
pedestrian motorway!) There was no sign of water on the ridge so, after
reading the dozen entries for today in the emergency shelter's visitors
book, we went on for the romantic and rocky Hen Hole. We had a long
view down the College Burn. A lamb led us to its mother, the messy ewe
being trapped by its horns in the boulders. The banks of the stream had
any number of tempting camp sites, so we decided to stay. It seemed
calm, but was the calm before storm, and soon big gusts were woofing
down the glen at us. At the least I would have to re-pitch the tent, so I

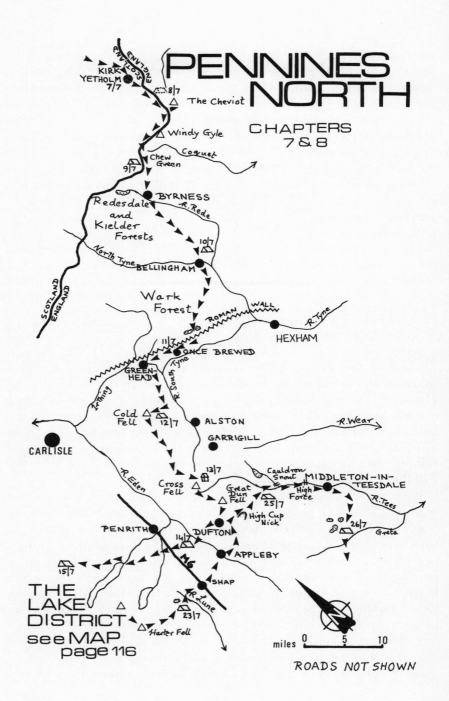

PENNINES
NORTH

CHAPTERS
7 & 8

KIRK
YETHOLM
7/7

🔺 8/7
🔺 The Cheviot

🔺 Windy Gyle

SCOTLAND
ENGLAND

Coquet

Chew
Green
9/7

BYRNESS
R. Rede

Redesdale
and
Kielder
Forests

North Tyne
10/7

BELLINGHAM

Wark
Forest

ROMAN WALL

R. Tyne

HEXHAM

11/7
ONCE BREWED

GREEN-
HEAD
R. South Tyne

Irthing

SCOTLAND
ENGLAND

Cold
Fell
12/7

ALSTON

GARRIGILL

R. Wear

CARLISLE

R. Eden

13/7

Cross
Fell

Great
Dun
Fell
25/7

Cauldron
Snout

High Cup
Nick

High
Force

MIDDLETON-IN-
TEESDALE

R. Tees

26/7

Greta

PENRITH

14/7

DUFTON

APPLEBY

M6

15/7

SHAP

THE
LAKE
DISTRICT
see MAP
page 116

R. Lune

23/7

Harter Fell

miles 0   5   10

ROADS NOT SHOWN

simply took the available easy option and, after supper, returned to the shelter. I like my sleep. The peg bag escaped when I was taking the tent down, shot a hundred feet into the air and vanished up the Hen Hole like a kite out of control. The tent did its best to follow so was bundled into the rucksack with scant ceremony.

I had changed to the old tent I used on the Munro trip. It had, since that venture, travelled from desert Atlas to deserted Arctic and even into the Nanda Devi Sanctuary in India. It was the best tent I've ever had, but is no longer manufactured. I'd left my Merrillite mainly because it was an all too-visible yellow. I also wanted a smaller, lighter tent. In Sheffield I hoped to pick up a lighter Tramp which has a deservedly famous reputation and is an unobtrusive but not sickly *green*.

My log book cracked: "On the whole the Hen Hoose was preferred to the Hen Hole." The shelter, if not a hen house, was unusual in being a railway goods wagon with sliding doors on the sides. It made a grand house and was quite dry and windless even with the east door open. I slept on the rescue stretcher rather than the stoorie floor and hoped no late parties would arrive and jump to wrong conclusions. The book was full of the agonies of northward-bound gangs, agonies doubly-enjoyed as their ending was a few hours off. There were few north-south travellers; later on somewhere I was even told off for doing the Pennine Way "the wrong way".

Monday 9 July   THE CHEVIOT AND THE BORDER LINE
The first words in Wilson's *Tales of the Borders* are as follows: "You have all heard of the Cheviot mountains . . . they are a rough, rugged, majestic chain of hills, which a poet might term the Roman Wall of nature, crowned with snow, belted with storm . . . like a huge clasp riveting England and Scotland."

We tramped up Auchope Cairn (the boundary of the old Eastern March) in cloud, but it cleared thereafter, except on The Cheviot itself, which was sulking in the clouds. The summit's eroded acre of man-trampled peat was mercifully dry and the term "ghastly" given to the walk to it was hardly true. Since realising how erratically the Donalds are listed I have been careful to visit everything vaguely 2,000 ft plus, both for topographical curiosity and to make sure in case future revisions spring surprises; so, from the marooned trig on Cheviot we made a circle of several toplets: to the north-east, then Braydon Crag and its cairn above the Hen Hole, from where it was easy to contour back below the level of the bogbergs and regain the Pennine Way via a snow gully.

There was an even larger grey remnant of snow on the south-west slopes of Auchope we saw later.

On the Cheviot Range we have a doubling-up of the lists of 2,000ers. The Scottish Donalds 'poach' as it were over the English border just to be tidy, but the Cheviot and all the rest of the 2,000ers south of the border are listed in George Bridge's *The Mountains of England and Wales* (Gaston/West Col). There have been other lists in club journals but as this is available in book form it seems to be the one everyone now starts to tick off. My *Donalds* collection, I saw, could be leading on for crossing *Bridges* – with the Irish peering over their *Walls*! In some ways it is a pity they are all so cut and dried now. In 1728 Defoe came to climb the Cheviot and feared it would be a precipice-girt pinnacle.

West from Cheviot gives high-level moorland walking on a large scale. The clouds were soon bannered in the sky, *argent* on *azure*, and we enjoyed our summit striding along the Border fence, cooled by a breeze and with extensive views to both countries. Pipits fluttered and piped and one grouse went scolding off. In *The Birdman* the author mentions taking a tame grouse from Aberdeenshire to the Thames. After a couple of weeks it vanished and he wrote to the keeper to say so, but the keeper was able to reply that the bird was back in Aberdeenshire, ahead of the letter. If we could navigate like that. . . .

We had a brew on Windy Gyle by an old tumulus which has been burrowed into by twentieth-century humans seeking shelter out of the wash of wind and rain. Names are an endless fascination. Some of our simplest outdoor words, *night* and *star, snow* and *wind* for instance, are among the words of man's very beginnings. What fear and wonder and dreams have come down in them, echoes of humanity caught by modern magic, as events long gone are caught by giant telescopes. You could almost reconstruct Border history from the names along this high walk: Black Hag, The Schil, Auchope Cairn, Scotsman's Cairn, The Cheviot, King's Seat, Butt Roads, Clennell Street (a pre-Roman road), Russell's Cairn (a burial mound), Windy Rig, Foul Step, Monzie Law, Beefstand Hill, Lamb Hill, Yearning Saddle, Dere Street, Chew Green, Coquet Head, Ogre Hill, Raven's Knowe, Windy Crag. . . .

There was another shelter on Yearning Saddle, full of self-congratulatory and do-gooding notices. I always find it sad that we so constantly foul our own nest. We go to the hills to be free of man's intrusive ugliness (and this day's walk is the most free of the whole Pennine Way) but then we will mark routes and build shelters and tame it, to suit the incompetent. You cannot make hills safe anyway – they are far more clever than we are – and by interfering we simply enlarge the problems.

Build a shelter and it at once becomes a magnet, an easy option (did I not take it the night before?), a debasement of the very challenge we go for. It may save the odd life, but it brings so many more people that lives go on being lost so in reality it saves nothing. If there had not been a shelter on top of the Cairngorms the worst tragedy in British mountain history would not have happened. If we take on nature for our irrational entertainment then we must learn to play it nature's way and not superimpose our own urban strengths and weaknesses. We demean something wonderful, something beautiful. In other spheres the word used is prostitution. Beware of the mountain pimps.

This is not just my opinion, it is the feeling of most independent hillgoers in Scotland. You may disagree entirely, but any part of a country has its own traditions. These are being attacked by bureaucracy as never before. The hills should be part of the Welfare State! Well, Scotland does not want it so, nor do we need the massed ranks of Ramblers and others. That may be the way for England, but from what I was to see I doubt it. The Pennine Way itself is now messy and worn because of the magical appeal artificially created by its special designation. It is a great route, wandering at its best and full of interest. But it is seldom done for interest. I wonder what Tom Stephenson would say if he saw it now?

During the day I met people at very irregular intervals, for this 'stage' is perhaps the longest and most detached from bases. We had a tent so were not chained to any set stages or overnight stopping-places. Today we ambled and had time to enjoy an evening by the tent, reading and relaxing. We finished the walking itself by wandering over Chew Green, an extensive Roman fort site on Dere Street, their main road into Scotland from York. It must have been a dreary and unpopular posting. The green geometry of its acres can still be seen.

I filled the water carrier from Coquet Head and went over to camp by the shelter of trees. The loneliness was a tonic though, as always, slightly sad, when man's past reminds. Here were the barely-buried bones of rough history, Stevenson's

> Hills of sheep, and the bones of the silent vanished races,
> And winds, austere and pure. . . .

Our day's walk had taken us virtually across the length of the historic Middle March, the centre region of three (duplicated each side of the Border) set up as almost semi-autonomous powers in an effort to have even bad government rather than none, back in the days of feud and foray. The truth is a deal less romantic than tradition and far more fascinating than fiction. Try *The Steel Bonnets* as a nightcap – and a change from *Flashman*.

Tuesday 10 July　BY DALE AND FOREST AND MOOR

We had a dew-dribbly tent to pack up the next morning. A trio were camping round the other side of the wood – which explained voices in the night. A succession of little hills led on, giving fine views down into Redesdale. Carter Bar (Carter Slap more anciently) is an historic route of travel and foray, of drovers and armies. Catcleugh Reservoir fills its head now, supplying Newcastle, 40 miles away, with water. There is an 'industrial' window in the old Byrness church in memory of the 64 who died constructing the dam, which took the labours of a thousand men for fifteen years. I was told this was the smallest church in England.

About 300 years ago one of the regular meetings of the Lord Wardens of the Marches on Carter Bar ended in fighting between the Redesdale and Tynedale men and the Scots. The latter were having the worst of it when a party from Jedburgh rode up, late for the meeting but delighted to charge in with yells of "Jethart's Here" – which they have been singing about ever since. Another tale is told of Barty of the Comb, a Redesdale Milburn who returned to his pele tower to find his sheep gone. They chased into Scotland under 'hot trod' dispensations but, not finding their beasts, made sure of returning with some others. The Scots sent two swordsmen to challenge Barty and his partner, Curly Jack. It was a desperate duel. Barty was wounded and Jack killed, but the wounded man killed his opponent and as he was set on by the second Scot swiped him a back-hander "garring his heid to sprang along the heather like an inon". Jack was slung over a shoulder and Barty delivered body and sheep in turn. The stuff of TV serials. I just wish the Pennine Way went over Carter Bar to finish in Jedburgh for, with its old abbey and associations of Mary Queen of Scots (who nearly died there after a mad ride to see her lover the injured Bothwell, at Hermitage Castle), Scott and the Wordsworths (Scott read them passages from *The Lay*) and Burns (who was given the freedom of the neat burgh), it is the logical northern terminus. Even the youth hostel is a fifteenth-century tower, Ferniehurst Castle. The tacking-on of the Cheviot is quite illogical. Perhaps if the Pennine Way is ever linked to foot routes up Scotland, Jedburgh can be given its proper place in the Groats End Walk.

Byrness was quiet and has done little to cash in on the presence of the Pennine Way, even to hiding the route fairly effectively. A friendly cafe

produced toasted sandwiches. By trial and error and the gospel according to Wainwright we wandered off into the vast forests for miles of hot,
hard-surface walking. Correcting Wainwright seems to be a Pennine
Way game. The route then swings over the moors to the Padon Hill
Monument, but I never reached it as I found an injured lamb and went
off to report it. The monument according to several guide books was to a
Scottish Covenanter who preached there, but the only Covenanters I can
trace are Sandy Peden or Capt. Paton. There is a Peden's Cleugh just
over the border. Of Alexander Padon I can find nothing.

We rejoined the official route for some soft moor and were thankful
the ground was suffering from lack of rain. We crossed a road into a herd
of cows which were milling about, and whacked our way through them
but, as the last cow turned out to be a black bull I metaphorically lifted
my hat to him and passed by instead. We rounded the hillside, found
water, and went up to camp, or bivy, rather, by School Crag, a rocky
eyrie which gave an extensive view over the Bellingham countryside. A
breeze just rustled the shading bracken and we snoozed on heather. A
party of lassies on ponies cantered by and sheep several times almost
walked on top of us. I felt like some hiding Covenanter myself!

In some ways I was hiding; by camping high and staying unobtrusive I
could stop anywhere and thus avoid the almost inescapable involvement
of an official way and its directives. The dog ruled out using youth
hostels, and planned camp 'sites' know little of quiet. Above all I liked
the solitude and peace, the tranquillity that allowed, on this occasion for
instance, baby wheatears to be fed by their parents, undisturbed, on the
rocks just a yard away. All the time there ran on an unending, exuberant
reel of lark song overhead.

Wednesday 11 July   TO THE ROMAN WALL
Camping wild also had two other vital advantages: it costs nothing and
time was kept as a servant instead of a frustrating master. I went to bed
by simply lying down on the tent. Later I crawled into the sleeping bag
and later still, when the last warmth of day had been sucked up by the
cold sky and its icy stars, I put the tent up. There was a touch of frost on
the crags while the fields below were saturated with dew. We fled soon
after breakfast when the midge *impis* descended on our *laager*.

We went down Hareshaw Linn Glen, a long wooded dell through
which a made path led to a hollow of overhanging rock, over which
squirted a depleted fall, shrunk to insignificance by the dry spell. We
made the most of Bellingham's good shops. It was a pleasant, unpretentious town, which seemed to say it had had its share of Border batterings

and wanted only peace. The church (*c.* 1200) has a massive stone roof and narrow windows, a reminder of those days. The town is pronounced Bellinjum. As the sun was high and hot I changed into shorts and walked on. It was to prove a 20 mile grilling and by the end of the day my ears were reduced to something like pork crackling.

Four solid youths passed and all day we Penwaymen kept leap-frogging each other. They had huge packs and strode on, guide book and maps in hand and their transistor blaring. I shambled after, reading a Neil Gunn novel, *The Serpent*, so we received some odd looks from the north-bound traffic. Every second party had a transistor going. There seemed to be few cheery faces. It struck me as all wrong. We must have seen a score of hikers in Bellingham and met over 30 heading to it for their overnight stop, which implies that through the height of summer a thousand walkers would be on the Way each day.

A bridge took us over the pleasant North Tyne stream and the slopes above were brutal in the heat. We took a short cut to the Shitlington Crags and watched the quartet go astray there. We had a brew by the Blacka Burn and then they caught up for a joint expedition through a field of cows – and a bull, of course. Storm is a great attraction to cattle, who tend to follow him, so time and time again we ended leading a herd, usually with a resigned bull following up his harem from behind. A friend of mine regards cows as one good reason for marriage, "I can always put my wife between them and me." He does, too.

At Linacres I took a photo of the pleasing stone buildings in Wark Forest as the farmstead was so typical, and gaily went off in the wrong direction, which allowed the foursome to overtake us. The route became a bit of a nonsense, going over endless styles and through farmyards where they were shearing. The pull up from Warks Burn was exhausting, but a brew stop was made hellishly unpleasant by swarming flies again. I read my way through much of the dull forest that followed (it's the largest man-planted area in Europe), brewing at the Sell Burn and then passing the other crew brewing at the next stream – our last contact of the day. As our two parties kept running into each other I was very thankful not to be travelling south–north with another 30 competing parties.

We joined the Roman Wall at the Rapishaw Gap and simply turned west, abandoning ideas of visiting Housesteads, an extensive and excavated fort, which I knew already. Returning from Norway one autumn, I spent several days exploring the Wall, which is also a fine natural walking route. The Wall's construction was begun in AD 122, but it was never quite made to the scale of the original conception. Towards

Camp by the Forth somewhere in Flanders Moss

The Forth bridges

A Cheviot shelter: Storm looking out from the railway waggon that
gave us a good howff

Hadrian's Wall on Walltown Crags, Northumberland

Greg's Hut on Cross Fell

Right: Lunch above Horton-in-Ribblesdale

Pennine bog: the slats put down are vanishing, and overhead a TV mast

Pennine Way crosses Motorway (the M62)!

High Force: the finest waterfall on the Pennine Way

The iron fountain in Middleton-in-Teesdale

Skiddaw

l. to r.: Lingmell, Scafell Pike and Scafell – below is the head of Wastwater

the Solway it was temporarily built of turf. The whole is 75 miles in length. At Roman-mile intervals milecastles were built, on which patrols were based, and there were signal turrets between – all very efficient. We joined the Wall where it was at its most impressive, running along the whin sill cliffs which face north. The *Fosse*, a V-shaped ditch, backed the entire wall line and Agricola's road from Corbridge to Carlisle, The Stanegate, served the whole. When Prince Charlie headed south in 1745, Wade's army was virtually marooned in the east, where they could do nothing. Wade then quickly built a military road to create a decent east-west line and some of it used the Roman Wall as foundation. You drive on it to this day. There is a superb Ordanance Survey Archaeological Map to the Wall and no lack of guide books.

Crag Lough was pleasant, giving views and shade, but the heat was desperate as we climbed on; we deserted Hadrian's Wall and descended to Twice Brewed Inn. It had NO DOGS over the door so was twice booed and we went on to discover Vallum Services (visions of Roman chariots rolling in for their MOTs), where the Moores and their St. Bernard dog gave Storm and me a real welcome. A bath was bliss, as was the chance to wash and dry garments soured with sweat. There was a camp site along the road a bit, but since the midges were even coming inside the house, it was another good night not to be camping. I read till all hours and rushed my log-writing over breakfast in the cool of morning. By 8.15 the tide was flowing northwards. The locals were not too enamoured of their Pennine Way clientele, who tended to be brash and conceited as if their doing the Way gave them some status. "But you must give us a meal, we're doing the Pennine Way" is not the way to make Northumberland friends!

My next day was to take me on to a wild camp on Cold Fell. I almost hoped it could live up to its name. Rain is wearing, but it is the sun that destroys. I'd had enough of the salamander existence.

Thursday 12 July   HOT HELL AND COLD FELL
If, as W. H. Hudson maintained, "all weathers are good to those who love the open air", then some are better than others. The sun all too soon shook off dawn's lethargy and set to work on the poor walkers again. I abandoned the Wall to walk into Greenhead (which is in a valley) to make sure of my parcel, then set off to shorten everything we could, the Pennine Way at this stage being described as "uninteresting". We climbed a long brae (the Maiden Way) and lunched on top where midges and flies joined forces to destroy its enjoyment. We had a delightful walk up the banks of the South Tyne for a while, stopping to

paddle below a weir which was banked with bright monkey flowers. Burnfoot led us on to the Maiden Way and moorland country again. The Pennine Way, for reasons best known to itself, funks the end of the Pennines proper and follows the Maiden Way right up the South Tyne to Garrigill before pulling up Cross Fell. The Maiden Way eventually crosses the Pennines at over 2,000 ft, just north of Cross Fell – one of the highest old routes, linking the Vale of Eden with the Wall.

From the crest of the track we branched off through the heather. A voice yelled after us, "Hey mate, you're going too high." (We had not quite dodged all the traffic.) We walked over the parched slopes to the Glendue Burn where we passed the afternoon hours of greatest heat either by, or in, the tepid water. At 5.45 we made our big evening meal: basically a tin of meat and piles of fresh vegetables – the favourite every time, add to it what you will. Going on after a big meal never seems to work out well. It began pleasantly enough following up my stream, but all too soon we ran into another rent-a-mob of flies which, combined with clawing heather, sphagnum bogs and a continuing Turkish bath atmosphere, reduced us to the ranks of the near-insane. In one-and-a-half hours we made three miles, not enjoying "the insincerities of summer" (Saki). If any one part of the whole trip can be regarded as its nadir, this was it. I really did question the sense of such walking, for I do not hold with the theory of "enjoying it all afterwards". It should be fun *at the time* – and this was anything but. There is a world of difference between hard work and hell!

In some ways we were trapped, of course: the flies would be equally foul whether we retreated or went on. We dodged, we ran, we tried every trick to lose the myriad host. I covered every inch of skin to escape the tactile horror of their crawling, but this was unendurable in the heat. I killed scores, till my shirt sleeves were stained with the slaughter. Storm was nearly frantic: snapping at them in the air or pawing them off his eyes. It was utter misery, for there was no escape. We reeled under their assault on our senses: feeling, sight offended and hearing battered till the brain was bruised and tired.

We followed up a side stream to the Butt of Blackburn, where it petered out in a shrivelled, bleached bog. The landscape was of featureless moors. There was not even a sheep track. I sweated on towards the sinking sun, vowing that we would never again journey like this in high summer. Suddenly there were no flies: at 8.30, precisely, they vanished!

A grassy knoll lay across the stream; we just set up camp there and then. The dog must have felt much as I did, for he went careering round and round, leaping the burn, diving in and out of the tent and generally behaving like a daft thing. I sat relishing the last cool hour of evening, watching the orange-red sun fade away like a lantern running out of fuel. The contrast was stunning: Heaven and Hell but a minute apart. A solitary plover was weeping a mile off on the moor. The only other sound was the contented bubble of our burn. The map still used *burn* and *glen* and, ominously, north of Cold Fell, was *Midgeholme*. No reading of guides or anything else had mentioned flies as a curse. We were abed at 9.30 and, a minute later, asleep – sleep which was dived into as into cool seas, down tangle-deep where fiery dreams swam and all the day's horrors were forgotten.

Friday 13 July   COLD FELL TO CROSS FELL
We surfaced again to coolness and plovers' pipings. It had not been a dream. We wandered up to the ridge with some impatience but backpacking cannot be hurried any more than darning socks. Once up we spread the tent to dry and then went off to the top of Cold Fell, 2,037 ft, which is the real northern end of the Pennines. The Pennine Way is no logical watershed-walk along the spine of England as so many imagine. We reached Cold Fell trig point set on a tumulus just as it began to rain, so careered back to the tent, but too late to save it (or myself) from a soaking. Storm thought this some crazy new game. We did not often have an opportunity to run. The mist came down, and we walked south in a blank milkiness of cloud virtually for the rest of the day – time for navigation practice!

I had read in an article about this watershed walk that fences could be helpful, which they were – except when they were missing or bifurcated – supplementing the compass work and dead reckoning. It was rough going. We dropped to Butt Hill (an odd name for a pass), made morning coffee; I estimated 1 p.m. from there to the A686, which in fact we reached with ten minutes to spare. As my deviation had been all bog, heather and moss, perhaps the Pennine Way does well to miss it. We were on to the road before we saw it, the 1,903 ft highest A road in England. A notice marked "cafe" delighted and I was soon sitting before a fire eating hamburgers, while the dog, tied in the entrance, did his best to discourage visitors.

The going was easier up the Gamblesby Allotments after that, a surprise with a hill called Fiend's Fell. (Cross Fell was originally Fiend's Fell till an early saint planted a cross on top and cleansed it.) On Melmerby Fell the weather began to clear. We were suddenly looking down on a patchwork landscape – as from an aeroplane. The sprawl of

Cross Fell lay ahead and even the Lake District's array of peaks lined the horizon. We met the Maiden Way again by Meg's Cairn and wended on over an odd plateau, rightly named Stony Rigg, where shepherds were gathering. Storm rounded up some wheatear chicks which could only toddle. The mother chakked her concern. One of the many sink holes on Green Fell had water in it, so I gave Storm a wash as he had earlier nose-dived into a very gooey slot and was mud almost all over. We crossed the Corpse Road, over which corpses were carried from Garrigill to Kirkland, and met the Pennine Way at Greg's Hut.

Greg's Hut was our night's shelter: a restored stone building (once a lodging-shop) among the decay of the Screeds mining ruins above Cashwell. Its major drawback as a bothy is stone floors, but fortunately one bed was available. I had not long settled for a brew when three out of the four North-South gang of two days before arrived by the path up from Garrigill. One had fallen out with a sore gut which they put down to a long night in the pub in Alston. They ate a meal and then set off over Cross Fell for Dufton, transistor still on. . . .

Greg's Hut was a memorial to John Gregory of the Mercian Mountaineering Club who died, aged forty, in 1968 in an accident while descending the Adler Pass for Zermatt during a ski tour. A portrait hangs on one wall. The mining goes back to Roman times, for the area is rich in lead ores. The Earls of Derwentwater once owned the Alston area, but one lost his head on Tower Hill after the 'Fifteen and his brother likewise after the Forty five. The confiscated lands still remain in the possession of the Commissioners. The London Lead Company worked most of the mines from 1750 to 1905. Greg's Hut has its historical associations.

There is running water by the north gable, which even goes on through a cludge. The Hut has a grand view down the Pennine Way path dropping towards Garrigill. I noticed Charles Knowles' name in the bothy book from a ski visit with the Castle Mountaineering Club back in January. About a month before a John Dennis had used it, his only bothy, on a Land's End to John o' Groats walk; "seven weeks gone, five to go". Someone else had used it while pursuing all the English and Welsh 2,000 footers. My eyes had been sore on arrival, and as there was a mirror in the First Aid box I had a look and noticed a bit of grit embedded in the left eyeball. I failed to remove it, but next morning it had gone.

Saturday 14 July   OFF THE HILLS

We went straight up from Greg's Hut, but the cloud beat us to Cross

Fell, 2,930 ft. The area had several alarming open shafts from the ancient lead mines, so the dog was kept beside me. The highest point of the Way (and of England outside the Lakes) was surprisingly clean and bare: the trig, the dry-stone shelter and one cairn. Perhaps we could employ the same firm on Ben Nevis, Britain's highest midden.

Tees Head, the first col down off Cross Fell, lies to the south which felt a gain. We had cleared the Tyne at last. Little Dun Fell, 2,761 ft, and Great Dunn Fell, 2,780 ft, were consciously relished for a keen breeze even if there was no view. In January 1968 a wind speed of 134 m.p.h. was recorded here – the highest known for England. Great Dun Fell is covered with signal towers, alas mistakenly described as "uniquely so" by Wainwright. I lost the path in its sprawl so took a bearing which saved trouble – and landed me in different trouble.

I hit col and road just right, only to be jumped on by a lady who leapt out of a car with a pile of papers. I was the first person they had seen after a long, cold wait. They were Tourist Board, doing a survey of the Pennine Way. Would I answer some questions? You know where you are? Where were you last night? Greg's Hut – where's that? How long have you been walking? What! You *are* doing the Pennine Way? Oh. Well where are you going? But you must know! Shall I say south? The Lakes, yes, that's south. Oh, west is it? Then you're not going along the Pennine Way? You don't know when you're going to finish? I think maybe we should skip? Would you like some coffee?

Descending Knock Fell I met the first of the day's opposition. They reported snow, and almost unconsciously I asked whether it was snow falling or lying. It was a big patch. The whole area was full of odd hollows and dozens of sink holes, rivers vanishing and reappearing and one man-made cutting or *hush*. Hushing was the stripping of the topsoil by releasing a flood of water from a temporary dam in order to see what lay below – using nature as a prospector. Lead was the lure.

The Way descends right off the Pennines down to Dufton, only to rise again, one of the odder quirks of a quirky route. Ahead was Nature Reserve – could that be why? The delightful descent gave a view to the conical pikes that mark Dufton from afar, crossing a tiny clapper bridge, using a sunken lane and popping out in lush farmland on the outskirts of a warm, red-sandstone village which itself was spaced round a large green, inn and farm on one side, friendly village shop on the other. Storm was left by the fountain. Mr Pickles, the shopkeeper, gave me some dog biscuits for him. It was tempting to stay, but we pushed on into this brosy land. Down the Long Marton footpath we paused to eat and have coffee by a stream. No rain, no sweat, no flies – blissful ease – a

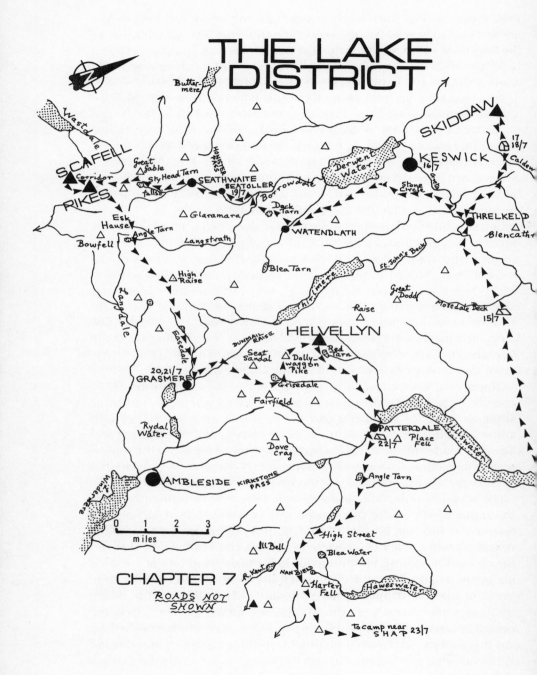

THE LAKE DISTRICT

SKIDDAW

KESWICK 16/7

Buttermere

Wastdale

17 18/7

Caldew

Derwent Water

Stone Circle

SCAFELL PIKES

Corridor

Great Gable

Sty Head Tarn

SEATHWAITE

SEATOLLER 19/7

Borrowdale

Dock Tarn

THRELKELD

Blencathra

fells

Esk Hause

Angle Tarn

WATENDLATH

St. John's Beck

Great Dodd

Mosedale Beck

15/7

Bowfell

Glaramara

Langstrath

High Raise

Blea Tarn

Thirlmere

Raise

Eskdale

Langdale

DUNMAIL RAISE

HELVELLYN

Red Tarn

Seat Sandal

Dolly-waggon Pike

20,21/7

GRASMERE

Grisedale

Fairfield

PATTERDALE

22/7

Place Fell

Ullswater

Rydal Water

Dove Crag

Angle Tarn

Windermere

AMBLESIDE

KIRKSTONE PASS

0 1 2 3
miles

High Street

Ill Bell

Blea Water

R. Kent

NAN BIELD

CHAPTER 7

ROADS NOT SHOWN

Harter Fell

Haweswater

To camp near SHAP 23/7

restorative ramble thereafter. In 1974 the redoubtable Joss Naylor covered Kirk Yetholm to Dufton (107 miles) in one day. We all make our own agonies and ecstasies.

We wended on, pausing by the bridge over the Eden to look at the clear sweep of the Pennines. So often, driving south, I had looked at them; next time I would name them off, remembering. Bolton had a church with the same Scandinavian elements as those in Caithness.

Above the Lyvennet Storm found a huge, but flightless, curlew chick which he sniffed all over. We puffed up and down to reach Morland, where I decided an enjoyable day deserved a proper bed. After finding several inns (on map and on their name boards) not to be inns at all, but pubs, I felt like invoking the Trades' Description Act. *Inn* implies a residential house. There was no accommodation at all. We went on a mile and a bitty and camped in the middle of a plantation where no one was likely to notice. Sufficient unto the day are even the pleasures thereof. It ended with good food, a soft bed, cool conditions and with the best of company.

Sunday 15 July   WEST OF THE M6
The early bird song was almost tropical in volume. We came out of our forest maze and descended from straggling Great Strickland to cross the M6. The village houses were solid, many dating back 300 years. All this delectable countryside shows the best of England, in my view. So much of the east lacks essential hills. The Lakeland Fells now loomed ahead and the Pennines became mere horizon swellings.

We came to the Lowther estate, fine, timbered countryside. We picked a dixi-lid full of wild strawberries, and scoffed them with sugar added. The dog found the hedgerows fascinating. He met his first mole and his first hedgehog and at one stage stood listening to a faint scratching sound which eventually I discovered to be caused by a wasp planing off a bit of dead willow herb stem for making 'paper' for its byke. We walked through the park with its extravagant and dead mansion. Mary Queen of Scots came this way on her journey of no return. At the old village of Askem we had a welcome break in the Queen's Head. When we rounded the end of the hills we were suddenly very much in Lakeland: Ullswater lay below us and Blencathra straddled the north. Pooley Bridge was a seething mass of trippers (Fort William had nothing on this) yet five minutes' walk beyond I sat by Ullswater to read a paper and could have been a thousand miles away. I think the statistics that show 90 per cent of the population never goes more than a quarter of a mile from their cars is wrong. They don't go nearly as far. . . .

We had to leap on to the bank to avoid a maniac driver on the wending lakeside road, so we left it and went up the hillside, which marvellously expanded the view. A family of quivering baby redstarts puzzled Storm and he was not at all sure of what to make of the black sheep. We came out by Wreay Farm and walked along for a mile or two before leaving the Ullswater landscape by a stiff pull up under Little Mell Fell. The visual door opened fully on Blencathra. Now, there is a hill I'd be prepared to barter for a few Munros!

Some harvesters were picnicking by the roadside. Storm 'comes' at once to a quiet bidding, but their dog would not for all the shouting he received. There were some interested comments. We chatted a while and then took the old coach road for Keswick. Several miles along it we camped by a beck.

Monday 16 July   KESWICK
It had rained most of the night and kept up a spiteful hard battering for the day as well. I dropped down off the old coach road to visit some prehistoric settlements, but there was little to see so we dashed over the race track of new road into Threlkeld to collect a parcel, then Mrs Hughes (Saddleback View, B & B) gave us welcome shelter till the 9.30 bus for Keswick arrived. A double-decker bus was new to the dog, so was the Queen's Hotel lift, and so too was an open-air meeting of the Keswick Convention. Had it been a sparkling day I would just have camped at Threlkeld, but there was much phoning to be done for which I preferred comfort. As I was returning to Threlkeld I was not breaking the pedestrian rules. Just having a night on the town.

It not infrequently rains in Keswick when I visit it, but as it has a good stamp shop one off day is always bearable. The last time I was there with the Dormobile the camp site flooded and we had to paddle 20 yards to dry land. The same distance further out a notice, just showing above the waves, read Children's Play Area.

Tuesday 17 July   BACK O' SKIDDAW
We were back at Threlkeld at lunch-time. Mrs Hughes kindly took some unwanted books and things as Ray was planning to stay there the next night. We walked up to Riddings, where the dog barked at the *stone* fox on top of the gateway pillar. The other pillar had a figure of a hound, John Peel's famous "Britain" bought by John Crozier, squire of Threlkeld, after Peel's death. Its descendants are still active.

Glenderaterra is an evocative name, its beck splitting Skiddaw and Blencathra and making a passage through to Back o' Skiddaw. Several years ago Wainwright began his series of drawings of Scottish mountains and was indiscreet enough in the Foreword to the first volume to complain at the complexities of Gaelic. "An English climber in Scotland thinks with nostalgia of the simple mountain names of his own Lake District. Helvellyn, Glaramara, Blencathra, Great Gable: lovely names and straightforward" (but equally un-English except for the last). Gaelic has rules. It is English which is the maddeningly confusing language. However, if we think our inter-tribal tongues can cause confusion, pity the poor French schoolboy, given an English newspaper to study, meeting in it the statement that a "*corpse* was pronounced *dead*".

After completing the Pennine Way I wrote to Wainwright, partly about that route, to which he had produced his inimitable guidebook, but also to say how much I had enjoyed his Scottish drawings, now complete; a pleasing change from everlasting photographs. This task, I may add, was carried out at well past pensionable age.

As we reached the burn below Skiddaw House the heavens opened and we had to dive into waterproofs for the 200 yards ahead. I joined a couple sheltering in a room which is left open for such occasions, but the rain went on and on. They had to leave. I stayed right there. I had a good book so was content.

The last time I had been there I had had Kitchy with me, returning from a glorious winter camp on top of Skiddaw. We almost decided not to have another dog after him for, devil though he could be, he had been a dog of character.

Kitchy lived to a good old age despite a thousand peaks having passed under his paws. A puppy unexpectedly jumped on him one day and he had a stroke, his rear quarters left useless and life slowly ebbing. The Siamese cat, Koko, crawled into the basket and faded away along with him. I was in Morocco at the time and friends coming out were instructed not to tell me; mother did not want to spoil my time there. Unfortunately the vet's bill for "putting down one dog, one cat" was addressed to Mr Brown, so was redirected to me in Morocco.

Returning from another trip to Morocco a couple of years later, I saw two marvellous Shelties near Rosslyn Chapel and, once home, rang Mrs Elder in Fife, who had promised to be in touch when she had pups for sale. The bitch had missed. We chatted on a bit and, almost doubtfully, she mentioned she had an *adult* dog which really should go. They bred and showed Shelties and this one was slightly too big, so they did not want to use him as a stud dog. Might I be interested in a two-year-old dog?

I went along to Coaltown of Balgonie. In the house six Shelties were milling about, but one came up and laid his head on my knees to be petted. You can guess the rest; I know it sounds like sloppy fiction!

"Which is the one you may sell?"

"The one that seems to have chosen you."

Storm has an oddly sad and serious expression and as he looked up at me I must admit I fell for him – as surely as he did for me. I have never been *possessed* by a dog before. As a family we have always had one, among other creatures great and small. I left the Coaltown with Storm sitting on the passenger seat, utterly silent and staring at me with that frown of his. A silent dog was something new, too. Mother was appalled when we arrived, unannounced, on the doorstep. Storm occasionally meets his previous owner – and he cuts her dead in a most embarrassing manner but then, could you expect him to want to go back to the show ring after the life he now lives on the hill? If by one of those twists of fate a lady in Rosslyn who has two Shelties ever reads this, then my blessings on you for being where you were when you were, and so stirring me to action.

The day had again vanished into varying shades of rain and we were thankful to have a shelter larger than my coffin of tent. It was a bare enough room with a couple of tables and a couple of chairs. The floor was creeping-damp concrete. After an hour with *The Brendan Voyage* I was forced to don breeches and pullover. The damp bit into one's bones more penetratingly than a frost. I marked an apposite passage in the book: ". . . as the harbour of Reykjavik came in sight, I felt a flicker of regret. Was it really necessary to be coming in to land with all its problems, its people, and its responsibilities? Life on *Brendan* was so relaxed, so peaceful, and so cocooned. . . ."

That was how I felt, in reverse. Tourist-seething Keswick was a million glad miles away already. I sat by the one window, with my coffee and my book, utterly content. The "lawn" outside was silvered with wet and before the stone wall the rooks paraded in groups, slightly ridiculous, a tipsy convention of black-garbed clergy. I could only see a few hundred yards of damp hillside before it was hugged into the sway of clouds. To brew the coffee meant collecting water, which meant climbing into waterproofs and wandering away down to a murky stream, one swollen suddenly after weeks of dryness. The house on its knoll, wrapped in trees, overcoated in cloud, would have made an excellent setting for a Hitchcock film. I had not been long at my book when my hair stood on end and Storm, lying on the table off the cold floor, leapt up. From outside came a great screeching. A kestrel rushed by and for ten minutes hunted and harried round the house. The rooks were disturbed but not disrupted from their strutting. It was just a noisy layman in tweeds after all. He seemed to have lost half his tail feathers. The clouds pressed down closer, so that I could hardly see to the wall, it darkened noticeably, in waves, and my page shadowed steadily.

I gave up trying to read and made supper: Batchelor's peas, fresh onion and carrot, rice and a tin of Shippam's *Chicken Supreme*. As usual I could not face the powdered soup. All reconstituted things seem to taste uniformly revolting – a complaint I'd just noticed in the *Brendan* book. Apple flakes finished the meal. I never tired of them. Bed was the table, my head to the window end, for the view, my pillow was spare clothes, my mattress the tent and my hot-water bottle, Storm. I was asleep by nine – a luxury not often experienced in frantic town life. Aye, if we could just keep to sea, or hill, rain or no. It rained all night.

Just before I dropped off to sleep the clouds lifted slightly and the view positively exploded in scale. The house faced down a long valley, the River Caldew, with big sweeps of hill plunging down out the mist: Great Calva, Coomb Height, Carrock Fell on the north, Blencathra and Bowscale Fell on the south. It was a grand landscape of wild and wetness. The clouds soon poured back in, the rain careered across and the trees sounded like surf. Faintly I could hear the kestrel crying again.

Wednesday 18 July SKIDDAW

Two lads who were fencing came in for a cuppa but the day seemed set to wild and windy. I began to work out logistics for *not* doing all "the Lake Threes" the next day. I also wrote up the day before with its diversion about dogs. The fencers gave up and chugged off on their tractor up the path to Dash Beck towards John Peel country. An old shepherd also looked in. His accent was so strong I could only just catch the gist of his conversation (a few teeth might have helped). In the afternoon I packed and went, but at 2,000 feet or so it was obvious camping would be hopeless on high, so I dumped the rucksack and went on for Sale How just to bag Skiddaw anyway. There was track enough once on to the ridge that I hardly used the compass. A big gale was galloping in from the west. The rocks were slippery and the summit was as cheery as a shaly coal bing in a Fife *haar*. If there was a miraculous clearance overnight I could come again tomorrow and continue for the rest of the 'Four'. One has to be as canny as a Swiss financier – and as ruthless.

People who dismiss Skiddaw are making no distinction between the dramatic and the graceful. Of course it is not as grand as the Scafells or as splendid as Helvellyn. If it was England's highest the song would be different for it has pure lines and a superb setting. Back o' Skidda conjures a dream image of emptiness impossible to visualise on the other urban Threes. As it is the nearest, geographically, to Scotland I may be biased. Our Wainwright sings its praises – and so did the Lake poets and writers: Wordsworth, Lamb (hardly an athletic type), Ruskin, Southey, Coleridge, De Quincey and the diarists Hutchinson, Budworth and others. Norman Nicholson's book *The Lakers* gives an account of these first tourists and writers, many of whom also appear in the equivalent book on Scotland, Maurice Lindsay's *The Eye is Delighted*. They were prodigious workers and wanderers, if often weirdly-driven.

Skiddaw is undoubtedly an easy ascent. I have always liked an ascent early in the day from Millbeck, by Doups and Carl Side, followed by a lazy wander down to the south-east (the most popular approach). The evening view off Latrigg looking to the breathy fields and silvered Derwent Water would make a poet out of a pig. There are good rounds to be made from Bassenthwaite as well. Only to the north and east is the summit far from moating roads and motorways. The true summit, a long crest of loose shale or slabbiness with a trig point on the highest of the toplets, gives an extensive view of Lakeland, with the Pennines to the east and Scotland spread beyond the glitter of the Solway Firth. Skiddaw rules O.K.

Back at Skiddaw House the sun came out but only long enough to mock us. Its bluff was called and the storm raged worse than ever. The wet was far colder-feeling than any frost and our sheltering cell was dank at best. We slept that night in a woodshed: an old mattress and dis- integrating peats were much more comfortable than the unyielding table. We could hear the hunting kestrels and the steady surge of the wind in the pines. Much later there were voices and steps in the dark, both in and round the house. It is used as an outdoor centre and ob- viously a gang had arrived. They chopped wood even – but did not come for peat.

Thursday 19 July   ANTICLIMAX

My alarm went off at 3 a.m. but I did not need to stir. I could hear the wind roaring in the trees, and mist blew through holes in the door. The plan had been to do Skiddaw, drop to Threlkeld to meet Ray at 8 a.m., then go for Helvellyn, meet Ray and food again (with his car in support) and then head for the Scafells, i.e. to do the English Threes in a con- tinuous walk in the day. I had told Ray I would only do it if the weather was right – I'd had my fill of the wrong conditions of late.

I had been unaware that this is a walkers' set piece, but, from the fun of planning, it was interesting to see that my final route would have been the same as the one which has evolved as the standard round. Most make it harder by starting and finishing in Keswick, but to add a great bash of road-walking down Borrowdale seems a masochistic way to finish a hill round. Having said that, we dropped down to Threlkeld – and walked up Borrowdale.

The really big challenge is not to just go round the four Threes but to crowd in dozens of peaks as well. Nearly 50 years ago a noted fell-walker, Bob Graham, set off from the Keswick Moot Hall to walk over as many tops as he could within 24 hours. He covered 42 and no one even tried to emulate the feat for 20 years. Those who do can become members of the elite Bob Graham Club. In 1979 there were 114 members, including two women. If the basic round is 42 peaks, 72 miles and 25,000 feet of ascent you can crowd in optional extras. Joss Naylor, a legend in his own fells, tallied 72 summits, 90 miles and 30,000 feet of ascent. Most of this I learnt from Roger Smith, who had just joined the club. His account, in the *Climber and Rambler of* April 1980, is well worth reading if you want to understand the outlook and feelings of the real athletes.

The youngsters who had been the night visitors materialised at 5.30 a.m. (mutual astonishment) but Storm and I had to be at Threlkeld for eight o'clock, so it was a case of "Hi! Goodbye!" We kept on paths high above Glenderaterra this time, Storm still a bit puzzled by the strange Herdwick and Swardale sheep.

I had just cleaned Storm up a bit at the entrance to the village when Ray appeared. We had breakfast with Mrs Hughes and were joined by David Hume from the Horse and Farrier, the pub across the road which has the date 1688 above the door and an anvil on the pavement. When we were ready to leave Ray took me along to meet Colonel Westmorland. I thought they were acquainted and there was a silence when he inquired, "Mr Westmorland?" of the gentleman who came to the door. "Colonel" came the reply. He had a fascinating collection of photos – and anecdotal memories – but we had to push on all too soon. We wondered if, for 65th, 75th and 85th birthdays, we would make Pillar as had "Rusty" Westmorland. The Colonel was slightly worried about his approaching 95th: "Might not be up to it." At a Fell and Rock dinner he was once introduced to an 85-year-old climber, then commented, "Ah, to be 85 again . . ."

Storm and I walked up to see the Castlerigg Stone Circle. It has 48 stones, so is quite a presentable site. We reached it by an oddly termed 'permissive path'. The setting was all of Keats "cirque of Druid Stones upon a forlorn moor", though stone circles are older than Druids, by centuries, and keep their secrets still. Keats had climbed Skiddaw and later scaled Ben Nevis, to the detriment of his health. He had reached the Ben on foot from Lancaster, no mean achievement, and one that rather alters the common pale-poet image.

Walla Crag gave views down to Derwent Water which, coming regularly from the north, I had come to know first, and still think the best of the Lakes. This high view down to it, with its blackness of background fells, was like some wild German painting. We descended to walk up by the Watendlath Beck on another 'permissive path' (do all modern word-creations or new usages have to be so ugly?). Every building by the Tarn had been turned into a cafe, so we had a coffee in this quiet rural corner, that could be nowhere but England. Somehow the Lakes manage to crowd their great and varied charms into a small area. 'Small' is relative, I suppose. The South Downs to Gilbert White were ". . . that chain of majestic mountains", yet a highland shepherd's wife will say of her man, "Och, he's on the hill", when he may be fighting a blizzard on mighty Mam Sodhail. When the Ultimate Challenge coast-to-coast event began Roger, Terry Smith and I had a week together welcoming into Montrose the sun-smitten participants. Almost everyone made awesome comments on the colossal scale of the empty grandeur. Here in Lakeland you cannot be more than a couple of miles from something of man; if lost, the simple following of a stream would lead you out in a few hours. I can understand the awe of those who had walked for days and never seen another person. There was something odd then for me to come from that to Lakeland's smaller scale. Lakeland is an exquisite miniature and it is something of a wonder that its jewelled beauty has not altogether been trampled underfoot. The charm remains as do the solitary places.

We went up over some rather wet moors to Dock Tarn (which managed to become *Duck* Tarn in my log). It looked like a strayed bit of the Highlands, even to the lilies in the lochan. Everything vanished in a haze of rain as we went down a steep, rough track to Stonethwaite. I'd agreed to meet Ray at the Chapel Farm camp site but was two hours ahead of schedule so, he not being there, we wandered on to Seatoller for tea and scones in the cosy Yew Tree Cafe. You do become spoilt in this mini-wilderness! The road winds on for Honister Pass, with Hause Gill tumbling down, as Hugh Walpole described it, "clearer, fresher, more assured of itself, and happier than any stream in the world". We turned back down the valley. I met Ray – brewing for the weary walker – and we then went and stayed with the Jacksons at Seatoller. Mr Jackson had been a quarryman and had a collection of minerals and fossils both of his own discovering and from all over the world. He displayed superb bird portraits engraved on the delicately coloured slate. Mrs Jackson apologised for not really doing evening meals, then produced a colossal spread. At Chapel Farm a memorial for the 1914–1918 War had 39 names on it: a devastating drain on the local population.

Friday 20 July THE SCAFELLS – NUMBER TWO

I was off first, *à pied*, by Thornthwaite Farm and the foot-track to Seathwaite, where Ray caught up by car. It may be one of the busiest of dales, but it is still farmed and much divided by stone walls (some ten feet wide) and with its share of trees. I think it is this compact, natural and man-made multi-use which gives the district its appeal. All of it could be popped into the void of Rannoch Moor: which I mention simply to set the contrast and give scale.

After Ray had inadvertently shown us some of the rougher Lakeland jungle he led on round to Taylorgill Force: a mare's-tail fall at the top end of a stony but tree-decorated glen. Once above it a barer landscape led by Styehead Farm to Sty Head, the col, which is one of the Lakeland Piccadillies.

We cut down below cloud level to pick up the Corridor Route and on round to Hollow Stones for Lord's Rake. There was little to see except swirling cloud as we scrabbled up the worn route, cut some corners and landed on Scafell. *Scar* or *sca* is old Norse for sheer or steep, which is appropriate enough for a hill bearing what Harry Griffin describes as the most remarkable cliff in England. The hill seems to have had an historical pre-eminence, "the Pikes near Scaw Fell" being the casual old shepherds' reference to the higher neighbour, another case of the Aonach Mor and Aonach Beag reversal perhaps. Scafell has a peaceful isolation denied to its big brother, partly perhaps because the direct route between is beyond most walkers' capacity and the alternatives still demand some route-finding and scrambling. There are easy slopes only to the west (Wastwater) or south (the Esk Valley), both rather peripheral places. The Pikes are only a little more accessible but beaten highways lead to them from Borrowdale (by Sty Head or Esk Hause), from Langdale (by Bow Fell or Angle Tarn) and from Wastwater (by Brown Tongue). They must be about the most comprehensively described summits in the world and with such aids as the Wainwright *Pictorial Guides* or the O.S. 1:25,000 *Outdoor Leisure Maps* or the West Col's *Esk House* special map, there is no excuse for going astray. For a first visit you could well take our route of today, or at least Ray's route, for we were to diverge later. I find a curious interest in such vastly known hills. Every stone, it seems, has a name and a history. You walk with ghosts and dreams.

There were only two other walkers sharing our misty summit. Storm eventually nuzzled us on to our feet. So young to be a Munro-bagger! We descended to Foxes Tarn to round the cliff, but avoided busy Mickledore col by scrambling along from it near Broadcrag Tarn, the highest tarn in these hills. The mist was shooting up from the Wastdale side of the Mickledore gap and swirling over like breakers on a reef. Scafell Pike, number two, was even more crowded than Ben Nevis. There must have been a hundred people within the immediate visual surroundings of the summit of England. Every track we had been on was taking sad punishment from the milli-marching feet and all due to this strange lure of "the highest", which in this case probably is the best as well. Each of our country summits is a mountain of character. Wainwright tells me it is pronounced 'Scawfle' and was sometimes written 'Scawfell' or 'Scaw Fell' or 'the Pikes' or various other things. Even the Ordnance Survey seem to have it wrong. Oh for the straightforward Gaelic. Even its easily-remembered height of 3,210 ft was reduced to 3,200 ft just before metrification.

It had been a day of no photographs and we were along and down to cold, windy Esk Hause before we came below the clouds. Ray went off down Grains Gill to return to the car, I continued down to Angle Tarn – chuntering off at about 3 p.m. Angle Tarn was like an eye hidden under the beetling crags. We tipped it a wink as we passed but were soon reduced to a stolid stumping along the wet slopes to Stake Pass. We skirted under Sergeant Man, to reach the Blea Rigg ridge, crossed it and raced down without being able to escape the rain which came sweeping in. We passed hissing Easedale Tarn for Sour Milk Gill. Coloured dots could be seen streaming and collecting and spurting on. It was obviously going home time on the fells. This inescapable human presence is something I seldom see, so it both intrigues and repulses. It is a personal choice or inclination, I suppose; I prefer Conival rather than Cairngorm and Corte rather than Chamonix. The passing of many feet had smoothed the rock of the path and the rain acted on it like soap. There were several displays of ballet from myself and others. It was sweaty under the skins so I took off most clothes underneath to stop them being saturated.

We found the hotel in Grasmere which we had booked by phone from Keswick – and found, too, our first taste of English hide-bound hospitality. I was told NO DOG and offered no help round the problem. If several other people had not been involved we would have moved elsewhere, as it was the very wet dog had to sit and shiver in the draughty entrance till Ray, Mary and the car arrived an hour later. We had a drink at the White Swan after dinner. This was the pub Scott used to retreat to for a dram now and then when staying along the road with the abstemious Wordsworths at Dove Cottage.

Saturday 21 July   DINNER AT GRASMERE
Most of the day dashed past in a spate of 'off-day' slavery: going over parcels before breakfast, spending the morning on mail, grabbing a lunch of strawberries and cream, visiting a few places of interest such as the old church where Wordsworth is buried.

Ray and Mary went walking, leaving their car for a kennel. The dog-ban from the hotel would have been a real nuisance otherwise. I'd just managed to clear the work when Charles arrived, with Pim and Mary Palmer, and they dumped another pile of mail on me. Ivan and Helen Waller and Harry Griffin drove over from their Lakeland homes so nine of us sat down for an enjoyable dinner – quite a change for someone as unsociable as myself. There were endless good yarns, good wine, and the hours flew. Ray, Charles, Ivan and Helen had already been involved in the trip. Just how time passed was brought home to me for, Ray having brought SMC Journal proofs to Kintail with my mail, Charles now brought a copy of the published Journal.

Harry Griffin occupies a unique position in Lakeland moun-taineering, having probably written more words about the district than anyone, a sort of definitive edition made flesh. He has now retired and is doing a new book only every other year. In his 67th year, he re-ascended every Lakeland fell over 2,000 ft, which gave us *Freeman of the Hills*, a useful guide as well as a story. My own favourite book of his is *Long Days in the Hills*, as this wanders to other regions as well, but keeps to describing only the *grandes randonées*, as the French put it.

I dealt with mail till two in the morning and resisted a new Harry Griffin book I'd just had autographed. Though today had been, in Wordsworth's words, a day "spent in a round of strenuous idleness", Storm and I had run up the first thousand miles on the Groats End Walk.

Sunday 22 July   HAILING HELVELLYN
The Sheffield contingent had been camping but were round early to collect non-wanted gear and papers and also to take my gear for the next stint round to Patterdale so I could enjoy a day without crawling along under my snail-shell load. They then wandered up from there to meet

Ray, Mary and me by Grisedale Tarn. We went up by the old packhorse road, and it shows the nature of the track that I read a Sunday paper most of the way. (It was full of Ballesteros winning the Open, which indicates this year for the golfer.) An endless stream of overdressed, overladen youths steamed past and collapsed, a progress maintained till they no longer overtook us. They had obviously never read the story of the tortoise and the hare, a version of which should be in all books dealing with the techniques of walking. The Hause gave a view down to Grisedale Tarn and out under the clouds to a landscape patterned by wandering rays of sun.

Helvellyn is the most frequently-climbed mountain in Britain (it was once even done by aeroplane, in 1926, so flat is the summit plateau), but manages to bear its batterings remarkably well. Harry Griffin had warned of the many additions. There is a memorial to a dog which lay beside its dead master for weeks. Both Scott and Wordsworth found copy in that tale (they and Humphrey Davy, later more famous as a chemist, made an ascent together in 1805). We saw a memorial to a fox hunter on Striding Edge. A tablet – inaccurately – commemorates the aeroplane landing. There is a stark trig point (3,113 ft), a feeble cairn for the true summit (3,116 ft) and a grubby shelter of crossed walls. The perfectly clear path up from Thirlspot to Browncove Crags has been given white-painted markers like milestones. Bad taste has reached the heights.

The long north-south barrier of Helvellyn forms the largest area of high land in England. It is a two-faced hill, a sort of Jekyll and Hyde piece of geography: all green and verdurous to forest-choked Thirlmere on the west and cove-bitten on the east. (The names of the coves read like a litany.) Half a dozen easy routes ascend through or round the massed plantations on the west, but it is the east which lures the walkers in their thousands by a score of lines, all good. It is a favourite summit for watching the sunrise. Our route up from Grasmere had almost a Pilgrim's Way feel to it. Grisedale Tarn is a pleasant resting spot.

After our rest, the six of us walked and talked an erratic course up Dollywaggon Pike, adding two young girls for part of the way. They were on their first hill venture and glad of some reassuring as we entered the swirling cloud. Helvellyn's contrasting flanks give an edge which makes navigation undeservedly simple and we undulated along to the bulky plateau summit, then sat to eat by the shelter. We all seemed to have brought a few 'special things' to eat, and did very well, including Storm, who had long ago found Ray all too ready to spoil him. My most poignant memory of Helvellyn concerned Storm's predecessor, Kitchy.

After spending half of his life as companion to my father, who only walked with sticks, he had become a dog of the hills for the rest of his days when Father died, a change made the more traumatic by being thrown in with the rough-and-tumble of Braehead School expeditions. After a year he lived for his hills and his kids. I could take him into the school and he would ignore all 'nice doggie' blandishments – until he met a boy or girl who had been away with him in the wilds: *they* were greeted with devoted enthusiasm. One tiny Fife lad left school and returned many years later as a tall, big, long-haired Australian. When he stood on our doorstep I did not know him, but Kitchy (a single-minded guard dog) shot through my legs at once, to give him a tremendous welcome. The school closed and I had a sabbatical, wandering and climbing in the Andes, Africa and from Corsica to the Arctic, so the Scottish hills (and dog) suffered a long neglect. Our first return was a ski traverse of Helvellyn. We ascended from the north and were wending over the bumps to the summit when Kitchy spotted the gaggle of a school party a mile off. He ran towards them, barking his joy at a reunion, but when he neared them and heard their Lancashire accents instead of the uncouth gutturals of Fife, his tail sagged and he turned back with a dejection which cut to the heart. Poor Kitchy!

When eventually we ended our Helvellyn high feast, Ray and Mary descended to Grasmere again, and I was handed over, like a parcel, to Charles, Pim and Mary; we descended east to take in Striding Edge, which was just on the lower cloud limit. A few straying walkers were assisted, and a few were demoralised by Storm. It really is off-putting to scrabble up some crest in an undignified manner and then be licked in the face by a dog who promptly trots down it with his paws in his pockets. Charles, being as notorious a chaser of English 2,000ers as he is of Scottish 3,000ers, force-marched us away out to some outlandish pimple before we were allowed to descend to Glenridding for ices and a laze by the shore of Ullswater, which I had thus topped-and-tailed in a week of wandering. Lakeland has a special allure but it is a leisurely, civilised, comfortable pull. Life can be too comfortable. It was time we pushed on for the south, time we returned to the spine of the Pennine Way.

I settled in at Side Farm and cleared the last of my mail so that the others could take it; they added Place Fell and were down for soup and coffee before returning to Sheffield. A lad doing Wainwright's coast-to-coast recognised my Tulloch tent – and had one as well – so we talked of Scotland and his doings with Dave Challis there. A car with a gang of drunks made sleep-destroying noises which the righteous anger of the other campers increased and prolonged. The solitary places – suddenly – were singing something of a siren song. The Lake District is a many-splendoured delight but it suffers from the over-concentration of civilisation, so called. A single tent on a mountain top sets no social problems.

VIII

PENNINE VERTEBRAE

I'll walk where my own nature would be leading
It vexes me to choose another guide;
Where the grey flocks in ferny glens are feeding,
Where the wild wind blows on the mountain side.
What have these lonely mountains worth revealing?
More glory and more grief than I can tell;
The earth that wakes one human heart to feeling
Can centre both the worlds of Heaven and Hell.

EMILY BRONTË

Monday 23 July   HIGH STREET AGAINST THE LIGHTS   *Maps, pp. 104, 116 and 137*

The forecast of showers failed for once. Showers are all too apt to become "of a continuous nature" as the BBC once described them. The day did not start in a dazzle either (which all too often means simply "too bright too soon will rain by noon"). More applicable today was the hillman's, "Away by seven gives a chance of heaven". A patch of blue is often a promise.

We went on green tracks by old slate workings to the col beyond Place Fell and on up Angletarn Pikes. The cloud had left Helvellyn, giving the view of all its upcrowding hills, all day, while ahead the whaleback of High Street surfaced. We had tea by Angle Tarn which was pale turquoise in the jewel-fresh morning light. The early timid patches of blue had bullied off much of the high cloud. Further on, we left the rucksack to wend up Rest Dodd, then on to Knott which gives a closer view of the long, flat breast and chiselled ribs of this warrior peak. The four Lakeland 3,000ers could be seen, as could the lapping southern sands and sea: salmon pink and seal grey. Cross Fell reminded me of our postponed Way – a mere waving of the blue horizon. Two people, who must have had a night in this fine fastness, came off High Street. I felt quite jealous. It was the best hill day since walking the Border two weeks before; a friendly sun, sharing its fires with cool clouds (huge shadow-spacing cumulus) and easygoing eastern breezes. High Street, 2,719 ft, was all homely hill happiness. The summit is known as Racecourse Hill

from the time when the dalesfolk held races up there, horse-races that
is, with much drinking and revelry. And 2,000 years ago the Romans
laid their road along its dry, safe, easy ridges, a link from Carlisle
to Ambleside built with sandstone slabs in many places. It is all
grassed over now. I am surprised no dig has been made to show something of it.

There were several high corries or cwms (why is there no equivalent
word in English?) lodged under the eastern crags. Their waters were
grabbing blue reflections from the sky. Brave eagles are regularly on
these fells, but we did not see one. How easy it is to lose wildlife species,
especially long-lived ones that breed slowly. Seton Gordon, in one of his
books, tells of an eagle shot in France which bore an engraved gold
collar with a date on it of 95 years before. Let's hope in 95 years hence
there are plenty of Lake District eagles. Our route passed by odd bony-
edges of protruding strata as we galloped down to Nan Bield Pass.
Kentmere Reservoir lay below a succession of tops like a smaller version
of the Kintail 'sisters', on one side, and Small Water was tucked in below
the other. People seemed to be coming up every valley approach, but
our early start gave us the grassy tops more or less to ourselves. Cars
glinted as they drove along the shore of Haweswater, rather bleak
looking with a tide-line.

The cairns on Harter Fell were all spiky with fence-posts – like some
poor bull quivering under a score of implanted *banderillas*. We went by
Adam Seat to Gatescarth Pass and lunched by the first water beyond.
The stove misbehaved a bit, but would have to last till Sheffield. Butane-
burning stoves now are very popular (an indication of affluence) but they
are desperately dangerous, which people seldom realise: potential
bombs which do not just flare, as a primus might, but given any leak,
explode. Almost all accidents I've seen have been with people making
careless mistakes changing cartridges in the presence of naked flames.
Melted faces and hands and chest are not nice to deal with. No one
changes a cartridge in my presence now. Either they go outside – or I do.

We added the off-route tops of Tarn Crag and Grey Crag above Long
Sleddale and, from Harrop Pike with its phallic-like cairn, we skirted
above the Little Mosedale Beck, our reward being to view several herds
of very rufous red deer. The dog recognised them. The calves were well-
grown now. Summer was slipping into the tawdry, worn clothes of the
sales' season. Asphodel, the sunny star of Scottish late-August moors,
was out already. Bedstraw and tormentil still showed – but not milkwort,
the third of that brotherhood of the grassy hill places.

Some tame, dried-out peat bogs helped progress till we picked up the

path from Mosedale (how many confusing Mosedales are there?) to Wet
Sleddale Reservoir. The path kept high, in the sun-washed clarity, but
later dropped to the dam, beyond which the M6 buzzed and a prob-
lematical camp would have to be found – so we turned to cut down the
Thornship Gill instead, and camped just before a water intake
swallowed its muted, warm flow. Pimento-spicy sardines from Morocco
were an enjoyed part of supper. We had left Lakeland; its best being held
for the end. All too soon (in phrases from *Job*) "the stars of twilight"
would become "the eyelids of the morning" and it would be back to
the Pennine Way.

Tuesday 24 July   TO APPLEBY

Grapenuts were an enjoyable start to breakfast, but not something to be
eaten in a hurry. Stepping stones crossed the River Lowther into Shap
where I posted things, then crossed the M6 by a pedestrian bridge to
return to fine rural walking, only three miles of which were on roads this
day.

Ragged limestone broke from the grey fields, an oddity to Scots eyes,
as was a wall slicing right through a small stone circle. The limestone is
quarried further south, which had rather determined my route. Shap
was once famous for its granite quarries, too. The Thames Embankment
and the Stock Exchange are built of Shap stone. The route wended down
to Maulds Meaburn which sprawls on the Lyvennet Beck. Its only sign of
life was one matronly cyclist. Climbing up the other side, the right-of-
way became impossible to find or follow, so we took to the road and at
once chanced on a loudly-complaining oyster catcher trapped under a
hedge. He repaid his debt to freedom by jabbing Storm on his in-
quisitive nose. An old track, a sunken road in places, ran Roman-
straight, through fields and woods to the outskirts of bright Appleby
which used to be Westmorland's county town. Its name sums up a
beautiful corner of England. It remains surprisingly hidden till the last
moment. Out of the haze peered a towered castle.

The post office staff, as so often in the wilds, knew all about my parcels
and chatted about the trip. In towns they just demanded proof of
identity ("Don't you have a driving licence?") and handed over food
and *Frolic*. We had booked in to the King's Head, beside the old bridge
over the River Eden, but ate at the Potlatch, a crowded restaurant which
showed that good food can attract customers. I did not dine out often,
so enjoyed a pizza, Chianti, and decent coffee. Rain poured down all
night, which did not help with drying the clothes I wanted to wear in the
morning.

Wednesday 25 July   BACK TO THE PENNINE WAY

I read Toulmin's *Blown Seed* most of the morning, until the rain stopped
and my clothes had almost dried. The road over the bridge was a
madness of big lorries, noise and fumes, so I thankfully cut up by the
station to gain the cuds. Road works of the new by-pass left my boots
clarty and heavy, the farm beyond had the notice "path to Flakebridge
Wood – through the yard and up the hill". It was delightfully mixed
walking through field and forest, gaining height all the time, to end with
a view of the Pennines, and an end of the delight. My old one-inch map
was not capable of showing rights-of-way, and we became infuriatingly
lost in fields where the silver-heavy grassheads soaked my feet as
thoroughly as a walk through a river. We eventually ended at Keisley,
which lay on the shins of the hills. A breeze blew away the irritants of flies
and drizzle. We brewed and relaxed.

   We followed a cart-track back to the Pennine Highway, joining it just
above Dufton at a stone gateway on which a pair of battered boots
perched. Imagination played with possible reasons why, as we wended
up and up the scarp of the Pennines. We passed the arched hollow of an
old limekiln on Peeping Hill. A corner opened up the view of the High
Cup Gill valley, a long amphitheatre running into the hills, a Whin Sill
rim, scree-skirted, and edged with the coloured beadwork of descending
Pennine Wayfarers. People passed for an hour, then no more appeared.

   There were several tempting camp sites, including the very lip of High
Cup Nick, for the updraught left the edge an area of calm in the
hissing, spraying wind. We looked for Nichol's Last, illustrated in
Wainwright, a small pinnacle, and relished the return to hills,

> ". . . Here, where the blue air fills
>   The great cup of the hills,
>   And fills with peace."
>   *A. Symons*

   The way over to Maize Beck was full of pockmarked holes, a lunar
landscape, and the beck was a black-lined gut; an odd area of strange attraction. After some miles of heavy rain, I pitched the tent near red
notices that warned of military things, dried the dog, then retreated
happily to books and brews while the rain lashed down and the wind
sprayed the noisy river into the air or over the tent. We fitted into our
hills as snug as a blackbird in its nest. There was smoked mackerel for
supper, one of the regular treats. Someone was once telling me of a
straying walker who, in thick mist, gingerly paddled out to cross Maize

Beck. A sudden breeze swept the fog away, and he saw he was not paddling the expected stream, but was wading out into Cow Green Reservoir.

Thursday 26 July TEESDALE AND SOUTHWARD

A 23-mile day, when drawn on my Youth Hostel map did, at last, show a marked gain southwards. The leisurely Lakeland diversion had eaten eleven days of July. I also passed the halfway stage of the Pennine Way during this tramp. We were off at 6.30, a more reasonable hour, following the squelchy Way over to Cauldron Snout which tumbles down stairs of rocky cataracts into a sweeping valley. I'd half expected Cow Green Reservoir, which blocked the valley above, to have killed this fall as the Hydro have destroyed several in Scotland. From the foot of the Snout the path under Falcon Clints lay on greasy duckboards, along which files of young soldiers stomped and slithered to a raucously sung *Ilkley Moor Brass Hat*. Storm and I paddled the Tees and cut over the hill to miss a long river bend, and the morning traffic. The Nature Conservancy Council had wired off plots to prevent erosion (caused by sheep, rabbits and humans), and the difference to the flora was dramatic: inside the wire were gardens of colour, outside there was just cropped grass and the grey sand of the 'sugar' limestone. We descended Skyer Beck to rejoin the Tees, passing a brutally intrusive quarry, the dust of which blew downstream like smoke.

High Force was the finest fall we saw in England: a rectangular cutting of water-rush set into the vertical Whin Sill rock barrier, flanked by trees and juniper scrub. A while later, Low Force was merely pretty. We had a cuppa perched on the rocks beside it, then followed the river down to cross it into Durham's Middleton-in-Teesdale, where we just managed to shop before everything closed. We spent our lunch hour on the square beside a canopied Victorian iron fountain, enjoying the pleasant town – and the rich, contrasting landscape of Teesdale after the scoured uplands. Middleton owes its neatness to Quaker ownership of its lead mines which closed only in 1905. The charter was granted by William and Mary in 1652. The church has a small detached belfry, built in 1557. Several guidebooks claimed it as the only such in England, but I met another on August 10th.

We took our own less hilly and less devious line to Grassholme Reservoir. At How we chatted to the farmer who had just cut hay (the air was rich with its scent), after which we were back to upland emptiness. We descended by High Birk Hat where there was a gate made mostly of string and old bits of wood, which seemed scant defence against the resident bull. A hot grind up to Clove Lodge led to gentle grassy slopes beyond. We were very glad to top the hill, and on the way down into Deepdale to find a camp by the Knotts Sike stream. It was a hot, grass-dusty evening, but free of flies and midges, and I was able to wash cheesy feet in the burn. The A66 Stainmore Gap road lay over the next rise to the south and its buzz was a constant reminder of the smallness of this solitude. The coming weekend was setting some logistical problems which had to be worked out over cups of Green Gunpowder tea.

Friday 27 July HAWES

Some lads were camping a mile downstream from us, by Deepdale Beck, and were rather surprised at our casual passing at 6.15 a.m.

"We thought we were good being up so early!"

We went over Ravock and down to Pasture End, and there had to deal with an escaped calf which was playing dangerous games with the A66 traffic. Fortunately a farmer came along, so we soon had the stray back in his field. The many roads cutting the Pennine Way allow easy access to it, and I'm sure much more enjoyment could be found by doing it bit by bit, over years if need be, rather than in one mad rush.

Limekilns I find a fascinating study, so was pleased to find one by God's Bridge, a natural crossing, two limestone slabs thick, over the River Greta. There was fine moorland tramping after that. Bowes Manor notices were signed by the 'Steward': a feudalistic touch which rather amused the Gael in me. The peat had largely dried out and quite often made for easy walking. We had a brew by Frumming Beck before Tan Hill, a pub rather spoilt by huge boozy notices. Must we have walls postered with "Drink the Pennine Way" as if it were some racing circuit? It claims, at 1,732 ft, to be England's highest inn, and commands a gaunt sweep of moorland country – some of the finest of the Way. The dog was kept to heel as the moors have open mine shafts, all that remains from a history going back 700 years.

Two older hikers, Cliff Hunt and Brother Anthony, recognised Storm and me, and had time to talk. A year later on the first Ultimate Challenge, Cliff Hunt met us again, after he had walked from Morar to Montrose.

We came on a high slope covered with what looked like stone *saeters*, and later reading proved Viking infiltration here. Did they just build the wooden barns of Norway with the available stone? It looked like it. The view down to Keld was one of the best. Could the lower reaches of Glencoe once have looked like this, I wondered? The sun glazed the green fields of Swaledale (the sheep are pronounced Swardle), and the

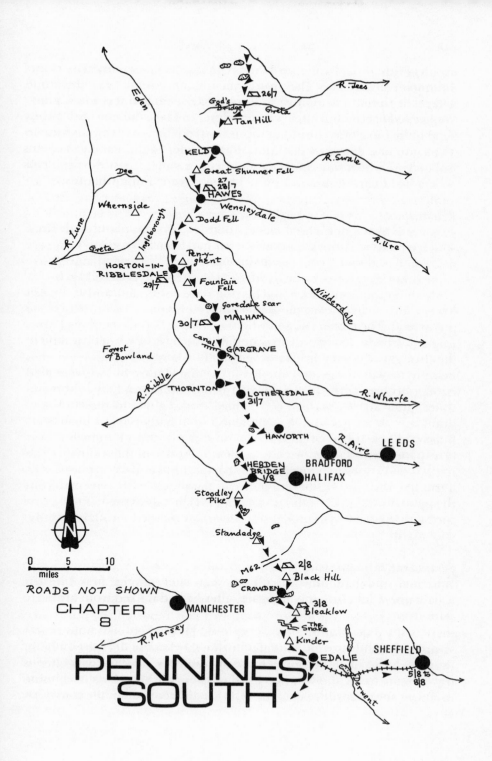

R. Eden

R. Tees

God's Bridge

◻ 26/7

△ Tan Hill

Greta

KELD

R. Swale

△ Great Shunner Fell

27
28/7
◻ HAWES

Wensleydale

Dee

Whernside △

Inglehorough

△ Dodd Fell

R. Ure

R. Lune

Greta

△ Pen-y-ghent

HORTON-IN-
RIBBLESDALE

29/7 ◻

△ Fountain Fell

Nidderdale

⊗ Goredale Scar

30/7 ◻ MALHAM

Forest
of Bowland

canal

GARGRAVE

R. Ribble

THORNTON

LOTHERSDALE
31/7

R. Wharfe

HAWORTH

R. Aire

LEEDS

BRADFORD

HEBDEN
BRIDGE
1/8

HALIFAX

Stoodley
Pike △

Standedge △

M62 ◻ 2/8

CROWDEN

△ Black Hill

N

0   5   10
miles

ROADS NOT SHOWN

CHAPTER
8

MANCHESTER

R. Mersey

3/8
△ Bleaklow

The Snake

△ Kinder

EDALE

SHEFFIELD

Derwent

5/8 to
8/8

PENNINES
SOUTH

erratic grids of walls climbed high on to the moors towards Great
Shunner Fell beyond. The river dances over several falls, the stone
villages are as natural as mushrooms. It is a corner to linger in for a day.
We headed for the hill after just managing to make the tiny back-room
shop before its noon closing. A whole bottle of lemonade washed down
some goodies. I needed the liquid for the long haul up and down this
isolated hill which takes the Pennine Way to 2,340 ft. Great Shunner Fell
covers 20 square miles and most people find it a long haul over an
endless succession of rising bumps. An account I read later had the F of
Fell misprinted as H. Or maybe it was not a misprint. The Pennine Way
crossing is nine miles. The slopes are dotted with signs of old coal mines
which served local limekilns once forests had been burned up. There are
also stark stone-men beacons here, which keep lonely vigil indeed. We
came down to Jinglemea Crag, Black Hill Moss and Bluebell Hill.

We caught up another lad and his dog as we descended, and watched a
hang glider soaring over the Buttertubs road. Once down, I had a big
pot of tea in the Green Dragon who then charged to see Hadraw Force,
England's highest single-drop waterfall, which was a pathetic piddle in
the drought whatever it may be normally. Slabs and styles led across
fields to an old bridge over the River Ure for Hawes, but we were glad
enough to stop at the Brown Moor Farm camp site; it had a shop and
water, after all. We washed out stained clothing, ate to repletion and
drank and drank and drank to replenish what had been lost in 26 heat-
pulsing miles. It had been as hot as on our march to Rannoch Moor.
(The paper next day reported it as the hottest day of the summer.) The
log was quickly written up and several maps, films and so on posted. On
a trip like this, you fight every ounce of the way. A gang returned from
the pub late and made a din till all hours. There always seems to be one
such group on any communal site. Sleep was relished through a windy,
cool night.

Saturday 28 July   HUMS AND HAWES
It became so wet and windy that I used one of my REST cards and we just
stayed where we were in Wensleydale. It would have meant a very early
start to make Horton before lunch (two lads reported the post office
there had a parcel for me), so we explored Hawes between showers and
sampled most of its pubs and cafes during the deluges. It cleared a bit in
the evening when we sat out to eat in the yellow, watery sun as it filtered
through the trees, and watched the day's Pennine Way disasters hobble
in. It was another wild, wet night, but that did not prevent the conscious

relishing of the body relaxing muscle by muscle into sleep. Sleep loves those who love life.

Sunday 29 July   BY DODD FELL TO HORTON

"I don't think it's rain, just wet air," somebody reported first thing. We were off early through a ghost town and had a look at hotch-potch Gayle with its wide banked beck, a pretty hamlet. We managed to lose the Way there, being on a path but not the right one. The dew was as wetting as any slushy track in winter, being a sort of Scotch mist that never quite got off the ground. A lad milking cows directed us, part of his route being "up the lane to the Land Rover, which might not be there". We went on by dykes through the cloud, passing Gaudy House, Rottenstone Hill and Ten End, and then bore up for Dodd Fell (2,192 ft). Our casual approach led to some wandering about in the paddy before we found the lonely trig pillar. My map showed the symbol for a viewpoint, but we could not see a hundred yards. It had been a breezy, cool ascent so I was not complaining.

The cloud broke and fled in ragged ranks as soon as we regained the main route again. We picked up the Roman road along Cam End. A post, part of a gate, was fluting eerily in the wind. An extensive array of *drumlins* spread in textbook clarity below our route. We began to meet the day's ration of walkers as we dropped down on the old Hawes-Settle packhorse road. Some bits were boggy, and well illustrated Brown's Law: "if there are more than four in a party, one at least will come a cropper at any difficulty." We skirted the limestone gorge of Ling Gill (it's a collapsed cave), and at Dry Lathe Cave met our first spelaeologists.

They arrived just as we were setting up the stove, so we had a grand view as several people abseiled into a 30 ft vertical slot, which they shared with the waterfall. The passage continued through the hill, I was told, "with some tight squeezes". From Old Ing we took a higher line and wandered about looking at various other holes. Ingleborough sprawled in the west with an extravagant complex cloudscape above its simple etched lines. The sun had tip-toed back and the afternoon was crisp as washed lettuce. I grudged having to drop to Horton-in-Ribblesdale to pick up my parcel. We met one quaking bog at the Sell Gill Beck and crossed to see Hull Pot, which was "just a big 'ole", according to one bystander. It is almost 100 yards long, 60 feet wide and 60 feet deep. In unusually wet conditions it may actually fill with water and even overflow like a beery tankard. Today there were just polite rumbles with no water at all. The water sinks just above the pot and emerges from a huge cave at Douk Ghyll Scar, a mile below. Hunt Pot, in contrast, is a narrow gash with a spraying stream stepping down to dive into it. The dog received a good wash and his enthusiastic drying-off on the grass just about rolled him into the 200 ft depths.

Horton Scar Lane (an old miners' track) led down between walls the two miles to civilization. We refreshed ourselves at the Penyghent Cafe where they produce Pennine Way-sized (one pint) mugs of tea. Peter and Joyce Bayes have really made something of the Pennine Way game with visitors' book, cafe, gear and books for sale, and interesting Three Peaks' exploits also recorded. Regular foot and cycle circuits of Penyghent, Whernside and Ingleborough are made in phenomenal times. It is an area one could become very attached to. Strange it has not produced its Scott or Brontë or Wordsworth.

We camped at the Holme Farm site where their customers all seemed to be doing the Way. Storm shared a tin of mince with me as we had had to buy the evening meal and breakfast, food and *Frolic* being beyond reach in the closed post office.

Monday 30 July   PENYGHENT TO MALHAM

Having collected our respective parcels first thing, I then had a heavy rucksack. There was a crowd champing at the bit for the shop to open at nine; a lack of business acumen somewhere. It was ten before we were off. We went along by the Norman church (it was *restored* in 1400!). The chunky, buttressed tower still leans out of true. Penyghent can be seen behind, rising, on one side, in a long gentle slope and then dropping in double-stepped steepness on the other. The Three Peaks were once given heights of over 4,000 ft, on old maps. We went up by Dub Cote Farm where we were given a cheerless forecast: "Nay views today, lad." Green tracks led to Churn Milk Hole where I left the rucksack and turned for Penyghent, *the hill of the winds*, which is 2,273 ft. The weather kindly cleared for us.

There were several groups toiling up it with their packs, right over the hill, such is the programming of the robots of the Way. Penyghent is no logical part of the Way really, as it can be skirted on perfectly good paths. Its lower step proved to be limestone and the upper, gritstone. A wall swept up from the south, stuttered over the steps and then traversed the scruffy summit to continue along to the lesser top of Plover Hill. We went out to this top and then quickly back the same way. An area of limestone pavement lay beside the road before we took to the dykes again for Fountains Fell, which owes its name not to the quality of the ground, but from once belonging to Fountains Abbey. It was muggy and thunder-dark, but we went on to narrowly escape a flanking storm, across by a tarn to a secondary top and down another wall to rejoin the Way. Both these hills had coal workings at one time. The miles to Malham Tarn and on to the Cove seemed rather wearisome, largely due to the weather change, something which affects us far more than is often realised.

Some climbers were on Great Close Scar, and when one was fighting over the crux a cow below let out a great bellow – which was not very well received. We walked down to see where Malham waters seep away, to reappear, not in the Cove as might be expected, but several miles further down, at Aire Head. What a mighty sight it must have been when water dropped sheer down the 300 ft cave wall. It juts out in a roof – an unusual artificial rock climb which is hardly likely to be freed of its aid. Underground courses are tested by pouring chemical dyes into sink holes and then checking likely places for the colour to reappear. Once, in the Pyrenees, this was done with a baffling lack of result, until a village fountain suddenly started spouting pink water – miles away from the expected resurgence.

We went along the Dry Valley (it felt like "the valley of dry bones") with its ribs of white walls, to see the famous eroded pavement overlooking Malham Cove, then descended to look at the Cove from below: two impressive natural features. The pavement looked almost like some whitewashed cobbling. Except for the Three Peaks and the Burren in Ireland, I can think of nothing like it. Down in the *clints*, the fissures cutting up the *grykes*, is the secret flora of lime-loving plants. The tarn above has not sunk away as it is held by impervious shales. At 1,229 ft it is the highest in the Pennines.

We pitched the tent, went in to Malham briefly, but fled its bustle to relax with the ducks at Back Hall over a very civilized afternoon tea on the lawn, before returning to the tent with eggs and milk bought at the farm. At a rather late hour we went off to have a look at the extraordinary cleft of Goredale Scar, which was almost a dry gorge, with its limpid stream reappearing to run past a delightful camp site. Dozens of wagtails were flipping about among the butterbur leaves. One walker I was talking to, there, was telling me of how he had had to run from a bull and had leapt over a high wall to sprawl on the ground in front of another bull.

Our site was made a misery by silly youngsters who never stopped their din *all* night long. Even heavy rain failed to damp their idiocy, and at midnight one of them ran pell-mell into our tent, breaking the main pole and collapsing its wet folds over us. Tent pegs and canoe tape made a weak temporary splint. I was up at six and gave the brats an ultimatum of either replacing my pole or my going to the police. Luckily they did not call my bluff. The pole I received was a bit short but was usable if perched on a stone. They were not being let off – that was for certain! I explained how to make a wooden plug to repair my pole which, cut down, would make a replacement for the one they had handed over, but a minute later I heard the owner say to a friend, "I suppose I can buy a replacement?" This scunnered me more than anything else. At sixteen I could not afford a tent, never mind being affluent enough to go boozing in the hills.

Tuesday 31 July   RURAL STRIDES
A cool, breezy, blue-and-white day was very welcome, returning me to "the calm that nature breathes" (Wordsworth) – needed after the soiled night. We had pleasing riverside walking below the Aire Head springs, criss-crossing the river down to Airton, then over a windy hill to Gargrave where there was a spick-and-span canal busy with long-boat traffic and brightly lined with geraniums. This is the 1816 Leeds and Liverpool canal, the only trans-Pennine one remaining in operation. Gargrave was linked to Leeds by canal in 1777 but the terrain on to Burnley slowed progress considerably. We had a poached egg on toast, just to enjoy Gargrave and the clean replacement weather. Yesterday had needed a good scrub.

All was very rural and pleasant. We came to a canal again at East Marton and in the fields beyond seemed to compete for every stile with someone coming the other way. The post office/cafe in Thornton-in-Craven was a find, with fresh baking and friendly service. We almost fell for a Bed and Breakfast there, but it was too early to waste sunny miles. Pinhaw Beacon, 1,273 ft, provided an extensive viewpoint, and the start of the Millstone Grit country. Heading for it we flushed the last cuckoo we were to see this year. Lothersdale remained hidden till we were almost on it. One mill still works but most of the buildings have been converted into homes. The result was a pleasing whole. We found Bed and Breakfast with Phil and Trish Robinson, just as the heavens opened in a cliché-loud thunderstorm. We went across to the Hare and Hounds for some food. NO DOGS. NO BOOTS. It seemed a welcoming sort of place. Inside was another notice. "Hikers once served, use room on right." I was clean, dry and tidy and in house shoes, but my breeches obviously damned me as a verminous hiker and I was asked to remove myself from the empty bar. I suppose if one throws leaves into the wind one is apt to get dust in the eyes.

Dufton: peaceful, despite being on the Pennine Way

Whernside from Old Ing

Horton Church and Penyghent

The canal across the Pennines at Gargrave

Dark satanic hills: the steaming peat bogs that guard the summit of
Black Hill on the Pennine Way

The hill out of Hebden Bridge

The donkeys on the Rudyard Reservoir leet

The desolate camp on Bleaklow

St. Peter's Square, Ruthin

Moel Siabod, on the edge of Snowdonia, from the south-east

Storm near the high camp on Snowdon

Across the Menai Straits:
looking back towards the mountains of Snowdonia

Anglesey: South Stack

A secret hollow in the Wicklows: the view down to Lough Tay

Glendalough: St. Kevin's Kitchen and the round tower beyond

Wednesday 1 August TO HEBDEN BRIDGE

In Lothersdale the Pennine Way sign-post had an additional sign pointing out a well-known brand of ice cream! The route began with a couple of over-and-down moves, farmland and repetitive. In Cowling, the Pennine Way sign pointed to the GENTS, but changed its mind to wander through someone's garden. A sense of proportion does not seem part of the Englishman's make-up. Perhaps we should forget rights more and deal with wrongs. The moors above were welcome. There were odd chalets on their edge, and one cottage, hidden away, which could have been a base for smugglers in olden times. The villages of the Pennines are all old and crowded into their haunts, full of individuality; a priceless heritage. In Scotland houses (never mind villages) of seventeenth-century date hardly exist. We sat out one heavy shower in the lee of a high wall, lost in a book. The wall led us down Bare Hill and Old Bess, then twisted down to Ponden Reservoir, coming into a valley of green fields and neat rectangular walls. We pulled up on to the moors beyond, which looked down to Haworth: Brontë country, the most visited of literary landscapes after Stratford-upon-Avon, perhaps as much for the human pathos of the Brontë family saga as for the works of Charlotte, Emily and Anne – astounding as these are in themselves. "There has been no English family like the Brontës. Half-orphaned in childhood; cooped in a remote place with an aloof father; tormented by a wastrel brother; exiled from their home and one another to serve as governesses; all dying young, all but one unmarried, and she to die soon after. I do not know any place so steeped in so many recollections of such untranquil emotion; nor any so resoundingly triumphant." – so writes J. H. B. Peel in *Along the Pennine Way*, the best book on its subject. Time perforce won over curiosity (the Parsonage Museum does not open until 11 a.m.), and we went on.

We passed a lonely farm and then swung up to Top Withins which is thought to be the setting for *Wuthering Heights*. A few trembling trees, a lone standing stone, a solitary house among the moors, it certainly feels right. "Pure, bracing ventilation they must have up there . . . one may guess the power of the mind . . . by the slant of a few stunted firs at the end of the house."

I suppose, as with Scott, more people know of this book's title than its content. Later in the trip I read it for the first time. What an extraordinary story it is to have been written by a young, unworldly Vicar's daughter. What a picture it is of human bleakness – and the despairing wildness of these hills. Let it be compulsive, if not compulsory reading for all who walk this way.

Some execrably bad restoration was being undertaken which has now spoiled the atmosphere. It is no longer a ruin to excite the imagination. All the roughness has been smoothed, all walls levelled off and topped with concrete, and it looks like a farmer's garage about to be roofed. It was a disappointment.

We left Top Withins at three o'clock and made Hebden Bridge post office just after five. Luckily they closed at 5.30 p.m. We tramped hard to make it, enjoying great cloud skies over the windy tops, then romping down to the Walshaw Dean reservoirs. Old cast-iron Savile Estate notices were so patronising they deserve to become museum pieces. A more recent one just said, "Please don't swim in your drinking water." The reservoirs were half empty but then I'm told every Yorkshireman has a good thirst. We followed Wainwright's recommended route down the deep, wooded Hebden Water. The miles of endless oak and beech forest became quite tiring, and the town never seemed to come – then suddenly we juddered down into it, its centre being huddled on the River Calder while long rows of houses tier along the steep valley flanks. For a basically industrial town it has a character which I liked at once. We had something to eat in a cafe, and took ice cream and our new parcel into the memorial garden to recover a bit.

We had no luck in finding accommodation centrally, and eventually we had to copy a list in the Information Office window and head for a telephone box. The first place we rang took us. I even remembered to mention the unwelcomed addition of a dog, but this caused no bother. When we reached the Beverley Hotel, two miles out on the Burnley Road, I found why: they had parrots, dogs, geese, donkeys and about a thousand African tropical fish! The luxury was a tonic, though by the time I had bathed, washed grim clothes, worked out needs, packed, done my log, prepared mail, phoned home, Roger Smith and Charles Knowles, I was ready for bed. Only 50 miles to go!

Thursday 2 August   INTO THE PEAT

The Pennine Way has a titillating variety of underfoot conditions. Today we were to discover peat. We returned to the town to shop and post mail, then, guzzling plums, crossed the dead Trans-Pennines Rochdale canal (1804) and staggered up the brae out of the Calder Valley. Hebden Bridge dropped out of sight in its sunny hollow, to be remembered affectionately.

Joy, so many coloured, best flows
When sun shines and wind blows.

We traversed along to pretty Callis Wood (the last trees of note till Edale) where we met painted acorn symbols once more. What a dark, stark landscape it becomes once off the limestone country. Stoodley Pike was quite crowded, being just above Mankinholes Youth Hostel. The monument commemorates Napoleon's abdication and the Peace of Ghent, and was begun in 1814. Forty years later it collapsed, but was rebuilt to celebrate the peace following the end of the Crimean War. Every now and then it receives another lightning strike, so choose your day for climbing it.

A friendly moor followed, with a view down to Todmorden and, at Withens Gate, a section of flagged path, built for relief in the cotton famine days. All through the last 50 miles of the Pennine Way there is a sense of the wasted moors being hemmed in by towns and mills, roads and traffic – as if they would like to swallow all the emptiness.

A concrete 'drain' dictated the route to a succession of reservoirs: Warland, Light Hazzles, Blackstone Edge. The waters turned, tone by tone, from silver to charcoal as the sky darkened. We nipped in to the White House for a Jura and chili-con-carne, which turned out to be a Pennine Way tradition too. The place was full of walkers with one old lad in despair. After three days of bogs he could face no more. There is nothing like Pennine peat to help discover one's frustration tolerance level. Perhaps the pub could frame the words of Psalm 69, verse 2 as a hint.

We continued along and up the so-called Roman road to Defoe's "Andes of England", Blackstone Edge, but black soil, black rocks, black sky were all soon swallowed by cloud. Over Redmires and Slippery Moss you could navigate by the hum of motorway traffic and the yelps of walkers finding the softer options. There must be some knack which I lack, for most of the youngsters who squelched out the mist had managed to acquire an adhesive blacking of bog. Some looked as if they had tried swimming in it. Ah well, one man's meat is another man's gravy. The footbridge over the M62 has a convex walkway so in its hollow you can find the latest peat growth. A surge of traffic was flowing through this Pennine artery, the main link between Yorkshire and Lancashire cities. The big Post Office mast on Windy Hill could not be seen until we were by its wired enclosure and then only its lower half. I nearly fell into a sopping area of moss. Keeping clean was obviously going to be as likely as a sheep laying eggs.

It was even wetter going south of the A672 up to White Hill. I had a spell with no map, but the beaten track left no room for doubt – so much for Wainwright's "faint trod". The rain came on so we drew into our waterproofs to plod, plod onwards, a sort of *slow, slow, quick, quick, slow* progression as we quickstepped round the bogs. We have a guid Scots word worth adopting hereabouts: *slaistery*.

I came back on to maps at Millstone Edge, and the A62 Standedge road was just ahead, with a book promise of a cafe. Peter's Cafe proved to have been burnt down several years before so we had to camp fast and fasting, before more rain swept in. A huge pile of car tyres made a windbreak. My mind ran on some words from the *Pilgrim's Progress*: "The way also was here very wearisome, through dirt and slabbiness. Nor was there on all this ground so much as one inn or victualling house, therein to refresh the feebler sort."

Under us was an east-west railway tunnel (Manchester-Huddersfield) and Outram's Huddersfield Narrow (1811) Canal which, with its length of three miles, was the longest-ever constructed canal tunnel. It was closed during the last war.

A last leg-stretch before turning in discovered a sprinkling of stars while downwards, westwards, a Chinese dragon of golden lights seemed to be wending over the land: town-lights, something we had not seen previously. Being aware of dusk itself was new for usually we were asleep by then; obviously this erratic summer was sneaking away from us already. August is the least spirited of months anyway, a snooze after the rich summer table has been cleared.

Friday 3 August   BLEAKLOW – AND BLEAK HIGH
We tramped off into the fogbog for Black Moss Reservoir and if we had needed any navigation aid the screaming gulls on it were a guide. It was reasonable grass-and-crowberry going, but by White Moss (white from the sheen of bog cotton?) it produced the worst section of the Pennine Way and perhaps of the whole Groats End Walk. The ground had the consistency of chop suey. It was a dish of saturated vegetation, black sauce and a hash of overcooked meaty hags. The A635 became the most desirable of attainments. We crossed a ditch which was another cotton famine project and reached the road as the cloud cleared.

Along a bit we plunged into more hags and deep-cut groughs, obviously into National Park country for notices proliferated, banning just about every activity. It made me wonder what or for whom parks were designed. They are often more restrictive than private land.

On Black Hill an acre or two of the summit is bare, bumpy peat, in the last stages of decay. It was steaming in the brief Friday ration of sunshine.

The trig pillar (1,908 ft) was right in the middle of it and required a devious approach to avoid the worst disaster areas. One gain from a million footprints was that they often showed where not to tread. I had neither anklets nor gaiters, and was determined to finish this route without covering my stockings with mud. So dome-like is the summit that a bearing was necessary to ensure going off down the correct channel. The Holme Moss TV mast to the south was a good navigational aid too. Soldier's Lump is an odd name but derives from surveying days. The soldiers did not enjoy having to camp on a "prodigious muckheap".

The long descent of Crowden Great Brook past Laddow Rocks was enlivened by meeting the two-day-old innocents heading north. They kept asking: "Is there any more bog?" Perhaps having several long, hard, excessively boggy days when starting (going either way) is a good thing. It noticeably thins out the ranks, a survival of the fittest effect which should evolve an interesting new homo sapiens perhaps, with naturally black legs, webbed feet and a plastic epidermis.

Crowden Youth Hostel, and the camp site in Longdendale, mainly serve we plebs of the pog; the end of the first Pennine Way day going north, and for some just the end. The Way swings round Torside Reservoir, one of the many which line this drowned valley. The A628 to Manchester was frightful. Road numbers milestone the Pennine Way. This one is Cheshire's Pennine Gap. A train clattered through as we waited at a level crossing.

A steep path took us up from Reaps Farm on to Torside Clough Edge, a pleasant ascent above a deep-set hill valley but the going became messy and sweaty up under Torside Castle.

At the stream junctions beyond, there were many paths but we folowed one marked *P.W.*, intending to traverse denuded Bleaklow and camp beyond, but a look back showed an inky sky dribbling over the blotting-paper landscape. We hurried over to a lonelier stream, pitched the tent in a grass-edged grough and laid in water just in time. The cloud and rain swept in. I felt sorry for the northbound, Day One walkers who would be receiving the storm into their enthusiastic faces on this bleakest of fogbogs. At the level crossing a linesman had warned me: "We have two kinds of summer here: the wet, and the terrible wet."

Saturday 4 August   EDALE ENDING
In the morning we faced the "interesting" situation of starting from an unknown point and, in thick clag, aiming to reach Bleaklow's vague

summit over its huge, desiccated, miry dome of peat. We travelled hopefully and, by feel and by fortune, arrived. So many people had strayed in every direction that footprints were no navigational aid. We first found the Wain Stones, two weathered heads of granite, one of which reaches out with moist lips as if to kiss the other. The Epstein-like sculptured group is known as "the Kiss" and is far finer in spirit and setting than many works squatting pretentiously in galleries of modern art. Wainwright's guide described them as "the only bit of sex in the book." Bleaklow has two summits, miles apart, both shown as 2,060 ft. The Pennine Way contents itself with one of them.

The summit was found easily enough, if *easy* can describe anything in this bombed, shelled and mortared battle-line of trenches. It is death or glory one-mile-an-hour country. We simplified our navigation as much as possible, using the Hern Clough stream and, once over Alport Law, having the sure line of the Devil's Dyke, an unusually straight channel. We could hear the traffic on the Snake Road before we saw it. The soft moor over to it had been laid with brushwood – just as the railway is "floated" over Rannoch Moor. The Snake Pass road was built in 1820 to link Manchester and Sheffield more easily. A snake is featured on the Cavendish arms, hence the name. Much older was Doctor's Gate, a Roman link from Castleton to Glossop.

The cloud which had covered Bleaklow now rolled away. We forsook the revolting path after crossing the Snake and almost forgot there was a Pennine Way as we made our own route along Featherbed Moss, a sere but serene fell. It faced the northern scarp of Kinder, the cliffs of which grew colossal in the moving, glowing mists. King Sun eventually won. From the Ashop Head Col with its view down to fat-bulging farmland and Kinder Reservoir we pulled up to join the edge of the scarp. A lad staggered past in a full suit of muddy orange water-proofs (shorts and a shirt sufficed for me), bearing an enormous pack which had innumerable parcels tied to it. For the rest of the day we were never out of sight of other people for long: weekenders and Penwaymen. It brought home just how many walkers there are from the surrounding cities and why the Pennines are so devoured by man and his doings. Urban society is itself an aberration perhaps, and one of the consequences is this unnatural pressure on the fragile high land. To be a free man only on Sunday is noble, but pitiable. I am not being elitist. This is superb, singing country, rich, variable, dogged with history, which I always delight to explore, when I can, be it a day's tramping or climbing on one of the ego-deflating edges. It is just so *peopled*, so over-peopled, which is an accident of history or geography (half of England's population lives within a two hour drive of the Peak), neither a shame nor a boast but, alas, an inescapable, grinding fact.

Kinder Downfall was a mere vertical thread of white among the tumbled rock-boxes. It really should be seen in spate, when the storm turns it into a spraying jet among the black glitter of wet boulders. Kinder itself must be marvellously desolate and difficult in wild conditions. It was almost sad, with the sadness of ending, to wend up towards Crowden Head through its dry groughs in the gentle morning sun. We floundered out, against the lay, to the map's 2,088 ft point which we hoped was the highest. There were tracks enough and the rim was dotted with figures. We returned to look for a trig point and when we had fully satiated ourselves with stuttering, poodle-footed, among the gulches and hags, we sadly descended Grinds Brook.

We met several hundred people. Perhaps a hundred of this Saturday's massed-start were aiming for Kirk Yetholm. Twenty, maybe thirty folk would make the 270 miles. The Pennine Way, if done in a single walk, is still a testing expedition. You can always run it, of course. It has a three-day 'barrier' as I write, just as once the mile had its four-minute challenge. A Rotherham lad, Brian Harvey, took an hour or so off Peter Dawes' time in 1979, his record – 3 days and 42 minutes.

We had a long lie in the sun by Golden Clough to dry out the tent and thoroughly clean Storm, then wandered down to Edale. We met one Pennine Way gang actually carrying gallon containers of water uphill. We had a snack and a Paddy in one of the pubs and were asked "Setting off on the Pennine Way, lad?" Obviously we had kept our stockings clean!

We took a train to Sheffield, an easy and natural act, but it felt most strange. Inwardly I was shouting for joy as the psalmist bids, outwardly we were just back from a day on the hills perhaps. Sheffield seemed noisy and hectic after the barren moors, banging us back to that other world of concrete and congestion – the lemming life of a city. I spotted a bus with the right number and climbed on to it only to head off in the opposite direction. The country bumpkins eventually reached *Chez Charles*. He had seized the chance of going off to Chamonix, but had kindly left his home at our disposal. A neighbour, Mrs Asher, gave me a key and we waded in through a deep litter of mail. First things first though: steak, raspberries and cream, wine and coffee; then sort out the mail and plan the days ahead which would be, as Kinghorn, a concentrated chaos out of which we hoped would come a trouble-free traverse of Wales. We bathed and by eleven went to bed as we were simply falling asleep anyway, despite the joy of Brahms' Fourth Symphony and a Prom Concert on the radio. Sheffield is the highest city of its size in Europe, and Banner Cross is high in Sheffield so we had not really suffered any come-down. Another stage was completed; as Dante says "to look back is wont to cheer climbing men." And walkers.

WEST THROUGH WALES

I must be rising and I must be going
  On the roads of magic that stretch afar,
By the random rivers so finely flowing
  And under the restless star.

NEIL MUNRO

Sunday 5 August – Wednesday 8 August   STOPOVER IN SHEFFIELD
Maps, pp. 153 and 204

It was an enjoyable change to have an omelette for breakfast – while listening to music on the radio, though I could not work out how to operate Charles' record player, which was frustrating. I had been looking forward to a glut of music, *starting* with his box of Beethoven symphonies. I cleared some urgent letters, posted them and returned from Banner Cross loaded with food, then washed every item of clothing before more letter-writing which kept me busy till Ray and Mary arrived for tea. We went down to the Manzil Tandoori for an enjoyable dinner.

Monday saw the parcel piles arranged early, then after a *Sheffield Star* reporter had been in I went to shop in the city centre. I bought training shoes for the walk to Wales to see how they would work. My second pair of Sesto boots were in Wales, so I left the ones I'd used to date in Sheffield to save carrying them. They were still in good condition and had proved light, strong and comfortable. The day went in a concentrated slog of little tasks, with constant telephone interruptions. Civilization palls quickly. On Tuesday the neighbours were fascinated by a Securicor van driving up to deliver three parcels of Storm's *Frolic*. It is as well the dog enjoyed his unvarying diet, for Pedigree Petfoods had sent us four times the quantity ordered. My estimate for the number of packets Storm would need had been based on the sample packet they first sent. The packets they delivered along the route were four times the size! Bill Wilkins of *Ultimate Equipment* came with a Tramp tent and I had a new rucksack to try out. A dash to the local bank failed to beat a flash storm that had the steep streets running like rivers. I sealed the parcels which I hoped to collect again in mid-September from rural post offices

in Wales, whose very names were a magical lure onwards. Freedom I'm
sure is the grandest of man's illusions – but we die if we are forbidden to
walk our dreams. I worked long into the night on a rough route Charles
had sketched out to lead from Edale to Ruthin: transferring it to the
maps and estimating likely daily distances and stopping places. His idea
of using canal towpaths was a help. It could have been difficult
otherwise.

Wednesday I simply had as a day off: dipping into the Knowles library
or enjoying odd snatches from the radio.

Charles' record player still defeated me, as it had done Ray the day
before. I went out to try the new tent and pitched it under the gaze of all
the old ladies peering through their lace curtains: it looked smart and
well-designed. No doubt it would be well tested. As a last gesture to
civilization I booked a taxi for 5.45 the following morning.

Thursday 9 August   RAIN FOR THE RETURN

Sorrow and ill weather come uncalled. It was pouring at five when we
woke but the taxi left us no option but to go. I read a paper in the train to
Edale and pretended the outside world did not exist. The illusion
drowned very quickly once we were dumped on an empty platform with
the swell of cloud ebbing past at a rate of knots. Ah, if we could only walk
yesterday's weather! Or tomorrow's. We splashed off to cross Rushup
Edge by the easiest line, Chapel Gate. A visit to caves and to Mam Tor's
prehistoric sites would have to wait. It was not a day for the ungover-
nable heights or deeps.

My training-shoes were soon soaked, but even boots would have
failed to keep dry in the weeping wetness of long grass. We kept to roads,
largely, by Whitelee to Sparrowpit where six roads met, then a nasty bit
of busy road with no verges so the A6 was actually welcomed for its
pavement even if we were constantly sprayed by blustering lorries.
It rained hard, hour after hour, with Achnasheen-like dedication.

> The cataract of the cliff of heaven fell blinding off the brink
> As if it would wash the stars away as suds go down the sink.
>   *Chesterton*

Buxton was a welcome sight. We went in to the Station Hotel as it
showed the first 'coffee' sign in town and had relays of coffee and toasted
sandwiches. The town was having a Scott festival but Storm would
probably not have appreciated *Lucia di Lammermoor*. High notes, even on

the television, set him yowling. Buxton's atmosphere of fashionable eighteenth century splendours hardly matched my breeches and boots. There was something incongruous about being in a spa, famed for its warm springs since Roman times, when it was named Aquae. Pavilion, Opera House, walks and gardens remain. You can even 'take the waters' in the municipal swimming pool.

The last time I had been in Buxton had been for a climbers' spree. I think it was called a conference, but jamboree would have been nearer the mark for such a collection of boy louts. The star had been Kurt Diemberger. He showed slides and films non-stop for about four hours

CHAPTER 9

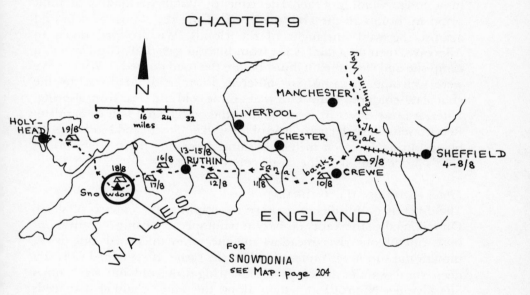

with the audience more than content. A Greenland film had one unforgettable scene. Several climbers scrambled out of their boat on to a double-topped iceberg but when they walked up to one end of it, it began to tip, so they raced down and up to the other end, only to make it tip in that direction instead. The subsequent see-saw was pure Peter Sellers with the climbers racing back and forth in an effort not to capsize their island. Eventually they made a break and ran down to leap for their attendant craft. There was a superlative close-up of facial expressions as the trio, in mid-air jump, realised they were wearing crampons – and were about to land in an inflatable dinghy.

A strong wind had shredded the clouds and, being dry, we pushed on up and out by the A53. The paths round the back of The Terret to the A54 brought a reward: we found a £5 note blowing across a field. (Later I was to find two £1 notes, one Irish, one English, besides several odd coins. In Scotland I found nothing at all.) The undulating moors seemed to have few grouse about – not very promising for the Twelfth. There were plenty of PRIVATE signs, however. Several sheltered nooks tempted us to stop but the wind made exhilarating walking. It was a strangely empty landscape and the Cat and Fiddle on its wild hillside could have made a film set for *Wuthering Heights*. The narrow road reached about 1,500 ft on the slopes where the River Dane rises, before dropping away in a long, winding brae. The cone of Wildboarclough's summit stood up boldly in the grey streamers of the sky almost as if braced against the wild onslaught of the clouds. We dropped down to Allgreave, then up again. A list from Buxton gave Hill Top Farm as a camp site and we came on it just before the road dipped to Wincle. We were welcome to camp, so slithered down fields to do so by the chocolate-coloured Dane. Our water came cold and clear from a spring. Later, it came direct from the sky, so the new Tramp had its baptism. Reborn senses are the perquisite of the walker. Storm and I just relished being out again; even in the morning drenching there was more of God's peace than in all the costly comforts of a city.

Friday 10 August   ON TO THE FLAT
The differences this day were more geographical than meteorological. On waking the landscape was hazy as paint spread meanly on canvas but once out of our river-meadow site the tones thickened and dried, though the sun never quite varnished the scene. It remained Corot: a deep rural wander down past Danebridge (the old inn sign shows Shackleton's Nimrod) and then along the water channel that feeds Rudyard Reservoir. (The lake gave a name to the author, not vice versa.) There was a fish farm bristling with security devices and later two grey mokes followed us through the soaking blackberry stems and reeds. We heard a busy road (the A523), then ran its gauntlet briefly before minor roads took us over an outlying salient of hill by the prehistoric site of the Bridestones.

A farmer helped us find our way through some trackless fields. He walked a horse and cart down with us for a bit, along with a scampering of dogs and children. It was a scene many imagine to have vanished. After wondering where it was we climbed *up* on to banks of a canal which we followed to the shops at Hightown. Fresh blackcurrant tarts and several cans of liquid were purchased for a canal-bank picnic. The tent was hung to dry from the grid of the aqueduct railing where the canal passed over a road. Once we left walking the canal we had some fun and games with nettles and hedgerows to reach little Astbury. Its ornate church has a free-standing spire. We had managed to round busy Congleton with almost no urban intrusion – a line which could well be used if a set path is eventually created to link the north end of Offa's Dyke to the south end of the Pennine Way as part of a Groats End Way.

An attempt to gain the M6 and Sandbach by rights-of-way petered out in a zigsaw of barley fields and other crops, a sweaty, frustrating delay in the heat of the day. We tramped off south to incongruously-named Hassall Green to pick up the Trent and Mersey Canal. We had much-needed refreshments and a wash at The Marina. What a peaceful world surrounds the longboat holidaymakers. The rush of ripples and the steady engine chug are almost its noisiest components.

Those soft thoughts of a *Wind in the Willows* existence modified after passing a few locks where some aggro was discernible with amateur captains (often dressed as such) yelling misdirections to wife-and-children crews. One poor wife was banned to the roof and lay there embarrassingly displayed, one leg in plaster. She told me that a few days before she had jumped for the shore, and missed.

Wheelock could provide no bed for the night so I filled up with water at a garage and wandered on till I found a quiet corner below the canal bank. It was interesting to watch, unseen, a gang of kids building a tree house on the other bank. I learnt some new Cheshire dialect words. After they squabbled off for supper only the occasional longboat chuckled by. The swallows were sweeping over the wired-off area beside us, warblers were willowing, mice squeaked in the jungle of nettles. We cooked a country meal (including 'windfall' potatoes we had gleaned along a country lane), had a vast mug of coffee which spoilt sleep and, with the wind changing direction, were all too aware through the weary grey night hours that the enclosure next door was the local sewage works.

Saturday 11 August   AN INLAND VOYAGE
My training shoes seemed largely made of cardboard and were rapidly falling to bits from dew or rain-drenched morning verdure. My left big toe was bruising – the shoes were turning out a doubtful gain on boots. We left the canal near a railway bridge south of Elworth where a train rushing overhead with the thunder of hurry startled the dog. We read many dull miles of flat, misty farmland on small roads, perhaps the least

interesting country of the trip, which perhaps explained why brick semis had names like Das Schloss and Coromandel. An Inter-city train screamed under a footbridge as we were crossing it. Poor Storm! Crewe was to the south of us but, like most towns of size, quite unaffected our view or route or even thoughts. Again, rights-of-way failed us (Cheshire seems bad) and we had more road-going to reach the Shropshire Union Canal. My book was *Lord Jim* and its style and my progression I felt had much in common: jumbled, not always clear but doggedly onwards. We brewed on the canal bank to dry out the tent. The day had a dust of gold as the sun won its way up the sky. We tiptoed past a fisherman who had fallen asleep on the job. The canal crossed high over the River Weaver. There were pretty locks with a trim house and garden. Delightful walking.

At Barbridge Junction we changed to the Shropshire Union Canal, and its banks were anything but easy to walk on. We had a rest at Calveley then did a cross-country race to reach Bunbury before lunch-hour closings. The name *Bunbury* fascinated. If the place did not exist it would be necessary to invent it. We made it by 12.20, proving the importance of being early. (Winning hours in the morning is the biggest single advantage of camping over accommodation, especially if the day is tormentingly hot.) Beeston Castle and Peckforton Castle, seen beyond thickly hedged fields and poplars, and quivering in the heat-haze, gave the scene the atmosphere of Provence. We skirted a low bastion of hill and from the breasting A534 wandered off up into Bickerton woods and fell asleep in their cool shadiness.

Storm woke me later by barking (a thing he seldom does) but his frustration was understandable. A grey squirrel had gone up a pine tree and the dog, following, had discovered gravity.

Sunday 12 August   INTO WALES AND INTO HILLS
  "Steal, if possible, my dear friend, one summer from the cold hurry
  of business and come to Wales."   *Shelley*

Partly because I did not have the tools to take it apart my stove had begun to leak, and over breakfast nearly went out of control. I climbed up Bickerton Hill, at six o'clock, in bare feet, to try to keep my shoes dry. When we came out above the filigree of trees on to the heather we could see over a haze-washed plain towards the Welsh mountains. Exultation in "the cold glories of the dawn" was tinged with the knowledge that the day's darg was to reach those scarcely discernible hills.

We dropped down through a jungly *maquis* to the hamlet of Brown Knowl, then on by paths which were marked, but their wet and luxuriant growth pointed to irregular use. Across the A41 the continuation proved to be a barley field but the next field led to a footbridge over a disused railway. Beyond it were vast acres of barley. I am too country bred to trample through fields of growing crops, I'm afraid, even if there was a right-of-way, so I merely ate some of the barley and also a few brambles (the first of the season), and our deviation by Broxton was rewarded with seeing an otter. A quiet walk took us on to Farndon where I bought a paper which I largely read by the River Wye – after crossing into Wales over the old bridge. Its buttressed, solid shape was reflected in the placid river. Every fifty yards along its banks a competition fisherman was sitting among the willow herb, each with a huge net basket in the water, optimists to a man for all they caught were tiddlers.

Llwybr Cyhoeddus proclaimed the first notice as we crossed into Clywd. As it was on the familiar green signpost, we learnt to recognise, if not to pronounce, our right of way. The fields were too full of thistles to revert to bare feet again so I was soon sodden and tingling from the knees down. The heat was stultifying, clamped down on the damp, odorous plain by a potlid of grey sky. I crossed the Alyn and followed it to Rossett where, thankfully, it was possible to buy drinks. I read a bit but a steep hill leading to a straight mile of heat-hammered road reduced me to a jelly. Storm is the stoic, his perfect patience always a rebuke under trying circumstances. We rewarded our effort with a tin of apricots before going down through Llay. A Miners Institute and a French-style farm gave it some architectural interest.

Cefn-y-bedd was a more suggestive name, a hamlet hidden in these first pleats of the first skirts of mountain and from which a Glenfarg-like road wound its way uphill. I had worked out a route to give us the easiest gradients, least road walking and so on but my first path proved to be a field recently restored from open-cast mining and having a surface as firm as my morning's porridge. A style lured me on to cross it but led simply to a gorge, choked in its own overgrowth. We fought down it, for the map showed a path by the river. There was no path. The greenery entangled every move, grasping like a miser. We more or less fell into the stream bed. It was almost impossible to move in any direction except up the quenched channel. This unconventional escape route at once paid off with blissful, tunnel-cool shade. When a desultory trickle of water appeared we stopped to eat and drink away some hours. There is no merit in making a road rough for oneself. "Jouk and let the jaw go bye."

Hours later we scampered up the gorge, found a long-forgotten path and had soon extricated ourselves. I then realised we had brought no water up. We stopped before Bwlchgwyn to camp on the lip of the forested Nant y Ffrith gorge. Jays chakked about in the trees. The heather was in bloom. This startled till I realised it was our distance south, not time, which brought it out a month earlier than expected. Bed, even without a last brew, was welcome. We had come 80 miles from Edale on our peripatetic perambulation.

Monday 13 August   CLWYDIAN BIRTHDAY
It was a raw-cold site and there was no tea in bed to relieve the gut feeling of early rising. Bwlchgwyn sprawled untidily along the hill crests and the country beyond was sparse and ochrous as if summer had passed it by. The furze cringed behind the walls and the blackberries were still in hard knots. We did our share of cringing to let a heavy shower pass up the long road to Rhydtalog ahead of us. We had our delayed breakfast by a streamlet before going through unspoilt Llanarmon with its cave and limestone quarries, castle mound, big church and old Raven Inn.

Only the postie was about, welcoming the mail van driver in a torrent of Welsh, a language which sounds like singing even when simply spoken. I envy almost any marked dialect, or language, for I have none of my own, having wandered too much when young. I hardly dared imitate the gutturals of Braehead even after a decade in the school. (When we had joint trips with Marlborough and Eton it was joked that I went along as interpreter.) More than once in the Alps baffled locals asked me what language the Fifers were speaking. Though these miners' kids had the accents, they were remarkably lacking a guid Scots vocabulary, due largely to the brain-washing of television. All of them first called *lochs* lakes, for instance, simply because that word was always used on the box. It was wasted shot to fire off *glaikit gowk* at some youth only for him to take it as a compliment. Lucky Wales then to have language's silvering on its soul.

The Clwydian Hills sprawled in a succession of paps. We walked up a leafy lane to one of the cols. There was a breathtaking view over the Ruthlin plain and a hint of big hills in the west. The sun had fought its way clear of the clutching clouds and dappled the landscape with chasing brightness. We left the rucksack and raced up Moel Llanfair, 1,466 ft, *the hill of St. Mary's Church* for a small but satisfying summit for my forty-fifth birthday. The year before I had taken Storm on his first hill day, a traverse of the Ochils of my own discovering youth. A mid-August birthday usually gave summits further afield: Pyrenees, Norway, Alps, Andes, Africa, India . . .

We left the apple-crisp heights with their pillow-fighting clouds to descend to the plain by a half-forgotten lane, crossing the Offa's Dyke Path – which winds along the Clwydian crest rather than on the actual dyke, which lies further east. The fields were full of huge bulls, chained out at safe distances from each other. Notices warning the public to keep out seemed rather superfluous.

Too bright too soon will rain by noon. We reached Ruthin, and sure enough the rain belted down for the rest of the day – but we were safely home. We stayed with Ann Roberts, who was taking the chance, with husband Eric away in the Himalayas, to have the house redecorated. Son Leo (6) had friends in, Ann had friends in, the shop bell rang constantly, Maureen Dodd was painting and decorating, lunch was served – all seemingly at once. I soon reduced my room to a shambles as I unpacked the goods for the parcels for the last stage of the trip. It was Sheffield over again, only companionable. Even Tigi Meow the cat seemed quite happy to accept a strange dog invading its territory.

Ann is just one of the nicest people I know, a lively compound of so many virtues most of us lack, being patient, kind, hospitable, hard-working, the calm centre for whatever wrecks and woes the storms may bring to others. Eric, in contrast, was mercurial, had climbed a pro-digious number of peaks, was a bookman and a night owl who would happily talk till dawn. We had climbed, skied and argued together in several countries and I suppose it had been optimistic to expect him, or Charles, to be at home in mid-summer.

When we went out later the streets were streaming. The town has a splendid site. It was here Owain Glyndwr first broke into open revolt, sacking the town one Fair Day in 1400 and for fourteen years bitterly fighting the intrusive English. Cromwell's cannon gave the castle a hammering in the Civil War so there is little old remaining in Ruthin, though the atmosphere remains with the square on top of the hill and the street running from it up to the castle.

I bought a Bluet stove to replace the leaking Vango, and the first stove we tried in the shop also leaked so had to be left outside to run out. Keith Thompson at The Bookshop sold me a copy of *The Story of San Michele* while dressed in jogging attire, and was working up to a plan to traverse the Offa's Dyke Path in three days. He also had a copy of George Borrow's *Wild Wales* in his shop; this is a book which has links with the whole country rather than just a single locality. It is a book which grows on one.

Borrow taught himself Welsh by twice reading through *Paradise Lost* in that tongue – at the age of sixteen. He could work in a score of languages and his early literary attempts were largely translations from German, Danish and Russian which were failures, but eventually The British and Foreign Bible Society engaged him to translate the New Testament into Manchu, which he had to learn for the purpose and which took him to Russia for two years. This led to several years of colporteuring in Spain, which led to *The Bible in Spain*, the book that made his name. *Wild Wales* was not a success to begin with. Too many travellers had published 'tours', but while most are forgotten, Borrow's account charges on, merit long outpacing mere fashion.

Tramping was a life-long addiction for this robust and restless man, who was probably more enthusiastic and alive than eccentric, as his contemporaries thought. As a young man he refused to visit Wales because the splendour of the country's literary and historic past overwhelmed him. When he made his trip in 1854 the route linked both the best of scenery and the homes of the great. It sparked off similar visits to other Celtic parts: Man, Cornwall, Scotland and Ireland, and also Wales on other occasions. It was the old Wales as well as the wild he loved, before Methodism made joy a sin, and before the people were herded into the industrial prison-house. He shares kinship with Scott (whom he disliked) but lacked the Borderer's security and calm. Zest was varied and prodigious: he tramped at a steady four and a half miles per hour, once walking (for economy) from East Anglia to London (for his interview with the Bible Society), covering 112 miles in 27 hours (at a cost of 5½d). Once wealthy enough, he thought nothing of demolishing a breakfast of "mutton chops, broiled and pickled salmon, eggs, fried trout, and potted shrimps". Borrow would have been an impossible companion on a trip; he would talk incessantly, barge into situations and commandeer and question all and sundry. This rumbustious escapade, however, has given us one of the most individual and revealing of travel books.

Tuesday 14 – Wednesday 15 August   RUTHIN "REST DAYS"
Tuesday was a day of gales which brought trees down and was a good one not to be under canvas, a thought that had sadder connections as the news began to come through of the Fastnet Race disasters; yachts dismasted, abandoned and sunk and a score of lives lost in the stormy seas not so far away. I plodded on with the packing but with plenty of diversions. When the weather moderated Leo took us a walk to show us his school. People were in and out all day and Maureen's voice could usually be heard yelling "Watch the wet paint!"

The caches were more or less ready by the end of the day so

Wednesday was spent in parcelling them up for Ann to post a few weeks later. The surplus *Frolic*, some Christmas presents, rejected training shoes were left to collect on the way home. Charles rang and I begged him to send my old Karrimor-Tiso rucksack to Dublin, the new one being most uncomfy. He said Chamonix had been a bit of a wash-out, a familiar climbers' complaint.

Ruthin each Wednesday had a Mediaeval Day with all the shopkeepers dressed for the part, the square occupied by market stalls and spinners, potters, corn-dolly makers, even an executioner, all practising their crafts, and even a genuine singing monk opposite the half-timbered Court House which was built in 1404. There are quite a few other old buildings, including the church which has a magnificent carved and panelled roof presented by Henry VII. St. Peter's church rings out a curfew each night as it has done for half a thousand years.

Convivial company made for a late night but, typically, when everyone had gone, Ann set to work in the dark room for several hours. Running a photographic business and Eric and Leo called for stamina of a special kind. The next time Eric went off on an expedition Ann planned to redesign and decorate the shop. It was her birthday the following Saturday so I had asked a local baker to deliver a cake as a surprise. We took our farewells that night as we were to slip off before anyone would be up.

Thursday 16 August   HIRAETHOG FOREST WALKS
A jewelled rainbow arched over the dark serge of hill as we walked on to Clocaenog and the vast forests beyond. We had a second breakfast by the secretive Afon Corris then strode on in the perfect combination of extensive views and delicious cool. We did not meet a car for seven hours and then only for a brief splutter by Pont yr Alwen as we crossed a road into the forests that surround the reservoir. Suddenly it began to rain hard and as we were only a mile from our planned stopping place we pitched at once. The rain poured for three hours, drew breath and then swept the dirt of the day under the carpet of the dark.

Friday 17 August   BETWYS-Y-COED
At dawn it started to rain again so we packed everything except the tent and lay reading Welsh short stories. There were letters to write but in the moisture-laden atmosphere envelopes and stamps would all have stuck together. A mosquito coil smoked away to keep the midges out of the tent. A lull at nine drew us out and off but it was an Edale exodus. I had

been vaguely aware of tinkling bells in the night so was relieved to find they were attached to real, live ponies.

Once out of the forest I was forced up to the trig point of Mwdwl-eithin (c. 1,745 ft) in order to find a fixed position. We followed a bearing to the Bwlch Gwyn, where the cloud began to thin but over Pen yr Orsedd the weather was so foul that we left the tops to follow a green road at a lower level. Several shepherds were making a big sweep of the Nant y Foel slopes. We crossed it at a fold and followed a massive *ffridd* wall to Maes Merddyn Farm. Starlings were perching on the sheep, just as oxpeckers do on African animals, finding food either in the fleeces or darting after whatever the host stirred up with its feet.

The rain switched off by the time we reached the Llanrwst road and walked along to Nebo (from which usually there is a wide view of the Carneddau, Moel Siabod and Cnicht). We had a couple of steep downs-and-ups before suddenly coming on a fine downward view of the deeply wooded slopes of the Betwys-y-coed valley. Old grassy paths took us down into Capel Garmon, a quiet village on the upper levels, then a steep road bullied down to Betwys in the noisy, touristy valley. The artist David Cox was largely responsible for its discovery as a beauty spot. There is a fifteenth century bridge of four arches over the Afon Llugwy which has a special beauty of its own. The Waterloo Bridge over the Conway is an early iron one, built at the end of the Napoleonic Wars. We used the camp site, collected the first Sheffield-posted parcel, cleared mail in a hurry and did some changing of plans. Just as *Hamish's Mountain Walk* had covered the Scottish Munros so this trip intended doing all the 3000ers 'Furth of Scotland'. I also intended to link the *Four* Country Summits (a novel scheme which had been kept secret in case it had to be sacrificed) so, as it was still a long way to the west of Ireland, I decided to push on for Dublin fast and take in only Snowdon, *en passant*, rather than use up several days over an attempt at the Famous Fourteen. They might just be done on the return to Snowdonia from Ireland before resuming the *Groats End Walk*, but alone, without transport, they would be really too complicated and time-consuming, nor was I going to sweat a rucksack over the route.

Today I found the frame could be removed from my rucker, which had become steadily more uncomfortable. It was one of these splendid modern ones so full of gimmicks that the practicalities had vanished. A sherpa simply wants a big sack to set on his back: no frame, no waist band, no pockets on pockets on pockets. I'd seen one recently advertised that called itself a *Yakpack*. Can't someone just make a simple – cheaper – *human* pack? And what about making one that is waterproof? A young girl stopped to pet Storm and slowly insinuated herself into the tent. We eventually managed to remove her by suggesting we take Storm for a walk, and returned her to her anxious parents who no doubt gave her a lecture about going off with strange men. I don't think I've ever been compromised by a five year old before.

Saturday 18 August   SNATCHING SNOWDON: NUMBER THREE

The A5, before most people would be at breakfast, is an attractive walk. The Swallow Falls, with plenty of water, were worth seeing though the Presbyterian in me rebelled at having to pay at a turnstile to see a natural object. It smacks all too much of commercialism and even blasphemy, as if casual accident gave creative rights. At the crossing to the Ugly House, Tyhyll, we turned off along the south bank of the Afon Llugwy where there is the site of a Roman fort. Too early for shops at Capel Curig we lay by the river to brew, or wandered along eating wild raspberries, then had to rush in to find the telephone kiosk where I did a brief interview with the BBC at Cardiff, the last such tie-up for the trip. I was amazed at how badly the radio and newspaper media are organised, with regions very much on their own. A trip like this could have been used in all sorts of imaginative ways, linking, as it did, all the countries in our islands. The visual impact too was completely missed, nor did any charity grab the opportunity of sponsorship. I never press for publicity in a big way but, as writing is the other half of my life, I was very conscious of the chances being missed. The gangrel in me smiled – and walked on.

The phone box was just behind the Joe Brown shop and we went in there immediately afterwards to pick up new Ultimate waterproofs in preparation for Ireland. A radio was on and as soon as I spoke, several eyes turned on us. Obviously I've more accent than I thought.

Capel Curig is *Curig's chapel*, Curig being a seventh century saint. Some Welsh names I noticed were close to the Gaelic: *aber* mouth of, *afon* river, *mawr* big, *ty* house, *cam* crooked, *du* black and so on. If Gaelic and Welsh are distant cousins, the Irish Gaelic (pronounced Gale-ick) and Scots Gaelic (pronounced gall-ic) are brothers, for speakers can understand and converse reasonably using them.

Borrow, on foot, felt ill at ease in a Capel hotel. We kept our refreshment to an ice cream, walking on west, past Plas-y-Brenin, the Sports Council's national centre, and the length of the Llynau Mymbyr. The tents round the knoll of Garth Farm were stabs of colour before a bruised sky. Clouds were pouring through the col of Pen-y-pass. We hurried (*festina lente*) for Pen-y-Gwryd, a bleak road junction. The P-y-G Hotel has a long connection with climbing, but if voices were already being raised 120 years ago about the growing mobs of trippers, one wonders what the early enthusiasts like Charles Kingsley or Charles Mathews would think of today's pressures? That was the period when the Alpine Club was founded (1857) and it was 40 of the P-y-G regulars who met in 1897 to consider a club — and the Climbers Club was founded the next year.

The tradition moved up to Pen-y-Pass and one wonders what that band of brilliant, innocent, exuberant brothers would make of a youth hostel there instead of their Gorphwysfa? Pen-y-Pass was *the* centre of climbing development at the time. The first world war cut great gaps in the ranks, the mountains took others, yet a remnant remained and the tradition lingered. It took another war for the Varsity domination to vanish. Climbing is an excellent guide as to how the world wends.

I had found and kept a length of white plastic which looked exactly as if it was a bit of cast iron guttering; this, sticking out at an angle, had an amazing effect on passing cars. Before then they were quite prepared to skiff us by inches but given the risk of scratching their paintwork they would swing well out. A few drivers even shook their fists at us. I would politely wave back.

At least we snaked up into the clouds of Pen-y-Pass unscathed. I had a glass of milk in an empty cafe and did not even object to the £1 per car charged for parking. Snowdon is free for walkers. We set off up the Miners' Track and slowly great breaks appeared in the clouds, giving brief views, as out of a window when the shutters blow to and fro. We found a surprisingly snug spot and as it was only a bit after three we pitched, brewed, and set off for *Number Three*, confident it would clear.

It did too. We scrambled up a crag for the view over Llyn Teyrn, a glittering eye under the cloudy brows of Y Wyddfa. The summit was blowing cloud like an active volcano. Lliwedd was a wall of shadow. We traversed along the castellated (and oddly nameless) ridge that separates the Miners' Track and the Pig Track, which we crossed at the Bwlch Moch, *the pigs' pass*, hence the path's name, which also appears as P.Y.G. sometimes, an interesting change. As we headed up Crib Goch we had Cwm Beudy-mawr the *big cow-shed hollow* below on our right to maintain the farming names. Below on the left were mining remains. Quite a contrast. The rock was greasy which sharpened the senses. We met an unhappy couple in shoes who asked me if there was not an easier way up Snowdon. Higher we saw a couple with a child traversing down the scree-covered flank, off any route and under anyone on the crest — and the crest was busy. One boy coming along it could not have been more than seven — all quite horrific and irresponsible.

My first traverse of Crib Goch had been made in wild winter conditions with Bob Aitken and fellow teachers Ann Winning and Annabel
Seidler. The weather was so wild that, on the way down, one gust blew
Ann over and she was left with her ice axe holding on to the railway line.
That day we had to call out a rescue for a school party who were already
numbed and showing the first symptoms of exposure. The valley com-
patriots of the incapable leader cursed us for 'interfering', yet, because
one lad was helped down instead of carried, his fingers were frostbitten
from dangling inertly round the supporting shoulders. It is inexplicable
that Snowdon does not kill and maim rash adventurers far more
frequently. Our blizzard day did have its moments of humour; at the
Bwlch Glas we caught another couple tagging on to us and when we
asked them where they thought we were going they replied: "We don't
know but can we please follow you?" Our foursome had become
fourteen by the time the summit appeared.

Snowdon is the only British summit with a railway to the top (Snaefell
in Man has a tramway) and if part of me objects to this mechanical intrusion the other is fascinated. All too often climbers, walkers, skiers or
whatever are as utterly selfish as the tourists and others they despise –
what could be more selfish than the downhill skiers' demand to extend
their mess on Cairngorm to corries west, or the pressures for a
Cambrian Way? Do they never consider there is an equal if not better
right to keep one major mountain chain free of a long-distance footpath? (There are a hundred as it is.) When it was proposed to build a
railway up Snowdon the landowner fought it off for years on amenity
grounds – yet he was the owner of the Dinorwic slate quarries, and
became first chairman when a company was set up.

The line rises, 3,140 feet in just over 4½ miles from Llanberis. Old
Swiss locomtives do the work: *Enid* No. 2, 1895, *Wyddfa* No. 3, 1895,
Snowdon No. 4, 1896, *Moel Siabod* No. 5, 1896, *Padarn* No. 6, 1922,
Aylwin No. 7, 1923, and *Eryn* No. 8, 1923. (The dates are when they went
into service.) No. 1, *Ladas*, came to grief on the first day of operations –
the only serious accident there has been. The train takes an hour to
ascend the rack and pinion track. There is a full system of telephones and
tickets with three intermediate stations where trains can pass. (Climbers
have been known to sit on boulders placed across the lines and toboggan
down Snowdon, though what happens on meeting a train is not told.)
On a busy summer day two dozen runs may be made. Wales has made
little railways very much a speciality.

I just missed reaching Crib Goch in time to photograph figures on the
ridge silhouetted against the clouds, so our traverse was done through

the milky vapours, as delectable as ever. It felt longer and more exposed because of the lack of view. The scrambling is delightful and the Snowdon Horseshoe round from Crib Goch, *the red comb*, to Lliwedd gives as fine a ridge-walk as anything outside of Skye. There is a dip at Bwlch Goch of red, crumbly soils, where study plots have been wired off by the Nature Conservancy Council, and then it pulls up to 3,495 ft on the rough *rim of the dish*, Crib-y-ddysgl, beyond which the going is easy. Crib Goch is not just a stroll and its knife-edge crest cannot be side-stepped much. It is the royal road up. Abraham in one of his books quotes a hotel visitors' book concerning the pinnacle above the Bwlch Goch: " . . . ascended the Crazy Pinnacle in five and a half minutes and found the rocks very easy." The next entry read: ". . . *descended* the Crazy Pinnacle in five and a half *seconds* and found the rocks very hard."

A twentieth century monolith had been stuck up on the Bwlch Glas to guide the incompetent. The reek of oil led us to the railway which we followed to the cafe and the summit. It was bitter cold on top and the only other sign of life was a miserable gull, so we simply walked round the cairn and fled back as we'd come to descend the zig zags to Glaslyn which has a monster legend like Loch Ness. Braehead parties had been up Snowdon on several occasions, usually going to and from Ireland, and I once set up a camera to take a summit group picture: Kirsty Adam, myself and about eight boys and girls of all ages. The picture was spotted by friends in Morocco who jumped to the conclusion that this was a family picture (a mistake the Irish often made too). They thought such fecundity marvellous for one so young. And such a number of *male* children. Allah truly had blessed me. To this day, each year when I return to the Atlas, I have to give a fictitious report on my family. I hadn't the heart, or the language, to correct the original error fifteen years ago.

Once below the cloud level Storm and I wandered about to peer down big holes and other remains of the mining that once must have made this cwm a noisy bustling scene. One spoil tip gave an excellent scree run. Odd iron spikes showed precarious stairs. Everything dripped and splashed – this is, after all, one of the wettest spots in Britain. Miners' lives must have been held cheap in those days. Glaslyn is *blue* or *green lake*, a colour due to the presence of copper, long mined in Cwm Dyli, the work only being abandoned early this century.

The path along glacier-gouged Llyn Llyddaw was being restored in defence against the pressures of modern wear and tear. It was an odd place in which to meet a JCB. Each walker setting off from Pen-y-Pass was being asked to carry up a bag of gravel to help the work. Llyn

Llyddaw shivered as cold dusk settled on the peaks. Lliwedd faded into the mist. We reached the tent at 7.30 p.m., about three and a half hours after leaving it. We sat outside to eat but it was soon too dark to read or write. Mid-August is not really midsummer: June is the peak, July holds on, but August has the touch of death in it, like an overfed, obese human, whose fatty heart is already doomed though he knows it not.

Sunday 19 August   ANGLESEY

It was only after we had bedded down that I remembered to con-gratulate young Storm on his canine 'first' of the Three Peaks, not that he cared, lying snug in the crook of my knees where he always slept – after first giving me a nuzzle in the face – difficult to avoid when pinned in a sleeping bag.

Once home I tried to find out more on the foot-linking of Nevis-Scafell Pike-Snowdon, for I knew the late inspiring Eric Beard had done it back in 1969 when he ran over 400 miles in 10 days and 12 hours. John Merrill linked them on his coastal walk. Eleven years after Beardie, the fastest time (7½ days) had been turned in by Arthur Eddleston, a Kent policeman (whom I met later on the way to Morocco) but once home I read the news that in September Ann Sayer (43) took eleven hours off his time, doing the three in 7 days and 31 minutes. An average of 60 miles a day on hard roads is impressive! Her record did not last a year. Martin Berry rang from London to say Arthur had just bounced back with a time of 5 days 23 hours 37 minutes for the 427 miles. Ann walked roads entirely (brave girl: think of Loch Lomondside or the A74!), Beardie largely ran, Arthur crossed the Mamores and the Devil's Staircase after the Ben, running down hills but race-walking otherwise. Arthur did nothing athletic until he was 30, by which time he weighed 16 stone. He was then cajoled into a Police walking race of about 30 miles, didn't finish it, predictably, and determined to do something about his fitness. By the following year he was down to 12 stone and winning walking races. He has raised many thousands of pounds for multiple sclerosis research since. Beardie's was a much less pressurised trip. He had one friend backing him up and sometimes just slept out. He used climbing gear on the hills, too, as he had nothing else. David Huby from York made a leisurely seventh linking of the Three in 1980 and I'm sure the numbers will increase ever-more rapidly.

Car records between the three peaks have a long history having been done in under 24 hours as long ago as 1926. I was later to have heart-failure reading that some one had added Carrauntoohil to the Three but recovered when I saw it was a road and air event. But cycling is genuinely self-propelled and personal, and the three have been so linked several times. In June 1980 Stephen Poulton (RAF) cycled them in 41 hours 51 minutes – twelve hours off the time set by Alan Evans of Kendal.

A most interesting link is the Yacht Race which has been held each year since 1977. It starts in Barmouth (home of W. H. Tilman) and is open to any yacht with a maximum crew of five, of whom two have to be 'mountain goats'. It is marginally quicker than walking, the 1979 time being 5 days, 8 hours. The 1980 race was won by a soul-searing eight minutes, Marines overhauling the RAF in the clouds on the Ben. Twenty-two teams finished in what promises to be a great sporting event. My statistics will no doubt all be out-dated by 1981 activities – but that was the state of play at the end of 1980.

Six-thirty on a Sunday morning was an excellent time to walk down the Llanberis Pass; it gave minutes per car rather than cars per minute and it was even safe to stand and stare at some of the famous crags like Dinas Mot on one side or Dinas Cromlech, Carreg Wastad and Clogwyn-y-Grochan (the Three Cliffs) on the other. We reached Llanberis just as the first toy train was puffing its way up Snowdon. Having frequently beguiled innocent Braeheaders up remote summits with promises of ice-cream stalls or chip shops on the top, when we came to Wales nobody would believe my proclamations of a railway never mind cool drinks. Their faces were a study when a train suddenly descended on them out of the mist.

Pete's Eats provided a welcome mug of tea and poached eggs on toast while I browsed through a Sunday paper. Later I realised it had been the previous Sunday's. The livid red sunrise over Moel Siabod in the morning had given its warning, and it was raining when we set off again. We went along Llyn Padarn, twice, for I had left Storm's lead behind when I donned waterproofs. Suddenly it was that sort of day. It rained non-stop for our plod to the Menai Bridge. "Dry with bright periods", the forecast had proclaimed. We crossed by Telford's 1826 suspension bridge, the first of its kind on such a scale – it still copes with today's traffic. Mock Egyptian towers suspend the roadway a hundred feet over the sea. There was no retrospective view of Creigian Eryri but plenty of confusing roadworks, as Robert Stephenson's tubular Britannia Bridge was having another deck added to its original railway span in order to carry road traffic as well. It too has an antique look, having been designed to complement Telford's masterpiece.

Once on Anglesey the road was crowded with Sunday afternoon nose-to-tail motorists as we wandered up to the unpretentious village of Llanfairpwllgwyngyllgogerychwyrndrobwllllantysiliogogogoch.   Few cars slowed long enough to catch more than the first couple of syllables. We chewed it over with the help of some chips and coffee in a cafe and a local translated what is in fact twin village names run together in asserting the longest name in these islands: *St. Mary's by the white Aspen over the Whirlpool and St. Tisilio's by the Red Cave.* Locally it is Llanfair P. G.

French climbers use the slang *exposer la viande* for taking a risk, which was apt for this suicidal bit of the A5. It had no pavement and I had lost our anti-car device. We took to country roads and by Llangefni were tempted by some soft accommodation, but pushed on to camp so as to use the A5 early in the morning when it would be less busy. We wasted much time thrashing about in a wood before finding water and space for the tent near Cefni Reservoir.

There was a rush to write up two days of log which was not helped by wanting to watch waterfowl and the sunset which ran a fiery path of gold to the molten doorway of closing day. We promised to avoid doing twenty-five miles of roadwalking in future. It is all too easy to become caught up in the treachery of speeding time. The world seems to be wound round with it like a ball of knitting wool.

Monday 20 August   ACROSS THE IRISH SEA

We were off by six, and the A5 proved as quiet as we had hoped. We had refreshment stops at Bryngwran and Valley and paddled in the sea once over the causeway to Holy Island. If Anglesey seems flat, this appendage can hardly be described as mountainous yet it has some of the finest cliff scenery, and climbing, in Britain. The South Stack lighthouse is perched on a skerry, and so high are the cliffs overlooking it that the light can only sweep the rocks below their edge. The steps down to the lighthouse are exciting enough for the walker.

At Holyhead I collected a huge mail which kept me busy on the afternoon boat to Dun Laoghaire. The *St. Columba* was scruffy, and having to leave Storm caged made me feel he deserved that treatment less than many of the revolting, fat, drinking, gambling humans on board. It is always a depressing crossing, somehow, but things usually warmed up on reaching Ireland. They were not to fail this time, either. But at least we had a calm sea.

IRELAND: SUNNY PERIODS

I envy solitude
and silence among the coloured hills,
I envy wind and stars
and all the gossamers of life
that man can see but cannot touch
or rule, or legislate.
Waves are not asked to queue,
Nor mountains wait.

Monday 20 August (continued) HOUSE-HUNTING *Maps, pp. 172 and 179*

For several days I had been trying, without success, to telephone my cousin in Dublin, for we were now several days ahead of our schedule. She had recently moved house and when I asked the ticket collector for directions to Glenageary, he waved northwards, "It's two stations up the line. Ask once you're there." Half-an-hour later I was becoming suspicious of these instructions as I knew the house to be only ten minutes' walk from the ferry. I bought an ice-cream for the pair of us and the shopkeeper told me Glenageary was indeed two stations from Dun Laoghaire, but southwards. With a colossal pack this was no joke.

An hour off the ferry and we were back at it, hot, sweaty and hungry. There was still no reply from phoning. A curry supper and a bottle of lemonade were taken to the nearest seat – the wall right in front of the church. We were just tucking into this when the church doors opened and hundreds of people came out from mass. We asked for directions which led to a ferocious-sounding argument ("You can't get there from here") so I took a vague consensus as to general direction and set off. We eventually reached the house.

There was no reply to my ringing and neither neighbour knew anything. However, the people across the road kindly took me in and rang the Lynches who would probably be feeding the cat and would have a key seeing Margaret was away on holiday. They produced welcome tea too, till Geraldine Lynch arrived. She had intended staying to look after the cat and house so simply handed over to me instead.

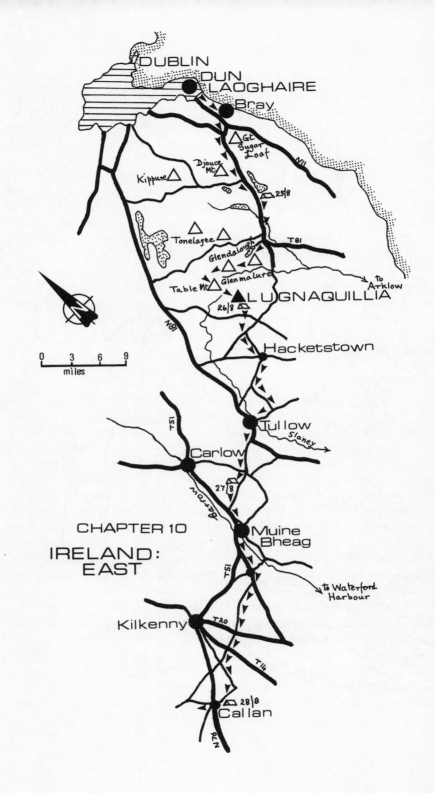

DUBLIN
DUN
LAOGHAIRE
Bray

Gt
Sugar
Loaf
N11
Djouce Mt
Kippure
25/8
Tonelagee
T81
Glendalough
Glenmalure
to
Arklow
Table Mt
26/8
LUGNAQUILLIA
N81
Hacketstown
T51
Tullow
Slaney
Carlow
27/8
Barrow
CHAPTER 10
Muine
Bheag
IRELAND:
EAST
T51
to Waterford
Harbour
Kilkenny
T20
T14
28/8
N76
Callan

0   3   6   9
miles

Tuesday 21 – Friday 24 August   DUBLIN DELAYS

I had a couple of days alone which broke the back of the organising and packing. Margaret's Moggy was not too sure of Storm but at least kept neutral. A few more days and they would have been playing. Margaret came back from Galway on Thursday and accepted her squatters and their chaos with Irish aplomb.

One unexpected thrill was to find in a bookshop a copy of R. L. Praeger's *The Way That I Want*, perhaps the finest thing ever written about the Irish countryside and its hills. I had quite a haul of Scottish books too. There was time to nip in to Trinity College to see the *Book of Kells*, which may have been created on Iona. So very little has survived from those days, when Ireland was the only light in a dark Europe, that its value is incalculable. Every day a new jewel-bright page is turned, so there is always an excuse to see it once more. The usual shopping, etc., seemed contrastingly dull. A new stove came from Alex at Nevisport but I'd already been forced to buy one in Ruthin. My comfortable old rucker arrived from Sheffield. We had procrastinated long enough. On Saturday we must set off.

Saturday 25 August   ROUNDABOUT TO ROUNDWOOD

The rain swept down all morning. It gave extra time for planning, and, as the Irish 3,000ers are probably the least known, a look at sources of information might encourage a few more Munro-baggers to add these good hills to their collecting. I am unashamedly in print as having called them among the finest hills of these islands, and if I was forced to pick just one hill it would be Brandon. I seem to be blessed for, on the whole, the notorious wet and cloudy climate of Ireland has permitted me many good days. (W. A. Poucher, in contrast, simply gave up trying to produce a photographic book on the Irish hills as he had done on Scotland, England and Wales.) *Climber and Rambler* for September and October 1979 and *The Great Outdoors* for August 1980 carried articles covering the Irish hills (with plenty of illustrations) and it would be worth obtaining photocopies if planning a visit. Just as Scotland has Munro's Tables and England has its 2,000ers listed by Bridges, Ireland's 2,000ers are pinned down in C. W. Wall's *Mountaineering in Ireland*. Just what constituted a *Separate Mountain* and what a *Top* is still a source of debate.

The Irish Munros are well scattered: three individual peaks and the Macgillycuddy Reeks which with their less certain number ensures that visitors traverse everything, which they should be doing for interest anyway. Recently Gill and Macmillan, under the general editorship of indefatigable Joss Lynam, have produced six cheap *Irish Walk Guides* which makes ignorance inexcusable. Volumes I, V and VI cover the Munros. Preparing for any unknown country or mountain trip is an indivisible part of the experience (as is writing about it afterwards for some addicts) so the above is more than sufficient to commence your homework.

Ireland's 3,000ers line up with a certain logic (a sort of banana-shaped curve), and to add Carrauntoohil to Nevis, Scafell and Snowdon, involves walking virtually across Ireland – hence my coast-to-coast from Dun Laoghaire to Dingle.

Dublin is fortunate in the way few other capitals are in having big hills on her back door step (Edinburgh follows with the Pentlands). The Wicklow Mountains contain one 3,000er in Lugnaquillia (3,039 ft) and many more over 2,000 ft. When eventually we set off this Saturday lunch-time we had to cut our planned high-level traverse to a fast road walk.

The Wicklow Mountains are rolling brown domes, cracked with black peat and flanked with dank bogs. At the Sally Gap and from Hollywood to Laragh (the Wicklow Gap) roads cross the range, and high on the east an old military road rims it. The deep, secretive, tree-planted glens have had their place in history, some of it bloody and not very old. Mining, forestry, waterworks, tele-communications have all left their mark, but the Wicklows remain serious mountains and their featureless miles demand respect and navigational skill in a way even the Reeks do not.

Romance lay even in the puddled pavements of the road leading out of town. We headed south by Killiney to Bray, which looks almost Mediterranean with its church on the hill and the blue sea below. We skirted inland, over the Dargle River and up to Glencormac under the Big Sugar Loaf, where we collapsed in the heat. Inland lay Enniskerry and Powerscourt Waterfall, one of the finest in Ireland, but they might as well have been on the moon, for a long traverse on foot cuts a very narrow swathe through a country. A slacker wandering, using local transport, or cycling, would see far more, but need more time, which is always the determining factor. If only we could buy the hours in which others are *bored*! Two ices, a *Pepsi* and a pint of milk set us on through a rocky gap up round the stony Sugar Loaf where a filling station provided more drinks. It gave a marvellous view over purple hollows up to shadowy Wicklow hills with Kippure in the background dominating with its TV mast. Across the road realistic aero-models were being flown. Against that background they looked almost surrealist. We completed a trying seventeen road miles at Roundwood camp site.

The Great Sugarloaf which welcomed to the Wicklows

In Dun
Laoghaire:
Storm hinting it
was time to be on
the road again

Above: Loo Bridge Youth Hostel, a converted railway station

Above, left: Foulksrath Castle (fourteenth century), now a Youth Hostel

Left: A richly decorated Kerry "front"

The rock of Cashel: one of the most famous of
ancient sites in Ireland

Galtymore from Cush

Cahir Castle

Haroldstown dolmen

Above, left: the prehistoric Turoe Stone – mysterious *la tène* carving

Above, right: Brandon, or Brendan, was an early explorer whose restless spirit took him on strange journeys. Brendan became the patron saint of my trip, Brandon perhaps my favourite mountain

Gallarus' Oratory: one fine example of the early Christian remains to be found on the romantic Dingle Peninsula

The Macgillycuddy Reeks from Tomies Mountain

One of the finest of corries: under the eastern cliffs of Brandon

Lough Anascaul in the Dingle Peninsula

Poulnabrone in the
west of Ireland

Irish travel on the
Dingle Peninsula

"Far, far in the West
Is peace profound"

Sunday 26 August THE LUG

The alarm went off at dewy 5.30 a.m. and we had it cool through Trooperstown Wood to Laragh and the Vale of Glendalough, *glen of the two lakes*, which combines beautiful scenery and a remarkable collection of early monastic remains. St. Kevin (died *c.* 619) established a hermitage by the Upper Lake and despite his desire for solitude disciples gathered and a settlement grew up. Its history is the standard one of fire, flood, Viking raids, 'the English', and ecclesiastical interference. Restoration, begun in 1873, has saved something of the atmosphere. Its setting, buried in the heart of the hills, usually means it is seen in monochrome with grey mist clinging to the tops and filtering through the steep forests, not that this detracts. Thackeray wrote in his *Irish Sketch Book*, "I don't know if there is any tune about Glendalough but if there be, it must be the most delicate, fantastic, fairy melody that ever was played."

Most striking of the remains is a Round Tower which soars a hundred feet above the trees. It is capped with a conical roof, reconstructed with the original stones. There are four windows at the top facing the cardinal points of the compass, and the door is high up above the ground. These towers were probably a mixture of belfry and sanctuary. A few can still be climbed to the top which really impresses one with the skill of the builders. Though all are basically similar in design, the differences fascinate and collecting Round Towers becomes as compulsive as Munro-bagging. We once rushed about Dublin in the dusk rush-hour trying to find Clondalkin Tower before going on for the Holyhead boat. Some one at last spotted it and eventually we arrived – at the foot of a factory chimney. There are about 60 towers left (out of several hundred) and they are all in Ireland except for one at Peel (Isle of Man) and two on the east coast of Scotland, at Brechin and Abernethy.

We brewed coffee at The Deerstone, across the stream from St. Kevin's Kitchen and someone from the first touring bus took off my Kodachrome slides to post. We went on through the magnificent oak forest to the ruins of Reefert Church which had several old crosses like the ones on St. Finnan's Isle in Loch Shiel. Various forest trails give attractive walking and a descriptive leaflet helped out the maps I had. Most Irish hills are shown only on Half Inch maps, and where there are One Inch maps the contours are 250 ft apart. You would be surprised how many 249 ft bumps can be hidden away in a misty landscape.

We walked up by what the book refers to as 'anonymous forest', passing the pretty Poll an Easa, and were glad of the mature trees for their shade. From the Prison Rock a path is way-marked over to Glenmalure. We went up Mullacor (*Mullach Mhor*) and Lugduff, 2,000ers which lie above the deep valley of Glenmalure and which look across to Lugnaquillia (*log na coille*, hollow of the cocks). The Lug is probably most often climbed from that glen via the Carrawaystick Brook – a name which is Ordnance Survey nonsense, a massacre of Gaelic *ceathramh istigh* (the inner quarter). To a Scot the Irish hills have a familiar sound; none of your dull English *Black Hills* and *Great Ends*. Give me Ballinafunshoge and Loch Nafooey any day. A friend once complained to me that Gaelic had so many different words for *white*, but this simply shows the inadequacy of our vocabulary for describing colours. Gaelic has many – differing – *whites*, we the one, unless you count *off-white*, which is hardly poetic.

To reach the Lug we had to rim round Glenmalure. The laughable One Inch map makes it look so easy, but it is all ups and downs, deep-cut bowls of hills, shockingly peaty and broken. The upper reaches of Glendalough reminded me of the Dubh Loch (without the Creag) while Glenmalure was like Glendoll with its smothering trees. There were odd tails from lead mining by the Glenealo River, modern geometrical patterns of the pumped-storage scheme on Turlough Hill, but mainly the view was of heat-shimmering empty hills. Tonelagee, north of the Wicklow Gap road, which crosses to Hollywood, stood boldly up as a hump-backed giant. Names again – Wicklow is Scandinavian (Dublin was founded as a Viking port) and Hollywood, like Baltimore and others, has travelled west over ocean. An American tourist on the Wicklow Gap once asked what lay west and being told Hollywood, gave a disbelieving stare and drove off. . . .

Because it was such hard going we made sure of covering every 2,000 ft bump as we rounded towards the Munro. The Lug gave a hot thousand feet up its stepped slopes. We met three older men descending. Had we been walking past Bray yesterday? "Ah, we recognised the dog." Two others, a gang on the North Prison and an old man on top made it a busy mountain for Ireland, but it was a sunny summer Sunday afternoon just an hour's drive from Dublin. We were not to meet anyone else on the rest of the Irish hills. The old man talked to himself, then raced off with his crooked stick, and vanished. A leprechaun?

The summit of Lugnaquillia, Percy's Table, 3,039 ft, is flat and the trig a stark intrusion. It was windy so we soon followed after the old man, but never found him, as we descended the bare slopes to the peat hags of the Col to Slievemaan. We camped at the first water as the slope dipped to the south to begin the Ow River valley – which led the eye south over endless peeping hills. It showed how rough the going had been that we camped an hour beyond the estimated time of arrival. From Slievemaan it is an easy walk over Ballineddan Mountain to reach the road, a good exit for a traverse.

Monday 27 August   OVER THE SLANEY RIVER

Daybreak had a death-to-summer coldness to it and we descended over Lybagh (2,089 ft) into a valley-held cloud inversion. It gave enjoyable walking to Hacketstown, a farming town overlooked by the small Eagle Hill, which was a landmark for miles in every direction. I changed into shorts and read Frank O'Connor stories as far as the Derween River. The Haroldstown dolmen, which was near, was the finest I've ever seen. Our riverbank lunch rather palled when we found a decaying dog in a sack floating below our chosen spot.

Up till then we had been going west, the trees yielding shade, but after lunch we walked into the sun and suffered all the way to Tullow on the Slaney (which rises on Lugnaquillia). We collapsed in its sloping square with ices and *Apla*. Storm had a liking for ices and a sharpened ability to find a dropped-one in every village we went through. The castle at Tullow was destroyed and the garrison butchered by Cromwellian forces. Our next stop was at Rathoe (rath, *ring fort*: the hamlet is built on one) and we sheltered in a grassy lane to cook and wile away the burning hours. We continued by the Fighting Cocks crossroads, to camp in a corner of a field at dusk near a ruined castle – one of many we had passed that day.

Tuesday 28 August   THE CROSSING OF KILKENNY

We were off before six and from the first rise in the road watched a red balloon of sun float out of the valley cloud-sea. We dipped, then up the next hill (the road ran up for ever) sunrise came again, as a golden disc, and then yet again as a burnished silver sequin among the flowing mists. We dropped off these odd little Carlow heights into the cloud and they protected us for a few hours from the beating of the sun.

Leaving Muine Bheag (Bagenalstown it is still called locally) I managed to go astray, not because of the fog, but from being in a stunned state from reading the *Irish Times* which was full of the Mount-batten assassination. Oh, the brave heroes that fight old men and children. I think there must be some kink in the Irish that they can produce such people: bombs thrown indiscriminately into pubs, children killed by booby-trapped transistors, and this callous murder of an honourable old man (a bitterly ironic choice for an anti-colonial gesture), and yet more children, because they were there. It's a madness which can only exist with connivance no matter how shocked, and shamed, the majority are. It is so pointless. If murder could gain anything it would have – there has been blood enough, God knows – but nothing has changed in years of horror. Even if every I.R.A. demand was met it would not end the bloodshed, merely change the players. Do they think the 'filthy Brits' like having the problem? Do they think two-faced Dublin would welcome it any more?

We left Bagenalstown, an innocent place for ever linked with the Mullaghmore infamy. We walked down by a squeaking mill on the delightful River Barrow and along country roads to Gowran. Storm led us straight to the ice-cream machine which every Irish town seems to have, along with other characteristic centres of refreshment. There was an impressive church. My log was testimony of the heat now fully switched on again: "Battle on, collapse and brew, read, snooze, catch up on this for yesterday. Shoulders ache. Feet ache. Sun no fun. Soul and soles being punished. A landscape of inescapable sameness."

Because of the heat the quickest route was chosen. Not even a Round Tower drew me aside. It must have been bad. When we eventually staggered into Callan, its ruins and history were ignored. We had a Paddy – served in the back of the butcher's shop (Victualler it called itself), filled our gallon of water, bought a *brack* and retreated to camp in the corner of a newly-cut barley field. It was dark almost at once and sleep was not easy in the stuffy heat which only slowly ebbed away as the dew fell hour by hour.

With hindsight now, I feel this day was one of importance, or rather the frightening events of the day before were. At a personal level, coming at an unexpectedly gruelling stage anyway, it took away the laughter from the trip. It was too near, too fanatic, too fantastic. And seen against a world more and more often being held to ransom by political hoodlums it was all too portentous. Good and bad alike appear to be floundering and struggling. Everything escalates, so it seems all sane controls become impossible. I think I began this trip an optimist. I know I ended it a pessimist. The terrible beauty is torn.

Wednesday 29 August   HEATWAVE HILLS

Perhaps it is better being a pessimist – it can only lead to *pleasant* surprises, whereas the optimist must constantly face disappointment.

The day was almost a copy of the two before, perhaps worse for the valley mists broke early and a sullen sky battened down on us for the weary miles of road. Any chiaroscuro had gone and one saw only fuzzy Turner images. If ever a coast-to-coast Way evolves I hope it will discount time and sweep further south to keep to hilly country or at least

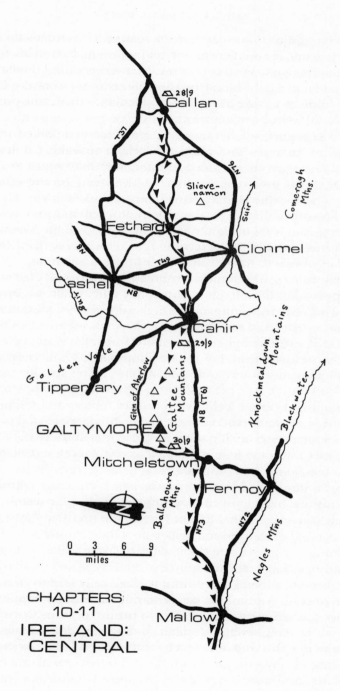

28|9
Callan

T-37

N76

Slieve-
namon
△

Suir

Comeragh Mtns.

Fethard

Clonmel

N8

T49

Cashel

N8

Suir

Cahir

29|9

Knockmealdown Mountains

Golden Vale

Tipperary

Glen of Aherlow

Galtee Mountains
△   △

N8 (T6)

Blackwater

GALTYMORE ▲

△   △
30|9

Mitchelstown

Ballahoura Mtns

Fermoy

N73

N72

Nagles Mtns

N
W   E
S

0   3   6   9
miles

Mallow

CHAPTERS
10-11
IRELAND:
CENTRAL

work out secret ways that avoid so much road walking. Roads are hard to avoid in practice as even very minor country roads tend to be surfaced. We were simply unlucky to run into such a succession of hot days over the longest bit of road-bashing on the whole trip. We were also pushing it in the hope of having a traverse of the Galtee Mountains in sunny splendour. We were not complaining, just pass-remarking with a certain wonder! No doubt it would rain yet before we stood on Brandon. It was also a pity to see so few historical sites. Ireland probably has more pre-historic sites, ruined abbeys and castles and so on than any other country in Europe; too many to cope with in practice, many are overgrown and desolate. There are no Roman remains at all, of course.

In Callan one lady in a shop where we stocked up with liquids (at 7 a.m.) broke into tears when the inevitable subject of the Mountbatten murder came up. There was a terrible apologetic shame in the reaction. People talked as if to try and clear their hearts. The coming visit of the Pope was pushed out of the press coverage. Millions were to flock to that man of peace, but the killings continue. We crucify Christ anew.

Cramp's Castle led us down into Fethard where we picked up fresh bread and cold turkey to picnic in the shade under a crisp, sun-dried hedge. Good bread is one of the pleasures of Ireland and most towns have excellent food shops. I remember stopping at a bakery once with a Braehead gang and stocking up with several loaves for our overnight stay at Foulksrath Castle near Kilkenny. The bread was crispy fresh and hot; a wee nibble as we went led to further nibbles and trying it with butter and honey and – and we soon had no bread left at all. Foulksrath may be a youth hostel but it is also a fourteenth-century keep, rather like Ferniehurst Castle near Jedburgh. On that visit, for our morning 'duty', the party was set to weed the moat.

Fethard is dominated by Slievenamon which the guide describes as a great sandstone hump, which is accurate enough, yet romance has set one of the legends of Finn McCool here. It was up these slopes that the fair ladies raced in competition to gain his hand. Grainne won this early hill race and her subsequent flight with Diarmaid is part of both Irish, and Scottish, folklore, and the source of the Tristan and Iseult romance.

We pulled up, and ups and downs marked the hot road on. It was too hot even to read. A couple of lads set a dog on us at a farm, and more than once tractors were being driven to the din of transistor radios. It seems even farming, even in Ireland, is changing. An old farmer who walked a mile with us did not think it for the better. The transistor on the tractor I found symbolic and dreadfully sad. If rural parts want to be part of the plastic age we are lost. The grey common denominator is all that is left: a regulated society, the antithesis of all that the remote places have always been. How can you love the sounds of it if pop music bellows in your ears? How can you smell the sweetness of it through the reek of diesel? This is the shift I see and fear: young people in the Highlands and Islands (and in Ireland) no longer care for the traditions, for the feel of their inheritance. Gaelic is dying. Old love is forgotten. The Clearances continue subtly and surely but the sad human flocks of the nineteenth century are now wild, errant goats, so knowing and so innocently led.

We were walking all morning towards the Galtymore range but because they were seen end-on through the wavering shimmer of heat they did not look big. We were glad to reach Cahir, *the fort*. I bought an ice-cream and as usual Storm found one. We collected our parcel from the Victorian brick post office and sat under the tall trees by the River Suir to brew and go through things. Weirs set the river laughing down by the Castle; it was a blissful hour of rest. Cahir has a Nash church but both the town and the country round are full of older religious ruins. The next town north is Cashel (one of the most celebrated places in Munster and its struggles throughout history) and never omitted from any itinerary – except now.

It stands on a stark white crag rising out of the plains and thus has a startling impact (like Edinburgh Castle). There is a round tower, cathedral, castle, chapel, high cross and much else, all squeezed on top of the Rock. Legend has it that the Rock was spat out by the Devil who had taken a bite out of the Devilsbit Mountains to the north. Dull truth proclaims these hills to be made of Silurian Grits and the Rock of Cashel is Carboniferous Limestone. We went off to look at Cahir Castle.

It is a 15th–16th century Butler stronghold, the largest of its period in Ireland, though small compared to the great fortresses of Wales, say, and its setting in the river made it virtually impregnable. Yet it capitulated on three occasions – to our benefit. Restoration work continues but even now it gives a clear picture of its period. It is small and delightful, with ward within ward, corner towers and battlements, portcullis gateway – everything one imagines a castle to be. It was captured by Cromwell, of course. Touring Ireland with English parties becomes almost embarrassing so often does one say of a ruin "destroyed by Cromwell". From Strongbow to the Black and Tans, Irish history is all struggles against the English.

We had another ice-cream and pushed on, for we wanted to camp on the hills above. The main heat of the day caught us as we reached the forested steeper slopes and no matter how the track zig-zagged we could find no shade. The map was quite inadequate; we could discover no water to pitch by and end the sweat bath. We turned up the hillside, on even steeper ground, towards a deep glen and rejoiced when the track approached its lip, but the glen watercourse had dried up.

We recovered from that shock and went on upstream. Five minutes later we came on miserable seepage pools rather than a flow, but it was water. We cooked in the cool depths by the stream. The sun is best enjoyed by those sitting in the shade. Storm had his usual game with a squirrel, a red one this time, but proved no better at climbing oak trees than he had been with pine trees. The evening light twinkled into our retreat, catching a thousand wings of buzzing insect life. The evening coolness came like a balm. The last few days had been grim work. Would it be rewarded? Just one more 'good' day?

We carried our gear up above the tree line and pitched by the grey slopes of burnt heather. Home is a hill.

Thursday 30 August   A GALTYMORE TRAVERSE
The logbook sounded somewhat different at the end of the day: "A walk of real bliss for a change! Even plenty of time and if proof is needed that road miles batter worse than hill miles today gave it; it was as hot but we ended fresh and strong instead of grilled and wabbit."

The early part of the day took us up a dried, rocky succession of hills. Much of it was beyond the map's rough delineating and there has been a great deal of planting on both sides of the range. The kindling sun rose in rather garish colours from a cloud sea which seemed to cover the whole country. There were some lush fraughans (*blaeberries*) to eat. The rock kept breaking out, like carbuncles, from the wounded flesh of the hills. It was rough as concrete and formed edges and tors. The first 2,000er was a mere bump but I was set on missing nothing over the 'Wall' height. Of course, not having that list, nor the new guide, I later found we had missed some outliers. Good, we can return.

Both sun and rain can so easily become bullies unless kept in their places by the wind. Today's bliss was largely due to sun and wind working politely together. The Irish miles were smiling. Every bump we climbed was higher than the last so the view eastwards reminded me of those Russian dolls, one inside the other; each peak had another, each paler in tone, smaller, fading away into the rosy sky of morning. It was superb.

Westwards, only one hill showed at a time: bigger, higher, unrelenting and seemingly endless in number. The going was good, on grass, while almost every col had the bogs filleted from past peat-cutting.

There was one particularly fine view over the inset Loch Muskry (a classic armchair corrie complete with water cushion) along to the cone of Galtymore. O'Loughnan's Castle was very clear: a squat, square, crenellated tower until it is approached off Greenane when it disintegrates, as if by magic, into a crumbly conglomerate outcrop. It *must* be a place of legends just as these are hills for the heroes of old. Greenane is An Grianan, the *Summer Bower*, which is suggestive, or maybe the name is connected with summer grazing in past centuries. A ruin at 2,400 ft may be a booley (our Scot's shieling) but the Famine in the mid-nineteenth century largely destroyed that custom. Turf (peat) is still cut, and stacks and bags of it line many odd corners.

This traverse was particularly rewarding as all too often, when with others, I had been the solitary car owner so had to turn back rather than go on. Our base was usually Ballydavid Wood, a youth hostel at the east end of the Vale of Aherlow which forms a green northern edge to the Galtees. It is a long white farmstead building dominated by a huge oak tree. The warden was telling me that a famous historian lived there and used to sit under the tree to work. She made it sound quite recent, but Father Geoffrey Keating died in the seventeenth century.

We skirted Galtybeg (though going over it is as easy) for we were looking for water to make tea, if possible before the well known spring on the pull up to Galtymore. This gush never seems to dry, though it does not descend to Loch Dineen below as expected but by-passes it. Galtymore Mountain, 3,018 ft, is the only point over Munro altitude, though a West Top cannot be far off it. It is a spendid summit and classically Irish. Today the weather was too hazy for far views, though the nearest big neighbours, the Knockmealdowns, rose high above the cloud sea. It is the downward view that is remembered, for the range sweeps up in a single rise from great plains – a patchwork quilt of green fields, stitched together with hedgerows, dotted with white farms and frequently hazy with the sweet turf reek, which I've often enough smelt on the summit, just as I've heard the clear laughter of children drift up. It is a beauty that has a poignancy for the Scot conditioned to his hills rising from a brown desert. Under different historical circumstances this might have been our view yet. Ignorant agricultural misuse and anything but innocent human abuse has made it otherwise. The gain is Ireland's.

There are various plaques and stumps of old storm-damaged crosses on top and a newer white-painted cross beside which Storm posed for a picture. This cross was erected by the Tipperary Adventure Sports Club in 1975. (Tipperary lies northwards in the rich farmland of the Golden

Vale, a town which seems to have sidestepped the worst of turbulent history.) Another memorial was to a James Blake from Golden who drowned in 1964 while life-saving at Tangier in Morocco. A text from Isaiah proclaimed, "Thus saith the Lord: Get thee up upon a high mountain" and in Gaelic was written *Buadha Barr na Binne* which led to one of those odd chains of connections. This translates *Victory on top of the Mountain* (Gaelic Ireland is as liberal with the term 'mountain' as Gaelic Scotland is prodigal) which seemed odd for a death at sea level, but in a book of Richard Hayward's which I'd bought in Dublin I discovered that this was the motto on the button-hole badge awarded to all members of the Kilfeacle Beagles who made an ascent to Dawson's Table (as the highest point is called) during a Whit meet. (Being off-season it is the humans, not the hounds, who make the ascent.) Hayward gives a description of one of these sociable events. The Galtees *the mountains of the woods* are, as he calls them, a "magnificent huddle of peaks". The last plaque I noticed was inscribed "Richard Hayward O.B.E., D.Litt., J.P. Belfast. Gentleman. Scholar. Naturalist . . ." He was a writer of a series of fine Irish Travel books, each delightfully illustrated with drawings. "The wilderness and the solitary place shall be glad for them" (which is also Isaiah).

A small cross is stuck in the cairn of the West Top from which there is a steep drop to some fine bog-bergs and a sinuous wall which runs over several summits to Lyracappul. Slievecushnabinnia had a tumulus on its East Top, and Temple Hill, later, was a huge mound of stones, a hundred paces in diameter about which no book I've checked has anything to say. Carrignabinnia is 2,697 ft, Lyracappul 2,712 ft, and Temple Hill 2,579 ft – and as the northern slopes are as steep as ever they give hill walking of continuing high quality.

Temple Hill is the last big peak of the range though the Ballyhoura Hills continue westwards. I had posted a parcel to Mitchelstown, which was to prove an error as we were forced into road walking again. We met a caterpillar vehicle wending towards the summit which turned out to be the Irish Ordnance Survey at work, catching up on what the British mapped 150 years ago. They were up to build a trig pillar. A year before, on the Knockmealdowns, our gang met some surveyors who asked if there was a trig on top. On being told there was, their reaction was, "Good, then we don't have to check" – a rather different attitude to our own Ordnance Survey.

There are many approaches to Galtymore from both south and north as the guide shows. A youth hostel to the south, at Mountain Lodge, can be linked with Ballydavid Wood in a good traverse. The best of the hills are covered by an annual west-east traverse on the last Sunday in June. "Stewards are in attendance and certificates are awarded to all finishers." The Irish go in for social hill days in a big way.

We sloped off to the south but the hazy visibility and the poor map left us unsure of things so we just descended to the forests, anyway. Any path south would eventually lead to Mitchelstown. We would camp at the first stream. The first stream was dry and we followed its course downwards feeling this was a repetition we could have done without. We heard the water ahead and came on it, a strong resurgence, which was a relief. To the south of the hills there are some big show caves so perhaps the limestone ran through here too.

We splashed in the burn, washed clothes and enjoyed our day's ebbing. Flying-saucer clouds spelt change and the haze turned to scurrying mist not far above us. It looked like rain, as Noah said. It poured all night: a close-run race across Leinster and Munster. Tally Ho for Killarney!

XI

IRELAND: SHOWERS

Hope is incomprehensible!
For, with sodden skin and blinded eye
And feet well mired from bog and brae,
This battered Hope looks up, to cry:
Tomorrow the rain will go away.

Friday 31 August ... TO THE RIDICULOUS   *Map, p. 187*

We fought through fog and forest to reach a road but had to make a diversion when a bull seemed likely to dispute progress – our only uncongenial encounter with the walkers' friend. We collected our parcel as soon as the post office opened and sat on the Mitchelstown square for the usual messing about. It must have been market day the day before – sweepers were busy clearing up the debris. They stopped to admire Storm. A garrulous drunk could not understand what we were doing, until I told him I liked doing my Christmas parcels early; he seemed quite content with *that* explanation. Two women came along, one obviously blind, and her sighted companion asked if I would allow her to touch the dog. Storm played up as Storm can, while the delicate hands ran over his face and fur. "Lovely, lovely," she quietly muttered. It was rather touching. They both thanked me profusely before walking on.

We took the main road for its verges were good and we wanted to 'eat' some miles. By Kildorrey, however, the local greetings were "Soft", which we took as referring to the weather rather than ourselves. It was hard 'soft' before long. We had an hour off during one bad spell by the Awbeg River. A *Blackwood's Magazine* was sacrificed, page by page, as I read in the drenching rain. We were back to a plod, plod progression, broiled in waterproofs as a change from being grilled. Mallow never seemed to come and nearly five hours of walking in the rain made us feel as if we had mallow even in our bones. Mitchelstown was 20¾ miles back according to a sign.

Mallow was a spa (Scott visited it), and a sort of medicinal cleanness still makes it an attractive town. Anthony Trollope was Surveyor of Posts

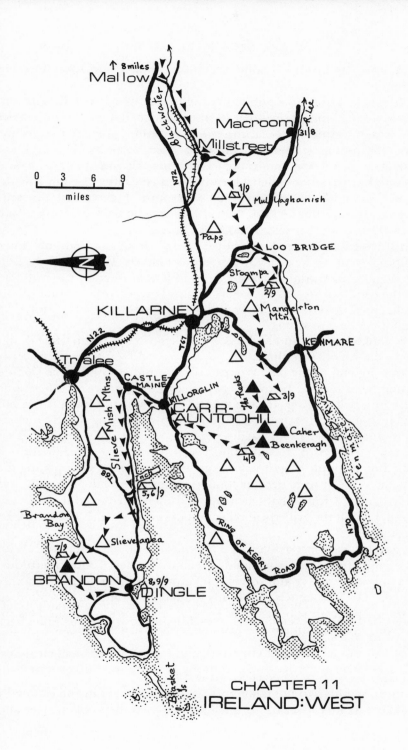

↑ 8 miles
Mallow

Macroom

Millstreet

R. Lee

31|8

0   3   6   9
miles

Mullaghanish

1/9

Paps

N72

LOO BRIDGE

Stoompa

2/9

Mangerton Mtn.

KILLARNEY

KENMARE

N22

Tralee

CASTLE-
MAINE

KILLORGLIN

The Reaks

CARR-
AUNTOOHIL

3/9

Caher

Beenkeragh

4/9

Slieve Mish Mtns.

N86

T67

Inch

5, 6|9

Kenmare River

N70

Brandon
Bay

Slievanea

7/9

BRANDON

8, 9/9

DINGLE

RING OF KERRY ROAD

Blasket Is.

CHAPTER 11
IRELAND: WEST

in Mallow. Its history is long and bloody, there are some fine old buildings.

We spent an hour in a pub to dry slightly (drinking Irish Cream) and then went on hoping a clearance meant a change. It did – to even heavier rain. There was no proper camp site I was told. I sheltered under the bridge (dripping stalactites), dithered over a lay-by that said NO TEMPORARY DWELLINGS, but by the Race Course I'd run out of steam and was standing irresolute when a tweedy, horsy type, after chatting a while, offered us a lift to Millstreet or Macroom. I explained my self-propulsion rules but he said, "Oh, I'll bring you back first thing." Ah well – there is some proverb about gift horses. . .

Millstreet was in the throes of preparing for an International Show Jumping event the next day so a bed was unlikely. We crossed the hills (the Boggeragh Mountains rising to 2,118 ft in Musheramore; names to suit the conditions) and one scruffy dog and owner were decanted at the Castle Hotel in Macroom. They took us in, and we were to be picked up at eight the next morning.

We funked dinner and had a skiddly picnic in our room while things dried a bit. An old war film, *Circle of Deception*, on TV made a ridiculously contrasting end to the day. We read till late and enjoyed some singing coming from the bar below. At two o'clock in the morning I became aware of a bell ringing. It rang on and on. It was not loud, it was not regular, but it was persistent and quite sleep-destroying. By five o'clock it was still ringing. I had hardly slept or, when I did, simply created nightmares out of it. I even wondered if it was in my imagination. I slipped on a couple of garments to go and investigate. On opening the door the noise at once became louder, almost like a telephone but was too irregular. I found light switches and then discovered it was a bell indeed, behind the grilled-off reception desk. An alarm? Then why had nobody come?

Thoughts were interrupted by a hammering on the front door. With some misgivings I was persuaded to let a man enter. To my querulous, "I'm only a guest here and you haven't given me much sleep," he calmly replied, "Oh, I'm a guest too. I only wanted in." – and off he trotted up the stairs – perfectly sober as far as I could judge. He was an object lesson in pertinacity if nothing else – just one Irishman, anywhere, will ensure things are never dull.

Saturday 1 September   TRAVELLING HOPEFULLY

My promised lift had not come by 8.30 a.m. so I went in and claimed a breakfast. At nine I set off to hitch. We crossed the swollen river and branched off, like the bear, for the other side of the mountain. Horse-boxes galore passed and then I was picked up by a lad going to the show. At the top of the hill I hid my rucksack and simply kept a carrier bag of waterproofs, some food and Nevil Shute's *No Highway*. Millstreet was milling. There was no bus to Mallow. After half an hour a reporter picked us up and politics, the Mullaghmore events and our doings were gone over in turn. I suppose giving lifts is one way of finding 'copy'. We were dropped off a yard from where we had started the overnight capers.

I felt I knew the Blackwater pretty well by then. We abandoned the main road at Lombardstown to escape being mowed down by a horse box and read most of the way back to Millstreet. We passed under Mount Hillary, at Father Murphy's Bridge we swung down valleywards again as our road ran on into a welter of wet-looking hills, then we companioned the railway which presumably would bring me eastwards again if I ever made it to Brandon. We fled Millstreet (after an ice-cream, of course) and the brae up was pleasant having 1. dry weather, 2. no perspiration, 3. no rucksack to burden and 4. a good book. I was glad to reach the rucksack to have a brew. Thereafter it was 1. wet weather, 2. sweaty going, 3. a burden of rucksack and 4. a book which I had just finished.

We ran into conifer plantings but eventually gained bare moors which were smoking like a battlefield, an impression accentuated by the peat cuttings and trenches. My boots slowly soaked through. In that wasteland the rain came down, not in twiggy showers, but heavier than it was to do on the whole trip. It was impressive: a tropical downpour that numbed the hand holding the compass and sucked all warmth out of the landscape. We ran into a tree plantation and guessed, correctly, that a road would run not far inside the forest. A mile or so on I was only too glad to pitch the tent, hiding it deep in the young trees for shelter. A gale was forecast.

Later it cleared, the cloud blowing in tattered flags across the sky. The rucksack and dog's towel were hung to dry and we went for a brief reconnoitering stroll as we had ended well up from the Clydagh River which we were supposed to be following downstream. Mullaghanish, 2,133 ft, sited above us, had a tall TV mast which gave an illusion of negligible distance to the top. We went up and if our legs were weary the view rewarded the unexpected effort: running into the explosive brightness of the west were The Paps, Crohane, Mangerton and the Macgillycuddy Reeks themselves. The magic west. "Thalassa!"

Sunday 2 September   BETTER THAN ARRIVING

Sunset from top of Mullaghanish meant supper by candlelight. August was away, the declining months were on us, the months of "rain-laden westerlies". There is an almost gruey cold ring to the repetitive *-ber* months – sighing September, brosy October, nasty November, dreary December – and we still had to reach the coast, climb the Welsh 3,000ers, walk Wales end-to-end, and on by the long limb of South West England. It was quite frightening, but as "ane by ane maks ane an a", we could simply plod on, day by day, mile by mile. If need be I could echo R.L.S., "Not to autumn will I yield, Not to winter even!"

We followed our stream down to the Clydagh which we managed to cross fairly soon. The waters had been as chattery and busy as an office full of typists but began to pause now and then in pools, quiet as tea breaks. We reversed the progress, for after dumping the sack we followed another stream up for Caherbarnagh 2,239 ft, a sheltered approach leading to a windy summit dome. Perhaps this was the gale we did not have in the night. It contested every step but blew the clouds away, and the descent of the Clydagh Glen became a joyous tramp taken in holiday mood. The air was pungent with the scent of bog myrtle, and the roadside walls and banks were thick with brambles and blaeberries. Even the dog took to picking the berries to eat. The glen descended between the Derrynasaggart Mountains to the south and The Paps to the north. Da Chioch Dhana (*the breasts of Dana*) both have prehistoric burial cairns on top and there are plenty of legends and superstitions connected with the region, but neither the new guidebooks nor Pochin Mould say anything about the hills I'd been up.

At the impressive gorge spanned by Poulgorm Bridge we lay and read for an hour before going along to Loo Bridge Youth Hostel, which is part of a long-closed railway station. The warden remembered our Braehead visit of almost fifteen years before. We had arrived from Brandon to find the hostel officially closed for redecorating but we were welcomed in nevertheless – and promptly given paint brushes. The warden baked scones for the gang and we all enjoyed our unconventional stay.

We walked three miles along to Aghnanus Bridge and somewhere above it perched the tent by a cheery waterfall deep in the sheltering wood. We were now into the wilder, rougher scenery of Kerry: scoured mountains with cauldron corries, deep furze-brittle valleys, and small farms, like crofts, which coaxed fodder from every bit of decent soil. It is very like some parts of western Wales or western Scotland.

Monday 3 September   MANGERTON MOUNTAIN

I set my alarm for five; the darkness was pitch black. A car's lights down in the valley winked like a fallen star. Pale, pearly day came at 6.30 a.m. Darkness had fallen at 9 p.m. It had caught me out the previous night and my log-book scrawl grew larger and larger and more erratic as I struggled, line by line, to keep the record up to date. We were loath to leave one of the bonniest sites of the trip but there were miles to go and promises to keep. Mangerton Mountain, 2,756 ft, really is a mountain: a great sprawl with Glenacappul and its three paternoster lakes perhaps only surpassed by the similar splendour of Brandon's eastern corrie.

The map did not show the huge afforestation barrier but by using the compass carefully, plus some luck, we took all the correct forks of the forestry roads to gain maximum height. A fire break then led up out of the forest with some difficulty as it went very much against the bold lie of the exposed rock strata. By the time we escaped the trees we were dripping with sweat. The tea was just ready when the wind dropped and the midges swarmed out. The tea was therefore drunk on the trot.

The landscape had the rocky, boggy mix of Sutherland and it was enjoyable to have to tease away at making a route. It was not a place in which to risk a broken ankle. We came over a rise to see a loch with Stoompa beyond – not on the plan, but temptingly near so we went for it – and discovered the great corrie on its flank: Glenacappul, *the Horses' Glen*, corrie inside corrie, each with its eye of water, a sweeping curve carved out by glaciers. Another corrie and lochan, the Devil's Punch Bowl, bites in from the opposite side, and a narrow crest alone separates them, pointing north from the boggy whaleback of Mangerton. It is a mountain which needs frequent visits even to begin an acquaintance. The guide book gives many routes but I did not have one with me, so I went over untracked wilds. Today was hardly even a reccy, for the mist gained Stoompa more quickly than we did.

The corrie rim simplified navigation for the return. We went out the northern ridge but it was not really the Carn Mor Dearg Arête I had hoped for. The bearing for Mangerton led over decaying peat bogs and gravels and pools, a tundra-like mixture, but we hit the cairn all right.

An irrepressible Irish lad once reached the top of Mangerton at two o'clock – he had looked at his watch to check. A plummy-speaking Englishman arrived just after and asked, "I wonder, old chap, can you tell me the time?" The other wet a finger and held it up, then peered dramatically to all points of the compass, knelt to pat the ground then looked up to say, "Two minutes past two." The Englishman wandered round the cairn and met another walker. "Can you tell me the time please?" he asked again. The other glanced at his watch, "Just after two." The Englishman gasped! Retelling the story later he said, "I know the Irish live close to nature, but that was fantastic."

Another bearing led us off towards the south west. It was featureless enough to make the compass work interesting, sometimes steering from tussock to tussock, but we came below clouds at about 2,300 ft. We stopped to work out what we were suddenly seeing from this other side of our mountain. It was a big, open view, sweeping from immediate roughness over many hills and lochs to the indeterminate horizontals of a sea horizon – the western ocean of our dreams.

I was so delighted to be on what felt like home ground that I wasted some more time collecting all the 2,000 ft bumps I could ascertain from map and ground. We did everything on the list but on Stoompa had missed out a Top – which is what you risk with unplanned escapades. There were plenty of red deer about or else we chased the same herd round and round and in and out that looney, lunar landscape. When sanity caught up (we had run out of all potential bumps) we had a paddle in Triangle Lake, a blue reflective pool which really was turquoise. The Reeks had cleared, and flowed, like a decorative Arabic text, between Purple Mountain on the right and the jumble of Kerry peaks on the left. This was encouraging. If it stayed fair we could surely lodge on or under them.

Not long afterwards we were in the toils. My logbook was plaintive but did not exaggerate one bit: "The hot sun was out, the midges were out, and the landscape was out – out to get us, with every known and unknown rough nastiness. For a solitary wanderer, laden, it was the most dangerous going I've ever known in our islands. Even Storm the sure-footed was constantly in trouble, beaten by the tangle of long grass or falling through booby-trapped holes into water. The best going was on the boulders of the stream, when there were any. It's a route I would thoroughly recommend to all my best enemies. I will not forget Galway's river in a hurry."

Hindsight does not reduce its position of unique nastiness though perhaps the Rhinogs tried. Few steps could be taken with any certainty of their outcome, a combination that destroyed all rhythm or mental relaxation. We found a breezy slab in mid-stream, just above forest level, so were able to stop for a brew and regain our composure. Our picnic is remembered with relish, so easily do good and bad step on each other's heels. Among the shady oaks we picked up the path to Shaking Rock and then a small road took us down to Galway's Bridge, with its church buried in a jungle of rhododendron bushes beside the busy tourist road above the Lakes of Killarney. A car drew in and I asked the couple if they would be kind enough to post a film and some letters for me. They would hardly wind the window down to talk, refused my request with obvious fear and drove off hurriedly. . . .

We walked up to Ladies' View, a spot made busy from guidebook instructions to stop and wonder there. The view is of a Trossachs-like mini-landscape of charming rather than grand scenery. There are scores better within a mile or two; but they require walking. Judging by the sunbathing flesh on display not many there would be capable of walking. We had a quick coffee, *Coke*, glass of milk and a ham sandwich and then fled, down the rough hillside towards the Upper Lake. Carrauntoohil was gathering clouds out of the clear sky. The oakwoods have wild growths of the *arbutus* (strawberry tree) and various plots were fenced off for botanical studies.

We followed a made path along to Lord Brandon's Cottage which was a Visitors' Centre and tea room. The latter was not open so we had a brew for I was suddenly feeling both weary and unwell. A trip into the rhoddies confirmed an attack of diarrhoea. Along the Cummeenduff Glen road we resisted Bed and Breakfast signs and an invitation to camp in a field where they were hay-making and the known charm of Black Valley Youth Hostel. Very slowly we bullied on to reach the stream from Lough Googh, our objective. As we felt a bit like the loch's name we did not make it. It was too late and I was too weak. We camped on a grassy flat and spent most of the night rushing in and out the tent with successive emergencies. The weather was revoltingly muggy and midgy. Coils were kept smoking all night. In the morning we went on simply because anything was preferable to staying where we were. It should have been one of the great camp sites of the trip. It was memorable, of course.

Tuesday 4 September   THE MACGILLYCUDDY REEKS AND NUMBER FOUR
By morning the worst was over and I forced down some muesli and milk for I had to try and gain some strength (such an upset is enervating) before the traverse of the Reeks. I had supplies enough, indeed had gained an extra night's rations, so was more worried at the weather's condition than my own. The clag was right down and it was ominously grim and windless. E. A. Baker, writing of the Reeks in the *Cairngorm Club Journal* similarly set off "in a Scotch mist that might have been distilled on the skirts of Ben Nevis."

We went up steadily and slowly, with frequent rests, each time pushing more food into a weary tummy and slowly, over the day, regained full strength again so that it was all forgotten till I sat by the tent in the soft sun of sunset to write up that day and the previous one in my diary. They were a right pair as the left foot said to the right.

The pull up was very steep. The cloud began to move when we were still below the crest – we could see Lough Gooch below us as if it were racing across the hillside. A wind welcomed us to the ridge, more or less at the spot I had studied the day before; I dumped the sack and set off with relief to tackle the titillations of the eastern end of the Ridge of the Reeks. If you go far enough east you come to the Gap of Dunloe. An annual traverse event begins there and it is a great place for tourists who go for rides in pony traps.

The Macgillycuddy Reeks are a glacier-eaten barrier of old mountain, high and long and positioned to catch all the weather the west may blow. Their full traverse is a grand walk with some good scrambling for topping and tailing the day. Carrauntoohil, 3,414 ft, Ireland's highest, throws our jagged sickle-shaped ridges to encircle a pair of spectacle-lochans in the resulting western corrie while running east is an un-dulating succession of Tops, the Ridge of the Reeks proper. To traverse the lot (as any Munro-bagger must do) is one of the best of ridge walks, in the top handful that seconds the Cuillin pre-eminence. From trial and error I would now recommend those with only one car to start and finish from the youth hostel to the north, an old schoolhouse by the Gaddagh River. Make for Lough Cummeennapeasta (in which there is a crashed American plane) and up the red boulders to Cruach Mhor. The names and heights of the eastern 3,000 ft extremity are variously given (Cruach, Cruagh Mor) but the peak wanted is unmistakable as it has a large cemented cairn on it. Some scrambling leads west from it, which can give trouble to gentler-walking types, but all too soon the green switchback starts which eventually leads up Carrauntoohil itself. Before going up this last rise, move across the flank to go out and back for the Caher ridge arm, then, after the summit, go on round the western corrie, again with scrambling (more easily skirted) to end on Beenkeragh. Descend carefully off it to regain the start. With two cars other varieties are possible but what they gain in some respects they lose in others. The above would be my first choice.

Our problem was that the Reeks lay as a great barrier across the general coast-to-coast line. Doing them and winning beyond would be hard work by whatever route and method used. If we had stayed at Black Valley and done them without a rucker then they still would have to be crossed. I took what felt like a reasonable compromise. It gave me the fine scramble to Cruach Mhor *twice* as we simply came back again after reaching it. It would have been enjoyed more had I not felt so fragile. The rising wind made it interesting. The gusts rushed up, gasped out exciting things, and ran off again to whistle along the crest. The game ended on the big, made cairn of the Cruach.

The hollow in it shows it to have been constructed as a shrine and it was in September, 1969 that a Braehead party arrived in cloud as thick as today's to find an old man on a ladder at work painting the niche. All the cement, water, paint, ladder, everything, had been carried up from his home at Ballyledder below. We debated whether this was an act of devotion or a penance. He thought we were all daft and could see no point in walking in the hills until one of the boys pointed out that I did it for my wages. "Ah, that makes it all right," the old man replied. On our next visit the ladder and paint pots were lying about and the niche was empty, and never has been filled. I still wonder if the old man had died, or what lay behind the abandoned task.

Storm delighted in the scrambling and needed restraint rather than encouragement. The easiest line in many cases is the exposed crest. In places the ridge is only a wafer of the rock strata in thickness. We arced back – down and up the splendid mile – to Knocknapeasta and then it was all grassy golf-course going with plenty of divots lying about to show where players had gone for a slip. The grass is not at all adhesive. Top followed top for the one man and his dog. At the col before Carrauntoohil (where the tourist route reaches the crest from Hag's Glen up the Devil's Ladder) it was raining and I almost considered camping for there is a spring not far above and I could do with some extra puff. It was very windy, however, and after some food and a brew we continued up and across to the Caher arm. It becomes quite exposed, too, but has a good path to the highest point on the crest. There is a conical, grassy bump of a Top beyond (Cahernaveen on some lists) which is easy to overlook in cloudy conditions. Coming up from the west in mist it is frequently taken as the summit proper, as E. A. Baker had discovered in 1907. We battled back into the wind, which had been assisting us previously, and five minutes from the top of Carrauntoohil the clouds tore apart dramatically. We raced for the summit cross and just failed to make it before the cloud returned. We collapsed in the lee of the cairn feeling utterly puggled – not the ending I had envisaged for the walk between the Four Country Summits.

Then we experienced a little miracle. The weather cleared. The clouds broke, not below us, but around and above so that we looked over a white maelstrom, the sort of view one often has from an aircraft, but here made glorious by tingling senses. Above us there were flying saucers of wind clouds in the blaze of sky. I whooped for joy and blazed away until both cameras ran out of film. No picture could capture it for the wonder was all-enveloping, it came and went, changing moment by moment, a surfing, tumbling, explosive marvel which called for worship rather than mundane photography. The cross on the summit was perhaps justified and is at least better than all the man-glorifying litter on so many other highest summits.

This cross (of metal-box construction) bore the date 1976, and originally a small windmill was installed to provide power to light coloured lamps on the extremities of its arms. The lamps alone survive. The cloud moved to give brief views to Beenkeragh, the other arm of the western horseshoe, and it kept coming and going while we made the most of the scramble between. Baker, and many since have failed to link them in mist. (The ridge is not a direct line, for there is a bite of corrie off-setting it.) Baker also made rude comments about the map – does nothing change?

Beenkeragh, 3,314 ft, Ireland's second-highest summit, rises boldly above the hidden corrie in its heart. The ridge is a chaos of sandstone structures which are easily enough bypassed but well worth scrambling over. At several places the fossilised ripple marks of a prehistoric shore can be seen, and what looks like Nancy Pretty (London Pride), the mountain flower, St. Patrick's Cabbage. We went on over a couple of bumps to Skregmore, 2,790 ft, but the cloud followed us, height by height, so we turned down towards the twin lochs, which look like a filled-in figure of 8. The wind was doing its best to empty the lochs, and spray dashed off the surface in all directions. It is a vast cauldron of a corrie and impressive in any condition.

We escaped down the Coomloughra Glen then swung north to follow an odd level ridge flanking under Skregbeg. We camped on a fine breezy, midge-proof hump, above the ridge-held stream, with a view over the patchwork Killorglin plains to the Slieve Mish Mountains and the Dingle peninsula. We could see our destination, though Brandon Mountain, like the Reeks above us, never cleared but spat up black clouds like an active volcano. Glencar lay below us – where Oisin, back from his 300 years in the land of youth, reined in his white steed and eyed the wild land for his Fiana band with whom he had so often hunted. The same tale is told of Glen Lyon and many other places. Our shared Celtic heritage makes me feel very much at home in Ireland.

Wednesday 5 September   ROUND DINGLE BAY
The exposed site caught the wind when it rose to a gale which gave the

Tramp a good testing, but I had no sleep for a second night and set off rather blearily for the fleshpots of Killorglin. The Reeks were holding back a great mass of cloud which every now and then broke over them like angry waves, or escaped round the ends to stream across the sky. We followed an old turf road which had juicy brambles in its unkempt hedges. Storm enjoyed sniffing out rabbits. I whacked a bull off our way – seen end-on I had failed to notice its sex. I don't usually go bashing bulls. In Killorglin we picked up a parcel. The bags of muesli in it had burst. Storm's towel had blown away on the Reeks so I bought a new one. Killorglin straddles the River Laune which drains the Killarney Lakes. It is an unpretentious place most of the time but has an annual Puck's Fair which attracts most of the gypsies in Ireland. A puck goat is hoisted to a perch high above the square (a rite going back to pre-Christian times) where it presides over the buying and selling of horses, cattle and sheep, and all attendant revelry.

As we left the locals were bringing in the milk churns by donkey cart or newer mini tanker-trailers. I had hardly seen donkeys this year. Ireland's agriculture is obviously doing all right, judging by the modernising we had seen everywhere. New bungalows seemed to be going up, though people still live in the country: the towns, which start and stop bluntly, with little in the way of suburbs, are simply markets, business centres, meeting places, full of character and never intended to deal with modern traffic. I hope neither town nor country loses its present character. Ireland's domestic architecture is unique.

We reached Castlemaine (the castle was destroyed by Cromwell) for lunchtime, and the long road walk to Inch is best forgotten for it rained most of the time. Verges of montbretia were soaking and overhung with hedges of fuchsia, the symbol of Kerry history: red drops from the green. Inland the bulk of the Slieve Mish were smothered in cloud. Murphy's Bar was the only bright spell. In it they were talking Gaelic. All the signs of the west.

We had hoped for accommodation, but the hotel was NO DOGS so we just camped behind the dunes of the Strand where there was a (temporarily?) abandoned camp site with caravans and tents still using it despite a lack of water. I read *The Riddle of the Sands* (the film was on in Killorglin) till my candle burnt out. The pounding of surf reminded of home. The scent of it even wrapped our sleep.

Thursday 6 September   THE MILES ON THE INCH
The miles of empty sand were not to be resisted. We stayed for a day of salt-breezed pleasure, wandering in to the shop with a German honey-

moon couple and their horse-drawn caravan, and wandering out along the four miles of this odd arm of sand that almost reaches the other shore of the Dingle Bay estuary, which is one of the many fjord-like *rias* in the south west. Storm raced about like blowing bracken, chasing sanderling along the foamy edge of the sea or romping in and out and over the dunes of marram grass. It was a barefoot day of bliss. On the concrete above the Strand someone had painted two lines:

> Dear Inch must I leave you? I have promises to keep
> Perhaps miles to go to my next sleep

Friday 7 September   "OCCASIONAL SHOWERS"
We set off in an absolute calm: a visual (and audible) grey that left us wondering what it meant. The forecast was the stock in trade "occasional showers". We followed along the *corniche* road. The fuschia hedges were high as trees at times, a rain of bruised colours in the treeless landscape. We swung inland to Anascaul, *ford of the heroes* (unknown), where the South Pole Inn hints at more recent heroes. Tom Crean came here after many polar adventures. He was awarded the Albert medal for saving "Evans of the Broke" in grim circumstances, he was in the party that recovered the bodies of Scott and his companions and he was one of those who made the boat journey with Shackleton (also Irish) which is perhaps the greatest of all true survival stories and made Shackleton my first hero, towering over poor Scott who made mistakes and paid a bitter price.

We left the village against the stream of the morning milk-collecting and the school-bound children who would fall silent at our passing and then gaze, whispering, after us. Winthrop Young in his poem 'Brandon Bay' catches the atmosphere and describes the "peat-brown children" watching from the walls, shy as seagulls.

We had a break by Loch Anascaul, where a robin was singing his autumn song, and sat out a sudden shower under some hawthorn trees before climbing steeply up behind Knockmulanune into cloud. I kept the dog close. The Irish have a detestable habit of poisoning their land and many a good dog has died in agony instead of the fox. We felt our way to a whispering lochan and edged up over a hill to Windy Gap beyond. We had brief glimpses of lochs down both sides and some wild empty country in the interior, a layered landscape, sweeping up from level to level until lost in the cloud. We climbed Gowlane Beg and then on to Croaghskearda which proved a bold prow overlooking the sea. We promised to come back some day and walk right along all these hills of the Dingle peninsula. Decayed peat hags littered the slopes. We wandered out north to visit another Top and collected just one shower, which lasted the day out.

At the top of Slieveanea the detail had been rubbed off my map, at the fold; I had to make a couple of casts in opposite directions to work out the lie of the land and identify the precipitous northern slopes. We broke down through them, south of Lough Doon, to the Conair Pass road below its summit brae, and swithered about what to do. In full water-proofs, our feet soaking, the time was only 3.40 p.m. so the weather could clear for a fine evening. Taking a flanker below the cloud to gain Brandon's base, the hillside down to Lough Clogharee in the Owenmore Valley was rough, with overgrown boulders, and the small stream flowing from the loch proved surprisingly difficult to cross. The ground was saturated by now, for our shower went on and on as if deter-mined to wash Brandon away before we could reach it. Down the Cloghane road we turned up over small furze-held fields of the moun-tainy farms to gain my favourite corrie, the heart of my favourite moun-tain, Brandon the blessed. Collie, Winthrop Young, Praeger and many others all thought highly of this sea-moated peak. Even Joss Lynam, a Galway man, admits its superiority.

There were no favours today. The jutting crags jagged blackly into the clouds and long tassels and veils of water hung down everywhere. We kept above Lough Cruttia, *the harp lake*, hoping to find some weak zephyr somewhere on the ridge. There was no wind. Up on the next shining level, near Lough Nalacken, *duck lake*, there was a clear stream dodging in and out the red boulderfield, and here I pitched the tent slowly and carefully, peeled off the wet skins and crawled in, looking forward to a drum-up and a chittery bite. I had just set a match to the stove when I received several bites. We had sat ourselves on top of an ants' nest. Willy nilly I had to don skins, take the tent down, find another spot beyond the range of the wee red devils – and start all over again. It had rained non-stop and simply wept on into the darkness; but at least, here, without the icy malignity of inland rain.

Saturday 8 September BRANDON MOUNTAIN
The rain stopped at 8 a.m. after a sixteen hour deluge which must have contributed to rainfall statistics. I wonder if weather forecasters are ever conscience-smitten about their erring prognostications? We had slept well and I had even dried out a wet dog and damp banknotes. Apart from a few day-nibbles we breakfasted off all the remaining food. A wagtail landed on the tent, to the dog's amusement – yesterday's main

wildlife interest had been a badger sett with six or seven entrances, sited high in the turf wilderness.

Briefly, Brandon Bay, Kerry Head and the fine strand of Ballyheige gave a delicate, shadowy view but as soon as we had packed and tramped the wind and rain continued in a squally storm. Keeping well up and traversing along above the invisible paternoster lakes, we picked up the Pilgrim path from Faha and Cloghane. In the last, innermost corrie the wind was so violent that I was sometimes sent sliding off along flat polished slabs of rock, yet the headwall was relatively calm and every pockmark in the sandstone seemed to have a fragile flower growing in it. The path twists up brutally. Triangular notices, as for motoring directions, warn AIRE – CNOC GEAR (Care – dangerous Hill) which a Braehead lad once suggested meant "engage low gear". The path joins the main, north-south crest of Brandon Mountain only ten minutes' walk from the summit. However it is a walk on the edge of a thousand foot cliff. The pilgrims must feel they have earned some reward. Brandon is another spelling of Brendan and Brendan is Brendan the Navigator, early Celtic saint and traveller. The ruins on top are of his oratory for it was to this wild height rather than an island that he would retreat to meditate. Obviously he heard two mighty voices for he sailed off, perhaps even to America.

St. Brendan was born near Tralee (the other end of this peninsula) in 483 and was buried 94 years later at Clonfert Monastery in Galway. He was baptized by St. Erc, founded monasteries at Ardfert, Brandon and Clonfert, drew up a monastic rule that lasted virtually to Norman times and made evangelical journeys to Brittany, England, Scotland and the remotest Hebrides. One of the vanished churches on St. Kilda is named after him and there is a Brendan Creek in the Faroes. It is his *Navigatio* however which has continued to fascinate – a Latin account of a voyage which reads rather like the Arabian Nights. This was much copied and translated even before the days of printing. Early Scandinavian voyagers knew of America as *Irland It Mikla* and knew of Brendan's promised land, to which heavenly guidance was given to the saint on top of this mountain. He was absent for seven years, having sailed off in a little fleet of "vessels ribbed within, covered with the hides of oxen tanned with oakbark, with the joints tarred and food in plenty. . .". An accurate description of *curraghs* which has come through all the overpainting of myth and legend, and there were other clues enough for the whole venture to be recreated – successfully – a few years ago.

The story is told in Tim Severin's *The Brendan Voyage* which had kept me engrossed back o' Skiddaw. The story of his search for the materials and the skills to build the *Brendan* is as exciting as the voyage itself. It is interesting to see how modern synthetics failed dismally where old ways and materials stood the strain. Physically the voyage was shown to be possible. Brendan did not receive his name *the Navigator* without justification.

Beside Brendan's oratory on the summit there are several mounds (probably beehive huts) and a well. There is also an ugly cross made of what looks like twisted scaffolding – definitely twentieth century. On May 16th, St. Brendan's Day, pilgrims still visit the peak. In 1868 twenty thousand gathered under the guidance of the famed Dr Moriarty. The line of the Saint's Road comes up the gentle south-west slopes from Ballybrack, my route down, which I followed by compass until below the cloud level. Brandon had been *almost* an anticlimax for I had seen really nothing of the great eastern cliffs and corries, nor of the wide view one expects from the furthest west of all Munros. On a clear day they say you can see America, which is perhaps as likely as a clear day. To be fair I have swum in those high lochs in October, and in April come up to a summit hoary with frost and dancing with sun.

My first visit had been on a blitz with friends Ann, Annabel and Bob when doing all the 3,000ers of Wales and Ireland to complete impatiently the first round of the Munros, etc. We had driven well up above Ballybrack, on steeper and steeper ground until we could go no further, even with the passengers walking. Annabel then dropped a contact lens and Bob and the girls were groping for it while the car was sliding backwards, though I had the brakes hard on. I tooted and tooted only to be given impatient waves by the crawling searchers. Eventually someone realised I was having problems as well. A boulder under a wheel stopped the car from being ditched. We found Annabel's eye. "*Bohreens* are best left for pedestrians", is the moral. On another occasion, alone, I took my Dormobile high on to Galtymore and while up there for two nights the foresters felled and trimmed pine trees over my road out. Having worked in a sawmill I had knack enough to be able to shift the trees and left them neatly stacked to one side. I often wonder what they made of that.

A bit beyond Ballybrack, which is only a hamlet with cow-laid road surfaces, lies Brandon Creek where I have also spent a night in the Dormobile. At some unearthly hour men came down and launched their black *curraghs* and hours later returned. Two women sat at the back of the creek, one above the other, lighted lamps in their hands, to guide the fishermen in. The scaly fish glittered in the pale moonlight as they were thrown on to the slipway and then one by one the curraghs were walked up, like leggy beetles, to be stacked. At dawn all that showed from the night's work were a few drying, blowing scales along the verge. It was from Brandon Creek that the *Brendan* set sail. She wintered in Iceland, where Tilman's battered *Baroque* joined her during the trip I did not make. What did they think of each other, I wonder?

The whole end of this peninsula deserves exploring. The small Oratory of Gallarus is almost like a stone *curragh* and must be one of the most perfect of old Celtic remains. Out on the wild seas beyond Slea Head lie the Blasket Islands which I first saw, on my first day on Brandon, over the haze of spring burnings on the Three Sisters. Local names ring romantic: Smerwick Harbour, Ventry Bay, Mount Eagle, Brandon Head, Dingle. . . . It is one of the Gaelic-speaking areas of Ireland.

Our walk into compact Dingle felt like the ending of our coast-to-coast walk over the Irish 3,000ers. Inch was an indulgent aside; the most aesthetic route would keep high along the spine regardless of wind and weather. Someone in the west was once asked about the Dingle climate. "Climate? Now I don't know if we have much climate. Just lots of weather."

Sunday 9 – Wednesday 12 September   BACK TO DUBLIN

Dingle seemed more lively on Sunday than the day before but there was no bus till Monday. The bus office proved to be in a pub. We took the bus from Dingle to Tralee and then the train from there to Dublin. On the Tuesday I combined with the Lynches to go to a Ben Travers comedy *A Cuckoo in the Nest* at the Gate, and on Wednesday Margaret had a dinner at home so it was a merry night and late. The border produced its share of tales, my favourite being about the problem the rural guards were having many years ago over women smuggling butter. They worked out a fail-safe system. They heated their rooms till they were oven hot and left the likely suspects inside for a while . . .

We were off for an early boat on Thursday – a mere ten minutes' walk this time. On landing in Ireland Storm had come out of his cage covered with fleas and, as these had chosen all the wrong moments to reappear, I was determined there would not be a second dose going back. We were allowed to sneak into a quiet lounge. "Sure, but he's a gorgeous fella."

WALES OF THE WELCOMES

There is pleasure in the pathless woods,
There is a rapture on the lonely shore,
There is a society where none intrudes,
By the deep sea, and music in its roar:
I love not man the less, but nature more,
From these our interviews, in which I steal
From all I may be, or have been before,
To mingle with the universe, and feel
What I can ne'er express, yet cannot all conceal.

BYRON

Thursday 13 September   CROESO CARNEDDAU   *Maps, pp. 204 and 216*
I doubt if the Carnedds are very often climbed from Dublin, but having
caught the early morning *St. Columba*, a train to Bangor, a bus to
Bethesda and a car to Llyn Ogwen, it seemed the natural thing to do.

The tent was pitched with its door to Tryfan just above Ogwen
Cottage (another historic inn which is now an outdoor centre for Birmingham) and we set off as the shepherds began to gather along those
slopes. As we wended our way up heartless Penyrolewen we could see
and hear the beasts across the valley, noisy, darting groups which
merged to form processionary lines, then erratically converged round
the gorge behind Ogwen Cottage before swinging down into the Nant
Ffrancon with the impetuosity of flood water. A solitary six were missed
by the score of men and dogs and jerkily wended back east towards
Tryfan. Some interpret Ffrancon as *beaver* and these beasts were
described in a first-hand account written in 1188 by Gerald de Barri.
They have joined elk, wolves and other beasts which man has destroyed
in Britain.

We climbed up into black clouds which just occasionally let in a flash
of gold. My usual Carneddau weather. From half a dozen wanderings
over its 3,000ers I have only once had a really good day.

Like Gaul, Snowdonia's Munro-region is divided into three:
Snowdon and its satellites in the south, the central Glyders and their

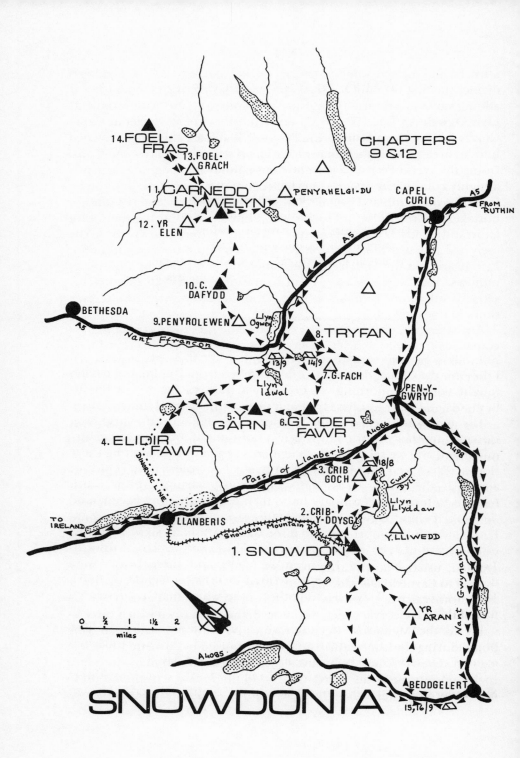

CHAPTERS
9 & 12

14. FOEL-FRAS

13. FOEL-GRACH

11. CARNEDD LLYWELYN

12. YR ELEN

PENYRHELGI-DU

CAPEL CURIG

A5

FROM RUTHIN

10. C. DAFYDD

BETHESDA

9. PENYROLEWEN

Llyn Ogwen

Nant Ffrancon

A5

8. TRYFAN

13/9

14/9

7. G. FACH

Llyn Idwal

5. Y GARN

6. GLYDER FAWR

PEN-Y-GWRYD

4. ELIDIR FAWR

Pass of Llanberis

A4086

A498

Dinorwic Line

3. CRIB GOCH

18/8

Cwm Dyli

Llyn Llyddaw

TO IRELAND

LLANBERIS

Snowdon Mountain Railway

2. CRIB-Y-DDYSGL

1. SNOWDON

Y. LLIWEDD

Nant Gwynant

YR ARAN

A4085

BEDDGELERT

15,16/9

0   ½   1   1½   2
miles

SNOWDONIA

outliers, and the sprawling, northern Carneddau. The Pass of Llanberis divides the first two and had been my route going to Ireland, so it was adding variety to return to the other great division, the Nant Ffrancon-Llyn Ogwen A5 line. The roads east from these passes meet at Capel Curig: the Fourteen Munros and Tops of Wales are therefore crowded into an area smaller than that of Lakeland's Seven Munros and Tops. Doing the Welsh Fourteen is an obvious natural challenge and remains a highly competitive event. A good account of what is involved can be found in the Thomas Firbank classic, *I Bought a Mountain*. If I am not mistaken the record set up by his wife Esmé in 1938 during their joint effort still stands. It was an hour less than the previous man's record. The men had reduced the Snowdon/Foel-fras time to 8 hours 25 minutes. Eric Beard did the Fourteen three times, the last being in 5 hours 13 minutes. Joss Naylor's 1973 record time of 4 hours, 46 minutes, 22 seconds still stands I think – in 1980. One lad has done the round three times in one day!

Any attempts at hill or distance records, now, are highly organised, of course, as in any athletic event: a challenge as different from ordinary hill walking as, say, an Olympic Downhill or Slalom race is from a ski-tour over the Cairngorm plateau. *Chacun à son goût* – as long as I don't have to run!

The logistics of doing the Fourteen as an unsupported one-man-and-a-dog team really ruled out any present attempt, but we could enjoy them as much piecemeal. Even the Carneddau shrink without a load on one's back.

Penyrolewen, 3,211 ft, *the hill of the white ravine*, has several false summits and a top that is rather dull and flat when there is no view to be had. Looking as it does into the dark, giant-hewn cwms of the Glyders, and with Tryfan set on guard, many regard its view as the finest on or from the Carneddau. We saw nothing, but, with the height gained, the walking could be enjoyed for itself and so were the brief views that were granted, usually downwards, to Ffynnon Lloer, *moon fountain*, as we walked to Carnedd Dafydd, 3,423 ft, *the cairn of Dafydd*. There were three prehistoric cairns on the way. The cliffs of Black Ladders steered us on round the huge corrie which drains to Bethesda, a town which owes its name to the Methodist Revival connected with the slate-quarrying boom during the last century. Gravelly slopes led to Carnedd Llywelen, 3,485 ft, *Llywellen's cairn*, which is second only to Snowdon in altitude, a rocky moonscape in the murk. It was odd not to find a trig point on so important a summit. (These brotherly names commemorate the last two defenders of independent Gwynedd against Edward I.) There is a fair descent out to the ragged top of Yr Elen, 3,152 ft, *deer calf*, which has always been a favourite since a snowy winter visit a dozen years ago. From here one can skirt round to the miles of green pasture which lie on the northern hills and plateaux, giving no sense of scale even on a clear day. They are windy heights, fair or foul. Some old exposed piles of rock, almost cairn-like, north of Carnedd Llywelyn, form tors on top of several outliers while others are genuine prehistoric tumuli. The group is well-named.

We had some food on the rocks of Foel-grach, 3,196 ft, *scabby hill*, then discovered a shelter-hut hidden below. A beaten path leads over a rise to the summit of Foel-fras, 3,092 ft, *rough or prominent hill*, which is the last of the Fourteen and must be a real thank-God cairn for those who have come that far. It has a trig point west of a stray length of wall. The ground is strewn with uneven rock – altogether an odd place. There was no view to the Great Ormes Head and the sea. We turned, and in less than an hour were back on Carnedd Llywelyn, *en route* being given the one splendid view of the day when the clouds shifted and Yr Elen appeared like some splendid Alpine peak, brooding over the bright tear-drop of its tiny "corrie lochan" – Ffynon Caseg, *the mare's well* – while beyond rose a symmetrical cone, Elidir Fawr. There are wild ponies on the Carneddau, many-hued, dainty creatures which must nevertheless be tough to live at these heights. Today's surprise was to see their drop-pings on the ridge above Fynnon Llugwy.

Rather than repeat any more ground covered we turned south east over new country, down to Craig yr Ysfa, *crag of craving*, an array of historic climbing crags above lonely Cwm Eigiau, beyond which we found a surprisingly narrow sweep of ridge overlooking clear Fynnon Llugwy. The ridge must be good in winter. It led to Penyrhelgi-du, 2,733 ft, *hill of the black hound*. Tryfan looked like Suilven: cloud-creating and bold. Onwards, to the east, were the *pass of the three knights* and the *slippery hill of the witch* but we had run out of time so simply romped down the long south ridge, picked up the Hydro road and returned to the A5. I met not one person on my round of these big hills which cover more ground than the Glyders and Snowdon combined. Only in the Rhinogs and Carneddau can you escape more than three miles from a motor road in Snowdonia.

Car lights were already beaming along the valley as we came off the hill. An hour's plod along past Mr Williams' farm of Gwern gof Uchaf, where I had camped many times and where a few tents now glowed in the night, brought us back to our tent. Llyn Ogwen lay in fish-scale glitter.

The wind had gone. It was too cold for midges. Tryfan lifted a dark and familiar shape against the ice-bright stars.

On most visits to Snowdonia we have camped under Tryfan. On that 1967 visit Ann, Annabel, Bob and I were without Kitchy (he did the Welsh and Irish peaks later with Braehead parties) so were at a loss why Ann should suddenly sit bolt upright in the tent in the middle of the night gasping, "But we haven't got Kitchy! We haven't got Kitchy!" We said we knew that. "But I just felt him walk across me." In the morning we found a kitten curled up in a corner of the tent.

Friday 14 September   THE GLYDERS
Our British climate suffers from a chronic instability. A "high" was supposed to be moving in but the expected brightness was blown away in a torrent of wind.

> Full many a glorious morning have I seen,
> Flatter the mountain-tops with sovereign eye
> . . . But out, alack, he was but one hour mine,
> The region cloud hath mask'd him from me
> now.
>
> *Shakespeare*

Storm was keener to be off than I was. We wended up our stream to Llyn Bochlwyd where novelty led to changing the plan. Tryfan was abandoned and we went up Y Gribin instead, a long-standing wish. We had seen a helicopter on it yesterday. No helicopter could have operated near it this day. The name means *serrated ridge* which it is, near the top, where the vegetation peters out and bare rock, wind and clouds seem scoured by mighty forces.

Glyder Fach, 3,262 ft, *the small pile*, always reminds me of a builder's yard – so much concrete material lying higgled-piggled – but in the cloud it can be an eerie place when the piles of boulders take on mysterious shapes and even the small Welsh sheep loom large as elephants in the gloom. Pennant visited both Glyders on his *Tours in Wales* (and also Snowdon and Carnedd Llywelyn). As this was a century before Telford's London to Holyhead road (the A5) he must have felt it extraordinarily remote. Kingsley described it as an "enormous desolation, the dead bones of the eldest born of time". Today's woofing wind and the flying sheets of cloud almost enhanced it. We played hide and seek in the summit hedgehog of rocks and then on the Castle of the Winds.

Glyder Fawr, 3,279 ft, *the large pile*, is marginally higher. Its interest lies in the weird "splintery stooks" of rock as Showell Styles calls them. There are three or four of these warts. Both Glyders are fine viewpoints being very much in the centre of the big hills. Storm took my word for it as we saw nothing. Llyn y Cwn, *the dog's pool*, on the next col was doing its best to blow away, so we kept on a safe course till up Y Garn, 3,104 ft, *the rock*, not that the path we followed strayed near the edge till we hit the rim of Cwm Clyd which we followed to the top. The beaten paths and proliferation of cairns are a pity. There are so many that they now confuse rather than help.

We trotted down the rubbishy slope and skirted Foel-goch for there are clear tracks round the head of the Afon Dudodyn leading on to the rising, Caher-like ridge of legendary Elidir Fawr. On it, with Bob, Annabel and Ann I had completed my original round of all the 3,000ers. Brandon had been reserved for the last, but on our outward trip we had had to omit the Glyders or miss our ferry and car hire in Dublin. Elidir was an Englishman who came riding into Wales and married a Prince of Gwynedd's daughter. The Prince died with no son to succeed and Elidir put in a claim only to have local support given to a bastard son who won the ensuing battle. "Carnedd Elidir" is his monument. The *fach* and *fawr* are map nonsense.

Both going and coming from Elidir Fawr we could hear the noise of the Dinorwic hydro scheme construction but the mist refused to shift to allow us to see how things had progressed. A year before I had suddenly looked down into Cwm Marchlyn to a scene which was pure SF. Marchlyn Mawr, *great horse lake*, was dead and the hollow shuddered to the noise of gigantic earth movers and other colossal machines and constructions. This was to be the upper level of a pumped-storage scheme. The power station is dug out underground, a huge hole as deep as a sixteen storey building and spacious enough for two rugby fields – one of the largest man-made caverns anywhere.

We took in Foel-goch, 2,727 ft, *the red hill*, and Yr Esgair, which has a sheer face and a knife edged ridge of character, but these far corries and tops are better for walking than climbing, and the flora is rich. We retraced a bit further and managed to break down perfectly easily into Cwm Cywion, *cwm of the chickens*, from which an easy descending traverse brought us down into Cwm Idwal. We ran into several orange-bright gaggles of walkers, quite a shock, for the last people we'd met on a hill had been on Lugnaquillia on the 26th of August. Carrauntoohil was the only Country Summit we had had to ourselves (and the only one which gave a view) and any one of the other three probably had more people on it than we met on all other hills combined.

The usual jet fighters screamed through the pass – an objectionable feature of this area of special recreational value. Llyn Idwal, 1,223 ft, is named after a son of Owain Gwynedd, Prince of Wales, who was supposedly drowned in its waters. Above it are the Idwal slabs and the great cleft of Twll Du, *the black hole*, more often given as the Devil's Kitchen, the blackest, most devilish cleft in these mountains of myth. Approaching the tent I looked once again on triple-topped Tryfan, a haunted mountain which even altered the flow of Llyn Ogwen's waters from east to west. In Scotland they plant a rowan tree by remote shielings to ward off the evil eye. One grew beside my tent.

As soon as I was bootless, had paddled and brewed, it began to clear. I had a vast curry and rice sitting in the stabs of sun, my back against an ice-carved whaleback of rock which was set at just the right angle. At six o'clock we packed up to reascend the Miners' Track to Llyn Bochlwyd to camp there, another old desire fulfilled. It was too cold for a swim, however, even though I had the privacy. The days when I would break ice on lochans and plunge a naked body into their blackness have gone.

It used to amaze me how Braehead kids could tolerate icy waters. Coming off a hill on Lagganside one sweltering day I was begged to stop for a swim and knowing a big pool we tramped over the dusty heather to it. As we neared the banks we could hear yells and screeches. We were forestalled. When we peered down it was to see an all-female cast enjoying the waters. They were all somewhat middle-aged, the sort of nudes Rubens so often painted. I suspect it was a Ladies' Scottish Climbing Club Meet. We diplomatically withdrew and as we went one Tom Thumb grinned at me, "Aw, sur, it's enough tae gie ye a complex for life".

The rowan trees were already yellowing and they were so laden with red berries that whole branches were bowed with their weight. The wind died away at dusk. Our crag-hidden hollow soon slipped from shadow into darkness. Snug in bed we enjoyed the outlawed majesty of the mountains. As if our modest evening climb had brought them nearer, the stars blinked and winked brighter than ever, perhaps they really were cold, for that gasping night gave the first frosts of the autumn, frosts that would soon occur regularly, setting the glowing colours to the cheeks of summer.

Saturday 15 September   TRYFAN–NANT GWYNANT-BEDDGELERT

The prodigal sun came home to the hills and the resulting party was to continue for much of the remaining six or seven hundred miles of the trip. Only something like six days out of forty were to produce meteorological tantrums. Wales became a romp, relished with a growing astonishment. Today had a touch of madness in it which I think stayed to the end.

We were up at five and an hour later stood on the stony col between Tryfan and Bristly Ridge which had so often been our route up Glyder Fawr. We left the tent spread to dry before galloping (fun over the endless boulders) up and down Tryfan, 3,010 ft, that prince of Welsh peaks, which from all angles, is grand and unmistakable. Legend has set the grave of Bedivere, last of King Arthur's knights, on Tryfan. (Excalibur was cast into Llyn Ogwen.) Its very highest point is a pair of trig-point-like monoliths, nicknamed Adam and Eve, which look down on the craggy west face, so the minor jump from one to the other becomes a test of nerves. The east face has a long history of climbing but the whole peak can give exploratory scrambling to reward an innocent. The summit is only half a mile from the A5 – but 2,000 feet above it. My last visit had been with an old Kitchy by that east face. At the foot of the monoliths is a wall which requires both hands, and Kitchy perforce was thrown up ahead of me. The scrabbling noise of his landing drew the eyes of the crowd on top, so that when I heaved up immediately after they were convinced the dog had climbed up unaided. There was a delightful air of disbelief. One lady peered down over the edge, then looked at us, simply saying "Impossible!" Had it been beyond his ability Kitchy had me well trained; he simply scratched my leg which meant he wanted to be carried in the rucksack. Once in it, whether on hill or cycle, if the day was good, he would insist on having his head out to watch things, but if it was miserably wet he simply curled up inside. Storm is several pounds heavier than Kitchy and I'm that much older so this system is being kept secret from him. Storm is very bold on rocks and Tryfan held him up not at all today. We had the summit to ourselves.

We had come up with morning's first light as the moon faded. The Carnedd summits were bouncing off white masses of cloud and there was a tingling, toothpaste-advert freshness to the day. We boulder-hopped at a trot back to our gear and as we continued took a series of pictures: of Tryfan's spikey shadow which enveloped frosty Llyn Bochlwyd and pointed to Foel-goch; of Tryfan, *lion couchant*, from the Miners' Track to Pen-y-Gwryd; and of the Lliwedd-Snowdon group as we descended the path to touch again my line of the Groats End Walk. This was the very land of *I Bought a Mountain*, the book which gives such a vivid description of what it is like to be a hill sheep-farmer in this rugged area. If all walkers were made to read it they might be a bit more appreciative of the shepherd's labours. Once started it is compulsive, for it gives insights and knowledge which we often miss as our contacts with reticent locals are few.

My immediate imperative was to reach Beddgelert Post Office before it shut for the weekend. We made it at 11.50 a.m., which was not really the way to treat Nant Gwynant which is the most beautiful of the valleys that moat Snowdon, deep set below the road on one side with the mass of Cwm Dyli and Lliwedd beyond, then running out to the flats of Llyn Gwynant, circled with trees and reflecting Yr Aran and *the hill of the hawk*, Moel Hebog. Yr Aran, *the height*, looks like the Pap of Glencoe. The Nant Gwynant perhaps looks like how Glencoe once appeared before it was ravaged by man. History, if it teaches anything, indicates that man simply never learns from the past. The Highlands are a grim desert as a consequence not of natural but of man-determined activity. The rest of my walk through Wales was a constant reminder of this; the scenery at valley level far excelled that comparable in the Highlands, because it has a long history of agricultural use and not pillage and misuse. The creeping bracken is a warning even in Wales, however.

My appearance changed at Beddgelert for new Rohan breeches and a Berghaus Goretex jacket were waiting there, besides the first of the parcels we had left for Charles to post from Sheffield. I did a quick-change to send home the older breeches and jacket, films from the day's sudden splurge, the maps I'd walked off, the books I'd read. . . After the post office closed, at 12.30, we relaxed over toasted cheese sandwiches and ice-cream. The tourist season was on the wane so Beddgelert had a quiet village atmosphere to it again. It is merely a hamlet at a meeting of valleys but has a tourist fame out of all proportion, for it is the setting of the legend of the slaying of Gellert, Llewellyn's faithful dog. The dog had been left to guard his infant son and when the master returned it was to find the cradle upset and blood everywhere. In a rage he slew his hound, only to discover its bloodied condition was due to faithfulness. A dead wolf lay in a corner. Some locals raised a stone to mark the dog's grave and some verses were written – and a legend was forged.

Joseph Jacobs in his *Celtic Fairy Tales* (Dover Publications) while admitting the early nineteenth-century origin of the now popular Beth Gellert story, traces it back to ancient India where it is still current in Buddhist folklore. One form came to the west in Crusader times, as a moral apologue against precipitate action, and is in "The Fables of Cattwg the Wise", probably a sixteenth century production. So it seems the Gellert legend was known in Wales generally before it became (craftily?) localised. There is a proverb "I repent as much as the man who slew his greyhound", there are other place names connected with greyhounds. In the days of Richard III a greyhound on a cradle was adopted as part of the national crest. E. Jones, in the second edition of his *Musical Relicks of the Welsh Bards* (1794), connects the legend to Llewellyn and Caernarvonshire in his telling of it, and mentions the date 1205, which Spencer did in his broadsheet poem of 1800.

Another specific Gellert story which already applied to the area, concerns a greyhound of Llewellyn which ran itself and a stag to death. Jones in his first edition of *Musical Relicks* mentions an epigram about it which looks as if he took this exploit of Llewellyn's Gellert and buffed it up with the general folktale which was known widely. Spencer then took it from Jones and his rather awful verses led to its popularisation. That is a brief summary of five pages of detailed study – which I find fascinating. The cairn raised by the landlord of the old Goat Inn was only what the tourist desired, and deserved, but if I smile at the gullibility of tourists, the scholars can err as well. As kids roaming the Ochils at Dollar, some of us gave names to local spots which meant much to us. "Paradise" is still in use and above Castle Campbell, our meeting place, "William's Stone", was given from the name of Bill Proudfoot, a boarder who lived almost next door to our home. Yet in a recent local book our name is set back into legend.

Moel Hebog dodged in and out of view as we walked up the quiet Rhyd-Dhu road which skirts the Snowdon *massif* on the forgotten south side. The Forestry Commission have a camp site a couple of miles out which was friendly and 'well-appointed'. The logbook had been dropping behind so I brought it up to date, writing in a common-room-cum-cafe before a log fire. The new breeches felt tighter than the ones they had replaced, which confirmed that I had gained, not lost, weight on the journey. This seems to happen during prolonged backpacking. Possibly the body becomes more sturdy to cope with the two or three excess stones it has to carry in the rucksack. John Merrill on his long trips also puts on weight.

Sunday 16 September   YR ARAN AND SNOWDON

Again a strong wind was the day's weather feature. We went up Yr Aran more or less directly, but constantly stayed below the cloud level to read, hoping the clouds would rise and break, which they did all too slowly. We gained Craig Wen and wandered on to the cone of windy Yr Aran from which we dropped to explore the old quarries on the Bwlch Cwm Llan.

As the cloud was slowly rising I decided to continue. I could not resist scrambling up a small crag and several times was left clinging to it while the wind tried to blow me off. A wild goat was grazing on the lee flank of the ridge. We could see across to the Watkin Path and the old mine beside it. The name comes from Sir Edmund Watkin who constructed the lower parts of the path in 1892. A plaque on a rock commemorates the spot where Gladstone (then 84) made a speech to a large gathering of miners on the topic of freedom for small states.

Snowdon is a classic example of a spoked mountain, the summit being the hub from which several ridges run out like the spokes of an old cartwheel. As the cwms between the ridges have been deeply eroded back by glaciation there are steep headwalls and the ridges themselves are often flanked by precipices. Most cwms have typical corrie-lochans. It is a grand mountain in every way, the four routes to and from the summit hub we managed this trip being but a sample of the possible lines. Each of the four Country Summits is worthy of its calling when you think of it. There are many books on Snowdon and its paths, and the National Park produces five leaflets covering the popular paths which give much interesting information. Rowland's booklet is useful and the O.S. Outdoor Leisure maps of great help.

We converged with the path coming up from Llechog and found a group on it who had come up the Watkin Path but then gone astray in the cloud to end down here though aiming for the summit. Bwlch Main was a narrow crest despite its name, and through odd gaps in the cloud we could see sun-spots wandering about among the Cwm Clogwyn lakes. The last pull up needed no navigational skill as the *chug-chug-chug* of the diesel engine beckoned. There are not many summits in Britain where you can have coffee and a hot pie on top, or a drink in a pub. The concrete buildings are not pretty but are built to cope with the warfare of vandalism. Today's conditions hardly enhanced the top but mentally I rejoiced as I was back on my Walk proper again. Pennant's description of his visit had a familiar sound: "A vast mist enveloped the whole circuit of the mountain. The prospect down was horrible. It gave an idea of numbers of abysses, concealed by a thick smoke circulating about me. Very often a gust of wind formed an opening in the clouds, which gave a fine and distinct vista of lake and valley." Borrow thought the scenery "inexpressably grand" and Belloc, who walked to Rome over the Alps, was more moved than by any corner of Europe. On a clear day you can see the Lake District hills and the Wicklows in Ireland.

I read for an hour in the cafe but the cloud refused to clear so we ambled off down again. The departure from a summit is where the most vital accuracy is needed in navigation and that applies even to well-worn Yr Wyddfa, more so perhaps, for the whole top of the peak where its many paths meet is trampled bare by the visitors.

In many ways it is a pity Snowdon has been sacrificed to these artificial, urban intrusions but, as on Cairngorm or the Cairnwell, it allows non-athletic types to enjoy something of the wonder of the mountains. Such people have their place and are equally entitled to their rights as are we selfish, solitude-loving types. My father was a life-long walker but ended as an arthritic cripple on sticks; his enjoyment of rough motoring, chair-lifts and so on, tempers my own outlook. Perhaps the motorist deserves east-west communications over Rannoch Moor or between Speyside and Deeside by Glen Feshie (a ribbon of tarmac would make little difference to the present ugly estate-roads), and bleak, forest-defended Wyvis is perhaps rightly developed for the growing northern population and to relieve Cairngorm a bit. To flatly deny *everything* is a mistake. Even conservationists can be ridiculously extreme and truth never lies in extremes.

We came out of Snowdon's cloud cap on the craggy edge of Llechog, and the descent to Ffridd Uchaf farm gave us views to the hills running from Moel Hebog to Mynydd Mawr. The Nantlle ridge of peaks facing Mynydd Mawr is one of the best in Snowdonia. Storm went into a stream to remove the mud before we walked back to the camp by pleasant forestry tracks. The Sunday papers had been delivered to my tent while I was away: real camp services. The Goretex jacket proved itself today. I wore it all the time because of the savage wind but did not drip with sweat inside it as I would have done with any other waterproof material. The big wind led to rain as it invariably does.

As we are now back on our devious John o' Groats to Land's End route it might be the place to mention some of its statistics. Like many people I first became aware of the route through the deeds and declamations of Dr Barbara Moore. Her style (honey and carrots) roused others (steak and chips) until in 1960 Billy Butlin turned it into a mass event with over 700 starters. The winner, Jim Musgrave, did 891 miles in 15 days, 14 hours, 31 minutes. The race began with just the wintry weather ours had produced – which thinned the field. The first lady home was Wendy Lewis, and it was only in 1980 that a 57-year old South African granny, Mavis Hutchinson, set 16 days, 22 hours as a new target. Along came Ann Sayer. The record, as 1981 begins, is still hers – 837 miles in 13 days, 17 hours, 40 minutes.

I mention one or two books in the bibliography. Walker's is a good yarn about the Butlin circus. Hillaby's I find disappointing: a third of it covers the South West, then it tails off. Scotland is hardly covered. Theo Lang is interesting. The Naylors' tome is firm favourite.

The route was cycled in the thirties in 2½ days. Jimmy Saville has cycled *and* walked it. Young teenagers have led donkeys along the line, I met a Kent schoolboy who did it with a friend one summer holiday – keeping off roads as much as possible. It is the inescapable road work which is both the make and break of such a trip. Each summer Cameron McNeish, who is warden of Aviemore Youth Hostel, expects to meet three or four a week on packing trips along the *Groats End Walk* – and "that does not include the barefoot walkers, the pram-pushers and bathtub brigades, the roller skaters and the rest." It has been hitch-hiked in little over a day. It has been done as a double round-trip walk. I'm glad I did not learn all this before starting. My illusions were intact!

Monday 17 September TO PORTHMADOG

If it had been a brilliant day we would have gone over Moel Hebog but as it was we just ambled down the Glaswyn Valley and by following an old railway line and tracks managed with a minimum of road walking. Whispering trees choked the pass and ice-borne boulders dotted the river. There were lots of 'things' in the woods: agarics, chanterelles, tufts, stinkhorns, boleti . . . We lunched opposite the climbers' crags of Tremadoc where various innocents were being introduced to the game. Behind us was the reclaimed estuary, 7,000 acres with not a contour line. We picked up a parcel at Porthmadog, looked at the small maritime museum (s. v. *Garlandstone*) and wandered on to Borth-y-Gest to spend a very enjoyable night with Pip (Showell) and Jean Styles. Being the home of a mountaineer there was a pot of tea at once, and then a restful talking the hours away over a good meal. Home comforts are doubly relished when far from home. Showell Styles is the Welsh equivalent of Lakeland's Harry Griffith; I felt privileged to have met both these *doyens* of mountain writing on the trip. Climbing books, historical novels and children's stories had given variety to a life of authorship, and with work, friends and places in common, we could have talked all night.

The Styles' house stood above the Glaslyn-Dwyryd Estuary, looking across to Cnicht, the Rhinogs and Harlech Castle. I was aware of a good old storm in the night as the sheltering Corsican pines sang to it and the halyards on a hundred boats tapped their impatience on aluminium masts. Once again a night under a hospitable roof had coincided with what would have been wild camping.

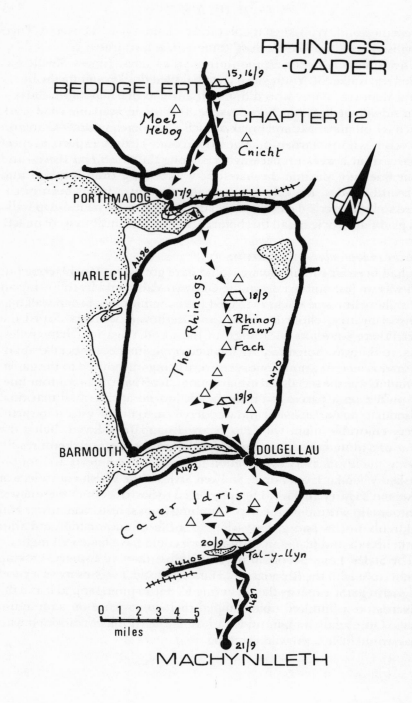

RHINOGS
-CADER

CHAPTER 12

15, 16/9

BEDDGELERT

Moel
Hebog

Cnicht

PORTHMADOG   17/9

N

HARLECH

The Rhinogs

A496

A470

18/9

Rhinog
Fawr

Fach

19/9

BARMOUTH   DOLGELLAU

A493

Cader Idris

20/9

B4405   Tal-y-llyn

A487

0 1 2 3 4 5
miles

21/9

MACHYNLLETH

Tuesday 18 September ON TO THE RHINOGS

A civilised breakfast was a change and we went off into a well-washed landscape. From Porthmadog we crossed the Cob as the mile-long embankment is called. It was built in 1821 thanks to the enthusiasm of W. A. Madocks, M.P. who has his name enshrined in the town's. On the other side of the flat is the house where the Shelleys lived and where the poet may or may not have come near being assassinated. The writer Peacock was a tremendous walker who found Shelley's enthusiasm not up to his own. T. E. Lawrence was born in Tremadoc, a far cry to Arabia.

The Festiniog Steam Railway and the main road use the Cob. The toll was on the far side but pedestrians were not charged. I bought and read a newspaper along to Penrhyndeudraeth for a second estuary with a toll bridge. When we stopped beyond to dig out a bar of chocolate we spotted a rather weird caterpillar. I made a quick sketch of it to try and find out what it was. At Hay-on-Wye, many days later, I bought a *Telegraph* and in it was an article of Maurice Burton's answering a reader's query about our mutual mystery. It was an elephant hawk moth caterpillar, the name being apt, for it has a long snout which makes it a very odd creature to look at. The snout is retractable and it has false eyes to frighten off predators.

There is always something new. In Kerry we had seen spotted slugs and later read that they were a rarity found elsewhere only in Spain. In the Nant Gwynant we saw orange-coloured slugs, about which I have not learnt anything. Not many Field Guides to the slugs of Britain and Ireland have been published. Jays, buzzards and kestrels were to be with me constantly in Wales. The red kite is the real rarity, the equivalent of our osprey, but it is not on display with AA roadsigns to indicate its locality.

A steep road took us up to a 'level' where we had lunch by Llyn Tecwyn-isaf. After another brae we found a green road which bore us up to the singing solo heights. It was a joy to have a sea view, even towards a cold, autumn sea. So much of our trip had been on spinal mountains inland and we would soon lose the sea view again as we penetrated into Wild Wales if I can borrow a phrase. I hope there is never an official Cambrian Way. These superb mountains deserve to be preserved for the imaginative not exploited for the feeble. High-level *Ways* are a contradiction in terms, in ethics, in desires. The *Offa's Dyke Way* gives perhaps the best low-level route in Britain. I think most Welshmen would regard that as enough. Now that there are a hundred Long Distance Footpaths, we are in danger of losing a fair balance.

We followed indeterminate paths through marshy reaches among knobbles of crag to another higher 'level' above which the tiers of the northern Rhinog peaks were dodging in and out of the clouds. Llyn Eiddew-bach was set in below them but I chose a more sheltered spot down by a nearby steam. After a brew we followed a track and then via Llyn Dywarchen scrambled up the west of Foel Penolau. From it we crossed to Moel Ysgfarnogod, 2,044 ft, *hill of the hares*, and already realised that the Rhinogs are a quite individualistic range, different from anything else this trip. There was a huge reservoir to the north east (Llyn Trawsfynydd) but as the clouds were beginning to drip we scurried off, as fast as Rhinog roughness permitted, back to camp. The daylight lasted only until seven o'clock.

Wednesday 19 September   THE ROUGH RIDE OF THE RHINOGS
Knoydart has nothing on the Rhinogs for rough going. In giving Scottish mountain rescue statistics Ben Humble used frequently to add 'English' to his comments, the inference being that anyone coming to Scotland would need new standards and skills. This might hold in winter, but otherwise only the scale is different. Pennine peat or Rhinog roughness will give all the training needed for anywhere. More English come to grief simply because their numbers are greater. Not that nationalism is entirely absent. There is one story of Bob Scott of Luibeg who reported an 'excellent' weekend: "Aye, twa royals in the mornin, an a bloody Englishman fished oot the Derry in the efternoon."

I thought the Rhinog revelation was to be denied us for it was cloudy when we set off. We opted to go by Llyn Eiddew-mawr round Clip to keep below the cloud, and this led us into a fine sampler of the landscape: ribs of rock moated with deep marsh, then heather-covered chaos before a flight down unstable screes to gain access to Craig Wion. We could smell, but not see, the wild goats. They apparently are banded in colouring due to the escape of a billy goat which was the film mascot of a regiment using Cwmbychan as the North West Frontier during the making of a screen version of Kipling's tale *The Drum*, though goats were, for hundreds of years, the main hill animal before the sheep. Seventeenth and eighteenth century wigs were made of goat's hair. The cloud had been careering round us with a promise of clearing, a promise fulfilled. Snowdon kept its cloud cap, but the Rhinogs, fore and aft, cleared rapidly. Cader Idris filled the southern horizon, an un-mistakable sweep of hill which is seen from far and near.

We descended a rough gully and complex route-picking led us to Llyn Morwynion, the first of the many small lakes that lie like navels among the bellyfolds of these hills. We brewed and dried the tent. A crag fell sheer into the water so we had to scrabble up vertical vegetation – mostly heather which could (and did) cover all sorts of ground expected and otherwise. The Welsh for ling heather is grug which sounds just right. The Rhinogs are very gruggy. The dog vanished through one Pooh-trap to splash into water hidden below. The escape off Mangerton Mountain alone gave tougher going this Walk. We crossed the so-called Roman Steps at the Bwlch Tyddiad and, by ways well chosen and badly chosen, passed Llyn Du to reach Rhinog Fawr, 2,362 ft. (Rhiniog means *threshold* but Rhinog is no more than the local pronunciation). The sandstone which produces the banded appearance on the way up has the odd name of greywackes.

From the top we looked to Rhinog Fach and Y Llethr across another deep bwlch. I had underestimated the ups and downs even if I'd expected one-mile-an-hour progress. On a rake flanking Rhinog Fach there was another lake which looked easy to reach. For Rhinog Fach I could nip up and down without rucksack. The descent to Bwlch Drws Ardudwy was made down a very unstable gully which cut through the curving ribs of rock that are such a feature of Fawr from Fach. Tiny Llyn Cwmhosan would have made a fine camp site as would the larger Llyn Hywel. A week's wandering to camp by every llyn would be interesting. We brewed by Llyn Hywel before scrambling up Rhinog Fach, 2,333 ft, which falls into its water in sweeping screes through which the bare rocks bulge to the summit.

We followed people up Rhinog Fach then met a lad on Y Llethr, 2,475 ft, as we scrambled up it. Our rocky route took my mind off the effort and the view, so I was surprised, once up, to find a complete change of terrain (to grassy and benign) and a sky suddenly black and boiling whereas half an hour before it had been biscuit-tin blue.

The nuclear power station by Llyn Trawsfynydd is a sore box of an intrusion in the vast view of what is a National Park. The view was perhaps the day's best because of the mix of good and evil: sun stabs to the east, clouds over Snowdonia and the hurrying dark ironing out the colours of the sea. We rushed along our ridge, glad of its protective wall, over Crib-y-rhiw, *the ridge of the slope*, and Diffwys, *the precipice*, then retreated from the sudden maelstrom to drop down into the east. All the ground below has been planted to add yet another texture to the rough cast of the Rhinogs. At the subsequent Karrimor Mountain Marathon that was held on these hills, they had surprisingly few broken ankles, but a high fall-out rate! We seemed to descend from one berry-laden bilberry bush to the next. The berries were becoming over-ripe and both of our tongues and my fingers were soon stained blue.

We had even rougher ground as we descended to the forest above Llyn Cwm-mynach so were forced to pitch on heather as there was only an hour of light left. We ate every morsel and read the candle out. When a gale blew up I half-packed, in case we had to flee, but despite the hammering and the pegs having no real hold, the Tramp held. We had had a memorable passage of the Rhinogs. The *roughs* of its description are deserved, any search for synonyms would be merely cosmetic subterfuge. The Rhinogs are superbly rough, quiet and strong. My log ended: "silence and peace are not luxuries as they have become. They are necessities and our civilization has lost them to its own hurt."

Thursday 20 September   DOLGELLAU

This was a rag-bag day of variety. We enjoyed our tramp down the Mawddach valley with a view ahead of Cader Idris but out on the flat I had to stop reading as the flanking wind was too strong. We were charged one penny to cross the bridge over the Mawddach.

I managed to shop and collect a parcel from the post office at Dolgellau before meeting Trevor Jones who wanted to take some photographs of our trip. It was a return to places where he had begun his climbing days. He whisked us round to Tal-y-llyn, a glacier-gouged lake like Loch Morar. It was wind-loud as the sea. We were left at the Cwm-rhwyddfor camp site, but as the day was set fair Storm and I took a ride back to Dolgellau there and then, with the farmer. It was market day and we indulged in some tasty home baking. The town is full of narrow streets and could have looked the same hundreds of years ago. The bridge over the Wnion was built in 1638 but I followed up quiet lanes by the Afon Aran, through a rich, tree-green world to the windy moors to round the butt end of Cader back to camp. The new road ribbons along the flank of the deep cleft of valley; but we took the original track in its foot by the quiet Afon Fawnog – a road as old as time.

Even 200 years ago roads and railways did not exist. You travelled on foot, if poor, on horseback if richer. Drove roads led over the mountains for the English towns. Communication by sea was easier to the continent than to London. Even the coast has changed. Harlech Castle could once be provisioned by sea. Nothing is static and I sometimes wonder if the conservationists themselves know just what period they are seeking to save. Any return to a pristine landscape is a foolish dream. Maybe we could fossilise the landscape as it is now, but a landscape can only go on from the present, not retreat into some over-romantic past. The

Irish and Welsh landscapes are superb *because* they are occupied by man. If Scotland's *land* had been given vital time, money and effort it would have completely altered her social and economic history.

Originally I had hoped to descend off the Rhinogs to Barmouth to look up Bill Tilman, had he not been away on some mad caper. Sadly, between the planning of the Walk and implementing it, Tilman had gone off on what was to be his last voyage. Strange, for a brief spell, how several of us had known him and Shipton, before these two heroes of my youth died. A gang of us had hopes of the plum Nanda Devi twin-summits traverse and because I was toying with joining Tilman for a *Baroque* trip, Eric Roberts (Ann's husband) and I drove over from Ruthin to meet him at Barmouth. Tea out of a silver teapot and toasted muffins before the fire was hardly in character. He was not loquacious, however, and long minutes passed between comments: "I've sunk my last three boats", "Nobody will insure me", "Do you still want to come?"

He later gave Eric helpful pictures for his ascent of Nanda Devi but others of us, when the lure of helping the traverse had gone, opted for an old men's expedition round the northern sides of the mountain. The tale of Shipton and Tilman breaking up the Rishi Gorge into the Sanctuary is one that endures. Tilman returned the following year and climbed Nanda Devi, a great feat, for he did not go well at high altitudes. Donald Mill, in London, was in touch with Shipton (then in hospital with cancer), and to both of them we hoped to bring back our photographs and experiences. It was not to be. Passing through London I went to an Alpine Club meeting and at it the chairman asked if anyone had heard from Tilman. I think it was his Nanda Devi partner, Odell, who murmured that he had had a postcard from Rio. Somewhere between there and the Antarctic they sailed their ship under.

My own *Baroque* trip had been a personal fiasco. I had lasted from Lymington to Falmouth before packing in, a stone lighter, and glad to reach *terra firma*. I had been endlessly sick, I think from the inescapable reek of diesel, for I'd been sick enough, but briefly, on the *Captain Scott* in her rough Minch waters. Playing dodgems with super tankers and fishing fleets while feeling like death, with our navigation lights blowing out regularly, and alone on deck, made my ten days of the Channel unforgettable. At Falmouth I handed Tilman some grand copy (used in his last book, *Triumph and Tribulation*) by being caught with my hands on *Baroque* and my feet in the dinghy with the two separating irrevocably. The storm which sank several single-handed yachtsmen in the transatlantic race (including an old acquaintance, Mike McMullen, who vanished without trace) damaged *Baroque* badly enough for her to head for Iceland, and then to make a brief passage to Greenland where she flooded and had other adventures. I'd left my Munros' trip tent on board. It was sunk twice, went to Nanda Devi, and still survived to help this trip. Only one Greenland peak was climbed by *Baroque*'s unhappy crew, and I have a fascinating collection of letters from both crew and skipper; the former, for instance, described their climb as sufficiently demanding in poor conditions, while Tilman wrote, "The three boys climbed a peak there, the same that we did in '64, and took an unconscionable time over it."

Both Tilman and Shipton have left us a fine collection of books, not only on their often-shared Himalayan journeys but on their divergent later careers, Tilman with his Bristol cutter *Mischief* in Arctic and Antarctic waters and Shipton with his second career in the southern tip of South America. The latter's autobiographical *Upon that Mountain* influenced generations of British expeditions. These memories may appear tangential but were equally part of my journey through Britain; they are a shared, if modest, testimony to two very fine men, whose adventures and outlook I hope will long be an inspiration.

Friday 21 September   CADER IDRIS
We seemed to be blessed by having our ration of wind and wet at night. It poured, and the ground was like a sponge when we set off – early, but at a time unknown as my watch had run down. We went along to the Cadair Gates, and a well-worn track took us up through attractive deciduous woodland into the Llyn Cau cwm. I waited on a vantage point for the sun to win over clouds and lost what photo hopes there had been. (Normally it is not worth taking mountain photos unless the sun shines.) We left the cwm and climbed up and along the ridge over Craig Lwyd, 2,251 ft, with some splendid effects south through the frame of the Corris Valley; it was almost as if sparks flew, the way the sun and clouds clashed over Plynlimon. The landscape was both bold and spacious compared to the Cader spine of mountain ridge or compared to the Rhinogs' mixed thrill. These hills of central Wales are full of individuality, each very different, and delightfully unspoilt after the picnic peaks of Snowdonia.

We flanked to Mynydd Pencoed, 2,513 ft, and on the way back up Craig Cwm Amarch, 2,617 ft, ran into a bit of hail which soon collected in the pockets of ground. Storm found it sore on his nose. The Goretex material showed its qualities and I kept dry and unsweaty. We flanked up again to cross the tourist path on *the Saddle*, as Cyfrwy is a 2,646 ft Top. Others beyond to the west we left for another day and turned to let the wind blow us up the cloud-tearing roughness to the main summit.

At 2,928 ft Cader Idris just fails to join the exalted, self-conscious Fourteen (it would really upset *that* game) but it lacks nothing for missing 72 ft. It is the *chair of Idris*, a legendary seventh-century warrior who was killed on the banks of the Severn. Showell Styles likens its shape to an eagle with wings outspread. Even in the mid-eighteenth century professional guides were leading tourists up it, so there are well-beaten ways. Pennant climbed it and botanists, geologists and surveyors explored every nook and cranny. Tennyson came up from the north and was given a day of rain to dampen inspiration. I always feel Cader Idris is a Cassius of a mountain – lean and hungry – yet it is one of the few everyone seems to know. We lingered in the summit hut for a long time, hoping in vain for the weather to clear. The wind had a piercing northerly bite to it, which drove us on to warm up again, rimming the edge with tantalising views into the depths. Descending off Mynydd Moel, it cleared as we reached the end bump, giving a good view to the Rhinogs and of our walk round from Dolgellau. I was discovering some of the best country of the trip. We descended a spur to regain the old Bwlch Llyn Bach road back to Cwm-rhwyddfor. There we dis-covered it was only 2 p.m. so quickly ate and drank away some surplus weight and set off once more in golden sunshine; Tallyho for Talyllyn!

It was in this quiet corner that the young Thomas de Quincey spent several days after running away from Manchester Grammar School and vagabonding through Wales, living rough on a guinea a week allowance, supplemented by casual hospitality often in return for the literary service of letter-writing. His Talyllyn days ended when his hostess' parents returned. He wrote, "talent for writing love-letters would do little to recommend me with two sexagenarian Welsh Methodists . . . so came away." In his opium-drugged latter days he was to remember that peace and liberty.

The pull up from Minffordd gave clear views back to Cader, a mountain which joins the Rhinogs as being, in the words of *1066 and All That*, a good thing. So was the descent walk of the Dulas Valley, even if it was all on tarred roads. Corris Uchaf, an old mining village in a good setting, boasts a railway museum. We criss-crossed the valley, which once knew the tramp of Roman legions, to cut something off the sweeping bends. At one point I was indiscreet enough to ask how many

miles it was to Machynlleth so learnt both the mileage and how to pronounce the name of the pretty town.

Time forbade a visit to the National Centre for Alternative
Technology, a fascinating place (which is open to visitors) where power,
buildings and horticulture are all seriously studied in the fight to save
the dwindling resources of a greedy world.

Simply because so much of this Walk was spent in remote, rural dis-
tricts, the irregular meetings with our industrial, urban car-dominated
society began to appear in a different and uglier light. We are steadily
destroying our world, so far as I can see, which could well mean we are
destroying ourselves. The message is being heard clearly enough. We
simply ignore it. Last year, in one year of peace, we used up more
precious oil than it took to fight the Second World War. One day
terminal sin will step on the heels of original sin.

A trip like this is humbling for it brings one down to realities. Our
needs are few. Harmony is a spiritual conception. The world has grown
fat in its own conceit, flabby from endless greed. We desire only to
multiply without being fruitful, for fruitfulness means a putting into the
soil and the sea and the sky and not just exploiting and pillaging for our
own selfish, immediate interests. For every tree we fell we plant a man in
its place. Experiments with overcrowded rats in a cage demonstrate
where that ends. We seem to be the only species unable to control our
numbers. Nature manages – but we have rejected nature. A walk like this
gives a half glimpse of that rejected serenity and hope but, at its end, we
returned home to find that during the months away man had
accelerated further along the road to destruction.

The huge Afon Dyfi (Dovey) was a blaze of silver in the westering sun
as we crossed the bridge, first built in 1533, to pull up Doll Street into
Machynlleth which is carefully sited above the valley flood level. We
booked into the Wynnstay Hotel, as once did George Borrow. He
climbed Plynlimon, visited Ponterwyd (where there is now a George
Borrow Hotel) and went on to Devil's Bridge, as I was to do in the next
few days. The hotel stood on the trim main street (Machynlleth was a
"planned" town back in the thirteenth century), conveniently next to the
post office and along from the Victoria clock tower which is a small
second cousin to St. Stephen's at Westminster. Borrow spent a day in the
court and gave a tongue-in-cheek report of the trial of a salmon
poacher. This delicate business led to a street riot in the 1920s. I was
assured everyone meekly pays the municipality for their fishing
nowadays!

We were very comfortable in the Wynnstay, and a TV set and tea-making facilities in the bedroom ensured a late night, first watching *Carry on Doctor* and then, in my music-starved state, relishing several hours of light music which was all ITV was producing because of a long strike.

XIII

CAMBRIAN WAYS

". . . Wish to die, indeed! – A Rommany Chal would wish to live for ever!"

"In sickness, Jasper?"

"There's the sun and the stars, brother."

"In blindness, Jasper?"

"There's the wind on the heath, brother; if I could only feel that, I would gladly live for ever."

GEORGE BORROW: *Lavengro*

Saturday 22 September   PLYNLIMON   *Maps, pp. 227 and 235*

Wynford Vaughan-Thomas walked through Wales to celebrate his seventieth birthday and by chance I heard one of the series of broadcast talks that followed: his description of crossing Plynlimon. I did not know where this fancifully-named hill was, but as every river in Wales seemed to rise on it, it had to be fairly central. It went on the list for this Walk, and with the Rhinogs and Cader Idris now forms a triptych of enamel-bright memories. The Arans and Cader apart it is the highest range south of Snowdonia.

I had already walked the dog before breakfast and finished eating just as the post office opened. We then spotted a second-hand bookshop which was no help to time-chasing. The hotel supplied me with coffee while I rushed off a dozen letters and finally left pleasant Machynlleth at noon. The information office is situated in the Institute which is part sixteenth century and reputedly on the site where Owain Glyndwr held his first parliament in 1402 at which he was crowned Prince of Wales. Envoys from several countries were present, the Church was freed from Canterbury, universities were planned. . . . In 1405 a 'tripartite indenture' with Mortimer and Northumberland aimed to divide the country into three well-balanced states. That Welsh parliament is one of those speculative ifs of history. Might we not all be happier now if it had worked? Alas, English nationalism is all too flint-hard and sharp. A *Glyndwr's Way* links many historic sites in Powys and would be an

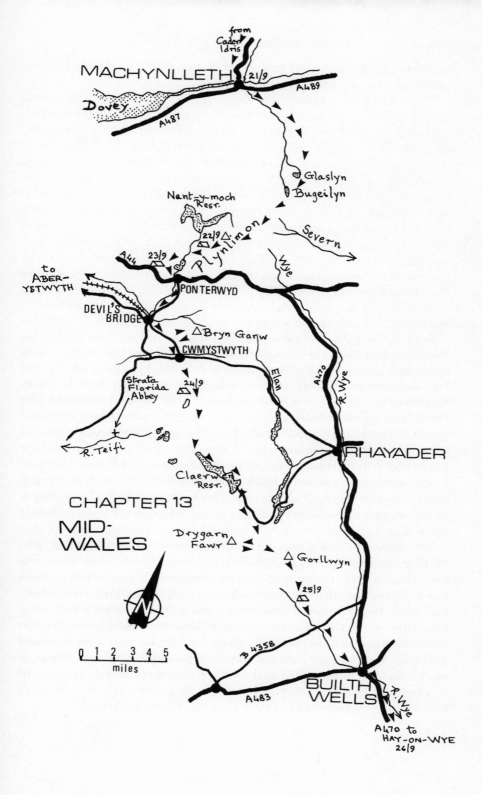

from
Cador
Idris

MACHYNLLETH 21/9

Dovey

A487

A489

Glaslyn
Bugeilyn

Nant-y-moch
Resr.

22/9

Plynlimon

Severn

A44 23/9

Wye

to
ABER-
YSTWYTH

PONTERWYD

DEVIL'S
BRIDGE

Bryn Garw

CWMYSTWYTH

Elan

A470

R. Wye

Strata
Florida
Abbey

24/9

R. Teifi

RHAYADER

Claerw
Resr.

CHAPTER 13

MID-
WALES

Drygarn
Fawr

Gorllwyn

25/9

N

0 1 2 3 4 5
miles

B 4358

BUILTH
WELLS

R. Wye

A483

A470 to
HAY-ON-WYE
26/9

excellent alternative to the Pennine Way. I carried off a series of leaflets about this ten-day trail.

There had been a biting frost overnight; we had felt the freshness of the air in bed. The sky looked as if freshly painted and the shadows were cool with the first breathlessness of the ageing season. (Never again will I do a big walk through July and August.) We followed the golf course to the hamlet of Forge on another Afon Dulas, and then kept up its valley. The frosty sun was reviving the sad greens of summer; in fact this first touch of hard autumn brought out all the bright softness of spring. It was walking at its best, gaining height almost unnoticed, then dropping with a flourish down to Nant y Fyda before a spur lifted us up above the cosiness of cultivation. The back lighting turned the rolling fields into a rumpled patchwork quilt, a "gaily chequered, heart-expanding view" (James Thomson). Buzzards circled and mewed constantly – we could see five at one time when we stopped for some tea and a long gaze to Cader, now filling the northern horizon. Only a short time ago it had been in the south. The Arans also stood out in rugged solitude.

We left the flanks of gorse and bell heather to gain the plateau of Plynlimon's hills by the edge of some deeply gouged and eroded cwms down which the infant Dulas drained. They were almost a desert feature. We wended over the tableland to Glaslyn and then over a hill to Bugeilyn, the blue waters already fading into silver. A marshy valley rather cuts off the Plynlimon summits on the north but we threaded across it surprisingly easily and zig-zagged up to the next expanse of country, now all peat hags and cold emptiness. This is the source of the mighty Severn. It reeked of fox and I was not surprised to hear later that Machynlleth has a pack of hounds, bred in mediaeval times from French and Moroccan beasts. It is a foot pack, for horses would not be much use in this countryside – unless you were prepared to get off your horse and carry it.

We hurried slowly up the interminable slopes towards Pen Pumlumon-Arwystli, 2,427 ft, the first of my summits on Plynlimon, but several times had to stop and don extra clothes as the sun faded beyond a mackerel sky and the cold blew back from the hold of dusk. Originally I had only planned to gain some height but a poor forecast for the next day drove us on. There were many tumuli-like cairns and a slate marked "1865 WWW". We chuntered down to the col past mere stumps of old peat hags, then followed a fence up to another top and this time we were on the slopes that give birth to the Wye, yet the map showed no name to this summit. *Wall* gives it Pen Pumlumon Llygad-bychan, 2,372 ft, after the *little eye* of lake set on it. Other derivations are not known.

It was too dark to read the map by now, but we went on from a cairn on a col to reach the easily-remembered 2,468 ft summit cairn of Pen Pumlumon Fawr itself just after eight o'clock when the first stars were already twinkling. Coastal lights were winking in imitation. A sprawl of golden brightness I took to be Aberystwyth. Below lay shivering reservoirs and the drainage of the Rheidol River, which hurries a deep cut course to the sea in contrast to the wandering miles of Severn or Wye.

I climbed into the shelter to fish out map and compass which I studied by torchlight (there were too many paths and fences). I wanted to camp not too far off so I could return for the morning view. Two small lakes gave a good line and could just be seen in the dark. We hit a stream just below them and at 9 p.m. were tucking in to a haggis supper. Plynlimon had been all Borrow and Wynford Vaughan-Thomas had led me to expect. We fell asleep under a cold gauze of moon-clouds. Somewhere today we passed our second thousand miles of walking.

Sunday 23 September   OFF PLYNLIMON
J. H. B. Peel, writing of Plynlimon, said he met only one person on its summits in five visits. "It was difficult to believe in the existence of traffic jams, cinemas, Moon probes, and betting offices," he wrote – and today he could no doubt add a few more horrors to the list.

A good kip led to a lengthy breakfast as the weather was soft and wet again. Milky clouds covered the summit and the murmur of the stream slowly increased. We kept to the tent till noon then in bright afternoon sun swung down off the yellow slopes of Drum Peithnant – with a view to the dam of the Nant-y-moch Reservoir – to cross the Rheidol at Aber-Peithnant. An old track took us behind a spur (with a prehistoric fort on top) where a gush of water poured through a gullet off the hills and made a perfect cover to read away the afternoon with *Wuthering Heights*. The chill drove us over to the edge of a wood above a ford on a minor road that carried no traffic that I noticed. The tent was rough with hoar before we turned in and we had a night of stars such as we had not seen in months.

Monday 24 September   INTO THE WILDERNESS
Dawn came red and unpromising but I still had to shake flakes of ice off the tent when I struck it. Dinas Reservoir was steaming as we wandered down past it to Ponterwyd. There are now two bridges and we watched the bubbles floating down between them until the post office opened. The people there very helpful, as all were. Being the village shop as well, they soon teased out of me what we were up to. "Would I like a bath?" was one reaction!

Wherever we stopped in Wales we met with great kindness. It was like being back in the Highlands, even to there being two languages. English was hardly spoken in the rural parts (until we came on the scene) and, again, Highland-like, there was a robust independence of outlook. A shepherd from Plynlimon would find himself one with a shepherd from Peeblesshire, or Skiddaw, far more easily than he would with any urban dweller. This difference between urban and rural outlook is still the greatest division in these islands, far more so than national ones. Rural Wales struck me as being well aware of its fine heritage: a happy self-contained people, dwelling in a singularly beautiful landscape.

The elderly attendant kept an eye on my rucker while Storm and I had a look at the Mynach Falls (*Monk's Falls*) below the ill-named Devil's Bridge. The first bridge on which two others are superimposed was originally built by the monks from Strata Florida and is more correctly the Pont y Mynach.

The falls were deep set and difficult to photograph through the velvetted mossy trees. The white water makes a small tentative leap into a pool and then, as if grown bold, crashes down through the black cleft among the trees. Its waters join the Afon Rheidol, hurrying from its Plynlimon source, and the whole wooded area is laid out with paths and brutally steep stairways – up which overweight tour parties were puffing for the cafe. We had a coffee, and they insisted on Storm coming in despite the NO DOGS sign. The Vale of Rheidol Light Railway ends at Devil's Bridge, having come up from Aberystwyth on the coast – the last of the seven little railways of Wales I was to see. (Showell Styles has written a guide for a train-walk journey to use them all.)

We pulled up to the Arch, erected in 1810 for the George III Jubilee by Thomas Johnes, an early agricultural improver who built an exotic mansion in the valley below. He planted four million trees (mainly larch or acorn-raised oak). Coleridge may have remembered Hafod when describing the pleasure domes of Xanadu. The Baldwin/Nash buildings were burnt down, and the dream turned sour. In 1958 the ruins were blown up and the site is now a caravan park.

I had originally planned to traverse Bryn Garw, *rough hill*, from Ponterwyd but the chance of seeing Devil's Bridge off-season led us there first. I hid my sack among the larches and went up and down this unexciting 2,003 ft hill in a couple of hours, by some long-winded forestry roads. Beyond the painted forest trails we had it to ourselves. There was a great sweeping view of the 'desert' to the south which lured us on irresistibly. We came down through jay-noisy tracks.

Joining a noisy crowd at one of the picnic tables, I found volunteers to bear off a packet of film, maps, books, postcards and odd things that always seemed to accumulate. We ambled down into the delightful Cwmystwyth valley and were glad of cold drinks at the post office. The shepherds were gathering across the river so we went on and paddled the Ystwyth a mile upstream. (Why is Aberystwyth so called when it is not really at the mouth of this river?) A small stream led us steeply up out of the valley, and we then wandered in and out of humps and hollows to end on the rim of a huge, empty, tawny basin, an extraordinary featureless bogland into which we picked our careful way to gain a stream that cut through it – the only object of any definition, and wandering as erratically as a butterfly in a gale at that. As so often in peaty, boggy country the stream gave by far the easiest walking line (you can forget the constant textbook adage about never following down streams) and also a selection of tempting grassy flats among the wrinkled, sodden wastes. At five or so we stopped, pitching more or less on the Dyfed-Powys border, by this gentle Ffaethnant which becomes the Afon Claerwen which in turn feeds a string of reservoirs down the Elan valley. What Birmingham does not take eventually joins the Wye. As we had crossed two rivers, that day, flowing to Cardigan Bay this felt like progress. It was all downhill to the Severn now! "Tail well up these days," I wrote before turning in after a benign and restful evening in the blessed solitude.

Tuesday 25 September   THE RHAYADER MOUNTAIN DESERT
There was nothing benign or restful about the next two days of turbulent wilderness. How quickly in mid-Wales the country changes from the plain porridge of domesticated rural valleys to the tougher meat of the sinewy uplands. A night of rain was steam-drying the moors for a dawn departure on the long miles of river-wending down to lonely Claerwen, a solitary house with guardian trees above an Ochil-like reservoir.

We planned originally to use the roadless south shore as it was less in-dented, but the going looked – and was – tussocky, which breaks the heart, if not the ankles, and the weather gradually turned wet and windy. We were content to follow the road from Claerwen, where the motorable track ends, though the path continues west over to Strata Florida, a long-derelict Cistercian establishment which once tamed some of the wilderness of the upper Teifi. Tradition makes it the burial place of the greatest of all Welsh poets, Dafydd ap Gwilym.

I am still not sure what the collective name for these hills is; any map of Wales tends to leave them blank apart from the wiggles of man-made reservoirs. *Bridge* calls them the Rhayader Mountains. They form a thirty mile, roadless, barrier to the south-west of Rhayader, their western flanks drained by the River Teifi, while their other slopes eventually drain one way or another to the Bristol Channel. Such an emptiness (which Defoe called "a kind of desert") was tempting enough in the original planning but since Charles had contaminated us with *Bridge's* disease (he had left this Sassenach substitute for Munro on the table when I used his flat) it lured with the offering of two summits above this perverse altitude.

It was on seeing these hills that a French Alpine guide exclaimed: "The Almighty has forgotten to put the tops on them." This guide, Jean Charlet, was brought back to the Elan valley in Victorian times by a 'lady alpinist' and later married another, Miss Stratton, which I'm sure set society talking.

The Claerwen Reservoir road is designed to give maximum frustration to the walker for when it is not going in and out big arms of water it is going up and down promontories of hillside. E. F. Schumacher's *Small is Beautiful* kept me engrossed. I had first read it many years ago, when it came out, and was struck by its warnings then; now, it made almost horrific reading as all the worst is coming to pass.

The Claerwen dam was more attractive than most, with a roadway on arches over it; and from the large centre arch a 'waterfall' dropped into the valley below where a farmstead snuggled down among trees. An ascent from there to the top would have given miles of rain-blasting on high so we held down the valley for another two or three miles. We had a picnic in the rain and watched the tourists drive up and away again without even leaving their cars, not that I blamed them. One dammed wet valley is very like another. The path on the non-road side suffered from being used by sheep, cows and ponies, all of whom had left their mark. Storm managed to go up to his belly in a bright orange goo. We sat out a deluge under a chestnut tree and went on in a fragile dryness. It was no state for a middleday dalliance.

Ascending the Rhiwnant we ran into sheep being gathered so perched on a knoll till they had flowed by and spilled off downwards. We exchanged friendly words with the busy shepherds then zig-zagged up by mining ruins on easy, if saturated, grass slopes, to gain the open miles of moorland. It was the sort of landscape that had to be read ahead and taken steadily, with guile, the type of going which shatters the innocent novice who still believes the quickest way between two points is a straight line. The wind was increasing steadily and I really expected a thrashing but for once we were lucky. Drygarn Fawr, 2,003 ft, was a bit like

Plynlimon with more outcrops or tumulus cairns or old mine workings (I was often unsure which was which), and an extensive view struggling to avoid being smothered under the dirty cloud blankets.

Gorllwyn, 2,009 ft, *ambush*, was under four miles on, but even with a tail wind took two hours to reach. We crossed the Bwlch-y-ddau-faen, a drovers' way to Rhayader from the Towy valley. We descended steeply into the warm valley to the east. Storm played hide-and-seek in the bracken, and also discovered a sheep dying with a festering hernia. All the paths or sheep trails were trampled into pockmarked ribbons as the beasts had been gathered. We kept to the river and had an obstacle course with new plantings to gain the minor road that ran up the valley. There was a field full of excited tups. After just one steep pull up we halted having covered 22 miles of complex packing. Enough! I pitched the tent by the Nant y Fedw, among bracken, which would be fired by autumn colours at home, but here still rose strong and green, taller than the tent. An erratic rain piddled down all night long. Every now and then a breeze would rattle the wet fronds on to the Tramp. The very uncertainty of a testing day had made it enjoyable.

Wednesday 26 September   WYE AND WHEREFORE
Brandon's sixteen-hour 'shower' was now surpassed. It had rained all night and continued to do so all day, not with Brandon's aquatic exuberance but with the very worst of wetness for walking, a fine, warm, vaporous rain that utterly soaked all it touched – and it touched everything. There was no wind so we had coils smoking while we packed inside our dank cell of a tent. Dawn merely changed the shades of grey. We set off through shrouds of steaming clouds and by the cross roads were soaked, Goretex or no. I have seen it claimed that this material 'stops you sweating', which is obviously nonsense. When conditions are right it allows sweat to escape. As today was equally humid outside and inside my waterproof there was no chance of the material percolating in my favour. On every little hill I almost blew up like an overtaxed pressure cooker. It was amazing how many uphills were squeezed into the miles down to Builth Wells. Builth is largely a market town, now that people no longer 'take the waters'. Historically, it was at Builth that the great Llewellyn met his end. Edward is a name no more popular in Wales than it is in Scotland.

We would have been quite happy to abandon the walking for the day had there been a bus to Hay-on-Wye but there was no way down the Wye except on foot. We ate poached eggs on toast in a friendly cafe and then sorted out some gear under the chestnuts on the Gro, looking to the eighteenth-century red bridge that spanned the muddy Wye. The next stage was not enjoyed as the road was busy and the verges inadequate. We escaped to the other bank for several miles beyond Erwood, where once the drovers swam their cattle over the river on the way to London, but thirst brought us over again to the knot of houses forming Llyswen. Oh, for the Irish ice-cream cones at every hamlet!

The flat going was welcome for I was nearly suffocated in my waterproofs. Little enough was visible in a world reduced to weary humidity. In places red soil ran into the river to fade slowly into the grey. The Black Mountains were completely blotted out. Aberllynfi on the map turned out to be the Three Cocks, a pub and cafe; both were used. As there was only a smir of rain I read the rest of the road in to Hay, which did my topical copy of *Kilvert's Diary* no good at all. It, along with most of my belongings, was hung up somewhere to dry that night in The Swan. We were booked in at The Crown and had mail waiting there, but, as in Grasmere, I had not mentioned a dog. In my sodden state I did not take the rebuff kindly, but the warm welcome for both of us at The Swan was restorative. We had a window looking on to a garden. In the gloaming the swallows were twittering and gathering on the wires. Evidently they considered it was time to be off to warmer climes. Weather makes philosophers of us all in the end.

> The gangrel disnae girn at wund
> Or warsle wi the storm;
> He coories doon tae bide a wee –
> There's aye the morn's morn.

Thursday 27 September   HAY-ON-WYE
We visited the post office for a parcel and also to collect a couple of boxes of slides (of Ireland) for I feared the winding mechanism was playing up. It was all right. The next call was the dentist who did a temporary filling. The view from the dental chair was over the fresh landscape of this rich valley, which has its addicts since Kilvert country appearances on TV – Clyro being a mile away over the river. He was curate there from 1865–72 and filled nine annual diaries, many, alas, now destroyed.

I had planned two days off here because of the particular attraction of Hay's new major industry – books. It boasts both the largest collection of any single second-hand shop in Britain and also more second-hand shops than any other town in Britain. Richard Booth, Booksellers, occupy several buildings including a cinema, castle and a mansion house. My Scottish, Moroccan, historical and climbing interests were

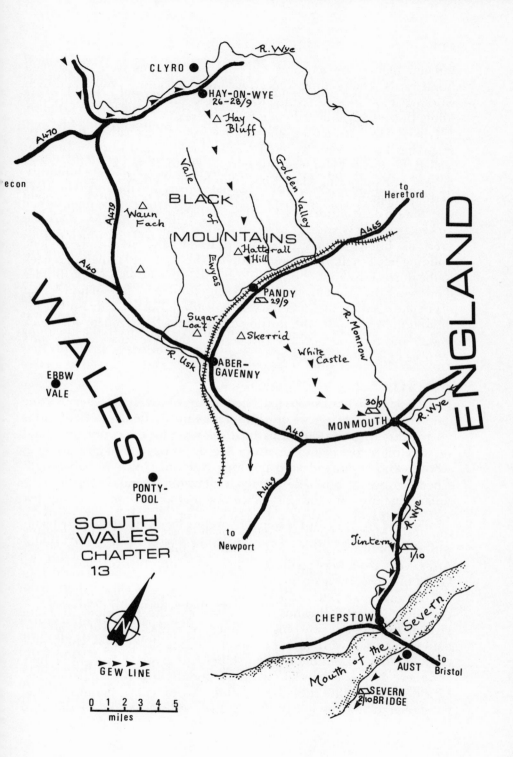

R. Wye

CLYRO

HAY-ON-WYE
26-28/9

△ Hay
Bluff

A470

Brecon

A479

Golden Valley

BLACK

△ Waun
Fach

of

MOUNTAINS

Vale

Ewyas

△ Hatterall
Hill

A465

to
Hereford

A40

△

WALES

Sugar
Loaf △

PANDY
29/9

R. Monnow

ENGLAND

△ Skerrid

White
Castle

R. Usk

EBBW
VALE

ABER-
GAVENNY

A40

30/9

MONMOUTH

R. Wye

PONTY-
POOL

A449

to
Newport

R. Wye

SOUTH
WALES
CHAPTER
13

Tintern

1/10

N

Mouth of the Severn

GEW LINE

CHEPSTOW

0 1 2 3 4 5
miles

AUST

to
Bristol

SEVERN
2/10 BRIDGE

satiated before the day was out and two cartons were dispatched homewards. The evening went in having a quick look round and then working at logistics. As Jerome K. Jerome said, it is "impossible to enjoy idling thoroughly unless there is plenty to do."

I liked Hay. Its setting and history were so typical of border or Highland Line places. Roger, Earl of Hereford and Lord of Brecon, walled the town and built a castle to resist Henry II, but kings seemed to delight in hammering Hay. King John burnt the town in 1216, it was destroyed again in 1231 by Llywellyn and was besieged in the struggle with Simon de Montfort. As if the Border barons were not enough it was sacked again by Glyndwr c. 1400 and a few years ago the castle (full of precious books) was accidentally burned, and its Jacobean-style building left a shell. It is being restored. The really old remains go back to the thirteenth century, built by William de Braose whose wife (bolder if not wiser than the barons) accused King John to his face of murdering his nephew Arthur and was starved to death in Corfe Castle for her indiscretion. A last walk with the dog discovered a Machynlleth-like clock tower, and we stood on the bridge over the Wye to watch the stars tremble in its moving waters.

Friday 28 September   BRECON BEACONS

The day spent in bookshops had been sunny, of course, so when this one dawned fresh and clear we quickly forsook the harder legwork of shops for the ease of grassy hills. I had half-planned for the contingency and we were off before eight in a bus to Brecon. It was full of girls going to school, who commandeered the long-suffering dog. We had a tight schedule once the bus had squeezed itself round several corners into the square, ending with the post office opening at nine and the Merthyr Tydfil bus leaving at five past. This swept us up a helpful 1,440 feet to the top of the Merthyr road where the Youth Hostel had a notice pleading with the public to realise it was no longer a pub (it had been the Storey Arms). At 9.30 we were on the Beacons, off-route, on an off-day, with the Welsh magic working again.

The range is an extraordinary one. I can think of no comparison for, though it is stratified sandstone vaguely like the Torridons, it is not jagged. Its lines are sweeping and pure, yet truncated, as if giants had battled against it with mighty weapons, cutting sharp edges above precipitous slopes. Even the steepest slopes had greened over, while here and there deep *kloofs* cut into its slopes and the *bergs* rose in flat topped *kopjes*. Perhaps the similes to South Africa came because I had remembered unconsciously that Brecon was the home of the 24th

Regiment of Foot which held Rorke's Drift in the Zulu war, a site and a story I knew from childhood in Natal. More VCs were awarded in its heroic defence than in any other engagement. The numeral XXIV is incorporated in Brecon's coat of arms. Some day I must make time to explore the town.

Storm set off a grouse which surprised me, for the hills were grassy rather than heather-covered and it was far south for this unique bird of the British Isles. We began on Y Gyrn which barely scraped its 2,000 feet at 2,010, but led on to the edge of a deep cwm full of moraine hummocks which held a small, round gem of a pool, Llyn Cwm Llwch. An obelisk on a col commemorated a tragedy in 1900: a miner from South Wales had brought his son Tommy Jones to visit his grandfather at the foot of the Beacons. They walked from Brecon Station, having a snack at a military camp, and later meeting the old man and a thirteen-year-old cousin. The lads were sent ahead, but five-year-old Tommy wanted his dad and turned back. He vanished and it was weeks later before his body was found, miles away and 1,300 feet up – at this spot.

From there we skirted out to Craig Duwynt, 2,704 ft, which was higher but hardly more defined till later when it showed as one end of the range's long scarped and scalloped flanks. Corn Du, 2,863 ft, *the blackcairn*, was more of a hill and has a warty appearance from a distance, and from it a swoop down and up landed us on Pen y Fan, 2,906 ft, highest of all the Brecon Beacons.

People seemed to be homing in on it from every direction so we went on to the next top, Craig Cwm Cribin, 2,608 ft, for a laze over the day's paper. Down in the cwms snaky lines of washed-out debris showed that it could rain here, too. Today was a day of glowing vigour, the wind coming from the south with a tang of sea and a taste of the cities in it. The sun throbbed white and diffuse, stabbed on to the landscape – one almost looked for a scrawled 'Vincent' in a corner. It was the day of perfection: yesterday had been a feeble recovery from the wetness, tomorrow could be too hot, or explosively wet – we would know soon enough.

We descended to a col with a big track which was the original bridle track to Merthyr and a Roman road before that. The valley to the south is now a succession of reservoirs as are all the south or east draining rivers. The map uses the word Forest on many areas here, meaning not trees, but wild country in olden days – such as the mediaeval hunting ground of Brecon's Fforest Fawr, or the Forest of Mamlorn in Perthshire.

I put on shorts before going up to Fan Big, the prow above, which had a big stone man on it. Beyond it the country changed. There were still big bites of corrie but the plateau was a mess of peat hags and the easiest going was on the edge. Craig Pwllfa/Waen-rydd has a trig marked 2,502 ft and a spot height of 2,504 ft; both had to be done; then a careful check showed Allt-Lwyd as 2,000 ft plus so we went *down* to it saying rude things about stray tops. As it was fine on high we pulled up the 400 feet back to bogland rather than descend to scenic Talybont Reservoir (Newport's water supply) and face seven miles of road.

We dropped into Cwm Cwareli and crossed the Nant Menassin just as the jungle began: great drying bracken slopes with plenty of trees and hawthorn and hints of past use in sunken lanes, ruins, and overgrown dykes. Two mares and their foals stood fringed with silver back-lighting under the oaks. A herd of cows had one bull who stared stolidly at us. We ended down a lane which led right into a pig sty.

We hurried into Brecon for a 5.10 bus and missed it only to find that it left at 5.50, giving time for a chip supper on the square. We sat in the gold of failing day, listening to a couple of women talking away in Welsh, it was so lilting that it sounded almost like singing. The hills were even clearer for the wandering journey back, only the shadows had changed from right to left. "From the rising of the sun to the going down of the same" – it had been good, a golden day which even memory has no need to burnish to recall its unalloyed pleasure.

Saturday 29 September   THE BLACK MOUNTAINS
Hay-on-Wye is on the Offa's Dyke path which we had last met on the day we descended to Ruthin. I wondered how Eric was faring on Annapurna, a very different sort of challenge to this stolid plodding yet so similar as well, for mountains are basically all the same. More people die on the Brecon Beacons than on Annapurna – and more find delight on Offa's Dyke than have ever seen Dhaulagiri. The challenge and the rewards are tailor-made, individually received. We do not wear each other's boots. We hedge our bets as far as we can for we love life more than most, love it enough, in the end, to put it at risk.

I had not noticed any waymark signs in the town and rather casually wandered up out of it on the road for the Gospel Pass, a name which may derive from the efforts of raising the Third Crusade in 1188. Once above this deeply agricultural belt there was a *machair*-like quality to the cropped grass, almost a natural golf course, even to having the hazards of bunkers and furze clumps. There was a splendid view along the Elfael Hills, the northern bluffs of the Black Mountains. The day's route was to give a seventeen mile walk to Pandy over the highest miles of the Offa's

Back to Wales: the Jerusalem Chapel, Bethesda

Wild ponies on the Carneddau

The view west from Tryfan: Y Garn, Foel Goch
and distant Elidir Fawr

The Rhinogs

Cader Idris: the summit
from the east

On the northern slopes of Plynlimon

Camp in the Rhayader wilderness – on the infant Claerwen

Chepstow: one of the finest of the Welsh Border Castles

Pen y Fan in the Brecon Beacons

Cheddar Gorge: Chris Bonington climbing "Coronation Street" gives
the scale (see crag on left at conjunction of both arrows)

The Cornish coastal path at Kynance Cove by Godrevy Point

Cornish granite at Bosigran, West Penwith

Land's End: a celebratory snack for dog and man

Dyke path. The rock is a hard sandstone known as *brownstone* but the peat is black enough unless churned up by ponies, the walker's unfriends. For many miles the path follows the Gwent-Herefordshire border.

We cut up to a rising track (*rhiw*) which scored across the prow of Pen y Beacon, 2,219 ft, leading us almost to the height of the trig pillar. A crowd of school children doing the Way still had the noisy air that betrayed their three-day-old status. By Clwyd they would be an efficient, quiet, team. I used to watch this transformation so often with the Braehead kids: the effervescent trip north with bottles of pop and crisps and the spew bucket coming into play and then the relaxed, almost sad return home when they were like sponges, saturated with new experiences. Three times, after long years of silence, men have phoned me to ask about accommodation in such and such a place where they had been a decade earlier, because they were engaged and wanted to go there for their honeymoon – a charming, unplanned spin-off.

The path was wide and clear despite book warnings to the contrary, but the peaty whalebacks would have marked quickly. Black Mountain, 2,306 ft, was the highest bump, but on Black Hill (2,102 ft and surely as much a Top as Pen y Beacon?), across a deep-cut valley, a helicopter was bearing loads and the dots of figures could be seen. The split nature of this range soon showed itself and the view into the deep Ewyas Valley which divides it gave the best prospect of the day – running down towards the Sugar Loaf which rose before a dazzle of sun.

For historical interest, walking the Vale of Ewyas would be rewarding. It has attracted people out from the world's bustle for centuries. In the reign of Henry I, William de Lacy, Lord of Hereford, found spiritual transformation in the valley and became an anchorite, living to see Llanthony Abbey established, change indeed for a Norman border baron. Now there are only extensive ruins left, for the decline had started long before the Dissolution under Henry VIII. The poet Landor bought the estate in 1807 and planted the trees which grace it, but his eccentricity and ill temper led to his being virtually driven out and he died abroad. His experiment in isolation had cost £200,000.

Hunky Hatterall Hill loomed up ahead. We met the local Park Warden who hailed from Southampton originally, so relished it here. He had a collie which made friends with Storm. We must have descended more than we realised for it felt quite a pull up to reach 1,743 ft. Below us the Herefordshire plains were neatly divided into small fields which rolled gently into hazy distance beyond the Golden Valley and Grosmont Castle. As we began to lose height rapidly an oddly-shaped outline held our attention ahead: Skerrid Mountain (Ysgyryd

Fawr), which is an old holy mountain, hoary with legend, and a trig point set on the ruins of an old chapel. South again was the Blorenge beyond Abergavenny with a more recent legend – on it is the grave of *Foxhunter* the showjumper I once trailed from London to Dublin in my horse-daft period. A kestrel flew over, then the air suddenly seemed to be full of wheeling birds – which turned out to be hang-gliders. There were over twenty airborne at any one time. It was fascinating.

The flurry and flutter excited the dog but as there were dozens of them, and people, and dogs, this new world was soon accepted. Storm and a boxer dog followed each other about and thought nothing of cocking a hind leg over some precious glider. We had everything laid on from instruction classes to a prang. (A lad made a timid rush to the edge and fell over it instead of launching into space.) It looked a pleasantly *cool* game and I felt quite envious. I was tempted to camp at a high farm for the spacious view but it was really too early. We dropped steeply down from a prehistoric fort site to Pandy. At one end of the straggly hamlet a wag had added a stroke to the P of the name, at the other someone else had added *Andy* before the *Pandy*. I believe it is pronounced Bandy and means *fulling mill*.

A site we had seen from Hatterall Hill proved to be for caravans only. A lad mowing grass in an orchard offered it as a site but we pushed on down to the Rising Sun which imaginatively offered all things for all men: pub, cafe, restaurant and camp site.

I suddenly realised that from here to Land's End we would not find any more land over 2,000 feet. We had more or less walked Wales from north to south, in what seemed no time at all, and it had been so very, very good. And the next day was the last day of September. No wonder the elderberries were ripe and heavy, no wonder the sun sank daily in a pale serenity – as if the air was being bleached by time, its pigments thinning like delicate water-colours. The rust of autumn would soon be on the land.

Sunday 30 September   AN OFFA'S DYKE DAY
As we set off we found a scattering of red apples along the roadside where a lorry had spilled them – so we had an apple every time we stopped. A road went grimly up to start with, and it was a relief to gain the Offa's Dyke Path across the fields to Llangattock Lingoed, the burial place of Morgan the pirate, Knight and Governor of Jamaica (his home in Brecon is now a hotel). The path officially went through the churchyard.

It was a day of rural strides once more, the sort of landscape where an

official, if contrived, path actually helps pick a line through the complexities of cultivation. A lark was in full end-of-season song. A green
woodpecker set the coombes ringing, living up to his Scot's name of
yaffle.

White Castle was disappointingly masked in trees and not open till
2 p.m. Wales is rightly famous for its castles. A surprising number have
survived, gaunt reminders of the grim old days. White Castle is the
finest of the 'Castles of the Trilateral' (Skenfrith and Grosmont are the
other two) which were established by the Norman Lords Marcher to
secure their debatable lands of Gwent. It was spartan, grim and no
doubt very effective, but after the Edwardian conquests gradually
crumbled. Its curtain walls and towers would be seen to greater advantage if it were not buried in trees.

We free wheeled down into the hamlet of Llantilio Crossenny (where
St. Teilo Parish Church is one of the finest on the Offa's Dyke Path) in
hope of a shop. There was one, but shut; our evening meal would
therefore be of scraps if I wanted to avoid the problems of a night in
Monmouth. I was becoming embarrassed by asking for accommodation
with the dog. Poor Storm; he would sit and smile politely, but it takes
more than that to melt the heart of a flinty landlady. After lunching
under a big oak we ran into dog trouble at The Grange. A Yorkshire
terrier came up as if to be friends then at the last second went screaming
off as if it was being beaten. A la-di-da youth then appeared and
demanded what *my* dog was doing loose. It was the only 'scene' we had
with Storm during the whole trip. I rather enjoyed it.

The route criss-crossed the Trothy River. We found a potato lying on
the track which more than supplemented our supper for it must have
weighed at least two pounds. I made tea by the site of Grace Dieu Abbey,
abandoned at the Dissolution and now completely vanished. We skirted
the Hendre policies and farms and the path led us up to the wooded
hills, the King's Wood, where I had planned to stay overnight, having
been told there was no camp site in Monmouth.

The plantations were both coniferous and deciduous, but surprisingly
lacked water. Eventually I saw a trickle and fought down a jungly bank
to reach it – only to find it too muddy for drinking. Upstream, at a small
spring, I filled the gallon container. On returning to the rucker we were
immediately surrounded by a cloud of angry troglodyte wasps. I had
dumped my bag down beside their entrance tunnel and they had come
forth to defend themselves.

In the end I pitched down the far slope a bit, in a corner of a wood,
which seemed to attract an endless passage of birds: unmannerly

magpies, woodpeckers which corkscrewed round the trunks to Storm's puzzlement, pheasants which honked or exploded at our feet, jays which flew past with their bursts of colour. In contrast we could hear the throb of distant traffic, the wind-drifted voices of children periodically and the Lara theme from Dr Zhivago being tinkled by a touring ice-cream van. Monmouth lay just along and down Watery Lane.

Monday 1 October   MONMOUTH AND TINTERN

September had slipped away in a second warm, calm, dewless night. What a difference to pack up dry, day after day. We were in Monmouth by 8 a.m. and before we even crossed the Monnow Bridge I had spotted a camp site. The Monnow Bridge has a unique fortified gateway on it. It looked as if it could be made of *Lego* bricks but is thirteenth century.

I liked Monmouth at once. To wait for the post office we went in to the first cafe we met. Finding one open at that time was a surprise. The lady running it gave Storm a dish of scraps which would have done a Great Dane. Grey squirrels apart, it was the only thing on the trip to defeat the dog. He was thoroughly petted in a second-hand bookshop (another parcel went homewards) and was invited into the Nelson Museum instead of sitting outside. This is probably the finest collection of items outwith the *Victory*, and a must for Nelson enthusiasts. After an hour I tore myself away from the working model of Trafalgar and collected my parcel from the GPO next door. We sorted our parcel on a bench in Agincourt Square (Henry V was born in the town) while the cleaners carefully swept round us. They took their time and were obviously dying to ask what we were up to. In front of the Shire Wall where we sat was an interesting bronze statue to Charles Rolls, of Rolls Royce fame. (His mother, Lady Llangattock, had given the Nelson collection to the town.) Rolls was a successful racing motorist, aviator (a year after Blériot he set a new Channel record) and balloonist. A special arrangement with the Monmouth Gasworks allowed him to make 170 ascents. His was the first British fatal flying accident in 1910. He is buried in Llangattock church.

Sociable Monmouth had stolen several hours, and, as so often, it would have been good to linger. In some ways a foot-journey is narrow, restrictive and frustrating, and belongs to the wide wilderness. Wandering at fancy's whim, with no rules, would possibly be best for more civilized, historically-interesting places. Perhaps we can try it some day. Having a mobile kennel would certainly simplify things.

We simplified the Offa's Dyke Path by refusing to take all its rather erratic ups and downs, and once we had walked out by the old school we kept along by the broad-flowing River Wye which always had a good path on one bank or the other. Designated paths soon tend to have official lines, official alternatives, suggested alternatives, marked unofficial routes, recommended alternatives and many other categories. To follow the wind and go free is still the best advice. Cool shade was welcome in the woods and there were masses of pink polygonum giving Himalayan dankness.

I met a couple who asked me: "Are you doing the *wey*?" Their accent left me flummoxed; did they mean Way or *Wye*? (And people complain at Welsh or Gaelic.) The answer was never given, for a stoat caught a rabbit just then and the latter's screams almost terrified the two walkers. Later a kingfisher, in shiny spectrum colours, glittered on the river as the day began to catch fire according to pattern.

By the time we reached Tintern Abbey it was broiling in the depths of the gorge. Tintern reminded me a bit of Melrose but the latter I liked more, for it is not commercialised. Everyone comes here with Wordsworth-Tinterned spectacles and is faced with massed car-parks, souvenir kiosks and turnstiles – a soiling of the rich setting which was chosen by its Cistercian founder for peace and solitude. However, the Abbey is well cared for and the Department of the Environment has worked away at the 27-acre site to lay bare many features of interest. A team of archaeologists were busy beside the car-park when we called, patiently trowelling, sifting and brushing down through the past.

There was no immediate camp site visible and I was not trusting a local's 'just up the road'. We collected our gallon of water in Tintern and lugged it up out of the valley. Wild camping in tame country always seems to present snags. We toiled up to a quiet viewpoint and made supper there, which reduced the weight of water for continuing and also let the day change into the cooler garb of evening. But then, after more climbing, we found the Offa's Dyke Path diverted and when we followed the new signs they led away *downhill* again – to such an extent we came back up in a huff and carried on for the Devil's Pulpit. It was dark by then so we soon stopped and gladly used a bit of flat grass under a huge oak tree. A brew restored equilibrium. The night again failed to turn cold or dew-wet but the valley slowly filled with creeping cloud and a dazzle of half-moon poured in under our canopy while the trees seemed to catch the stars in their reaching branches and sway them, glittering, in gentle lullaby. The bracken tangle round us was still green. At home autumn would be setting her fiery colours to the bracken braes; here, on the edge of the Forest of Dean, nature still hovered with brush poised, as if awaiting the first nudge of cool inspiration.

Tuesday 2 October   ACROSS THE SEVERN

We were about a week ahead of schedule by the end of the day, but that was from believing the Wye walk from Monmouth to the sea to be 60 miles, which gives a hint of how casual my homework had been. I forgot to wind my watch again but woke to the foul noise of heavy traffic in the valley below, so took that as a hint.

The whole Wye trench and several tributary valleys were filled with mist. Thus must things have looked in an ice age: the flowing glaciers with the higher ground rising bare above them. We had just won up the slopes enough to avoid being engulfed by this temperature inversion. Below it no doubt was cool enough and damp enough. Autumn sneaking in?

We gained Offa's Dyke and the valley rim with no problems. Some felling had caused the diversion but nobody was working as we passed. The clearing gave a view which would otherwise have been blocked by trees. Badgers had taken up residence in the Dyke, and Storm would wiggle into the sett entrances till only his flag-waving tail showed. The line of the Dyke was very clear and the path usually ran on or beside it. The Devil's Pulpit turned out to be a small pinnacle set out from the path, but the trees around it and the clouds below made it an anti-climax as a view point.

The Way cunningly avoided tarred roads: wiggling over fields (saturated now as we had lost our warm heights) and dodging behind houses to the dramatic lip of Wintour's Leap – so called as Sir John Wintour is supposed to have evaded Parliamentarian pursuit in 1642 by leaping his horse down it and swimming the river to freedom. Escape to France he did, but not down a 200 ft sheer cliff, I'm sure. The limestone cliffs are precipitously eroded and overgrown, with the river meandering in the depths. We twisted down to Chepstow as the last mist floated off the Wye where it curls, tidal and dank, round the buttressed might of a great Castle. Chepstow stands on the 'disemboguement of the Wye' as Borrow puts it, the end of his Welsh walk, and mine. The name comes from *cheap* (market) as in Cheapside. After the Norman conquest one of William the Bastard's followers, de Clare, built a huge castle there to contain the unruly Welsh, but it is most famed for being the birthplace of Strongbow who spent his time sorting out the equally unruly Irish. The castle was palely reflected in the Wye, with long ramparts (250 yards) behind which lay a succession of baileys, joined end-to-end, a plan forced on the builder by the ridges on which it stands. It was built from the eleventh to thirteenth centuries and has been little altered since. In the civil wars it was twice held and lost by the

Royalists – but at least was left standing. Jeremy Taylor was one of its renowned prisoners and after the Restoration Sir Henry Marten endured a twenty year captivity for being one of those who signed the death warrant of King Charles.

The bridge leading into the town was being repaired. It had certainly not been designed for today's juggernauts. It was built in 1816 by Rennie and was one of the earliest cast-iron bridges to be constructed. It leads to the castle by the river and the huddled town beyond on its hill.

We spent two hours in Chepstow with its old walls, which are well preserved. I had to swop stoves there, but the Ruthin-purchased one, sent from Bangor in North Wales, had not turned up. The one we had would not take the fuel waiting along the route so, perforce, I had to buy another one. The post office gave me forms to fill in about the missing one and the following spring, in Morocco, I was amazed to receive payment against my claim. We had a lunch snack of toasted cheese sandwiches and set off at noon.

It was hot enough to change into shorts and walk with a bare torso, even across the bridge out of Wales. Any feeling that the trip was nearly over had gone in a quick look at the map: from Snowdonia to Severn was a shorter distance than from the Severn Bridge to the nearest part of Cornwall.

Having drunk at the source of the Wye, Borrow ended his wanderings by having a drink from the waters at the mouth of the river. (He would have reservations about doing that today.) He then drank a bottle of port before the fire in an inn, singing Welsh songs till ten o'clock when he paid his reckoning, "amounting to something considerable", and went off to catch a train (first class) home to London. Lucky lad. I still had further than the length of Wales to walk before there could be any celebratory bottle.

The Severn Bridge, built in 1966, with towers soaring 400 feet above the sea, has no 'gaps' for airflow between the various lanes or footway. It seemed to bounce more than the Forth Bridge, giving an odd softness to the walking that matched the dry peaty miles of its source on Plynlimon. The pathway swayed to the grind of traffic. We walked with the feeling of a sailor on dry land again or a cyclist afoot after many miles in the saddle. What an unusual source-to-sea link we had made. We still knew next to nothing of Britain's largest river. We strode over, a hundred feet above the sea, the estuary beyond a "sulky old gray brute" as it has been called. On the Forth at least we had used the river, and been used by it.

The bridges themselves were the common factor and bridges, old or new, are the constructional glory of engineering, for devotion rather than vanity decorates their functional qualities. Telford is greater than Inigo Jones. To try and glean some facts about the bridge I looked up John Merrill's coast walk account only to discover he went round by Gloucester as he had set himself a rule of no motorway bridges. He used the Forth Bridge and he tried to wangle a crossing of the Humber Bridge catwalk during its construction. I failed to see the logic of his discriminating against this marvellous bridge. The Severn is over a mile wide here and the tidal range can approach 50 feet, a fact used in constructing the box decking. Sections were floated down from Chepstow to be lifted at high tide. The bridge crosses the Wye as well as the Severn. Brunel's suspension bridge (the Wye railway bridge to Chepstow) has been superseded in the scale of daring engineering. I'm biased towards bridges, of course, for my mother's father built many of Thailand's early bridges, but I still think older is better and plain stone is best of all.

All the way from Hay I had been on the border of England, had indeed crossed into it unknowingly on Wye banks, but it was crossing Severn that really made me know I had departed Wales. The English shore gave a fine cliff formation. Aust has become a forgotten town now, with the days of ferry gone and the Motorway thundering by. We had a feed of brambles, then followed a path along sea dykes by Northwick Ooze but had to abandon it as a firing range was in use. It was homely to have the smell of the sea again. The bridge rather lacked a scenic background or else the heat haze hid it from us. I can see the Forth Bridge from the garden at home so am no doubt prejudiced. The adequate paths, here, again made me think that the South West Coastal Path could so easily link on to Offa's Dyke Path as part of a grand Groats End Walk. Not that it would be scenically outstanding. Shocks lay ahead.

Severn Beach was the first camp site we found. The resident cat gave Storm a sock on the nose as welcome. Everything had shut down, for the summer was officially over. The sunny evening simply made it look all the more forlorn. We went off to have a session in the telephone box, first to check about the Motorway Bridge at Avonmouth (yes, pedestrians could cross it), then to Bill Sommers with whom I hoped to spend a night soon, then home, where everything was fine but Charles had left a message for me to ring him urgently. My immediate thought was "Eric!" As I had only one coin left, Charles had to ring me back more or less as soon as I could give him the number. It *was* Eric: he and two Americans had been killed on Annapurna.

XIV

BY SEVERN SHORES

Only the road and the dawn, the sun, the wind,
    and the rain,
And the watch fire under stars, and sleep, and
    the road again.

              J. MASEFIELD: *The Seekers*

Wednesday 3 October   OVER THE AVON, UNDER THE MENDIPS   *Map, p. 248*
Ray had also been trying to contact me from Devon but I kept eluding
him by going ahead of schedule. A friend of his, Barry Clark, had just
been killed in Snowdonia and Ray's 'Two Moors Way' was being interrupted for a second time. So it was not the most cheerful of evenings.
Remembering Storm's performance at Melrose I took him into the
shower with me and left him perched on the bench above the wet. There
he fell asleep, and tumbled off the bench to splash into the water.
Perhaps he did it on purpose, to cheer me up.

Charles was only able to give me the briefest of news about Eric. It
seemed he and Gilbert Harder (whom we'd met at Ruthin) and another
American opted to remain up at Camp IV when the rest of the party
descended to sit out what was to prove a five day storm. Later, more
news filtered through. The avalanche passed something like a hundred
yards away from Camp IV which had been sited on top of a rib which
forms the safest link between lower and upper parts of the mountain.
Camp III was 1,200 ft below, at the foot of the rib, and there, too, the
force of the avalanche blast was felt, and collapsed one tent. Camp IV
was hit by the devastating wind-blast which bursts out ahead and around
an avalanche, and can be travelling at several hundred miles an hour. (If
you want the horrific statistics consult Colin Fraser's *Avalanches and Snow
Safety*.) This blast simply blew Camp IV off the mountain leaving the site
bare and empty. A battered tin of food was found one and a half miles
away from the camp and a section of the fixed ropes (breaking strain
2,700 lbs which is about $1\frac{1}{2}$ tons) was missing, the broken ends of the
nylon looking as if they had 'exploded'. It is this wind-blast which does
such damage, even in Alpine regions: it flattens forests and explodes

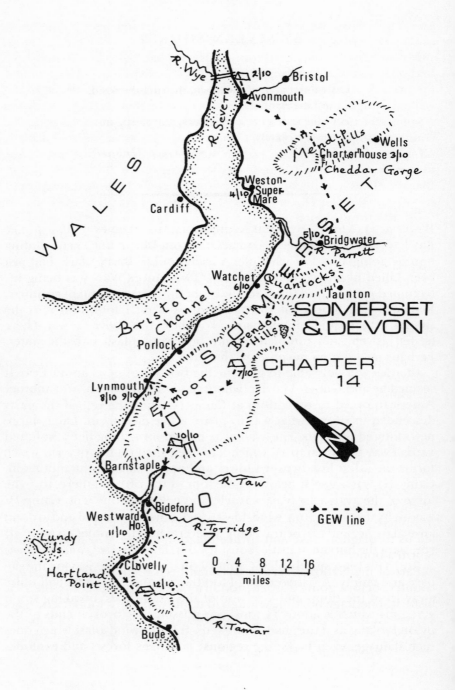

R. Wye

2|10

Bristol

Avonmouth

WALES

Mendip Hills

Charterhouse 3|10

Wells

Cheddar Gorge

R. Severn

Weston-Super-Mare
4|10

Cardiff

SOMERSET

5|10 Bridgwater

R. Parrett

Watchet
6|10

Quantocks

Taunton

Bristol Channel

SOMERSET
& DEVON

Brendon Hills

Porlock

EXMOOR

CHAPTER
14

7|10

Lynmouth
8|10 9|10

N

Barnstaple

DEVON

R. Taw

Bideford

Westward
Ho
11|10

10|10

Lundy
Is.

Clovelly

R. Torridge

- - → GEW line

Hartland
Point

12|10

0   4   8   12   16
miles

Bude

R. Tamar

buildings. No wonder our ancestors regarded mountains and avalanches with superstitious horror!

My own fascinating horror came early in what was to be a 26 mile hike to the Mendip Hills; early in that I was off by six and early in that it filled the first six miles of the day. We had been warned not to try paths, so walked straight into Avonmouth. What a setting there is ready-made for a Science Fiction film. I found it so utterly appalling as to fascinate the country bumpkin: dockyards, chemical works, gas works, fuel depots, oil refineries, timber yards, railway sidings, smelting works and so on; they were all fighting it out as if in some surrealist *Death of the World*. Blackpool has nothing on it for illuminations – and I hope the variety of its olfactory experiences. It was the ultimate I had ever seen in industrialisation, rendered the more menacing by the queer enveloping mist through which a poisoned sun failed to make its way. Avonmouth was not so much a place as one vast anti-pedestrian roundabout. The juggernauts rule there. We fled over the bridge, leaving it an arcing tail of lights in the failed dawn, escaping on to a path signed "The Avon Way". (The mind boggles!)

To be fair I suppose the sacrifice has been made where there was little to destroy, but even beyond Lodway, spilling out its frantic human ants who work in this black nest, the morning mist reeked of fumes. We walked up a wooded valley, loud with water and lost among the pulses of vapour banks. We made our exit among explosions of tail-less pheasants.

The detail of that day has gone. We seemed to wend uphill for a long way only to lose it all again. The blackberries were no longer tasty. "The Devil has pissed on them", as they say in these parts. We made some superb coffee in a wood on Barrow Hill above Lulsgate (Bristol) Airport where the cloying clouds which had given us such a limbo-walk were just beginning to clear. There had been no refreshing night rain (a grumble of thunder and flickering skies over the Bristol Channel) and the atmosphere was burdened with a week of weather-goodness. A bridle way led us to Blagdon Lake and spruce Blagdon village. The butcher gave Storm a bone.

Part of my National Service days had been spent in this part of the country, before going abroad; too brief a time to appreciate the rich historical heritage but time enough to doubly-offend a local friend who shared my room. One evening he suggested, "Let's go for a walk up the hill." Quite innocently, after a look right round the flat landscape, I asked, "What hill?" He pointed out what looked no more than a greened-over coal bing. On our one free day we went for a run in his car to the Cotswolds, country which I liked very much indeed but again my tongue tripped me up for I asked at one stage, "Where are the hills?" We, apparently, were *on* them. This English concept of hills being cultivated right over even their highest parts was simply one the Scot had never met. Even Ben Nevis to us is just a *hill* for the term mountain is not used at all. Just how ingrained my background was came out later, in East Africa, when a gang of us went on safari south of Nairobi. A dawn view of Kilimanjaro up, up, up, like a pink cloud above all pink clouds, had us all marvelling. "What a hill!" I gasped. Someone turned to me with a smile: "You must be Scottish," he said, "anyone else would call *that* a mountain."

So this time, 20 years after, I was quite prepared to have Mendip *Hills* that had fields right over their tops. Only on the very highest ridge (old red sandstone) or where the dough-grey limestone surfaces was the landscape not cultivated. I did a circuit to bump into the Charterhouse Centre where the Warden, Tom Elkin, was an old *mukka* of John Endicott, the Warden of our Fife Outdoor Centre – which happens to be in Argyll. (Incidentally, if a Scot can tidy up an Anglo misconception, we only add -shire in county names where this is needed to distinguish from a town – as Clackmannan becoming Clackmannanshire. There is no town of Fife or Argyll so to say Fifeshire and Argyllshire is nonsense.) We had a good crack over tea. Supper, in the hall of this converted rural school, reminded me very much of Braehead, except for the accents, which were buzzing Taunton. Derek Whalley and Tessa Sherriff were taking a gang off caving after supper so a Danish exchange teacher and I were invited along too. Storm was left asleep on his towel beside my pile of gear, which he was quite happy about, in fact he very soon became so defensive that Derek was hardly able to go into his own room!

We were all issued with boiler suits, safety helmets and lamps and drove off in the rain to visit Goatchurch Cavern in Burrington Coombe, an easy cave but giving the kids a good feel for the fascination of this game. I enjoy it at that level, too, but rather opt out when the going becomes over-wet and muddy. I have enough of that above ground. Derek's deep, commanding bass voice duly instructed the novices, and the professional touch of authority and humour soon had the Priorswood boys and girls enjoying their new experience. I noticed it had its practices and procedures, its language and mystique, like any other sport. Two hours went all too quickly underground. We returned to cocoa and bacon-butties in the kitchen and talked till all hours.

Thursday 4 October   CHEDDAR

It was interesting to see the centre come to life but odd not to be of it, so familiar were the routines. Tom Elkin came up later and we had a chat over coffee. He gave me a copy of his *Mendip Walks* booklet which I could have done with earlier. From Glastonbury and Wells, by Wookey Hole and Cheddar, right to the sea, there were fascinating places, caves, walks and antiquities.

A wind after the night's rain made for a pleasantly clear day in which we did little walking really: down Velvet Bottom (with old lead-mine spoil on which flowers refuse to grow) and along the breezy crest of Cheddar Gorge. The cars on its wiggly road looked tiny. It is a little feature, but on a grand scale, and an important low-level rock climbing area, with steep limestone faces of up to 400 ft.

A vast plain spread out from the hills, the Somerset levels, across which we would have to tramp for the shadowy Quantock Hills beyond. Cheddar Reservoir lay like the round disc of a mirror and the Bristol Channel and the Welsh coast merged along the northern horizon. I would like to have made an arc round by Wells Cathedral and Glaston-bury, but, as with the Cotswolds and Slimbridge, they might as well have been in Norfolk as just a few miles off our narrow way. I had even had to choose whether to walk along the crest or along the foot of Cheddar Gorge.

We trotted down the 322 steps of Jacob's Ladder into the gorge. The setting of the caves is completely commercialised and could as well be in London. Cox's Cave was shut (half day), the Waterfall Cave second rate and the Paleolithic Man Museum disappointing, but the visit was redeemed by a walk through Gough's Cave, which was marvellous and has not been ruined as so many caves have been by lurid artificial lighting and raucous piped music. This spectacle would be worth a big diversion, for it is a wonderland ranging from tiny corners of delicate statuary to vast petrified waterfalls of many-tinted, natural, colours. Storm was welcome to walk round it all. We then fled the Grotto Bar and Cave Man Restaurant, the stalls of cheese and the pokey holes selling cream teas, walking into Cheddar, the town. The people's wedding present to Queen Victoria had been a cheddar cheese, to be sure – but it weighed over ten-hundredweight.

I was sitting on a bench reading a paper when Bill Sommers arrived to bear us off home in his car, going by scenic routes to Weston-super-Mare. We had a walk on breezy Sand Point before supper. The navy have a small place there which Bill explained produced explosions in the sea once in a blue moon. As he finished his sentence the sea shot up in a great spout, quickly followed by the noise. I considered *that* was really laying things on for the tourist.

Bill was a school teacher and had, until a recent heart attack, done much in the way of outdoor activities. He put me on to the Charterhouse Centre which had been a pleasant break. Bill was also a Crusader Class-Leader, and I could claim past association with the Nairobi Crusaders in 1952, when that branch was the largest in the world under the leadership of the Jarvis family, whose house was open-home to so many service lads. Learning to make meringues was one result of being a Crusader. Anyone free on a Thursday night helped to bake, as classes ended with tea in the Jarvis garden – for sometimes hundreds of hungry lads. It was nice to have a reliable climate in which to plan outdoor activities and be certain rain would not stop play.

Friday 5 October   THE SOMERSET FLATS

A bath, after tea in bed, was a very civil start to the day. Bill and Molly's son was heading by Cheddar so gave me a lift back to my Walk line. A hot sunny day spent largely on tarred roads gave the feet a bit of a hammering. We walked fast to Blackford while it still had a touch of coolness. The name *Moors* for these green billiard-topped acres was an odd one. The fields were often bordered by ditches rather than hedgerows and these *drains* were frequently covered over by floating greenery. Storm assumed this vegetation was as solid as any other and his error of judgment led to a rather messy swim. I washed him in a trough and he soon fluffed out again in the sun. Somerset's most famous walker was Thomas Coryate who walked from London to Venice, 1,975 miles, one May to October in 1608.

There was actually a rise to the Polden Hills after we crossed the River Brue, and we followed the line of a Roman road. At Cossington we found welcome liquid, and tracks over fields took us to King's Sedgemoor Drain only to lose us beyond. *Chedzoy*, *Penzoy* and *Weston-zoyland* were buzzy Somerset names round the battle site.

Sedgemoor was my first contact with *Lorna Doone*, its hero having been mixed up in that battle which started and finished the Monmouth Rebellion in 1685. The Duke of Monmouth, glorified illegitimate son of Charles II, had been proclaimed king two weeks before in Bridgwater. He died (a messy execution) in London and Judge Jeffreys ruled the rebellious west. However, enough was enough. In 1688 James II was in exile in turn. The Stewarts were an ill-fated line, legitimate, bastards, pretenders and all. Killiecrankie was in 1689, the Battle of the Boyne in 1690 – and those contentions last to this day.

We felt a bit 'heady' with several hours of walking into the glare of sun, and the landscape itself disintegrated into a motorway crossing and endless suburbs entering red-brick Bridgwater. We made the post office before five and sat beside a statue to Admiral Robert Blake (seventeenth century) to fillet the parcel and send things off quickly. The day had a soft end as well, staying in the Bristol Hotel and watching the Horse of the Year Show on TV. Storm's late-night walk was enlivened by meeting a Chinese dragon in a back street. From a house overlooking the rushing River Parrett I could hear a record of Grieg's Piano Concerto so we lay on the grass and relished an old favourite which I had first heard, live, at a concert in Lima of all places. All through this Walk the haunting *Eriskay Love Lilt* had been my recurring theme. I must have made up scores of homesick verses to it, which have all gone again . . .

Saturday 6 October   QUANTOCKS

We left Bridgwater by Durleigh Reservoir and were forced off the planned route as there was a field of maize planted over the right-of-way. A farm near Enmore offered "Goat's milk, Yoghurt, Farm Manure, Cheese." We brewed behind a wall by Hawkridge Reservoir. The map showed a right-of-way across the middle of it – no wonder English walkers have problems! A delightful path took us up by the edge of a wood overlooking heathery Aisholt Common, to Wills Neck, 1,261 ft, the top of the velvety Quantocks.

A path along the crest of these hills gave hazy views of rolling Brendon Hills on one side and the vast flatland on the other. The flat gave much more demanding walking. We descended a coombe to tiny Crowcombe where we were to meet Ray and Mary at four o'clock at the church, a rendezvous I'd hastily fixed when Ray phoned us at Bill's two nights before. They were returning from Barry's funeral in Llanberis. As we had time in hand we hid the rucksack and had a circular stroll to Higher Vexford across what felt like a Yorkshire dale. The day had been grey and windy and at four o'clock the rain came on. We sheltered under a yew tree outside the church. A leaflet said it was a "Perp. with good bench-ends and crosses (12c and 14c)" We were given half an hour of campanology at close range before Ray and Mary arrived. Bell-ringing, like bagpipes, is best appreciated from a certain distance (about ten miles the cynic would suggest). We fled to the coast at Watchet – where Coleridge began *The Ancient Mariner* – but it still rained. We booked in at the Downfield Hotel where the pleasant elderly owner seemed equally part of its olde-world service and furnishings. An excellent dinner at the Jolly Sailor rounded off a hilarious evening. In retrospect, all the nights spent off-route had an odd unreal quality. They were beads which had escaped from the necklace we were threading, to run off into a dark corner, there to lie in solitary brightness.

Sunday 7 October   BRENDON HILLS

The night of storm led to a showery day which was not unpleasant. The sunny company cheered as well. And a rucksack-free climb up on to the spinal ridge of the Brendon Hills was relished. We went over to investigate Elworthy Barrow and talked and walked the miles away. Mary caught up for coffee at Raleigh's Cross, then we had a picnic lunch before they drove off. My Berghaus Goretex jacket worked well and it was ironic that Ray, a great exponent of the brand, had left his behind and perforce made do with Mary's cagoul.

Storm and I walked on, through Kennisham Wood, on good tracks, but lost our line beyond as we wandered up Lype Hill, 1,390 ft, the Brendons' highest. Quantocks, Brendons, Exmoor formed a pleasing succession of ridges, each loftier and wilder than the last. *Lorna Doone* was now my reading, another of those books that had nagged the literary conscience ever since Kenya National Service days when a friend John Cates used to read it avidly. I discovered why. It is immensely readable and as full of sex and violence as any modern novel!

We had walked with steep coombes dropping to the sea, but Lype Hill was an isolated dome swept by wind and rainbow showers. Flocks of shivery-voiced goldfinches passed. The swallows seeemed to have vanished. We followed marked paths over White Moor to Wheddon Cross and camped that night below Dunkery Beacon, at Blagdon Farm. Candles were needed to read after seven o'clock. There was a sense of acceleration in the Walk, now, as if I was a wandering space-craft feeling the force of gravity. All too soon we would come down to earth. I was made thoroughly homesick by hearing, again and again through the dew-cold, moonlit night, the rutting roar of red deer stags, a sound I had more or less given up hope of hearing this year. Perhaps only the maniacal crying of loons or the soul-curdling calling of curlews can match the roaring of stags for emphasising the wilderness of the northern lands. It was almost unreal to hear the repeated roar in that softer world of green Somerset hills. I almost wrote Devon hills.

Everyone seems to think Exmoor is Devon and it looks and feels it, too, on the spot.

Monday 8 October EXMOOR

We were on top of Dunkery Beacon, 1,704 ft, at eight o'clock. There was no view on the top of Exmoor today. The mist oozed about, and imagination crouched with John Ridd watching the Doones ride by – the opening of *Lorna Doone*. He was a lad then, riding home from school in Tavistock after his father had been killed, and here, by the light of the flaming beacon, he fearfully, secretly watched the raiders pass. There is no beacon now; just a trig point and a proliferation of notices. As the weather felt, and was forecast, bad, we scurried off westwards with the cloud clinging wind bullying us along the common. This was the last day of real hills, in the Scottish sense of open moorland above the gentle green stroking of arable farmland – which rather gave a sense of ending too: the Exe, Y, Z of England. It was a landscape as unsubstantial as dreams: half remembered kindly and half forgotten, tantalisingly.

Before Elsworthy Common, (a good *Lorna Doone* name) we saw a Bomb Disposal Team vehicle parked by the roadside which gave speculative thoughts. There was a thundery haze over everything so we took every helpful road, track or path we could to push on. Off-track the grey heights were marsh and bog. We kept above Warren Farm and the valley of the Exe, and if our going was wet and rough the other side of the hill was more so. It was drained by the Badgworthy (Badgery) Water and across the map was written Doone Country. The grey, creeping clouds and oppressiveness were eminently right. A sunny stroll would have been meteorological miscasting.

There is an intriguing mystery as to whether the Doones ever existed. A John Ridd was churchwarden of Oare Church (where Carver Doone shot Lorna) as recently as 1925. Blackmore wove his tale as tightly with this area as Scott wove his with the Borders and the Highlands. *Lorna Doone* was originally rejected by several publishers, and Blackmore rather resented its popularity. He was much in demand as a godfather, especially to children called Lorna. When several godchildren had died young he refused so to honour another child, whose parents lived nearby. He thus turned down Noel Coward. He never enjoyed good health, and died on the same day as John Ruskin. Ruskin was given half a page of *The Times*, Blackmore half a column.

Exmoor may have vast heather moors but it also has woody valleys with exquisite villages hidden away in them, and to the north the moor

tumbles down to the sea. If it all was Royal Forest in King John's day it is
Everyman's National Park now. Stag hounds are still used for hunting,
however, and there are markets (where wild Exmoor ponies are sold),
sheep dog trials and traditions going back many centuries. Jack Russell
may be a dog now but he was once a hunting clergyman from the banks
of the Taw. Winsford, in more modern times, was the birthplace of
Ernest Bevin.

At Blackpits Gate (on the Simonsbath-Lynmouth road) a condescen-
ding notice allowed us on to pick up the Exe Head path, and a grand
cow-churned coming we had of it. Once we were down in the coombe we
had a brew and dried out the tent for Ray had insisted we had a night in
Lynmouth, a diversion I was quite happy to make. At Hoar Oak Tree an
abandoned farm was surrounded by superb beech trees but the moor
beyond was all tracks and no track, so we had to thread a maze of fields
and little bumps to end on a perch high above the sea. It really was sea
now. The estuary feeling had gone.

A track, overhung with foul old blackberries, led to Summerhouse
Hill from which we could see Lynton on its shelf 500 feet above the sea.
The Foreland juts into the sea in a 900 ft, reddish-orange tinted cliff, the
highest in England. Somehow the East Lyn River has carved a deep
trench between, and thereby, over millions of years, prepared for the
disaster of 1952. We zig-zagged down Lyn Cleave and debouched almost
at the entrance of the Bonnicott Hotel. A lady was unpacking a Great
Dane puppy from a mini. She looked up and saw us. "Hamish and
partner?" Ray had phoned and given a Storm warning. Mrs Rainbow
and Wellington led us up to their hotel which clings to the hillside and
faces out to the sea. It was as comfy and friendly as Ray had said. We
stayed two nights and were much refreshed.

Tuesday 9 October   LYNMOUTH AND LYNTON
We had quite a mail at Lynmouth post office. Every shop seemed to be
selling *Lorna Doone*, just as Keswick was full of Hugh Walpole titles. Here
too were several booklets about the 1952 spate. I was able to read up
what I remembered visually from one of the early bits of dramatic television reportage: an unusually wet summer had left the boggy summits
waterlogged; when nine inches of rain fell in 24 hours the land virtually
"exploded", as one local put it. The East and West Lyn waters fall 500
feet in just two or three miles and are deep, wooded, gorges. It was as if a
dam had broken, and this joint flood swept through Lynmouth. Trees,
houses, hotels, bridges, streets – everything – was washed away into a
raging sea. The town has been largely rebuilt (even to the Rhenish Tower

on the harbour arm) with much careful construction to ensure future safety. Shelley, newly-married, stayed in Lynmouth (the cottage now rebuilt) but, having written a revolutionary pamphlet, had to escape by boat to Wales to avoid arrest.

We walked up to Lynton (once the home of Conan Doyle) then descended by the unusual cliff railway which has operated here since 1890. The first increase in fare came only in 1955. Its fascination lies in the operational mechanics. The movement of the cars is controlled by water tanks, each with a capacity of 700 gallons (3 tons). This weight, and gravity of course, moves the car downwards (on a gradient of $1:1\frac{3}{4}$) where the water is emptied, while at the top the other car's tank is filled. . . . Simple and effective. In the early days of motoring even cars were taken up and down the 500 ft hill on which Lynton sprawls.

The night before (and tonight) George and Pam Rainbow had produced a dinner both large and excellent, and before it, in the friendly lounge, George had been playing records. The music was too great a temptation. Next day I bought a small transistor radio. I have always scorned walking with a radio, and still would, if it were to intrude; for music, like mountains, is a personal matter, which is perhaps why I find *loud* music, blaring in crowded surroundings, almost a betrayal of music, and why pop is so out of place on the Pennine Way. Like many people, for me landscape (including mountains) and music have close affinities. There are many Munros to which, if mentioned by name, my reaction would be to name a piece of music. The connection could be of mood or moment or even company. Braehead so often thundered off hills yelling the march from *Aïda* that all rapid descents recall that piece of music. Braehead days took in the Beatles' decade, and *Telestar, Chains, Chains, Puppet on a String* are as likely to be linked to a peak as Sibelius or Wagner. My youthful Ochils have corners which I associate with *Cruising Down the River* or *Put Another Nickel In*. That really dates me! I partly justified the transistor because the Devon and Cornwall walking was going to give mainly coastal ups and downs which would largely rule out my pedestrian reading. The truth was that I was music-starved.

At dinner I had overheard two old regulars complain to George at the way time flew: "It's just one darned birthday after another." And I heard about a local epic from a hundred years before. It sounded like yesterday's deed in this timeless corner. In January 1899 a westerly gale had a ship in trouble off Porlock Weir, a hamlet to the east and reached by a steep winding road which still demands motorists' respect with its gradients of 1 in 4 at either end.

A telegram was sent to Lynmouth Lifeboat Station (the quickest way of sending a message), but it was quite impossible to launch the lifeboat, nor could they even reply to the SOS for the wires had been broken by the storm shortly after the telegram was received. In desperation the crew decided to take the lifeboat *overland* to Porlock. An hour later she was off: lashed to a cart and dragged by men and women and horses. A wheel came off the cart on the moors by Countisbury, a thousand feet above sea level; at one point the road was too narrow and everything was dragged over the fields; once down into Porlock the wall of a cottage had to be demolished to let them through (to the initial consternation of the owner) and a huge laburnum tree had to be sawn down. Despite mud and darkness, wet and wind, the superhuman all-night feat was accomplished, and the lifeboat launched.

They found the rudderless victim, which had been on tow; then her tug appeared and they linked the two again, but they could not make way into the gale. A second tug was sent for. The lifeboat stood by till it came, under oars, for she had no engine. Eventually all made the safety of Barry on the Welsh coast, at six in the evening, 23 hours after the call for help. The crew had not eaten in that time. The coxwain's log record did not even mention their overland, overnight voyage and ended: "We got back to Lynmouth the following day. A steamer gave us a tow for part of the way."

Wednesday 10 October   INTO DEVON

The weather was a repeat of the Exmoor crossing day: all threat which on the whole failed to go beyond the bluster stage. We crossed the rump of the Exmoor Hills by Parracombe which lines a hidden stream in a coombe. Its streets are all uphill. My transistor was first tried on the long hill out of the village. 'Baker's Dozen' took us to Blackmoor Gate. We lunched high then slipped down by White Cawsey into the Lee Valley, a landscape like a patchwork quilt on which children had been having a rough and tumble. We had a cultural evening thanks to the new toy: a good short story, 'Homeward Bound', 'My Word', a Chopin Recital, a programme about The Princes in the Tower and to end, appropriately, Tchaikovsky's *Sleeping Beauty*.

Thursday 11 October   WESTWARD HO

We had camped under an oak tree beside a forest-tamed stream. A cool, starry night, loud with owls calling, gave promise of another fair day, though such soft promise is about as reliable as a politician's intentions. The cool silence was so marked that the fall of an acorn on to the dry leaves made me jump as if a car had backfired beside us. Storm watched a mouse picking up crumbs and was content just to watch. He has no desire to kill things as men do. For a thousand years very few creatures have been made extinct, but in this present generation so many will vanish. The world is so fragile. For all the walking of this Walk, the sturdy oak I leant against, would scarcely add a ring to its growth in that time. Before setting off I worked out the miles to the finish. Oak tree to Dr Syntax's Head was 142 miles. Imprecisely.

Barnstaple was so crowded and noisy with commuters' cars that we more or less hurried through the historic town until we came to the well designed, many-arched bridge over the Taw. The bridge was built by public subscription seven centuries ago. Benefactors would be rewarded with "a mass solemnly sung", the prospectus promised. It called the river a "great, hungry, mighty, perylous, and dreadful water", which sounds like the description of a motorway. Bideford and Barnstaple have long been rivals. Each claims to have sent a greater number of ships to fight the Armada. Barnstaple's most distinguished son is John Gay, of *The Beggar's Opera* fame. He, Pope and Swift formed a trio marking one of the peaks of English literature, not that there is any sign of it in the town. He wrote his own epitaph which can be seen in Westminster Abbey:

> Life is a jest, and all things show it;
> I thought so once, and now I know it.

We were in Bideford for lunch time. This end of the country seems to set the visitor as many pronunciation problems as any other. Barnstaple had not been spoken as written, neither was Bideford and what does one make of Clovelly or Tintagel first time? Bideford is the "little white town" of *Westward Ho* – which was built later as a spa and named after the book. It looks down on the Torridge, and the sea has long been its way of life. In Elizabethan times its fishermen fished for cod off Newfoundland. Sir Richard Grenville's *Revenge* was crewed by Bideford men. Its long bridge was built in 1460 and the main street is the Quay. I walked along it to collect a parcel and sat on a bench to sort it out. Two old men were sunning themselves and I enjoyed trying to follow their Devon accents which I am sure have not changed for centuries.

There is in some respects a fantastic conservation in local speech. My Braehead kids lived in what they pronounced *Buckhynd* though the map has *Buckhaven*. On seventeenth century maps it is written Buck-hynd or even Hynd of Buck. And today quite a few of the despised 'Americanisms' turn out to be of older, purer English, preserved in more rural, unchanging America, words which went out with the

Mayflower and returned with transatlantic TV films. Queer you reckon? I guess so? Those are Devon phrases!

Westward Ho was disappointing, being anything but *Stalky* country, a shanty town added to a failed Victorian spa – a sad bathers' *bidon ville*. The best of it was a quiet camp site, if that is the correct term, for we shared it with several geese, goats and sheep. Ho is hogh, *the high place*, as opposed to combe. There was a great deal of both ahead. Kipling was at school here before his Indian days. When he finally settled in the soft south of England he was to write, "Then we discovered England which we had never done before . . . and went to live in it. England is a wonderful land. It is the most marvellous of all foreign countries that I have ever been in."

Friday 12 October CLOVELLY WITH BAD BELLY
Some good coastal walking could be expected from now on, for the dramatic South West Coastal Path was the obvious line. I had no intention of following it slavishly; my objective was Land's End, not an artful creation in a guide book, fine as it is. Some swotting last night had already made me realise I'd have to cut out Hartland Point (which looks out to Lundy Island) if I was going to make Bude (post office and parcel) before Saturday lunch time. The coastal path begins in Minehead in Somerset but I had kept to hills so had not really met it before today. It runs right round the coast of Devon and Cornwall to end at Poole in Dorset: 500 miles of it, which is twice the distance of the Pennine Way. It is very different in character, and historically it was re-opening what were once patrolled coastguard paths. Stone stiles, cottages, steps and cuttings have been dug out of the wind-woven *maquis*, and others created. It was 'opened' in 1973 with bureaucratic trumpets blowing. Some day it may *even* be completed.

With all the lights seemingly set at green we unexpectedly (and inexplicably) stuttered and stalled through this day. We had had a dreadful night and while packing up I seemed to be all fingers and thumbs. We took to the coast path by Kipling Tors but the rucksack seemed to weigh a ton and the ups and downs of a path suffering from hiccups soon had me reduced to a sad state. At Clovelly I was ready to call it a day but that was still too far from Bude. For only the second day on the trip I was actually ill, though *that* reason did not dawn on me till evening. There was no obvious cause – probably a bug from something eaten in Westward Ho where ice-cream, fresh fruit and a good dinner had been consumed.

Clovelly is one of those picture post-card places: a single street which drops down between the perched houses to a tiny harbour with a protective arm like Crail's. The cobbled street breaks into steps at times and the only alternative to walking is a donkey. Even the postie uses one. The houses are white and bright and at the season's end still had splashes of colour in the window boxes. Post cards showed overweight mobs packing the street so I was glad not to jostle through crowds – and cream teas I regard as one of the most overrated of gastronomic temptations.

At the top end of the town there were large car parks and souvenir shops, but no shop that sold proper food. It was Bude or burst. The road kept high on big whalebacks with the drainage going alternatively to the Torridge and the Tamar. The latter rises only about three miles from the north coast yet almost moats Cornwall as it flows south to the English Channel. Slowly the landscape was changing. It was as if it tightened its belt and rolled up its sleeves. The lush Somerset moors had become the smaller, tilted fields of Devon, but now the sea's effect was noticeable. It was a tougher world, gritty as its granite heart, suspicious of ease, introspective, combed and neat with labour but unkempt and wild where left for any time unworked.

We were tempted to camp by one of the Tamar's head streams but a bad headache and an inability to concentrate properly drove me on, continuing more or less on automatic pilot. At Welcombe Cross (most welcome) we turned along to Upcott Farm and descended a path into the wooded Marsland Coombe where we could camp on the Devon–Cornwall border. We needed water and shelter from a blow of wind.

There is nothing like kicking a man when he is down. The path proved a popular bridleway through an impenetrable tangle of trees, nettles, brambles and such like. It was sometimes feet deep in mud and to climb up it, once involved, was beyond me. We floundered on, quite demoralised and feeling really unwell – and only then realising I had been ill all day. A slight clearing near a small trickle of water had to do us. The place was as cheerless as the steamy Malayan jungle I knew as a kid. It was dark before I finished pitching the tent and cleaning poor Storm. I had a brew and thankfully lay down. Almost casually I switched on the transistor.

". . . and direct from Chicago, George Solti conducting Beethoven's Ninth Symphony." What a choice of music. Can any other symphony surpass its sweeping estuary of sound? My sordid site in Marsland Coombe has been added to several other hill associations connected with that healing masterpiece. After an hour of Beethoven, and aspirin, I was actually feeling hungry!

The winter before I had had a rather grand music-and-mountain association. I was visiting Janet and Reg Popham at Glenmore Lodge, then shut down for holidays, when there was an avalanche accident in Coire an Lochain. Reg, Tim Walker and I were the only climbers available, and once the doctor had arrived we were bundled into a Sea King helicopter and lifted up to the Cairngorms' most dramatic northern corrie. The Sea King is huge and its powerful searchlight beams lit up the ice-draped cliffs in dramatic fashion. As we were winched down I was hissing Wagner! (*A propos* another topic, it was interesting later to read the garbled garbage written about that call-out. Not a single paper had picked up the one real story. It had been the first time a big Sea King had been used in a *night* rescue.) As nobody was desperately hurt the setting was consciously relished at the time for its grand opera atmosphere: a frozen backcloth of the gods.

I wrote up the day by candle light: "Tomorrow I begin another tune – of Cornwall, the last county of our syncopated stravaig." My feelings were sadder than my notes made out. I hate endings.

XV

TURN HOME AT LAND'S END

. . . . find,
Wherever nature's still untamed, unplanned,
The native country of his heart and mind,
And there his age forget; older than he
Dewfall and thunder, mountains and the sea.

W. K. HOLMES

Saturday 13 October   BUDE AND BEYOND   *Map, p. 264*

We had a steep pull up on the Cornish side of our jungly valley. An old
mill and forgotten hamlets looked ageless. West lay Morwenstow made
famous by being the home of the Rev. R. S. Hawker ("And shall
Trelawny die?") who held eccentric sway as vicar from 1834 to 1875. The
dish aerials of a satellite-tracking station looked like obscene grounded
moons and were visible for miles along the coast. From Duckpool to
Bude the cliff-top walking was easy, and a big surge painted an endless
pattern below us. I was feeling fit – and hungry – after a good sleep and a
mean breakfast. Storm had room again to race, and most of the
downward slopes were taken full tilt by both of us. We collected our
parcel in Bude and bought a pile of goodies which we demolished over a
picnic by the old canal. A town wren scolded like a frenzied housewife:
tea, tea, tea . . .

We made a desultory overfed wander out to Widemouth Bay, a good
reach of sand hedged with NO notices. As water was a camping problem
we filled at the shelter, read out a shower, then toiled on up with the
extra ten pounds of weight, hoping for a camp site, an odd corner or
even a B&B sign. We could not leave the road till up on the Penhalt Cliff
where there were some poised ledges above the sea that gave a grand-
stand view of people surfing off Millock Haven. When they swam out I
thought they were seals but all at once the tiny black dots stood on end
and went surging shorewards. Not even performing seals do that.

We stayed there until the sweeping, coloured sky darkened. I had
intended to move into a field and camp once it was dark (as we would be
off before anyone was up this seemed the best scheme to work to). I was

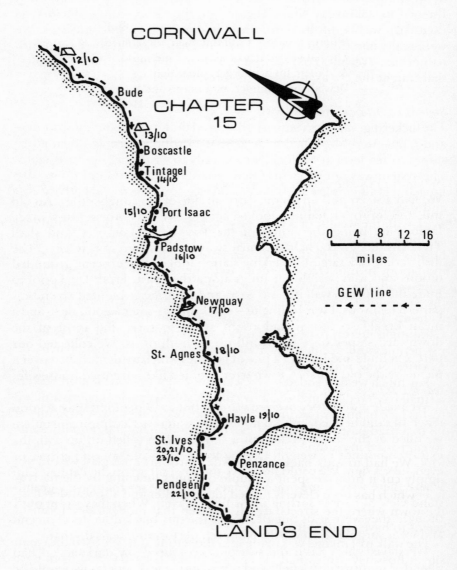

CORNWALL

CHAPTER
15

12/10

Bude

13/10

Boscastle

Tintagel
14/10

15/10 Port Isaac

Padstow
16/10

Newquay
17/10

St. Agnes   18/10

Hayle 19/10

St. Ives
20,21/10.
23/10   Penzance

Pendeen
22/10

LAND'S END

0   4   8   12   16

miles

GEW line

packing the dixies when a flash of lightning warned us off pitching as the highest object in many miles. We camped several fields lower, wedged in between furze bushes; and to try and distract thoughts from lightning, listened to 'Saturday Night Theatre' on the radio – unsatisfactory, as each flash was faithfully reproduced in crackling on the transistor. We were really into the old Cornwall now and nature raw seemed right with names like Trewint, Foxhole Point, Dizzard, Mineshop, the Strangles, that caught the eye as it studied the onward route on the map.

Sunday 14 October   TO TINTAGEL
The flickering, silent dry storm had cleared the air, and later the ground – and tent – were drenched with dew. We dropped steeply down gorse slopes to sea level at Millock Haven, only to go toiling up once again. The system was not efficient. On a mountain walk ups and downs are long and gradients are self-chosen and easy, on this coastal path the ups and downs were constant but irregular, rhythm-destructive and hard work with the weight of a camper's rucksack. I would not recommend camping to anyone doing the Coastal Path. There are many youth hostels available and the few gaps could be filled with other accommodation. In mid October such camp sites as there were tended to be shut, youth hostels were impossible with a dog, and wild camping has the snags of either seeking permission (time-consuming) or doing without (as we did) and facing problems finding drinkable water. Camping is merely masochistic on a coastal route. That night I counted my pennies and decided I would change to trying out these hard-won theories. Now, with hindsight, I'm sure they were correct.

For lunch we descended off Pencannow Point to Crackington Haven, a small bay, wedged in the slabby cliffs. A solitary surfer kept us amused by his lack of ability to win out against the breaking waves. We climbed up to a road past High Cliff, at 729 ft Cornwall's highest, and I became so engrossed in reading that we went away inland beyond our intended fork. We had to walk back to Boscastle Harbour. I am glad we did not simply cut it out. We spent a couple of hours lunching by the narrow inlet which has been cleverly turned into a shelter and also wandered up the town where the streets are all so steep that modern development seems to have avoided it.

The walk to Tintagel was made into the setting sun. We used the camp site at Bossiney (which had Sir Francis Drake as its MP) and from it we went to explore Tintagel and its historical-fictional castle on The Island. This is the English pilgrim place for the quest for Arthur. His following in Wales and Scotland is muted in comparison. If Geoffrey of

Monmouth, in the twelfth century, had not invented half his history, would we ever have had an Arthurian industry? The stark castle-remains straddle the neck of the peninsula (built by unromantic Earls of Cornwall) and a Celtic monastery-site tops this rocky knuckle in the sea. Tintagel is one of those places which had to be invented.

The mileage only just reached double figures today. I phoned Ray and Mary. Ray was going to finish off his interrupted Two Moors Way, then join me at St. Ives for my last couple of days. Fixing this rendezvous made me realise there was an ending, and not far away. I did not like the idea. However, endings are invariably beginnings for something else, which I'm sure is history and philosophy, as well as Resurrection reality. That night we had the last midges of the trip.

Monday 15 October   PORT ISAAC
We picked up the coast at Hole Beach with its view of black Penhallic Point. There were old quarry holes and man-made fingers of rock, also some fine fishbone walling which I hope is not going to be allowed to disintegrate from neglect. We slithered down to Trebarwith Strand, a short pitch of sand with the Bird Rock offshore at first slip. An up-and-down led to Backways Cove, then we had a couple of miles of easier going. It ended with four ups and downs in succession, the paths liberally overgrown with furze, slippery mud and with plenty of barbed wire strategically placed for emergency grabbing. I hope any injured walkers duly sue for damages. The last lark of the trip was singing above the wind-combed scrub. A surprising number of grey squirrels inhabited these three-foot high 'forests'. Just as Highland eagles are apt to turn out to be buzzards, all my Cornish choughs turned into jackdaws. Despite being in several chough areas I did not see one. The names rang rough and rude as bells: Tregonnick Tail, Trerubies Cove, Jacket's Point, Delabole Point, Barrett's Zawn.

We had a snack by an old watch tower and wandered into Port Isaac. There was no camp site to be seen so we had lunch and thoroughly dried out the tent in order to post it home. The Bay Hotel proprietor came from near Glasgow and used to take Scouts camping to Kinghorn. A bed was very welcome. It was a cold clear night with another lightning storm flashing away under The Plough. The Bristol Channel was having this dogged 'bad spell', which we had just avoided. Our last serious rain had been on the march to Hay-on-Wye – weeks ago, now! The forecast was for several more fine sunny days.

Tuesday 16 October   CAMEL CROSSING

We managed to be off early enough to hear Part Two of Stevenson's *Pavilion on the Links* and also to make some miles before the sun set shackles on our feet. Port Isaac looked an attractive hamlet which has not yet sold its soul for holiday shekels (it is too steep and narrow for cars). Everywhere I went I kept being told we were lucky not to be there in summer. The village is *porth izic* in Cornish, *corn port*, which tells of its past. It has spilled over, out of its tight bay, and my lodging looked out to sea.

A farmland stretch led to Port Quin, a tiny inlet defended by National Trust ownership and a 1 in 5 road approach. Doyden Point had a folly of a castle on a green spur of land. Several deep holes like mine shafts pierced down to the sea: scenery on a grand scale again. We brewed on Trevan Point from which we could look into the triplicate arcs of Lundy Bay. Polzeath brought a change; it seemed all caravans and crowded houses. We slipped down to the shore and walked the sands round by St. Enodoc's Church which, up to a hundred years ago, had been so covered in blown sand that the parson had to use a hole in the roof to enter and hold the services that would justify a claim to the tithes.

The River Camel is a major *ria* or drowned river valley across the mouth of which the Doom Bar creates a barrier to major craft. (The Bar was formed as a result of a local man shooting a local mermaid, and the Mermaids' Union blocking the port forthwith.) There is a long history of wrecking here, as almost anywhere on the coast. One trick was to tie a lantern to the neck of a grazing horse and so give the impression of a bobbing boat – man was not altogether adverse to helping nature. Our coastal path was built in the battle against smuggling.

The Camel, thankfully, does not have to be walked round: we joined a group of people on the sands at Rock and the ferry launch came and bore us all over to Padstow; we reached the post office just before it closed. I would not recommend my system of sending parcels to post offices as opening hours and weekends start dictating one's life. On a wander through the town we saw a Siamese cat by a B & B sign, and tried there for accommodation, successfully. Later we called on David Platten, a school teacher and outdoor enthusiast, who had recently done some navigation articles for *The Great Outdoors*. We had a pleasant sociable evening. When I opened the parcel that night I found it contained the maps needed right on to Land's End.

Wednesday 17 October   NEWQUAY

We had a pull up to leave Padstow, cutting sections off the day's walk round by Trevose Head, as the drive to win on, through this never-never weather, now dominated. The countryside all morning was far less broken by ups and downs, an altogether sparser landscape, still a patchwork of fields but with few trees. The farm town of Treator gave the first of the day's many *Tre's*. We wiggled on to Trevone, Hartyn Bay (brew spot by the sands) and Constantine Bay – a very *pukka*-looking world of golf, caravan sites, all with post-season paint peel, as if the Raj was in decay.

We kept inland after that, but the roads were quiet enough for Storm to walk off lead. Too often we were hemmed in by sunken lanes so returned to the coast at spectacular Bedruthan Steps. The cliffs here break into a wild jumble of crags, gaps and pinnacles – a scattered shark's teeth array at high tide, which have given the giant Bedruthan his jagged stepping stones along the bay. Mawgan Porth had a good bay but with a background of closed tourist buildings. A brutal escape led up in the hot sun of our continuing Indian summer, only to drop us down again to Watergate Bay which came as a complete surprise for it gave *miles* of long empty sand – akin in scale and quality to Sandwood Bay or Inch Strand. We were seeing it under unusual conditions of course: in perfect weather and lacking the milling mobs of the Newquay summer. We had tea in among some rocks by Stem Point and then walked the miles of the bay barefoot, passing Zacry's Islands, stranded in the middle.

The beach ended up against the sea cave-carved promontory of Trevelgue Head, where we climbed up a staircase into a suburbia of hotels, guest houses and B & Bs, but had to try several places before signing in at the Godolphin Arms. In summer a 'single' would understandably be difficult to obtain. It was oddly difficult now because so much was shut up. "We don't expect people at the end of October" or "No dogs" I was rather ungraciously told. The town was the least attractive I'd seen on the northern coast. Tourists are obviously its major industry and when any place concentrates only on one activity, it becomes unbalanced.

Thursday 18 October   PERRANPORTH–ST. AGNES

My logbook entries were becoming increasingly sparse as we walked unrelentingly through Cornwall. It was all in books anyway. What could I add? The landscape is no longer a wilderness; it is too accessible, somewhat pseudo, often arty and artificial. There is much more to Cornwall than cream-teas though a casual visitor might not notice. Perhaps that *is* the way people like it. Even its wild history has been

tamed by grey time. The scenery is outstanding, the climate soft, but the
human contacts disappointing. The Celtic, too, lingers on only in names.
A river could still be *avon* and words like *carn, ty, cam, du, glas* are familiar
enough at home; they are basic words, reaching far back into history,
while others ring with Welsh: all the *tre* (hamlet), *pen* (headland) and
porth names for a start, for Cornish is more closely related to Welsh than
to Gaelic. As a language Cornish died out in the eighteenth century.

We were a thoroughly disgruntled pair by the end of the morning
session. To avoid the town and the deep-cutting Gannel (another
drowned valley) we turned due south to Trencreek, only to be con-
tinually set back by impossibly overgrown or infuriatingly non-existent
rights-of-way. Nearing Cubert several successive failures sent us two
extra miles to end half a mile nearer an objective. Even the coastal path
comes feebly inland here, as if inspiration, official or otherwise, was
doomed in this enclave of country. We took the quickest road to Perranporth, about which I can remember little except the vast Penhale Sands
on its northern fringes where there are ruins of St. Piran's Oratory, a
seventh-century Irish missionary-church which was probably swallowed
up by the dunes soon after being built. The dunes are the highest in
Britain. Reading the various guide-books afterwards I was glad to see
that they, too, were seldom enthusiastic about Newquay or the Ligger
Bay miles.

The going beyond Perranporth became much more interesting as it
led to good cliff scenery and also the first of the mining stacks and engine
houses, which were to become an inescapable part of the landscape from
now on. The unplanned, wholesale, ugly exploitation for tin and copper
is sufficiently overgrown and decayed now to create an industrial-
archaeology interest. The coastal path largely misses the more recent industrial mess of china clay extraction. Just occasionally a white alpine
range would be noticed inland. Let us hope, if mining becomes viable
again, it is less destructive of landscape. I was going to add "and of the
people", but the grim working conditions of the miners are not likely to
be repeated. In the eighteenth century their lives were horrific: whole
families lived in damp hovels, walked miles to work, suffered privation
and disease, and had a life expectation of 45 years. Mines could be a
thousand feet deep and reachable only by ladder. The miners worked
outside the ordinary laws of the land, with their own parliament and
courts. Stannary towns were set up for the testing, taxing and sale of the
tin. Dolcoath, which operated 1720–1917, produced 80,000 tons of tin
and 350,000 tons of copper and had reached a depth of 3,000 ft. By 1850
there were over 300 mines employing about 50,000 people, but easier,

larger, cheaper sources abroad brought the collapse of the industry. Tens of thousands went abroad. Methodism became firmly established, with John Wesley sometimes preaching in the open air to 20,000 people. The evangelical revival may well have prevented the upheavals which took place on the continent. It was a long, grim story, anyway.

The slates and shales, which had given the colourful and streaked cliffs (cross-sections of geology) gave way, briefly, on 300 ft Cligga Head, to granite. The granite intruded several times before it took over entirely as the 'foot' of Cornwall that holds back the slam of the Atlantic. It is a desolate country, ravaged by weather and mining but strong enough for men still to farm the lower coastal strip. The south Cornish coast is sheltered and boasts of itself as a riviera – which is why I chose the north coast to walk on. It is the wild that draws, irresistibly.

St. Agnes is a double town, with its lower buildings forming a line along the old harbour inlet and the main village sprawling over the slopes above. We made several circuits in search of any Bed and Breakfast places still functioning. Even in summer there cannot be many. The St. Agnes Hotel, facing the parish church, was open, however. The stairway was decorated with big-game mementos and the bar was full of model ships and nautical souvenirs. I kept to my room as there was a good concert on the wireless. The skin under my watch was showing whiter, which meant that I was tanning browner, even in October. I phoned Mary to see how Ray was faring, to find he was not faring at all but was just recovering from some bug. He reckoned there was a Two Moors Way jinx on him. He had decided to come down on Sunday by car; then, if he was fit enough, Mary could motor down as well so they could nail their adjectival Way thereafter. I could use his car to return via Ruthin to Sheffield where he'd collect it on their way north.

Friday 19 October HAYLE AND HEARTY

A rather late start was not helped by my being in such a *dwam* that I had wandered away inland and had to turn west to reach Porthtowan – and promptly did the same again so reached Porthreath from inland! It had no bank, which could have caused snags with the weekend. We returned to proper coastal walking after lunching by Basset's Cove. A recorded Buxton Festival Concert tempted with Beethoven's Violin Concerto and Mendelssohn's Scottish Symphony, but when I met another walker in full panoply of shorts and stave, and his charitable intentions printed large on his rucksack, I slunk by with the volume turned down. What would such a professional think? From Ralph's Cupboard the scenery was good once more. Reskajeage Downs (a raised beach) gave almost level walking along the furzy edge of sheer cliff as far as Deadman's Cove, then from Hell's Mouth the coastal path rounds to Godrevy Point by Kynance Cove which has rugged rocks whitewashed by the surge. A lighthouse shone cleanly on an offshore islet. We descended to the Red River (from the mining spill that coloured it) and on to the Towans, the long strand that ran all the way to Hayle and which gave us another enjoyable barefoot walk. Hayle is *hayl*, Cornish for *estuary*.

We cut in to Hayle, as I could not tell with certainty whether pedestrians could cross the mouth of its estuary to the Porth Kidney Sands. A ferry once operated, but no longer. All the books were dismissive, Hayle was just an industrial town at best. Possibly because of this, it was more friendly and natural than the dried-apple tourist places. We found accommodation at the fourth try, with Mrs Pollard on Commercial Road overlooking the River Hayle. She keeps open all year and welcomes walkers. The dog and I had supper by the shore and watched the tide race out to expose the black mud which ate away at the red waters of a mirrored sunset. From our bed we could hear curlews calling, the friendly talk of ducks and the machine-like swish of swans' wings.

Saturday 20 – Sunday 21 October   AS I WAS GOING TO ST. IVES
We had to rein-in a bit for Ray's coming, though, on leaving Hayle, when I saw a notice LAND'S END 20 MILES (via Penzance) it was tempting to go and do it there and then. The weather could not stay dry for ever.

We went round by Lelant and then cut down by the church to the Porth Kidney Sands, which grew uncomfortably soft for walking so we forsook them at Carbis Bay. This was the bulge of the hammer-toe that is the extremity of the south-west limb of England. The route to St. Ives was solidly built up but somehow retained the character so lacking in Newquay. Again, we were seeing it at its sunny quietest. One sign pointed to a car park for a thousand cars. Cornwall is on my list of places not to visit in July and August.

The last parcel had received some bashing, and a tin of smoked mackerel had leaked. We dealt with that (it had even penetrated into film cassettes), and a shop helpfully cashed a cheque to relieve my worries. We then spent some time playing a mad game of trying to find the digs where Ray was going to join us. To within a hundred yards I knew where the place should be; but nobody had heard of *Goole* House (Ray had spoken the name over the telephone). It eventually turned out to be *Gull House*. The street-name Ray had spelt out: T-H-E-D-I-G-E-Y. Nobody had heard of *Thedigey*, either. It eventually turned out to be *The Digey*. After this word game the planned digs were all shut-up, anyway.

We tried half a dozen Bed and Breakfast places and met with such hypocritical excuses or blunt NO DOGS from sour women that we walked off furiously. Across the bay we caught the name Kandahar, which at once conjured up a mixture of Afghanistan (Lord Roberts) and ski-ing (the Kandahar ski club, founded in his honour). The latter *was* the connection for the Masons were members, and, perhaps a reflection on people having other interests, we were welcomed. They were incomers, of course, so lacked the megalithic Cornish outlook. The house wall was also the sea wall, and at each high tide the waves lapped just below the window with its view across the harbour: an arc of clean houses, outside stairs, and narrow lanes. By dusk the north-east wind was crashing the waves on to the wall outside. There were some loud bangs and the lifeboat was wheeled out and along the bay to be launched. Ray arrived on Sunday evening. And still the weather held dry.

Monday 22 October   PENDEEN PENULTIMATE
Perhaps Ray is jinxed or perhaps the British forecasters should copy the Moroccan habit and introduce their programmes with an *Insh' Allah*, which means *God willing*. It is no consolation to know that the rain falls on the just and the unjust. It just fell, with a dedicated indiscrimination, as soon as we rounded out of sight of St. Ives. This was a pity as the day's walk through West Penwith took in some wilder coastline which we simply could not see for the blast of rain. The Carracks attracted us because of the seals' hooting on them (it sounded very like laughter). After Wicca Pool we dodged inland to Zennor and had a lunch divided between pub and church. One of the pew ends was decorated with a mermaid carving. Something like 5,000 people had signed the visitors' book since May.

We broke down to Porthmeor Cove and on to Bosigran which climbers tend to describe as a sunny paradise of rough granite routes above blue seas, a veritable Calanques. It was being pounded by angry seas and a flood of rain, a rough beauty in its way, but forbidding too. We scrambled back to the road as soon as possible and walked into Pendeen. St. John's House was the first establishment offering accommodation. Mrs Olds took us in, gave us tea and bore off some damp garments. Supper was found in the Trewellard Arms along the wet road. It was appropriately decorated with pictures and posters of shipwrecks. The stone-walled hills above were being water-blasted so we had to forgo explorations up over Woon Gumpus Common to see the cromlech of Chun Quoit and the huge prehistoric hill-fort. Wheal Bay lay up the road, reminding that we were on the edge of the St. Just mining area, while towards the shore was Geevor which is one of the few mines still functioning. Dusk staggered in long before it should have done; bruised and mulberry-dark, and leaving the bare rumps of the hills to the wind and wet.

Tuesday 23 October   LAND'S END

We cut down to the coast through Geevor Mine and for most of the day were seeing the dereliction of old abandoned workings. Their fascination was such that I did not find them a sad intrusion as everyone had warned me. There is a certain grace and character in the old stacks and engine houses. We next passed the Levant workings, famed for running a mile out under the sea and to a depth of 2,000 feet. The National Trust have preserved a beam engine and public interest has now ensured that a good selection of sites are saved for posterity. Botallack was extraordinary with the ruins wedged and perched in fissures and pinnacles among the cliffs. Even Queen Victoria visited it – and Albert made the descent into the mine. The commonality was charged ten shillings a head to do the same.

We wandered out to see the promontory fort of Kenidjack Castle but most of it was hidden in a thorn coating of scrub. From there, however, we could see Cape Cornwall, a triangular shape with a mine chimney on top, which was unmistakable. It is the only *cape* in England. Cape Wrath felt a long way off and the two could not have been a greater contrast. The only link was that each had been a prehistoric site. We tumbled down into Porth Ledden and up again above the Cape. From there we could *see* Land's End.

I felt more depressed than cheered. It was a grey day, cloudy and gentle, and clear enough to make out the Isles of Scilly on the horizon. I can remember little of the rest. I just wanted to be done with the Walk, now, so pushed Ray on, down shortcuts, to Whitesand Bay which we walked to Sennen. Ray won a pub visit, I won lunch by the Lifeboat Station, and Storm romped as ever, happy as a frog in May. We followed well-worn paths to relatively quiet, and vastly overrated Land's End. We took ourselves out to the rocks of Dr Syntax's Head and I fished out our celebratory bottle of champagne, which, having been shaken since St. Ives, ensured we thoroughly sprayed each other when we opened it. It was our only recorded gesture to mark the end of six months of stravaiging. The end was not there, somehow, even though we looked out over the furrowed fields of the sea to the Longships Lighthouse and its wheeling gulls with nothing beyond. We took our champagne-doused presence off for a green bus to Penzance. A double-decker, full of chattering school kids, shuddered and juddered along to St. Ives. We walked down from the Malinkoff to the Warren and Kandahar – to the same beds above the sea surge. Perhaps the last two days had not really happened? We wined and dined appropriately at the Chopping Block where Ray, full of Ley-line theories, stirred up a splendidly argumentative evening – which must have puzzled other diners. I phoned home, to Charles, to relatives at Veryan – and very flat and silly it felt. A Scots fishing boat called in at the harbour and then steamed off on a silvery sunset path. I suddenly longed for the spaciousness of the north where the stars have weight and the winds kiss cool and kind. Let the end be in beginning.

Wednesday 24 – Sunday 28 October   THE REAL ENDING

The next day we drove to Veryan, where mail had been forwarded to my Hong Kong brother's wife's parents, then on to see Mary's sister and husband Michael at Hatt, in Devon. Ray then dropped off at Buckfastleigh where Mary joined him to complete their much-postponed Two Moors Way. I came down with a bang having to drive myself and Storm (after a six months' abstinence) up the M5, through Somerset, Avon (brief memories of a dawn crossing of the Avon Bridge three weeks earlier) and on into darkness for Gloucestershire where we stopped at Slimbridge Youth Hostel. Ducks and geese replaced gulls as the *kleine nachtmusik*. There was a continuous beating rain. I missed Storm who was sleeping in the car, and from his ecstatic welcome in the morning he had obviously missed me. It was a poor night's sleep in the claustrophobic surroundings. How many stairs do you descend to the empty cellars of endings? But start and finish were balanced in the magnificence of their coastal scenery, and while in the former I had rejoiced in the storm and the freshness of beginnings, by now I was weary of the clinging summer. The differences went deeper too: in Sutherland we walked with Hope, here with the spoils of man's dereliction; Sutherland was a storm-smitten, scoured, secret world, this was a man-afflicted, stale, commercial world. Both the similarities and the differences made me long for the bracing northland.

We breakfasted with the companionable ducks enjoying duck weather outside. It was not a morning for visiting Peter Scott's Wildfowl Centre down the road. We did not enjoy the M5, nor the A5, in the bullying rain. Approaching the Horseshoe Pass from Llangollen we had run into autumn colours, fiery and fresh after the rain, a reminder of the rich Welsh countryside and miles gained northwards towards winter.

We collected our leftover gear and surplus *Frolic* from Ann at Ruthin. How poignant the hectic days in August now seemed: expectations which can never be filled, dreams like mountain mists . . . The day before going off to Annapurna Eric had delivered to his publisher the manuscript of his long-researched book, *Welzenbach's Climbs*. Eric had Swedish-Welsh parents and German godparents, studied languages and had lived and climbed a great deal in Eastern Europe. He had a large collection of books and archive material. So much more could have been written. His loss diminishes all of us. One rather sorry fact came out during our visit. The first news of Eric Roberts' death was not given privately to Ann, but simply broadcast on the radio – which is inexcusable.

The return to civilization was oddly accentuated by criss-crossing my line back to Sheffield. The Mam Tor road had slipped away and it was teatime before I reached the city and thankfully parked outside Charles's. That day's driving I'm sure was far more dangerous than the full accumulation of risks over the previous six months. We spent the night at the Castle Mountaineering Club's premises in the back yard of The Rising Sun.

A climbing wall has been built as part of the crafty conversion. (Perhaps the Alpine Club could follow suit). I had a busy Friday while Charles was at the office (he is an insurance surveyor with the Commercial Union), but at least I had discovered the secret of his record player: he had removed the driving band! Glutted with music and ready-packed I was able to sit back and watch Charles pack in the evening, and the next morning he drove us and our incredible accumulation of books, gear, *Frolic* and so on to Kinghorn. Mother had lunch ready and in just over a couple of hours we were off up the A9 which, for once, I revelled in. I had not been on it since Hogmanay and in the swanking autumn colours it was looking pretty as a maid. We called in to see Cameron McNeish at Aviemore, spent the night at Inverness Youth Hostel (with Storm kennelled in the car), met Donald Mill below Wyvis (kennelled in *his* car), and ended at The Smiddy, the JMCS hut at Dundonald. The impatient flight north was over. Home is a hill and during the next two days we lived our hours in a return to the Deargs: going in over Am Faochagach, Cona' mheall, Beinn Dearg and Ceapraichean, and out to Inverlael after collecting Clach Geala and Seana Bhraigh. The stags were still roaring and flocks of blowing snow buntings went by imitating their lovelier, older name of snowflakes. How we need to live the present. A year later Donald drowned when trying to leave Knoydart. These were our last hills together.

The long night gave alternate spells of wan moonlight and swirling snowfall. A flock of geese went overhead passing low enough that we not only heard their dream-tingling cries but could hear the beat of their wings. We could hardly see the wind-harrowed waters of the lochan that surrounded the wee promontory on which Donald had pitched to try out a new two-man tent. The four of us were cosy enough, no doubt as sardines are inside their tin. At one stage I woke to see Storm, lying on his back, paws straight up in the air, having been wedged up from between two of us much as a boat is pinched in an ice floe.

That camp, with old hill companions and shared experiences in many parts of the world, with the snow blowing past as it had done for our northern beginnings, with the vast, formidable, yet familiar, landscape – a sweeping Sibelius setting – with the death-touched season yet flushed from summer racing, with wild evening so quickly nudging day aside, THAT was consciously, and with fulfilled expectations, the irrevocable ending of the Groats End Walk. In the retelling here it has simply been tidied away finally into the cupboard of our yesterdays.

O, some grow old and dream no more
But some yet dream by day, lad,
And some put feet upon their dream
And have a song to sing, lad.

Our life is short as one long day
And dew, it cannot lie, lad.
So climb the mountains while you may,
The sap is in the green, lad.

The names of friends I see no more
Who paddled in the stream, lad,
But waters deep, with crafty sweep,
Have washed away their dreams, lad.

For some grow old and dream no more
And some yet dream by day, lad,
Then some put feet upon their dream
And have a song to sing, lad.

APPENDICES

BIBLIOGRAPHY

INDEX

SUMMARY

IN PLANNING A big walk one thinks in days rather than miles. When I set off on this *Groats End Walk* the logistics had been rushed and skimped, partly from being away in Morocco so long and partly as a reaction against the meticulously planned trip described in *Hamish's Mountain Walk*. Because so much of the organising is described in that book I refrain from repeating it here. This is just a summary of the statistics some think so vital and a brief outline of the route for handy reference – something I only pinned down, for myself, *after* the walk, when I described it for the *Scotsman*.

Storm and I were walking from May 2 to October 23 – 175 days, of which 29 were actually spent *not* walking (mainly organising and packing, but a few purely 'festering'). The 146 walking days covered 2,500 miles and gave 250,000 ft of ascent, a daily average of 17 miles and 1,700 ft. The Walk fell into natural sections which partly form the chapters of this book. They were as follows:

(1) The north coast walk, which snow turned into a mere road plod and not the clifftop dander envisaged (chapter II).
(2) A north-south walk over 33 Munros from Ben Hope to Ben Lomond. Having gone south-north, east-west and regularly west-east (which gave me the idea of the annual *Ultimate Challenge* event) this had been a long-standing plan (chapters III, IV).
(3) The West Highland Way, which Ray wanted before it becomes the soiled – unnecessary – creation of bureaucracy (chapter IV).
(4) On Ben Lomond completing a sixth round of the Munros. Clearing off a few Munros off-route (Grey Corries, Klibreck, Wyvis) had eaten into the brief days of preparation (end of chapter IV).
(5) A canoe run down the River Forth, another long-standing intention, but always postponed as more interesting rivers and seas lured (chapter V).
(6) A Border Walk which was a grand mix of pleasant wee hills and history. This was inescapable as it joined (5) and (7) but gave a type of stravaiging I will certainly return to increasingly in the future. (chapter VI).
(7) The Pennine Way. I have been so rude about this walkers' M1 that

there was almost a moral obligation to walk it. Now I can be as rude, but from personal experience. Such Ways should be kept for low agricultural land. Wild country is not the place for bureaucratic promotions (chapters VII, VIII).

(8) The English 3,000ers (chapter VII), which gave a diversion from the Pennine Way, from which we then went on to Snowdonia so that

(9) The Three Country summits were linked, something done by only three others at that time, but the number is growing with the fascination of *racing* them (chapter IX).

(10) Coast-to-coast across Ireland which deserves to become a recognised expedition (chapter X).

(11) The Irish 3,000ers which really dictated my chosen line for (10) (chapters X, XI).

(12) The walking link of the Four Country Summits, which I have not heard of others having done, logical though it would appear (chapter XI).

(13) The Welsh 3,000ers which, like the English and Irish, I have done often enough but wanted to cover in this book as a complement to the Munros in *Hamish's Mountain Walk* (chapter XII).

(14) A north-south walk through the Welsh hills: Snowdonia, Rhinogs, Cader Idris, Plynlimon, Rhayader Hills, Brecon Beacons, Black Mountains and down the Wye (chapters XII, XIII).

(15) The South West (chapters XIV, XV), using hills (Mendips, Quantocks, Brendons, Exmoor) and then Coastal Path, or variants, to sew it all together into a personal

(16) Groats End Walk.

Perhaps I shall gain an entry in some book of records – for the slowest, most devious linking of those two over-exposed ends of our Isles.

NOTES ON FOOD AND EQUIPMENT

A TRIP LIKE this, alas, does not just happen – like a sneeze or something – it has to be worked at for a long time before and even afterwards. This is part of the game and long may *we* remember it is a game. We are disgracefully treated by the trade on the whole, being conned into more and more expensive equipment and in the long run gaining very little. I am sure I carried about the same weight 30 years ago. Half our super foods taste like dust. This is a subject on which I could fill another book – for it concerns all of us. Of course there is good gear about, and I am fascinated by its development, but selectivity seems to be entirely lacking. The majority of hill walkers, never mind climbers, are vastly overgeared.

Travelling light is an art, by which I mean it is something more to be expressed than learnt. Some people have the knack, some do not. I have a friend who, in any party, will invariably own the heaviest rucksack: a source of constant amazement to himself and wonder to the rest of us. This trait can be useful at times. A discussion on top of A'Mhaighdean about possible London trains from Inverness will be settled at once by Dave pulling out a wad of timetables from his weighty jacket. The topic is discussed endlessly in tent and pub and bothy. The weight that it is most vital to cut down on is the weight that goes with you all the way in permanent items like tent, sleeping-bag, stove, rucksack. Food luxuries are usually impermanent ounces. I am neither very able nor good at carrying loads and being a hard perspirer does not help. I have to fight every ounce of the way. These notes just show how my gear worked out. Neither my gear, nor my thoughts about it have changed much over the years. I do not offer it as a perfect list by any means. Inexhaustible wealth would be needed for that.

I had vaguely hoped, during the early planning, that I could do without a system of parcels sent to await collection along the route but this cannot really be avoided. It was impossible to carry 70 maps and several hundred spools of Kodak film, then all sorts of foods (sugar for instance) are sold only in large or heavy quantities, so all these items had to be broken down and distributed along the route. Books were a vital item, and I averaged about a couple a week, as well as newspapers and magazines. Even stamps and packaging had to be available for returning the finished bits and pieces.

Fiddling with these logistics was a daily chore and as vital to smooth walking as the constant trimming of sail at sea. I remember a shepherd once rebuking his assistant: "Weel Billy, you wilna gether sittin on yir airse." Even Storm presented problems. His *Frolic* had to be available along the route, and his day-time nibbles of dog biscuits had to be broken down into half-handful quantities. One chaotic party involving friends, and much slaving by my mother and me saw this process done. Mother and Nevisport sent odd replacement items and at Kinghorn, Sheffield, Ruthin and Dublin there were days of chaos in other peoples' homes. The actual walking was a picnic – but that was what all the hard work was for. It also depends what you mean by a picnic.

One thing I dislike – and will no longer tolerate for myself – is the use of vivid colours for items such as tent and waterproofs. This has lingered due to a fallacious desire for 'safety', an argument that would apply only to solo travellers, if valid; yet we still see endless queues of belisha-beacon bodies marching over the fells. Most solo walkers would carry a bright orange bivvy bag (or something) which could attract the eye *in an emergency.* So, have mercy on the wilderness! Boycott bright colours.

TENT.   Over the first Scottish months I used a Black's 'Merrillite', modified by them in the light of various personal suggestions. This is a sturdy, good, lightweight tent for two people. John Merrill used it for his long coastal walk but its weight had me abandoning angle poles and ridge before the start, and when I set off again from Kinghorn I took the old Tulloch Mountain Croft tent I'd had on the Munro trip described in *Hamish's Mountain Walk*. This change was partly to reduce weight but mainly to use a discreet colour instead of yellow. Quite often I camped where I preferred not to be seen! At Sheffield I picked up a new, really light tent, an Ultimate 'Tramp' which is deservedly one of the most popular on the market.

RUCKSACK.   Karrimor had long discussions with me on rucksacks which I insist should be 1. canvas, 2. simple. One of their 'Jaguar' range seemed the best but was left at the last moment in favour of the Karrimor one I used on the previous long trip – it weighed several ounces less. However, after the constant sweat baths *en route* to the Lakes, I had mother send on the 'Jaguar' to Sheffield. In practice it proved the wrong size for my particular shape so I went back to the old one. Only later on did I try a Berghaus 'Phantom' – and felt I had found the personal choice I'd been looking for.

STOVE. Vango '7000'. This combined super lightness with steadiness and the use of many makes of cylinder. It folds into a tiny size but I usually left it assembled. A great wee stove. Self-sealing cartridges were difficult to obtain in Ireland so there I went on to a Bluet. Ray Swinburn supplied the cartridges which were used in Scotland, the rest had to be picked up *en route* as available.

WATERPROOFS. Nevisport for the first half, and Ultimate later, provided jackets and zipped overtrousers, and after Ireland I tried out a Berghaus 'Goretex' jacket. It did not have very severe testing but under some circumstances was much better than ordinary waterproofs. Those who have used Goretex extensively praise it highly. It is costly, though.

SLEEPING BAG. A Black's 'Backpacker' throughout. This down bag weighed only 2 lbs and took up little space: great for the job. I did not have a Karimat as it is bulky, and newspapers, etc., could serve for insulation, if needed.

CLOTHING. The extremes of May blizzards and July heatwave tested ideas here. Next to my skin I wore a Damart vest and underpants. Damart I regard as one of the real boons, being soft, warm and able to pass sweat through, so it does not lie clammily next to the skin (as does wool). A Damart polo-necked shirt doubled as pullover and spare shirt. A cotton tartan shirt from the local army-surplus store did every bit as well as all the expensive ones in the specialists' shops. Nevisport supplied me with Devold stockings which did about 1,000 miles before wearing thin at the heel. They reckon them about the best. I wore cotton shorts wherever possible, otherwise Rohan Summer 'Striders', the first breeches really to be designed for summer walking, being smart, light and with zips to allow them to go on and off over boots. I also carried light nylon trousers and socks for evening wear in hotels – usually while day wear was drying after its weekly wash. A handkerchief was useful for many jobs, and I carried a spare. A Damart tracksuit kept me super-warm in the bitter snows at the start, later I had a light pullover. For indoors I first used my old highland dancing pumps, but canoeing in them finally brought their 20-year-old life to an end. I managed to find light leather slippers to replace them. I could thus change completely, if need be, and make any number of combinations – all with remarkably little weight. Most people I suspect carry far too much in the clothing line.

BOOTS.   Nevisport put me on to, and supplied, two pairs of Dolomite 'Sesto' boots from MOAC. They needed little breaking-in and were the least troublesome boots I think I've ever had. They were light but strong enough (if too light you bruise, if too heavy they tire you) and gave no blisters, ever. They were roughly used, receiving no treatment at all, yet two years later were still my regular walking boots. After about 1,000 miles of constant use I changed over from one pair to the other. I used old cloth *stoptouts* (anklets) on heathery or muddy going, but eventually dispensed with them. (They are a classic example of the rip-off we suffer. I have a ten-year-old stock – but you try and buy these simple, cheap items now! They are not made. Instead you pay through the nose for fanciful gaiters – quite the wrong thing for walking.) Boots need to be chosen carefully for the job they are to do. An expensive winter climbing pair should not be used on acid peat-plodding. Wellies would be better for that. ('Whernside Wellies' have vibram soles.) I also use super light 'Bogtrotters'. A pound on your feet is the same as four on your back. Have you ever weighed your boots?

KITCHEN.   I used up my last two one-gallon square, squashy water carriers this trip. I have not seen them for years, nor anything so good. Nevisport gave me an 'Optimus' water-bottle which was light and water-proof, but later I replaced it with a 'Twinco' as I also used it for soaking vegetables, etc., and wanted a bigger mouth. The smallest dixi of a three-nesting set did me as cooking pot and mug, and a saucer-shaped dish did the dog and acted as a lid when I was using the dixi-lid as a cup. I had a spoon and a French 'Opinel' knife (a simple blade with no gadgets). Jam went in a large medicinal tin and all other foodstuffs were simply in polythene bags. Quarters of 'Goldilocks' scourers were ready in each parcel. I seldom fried food so avoided greasy dishes.

TOILET AND MEDICAL.   A toothbrush was my total equipment. Parcels always had toilet paper, but soap I used only when available. A comb was one luxury item. I also had a comb (another) for the dog, his lead, and a small dog towel – in self defence as we shared a tent. I carried one wound dressing, one elastic bandage, various strips of Elastoplast, a few swabs, two safety pins, a few aspirins, and the following ointments, all in tiny quantities: Whitfield's (for athlete's foot), Sulphur (sores, an-tispetic), Anusol (piles), Vasogen (for sweat rash), Flypel (anti-midge).

PHOTOGRAPHIC.   I had two Rollei 35S cameras, one for slides (using Kodachrome 25 or Kodachrome 64) with a U/V filter, one for black and white (using Kodak Plus-X, ASA125) with a yellow filter. Excellent small cameras but fragile and the servicing for their repairs, spares and parts is disgraceful. A spare cell, brush and tissues were carried.

One cloth needle, one stocking needle, plus some threads and wool, a button or two and some canoe tape, with tiny scissors, did for any running repairs. I wore an alarm watch. A jiffy can-opener, one spare boot-lace, whistle, odd bits of cordage, a bit of candle (late in the trip), some pieces of mosquito coils (early on), my log book, some stationery, stamps, etc., biro, diary, current paperback, money, cheques, Bankers Card, NTS and SYHA cards and tiny New Testament I think completes my list. It looks a great deal but my rucksack was never full, a good test. A few medical items apart, it was all used, as I knew it would be from past experience. Again I worked to a list, a habit I recommend. Copy this one if you like as something to start from. A *simple* Silva compass and a wide variety of maps were used. I had Bartholomew's new 1:100,000 maps (the old Half Inch) covering the entire route, which were excellent for showing the whole landscape. (Pennine Way guides have infuriating narrow strip maps which tell you only where to put your feet!). I'd accumulated cheap old One Inch OS maps for areas that would only be crossed this once, Nevisport provided OS 1:50 000 maps where more recent information was required (on rights-of-way for instance) and the local 'Book House' in Kirkcaldy met all my last-minute panics when parcelling. Binoculars and altimeter I sent home as they were not used enough to justify their weight. Sometimes rather missed, but . . . In the end I carried a tiny transistor for the sake of hearing some music in the evenings.

FOOD. "Some people have a foolish way of not minding, or pretending not to mind, what they eat. For my part, I mind my belly very studiously, and very carefully. . . ."

Amen to Dr Johnson. I wonder how he would stomach our plastic dehydrated stuff today. Most packet soups and meals I find quite revolting, and have simply reverted to eating as normally as possible. I do not think it even makes much weight difference. If you have to simmer something for ages you are burning up fuel weight. If you must burn fuel the end product might as well be palatable. There have been some excellent instant meals developed of late but they are prohibitively expensive. Natural is not only kindest and best, it is usually cheapest. I hoped, originally, to buy most of my food as I went along, but this presented weight problems, as many items could only be bought in quantities quite ridiculous for one person. A kilo of sugar would have lasted weeks, for instance, yet I liked a little on my apple flakes and used it in coffee. So sugar, soup, apple flakes, some dried Batchelors' vegetables, rice, pasta, potato powder, salt, coffee, tea, drinking chocolate, a home-made muesli, Knorr cubes, spices, milk powder, etc., were broken down into smaller portions and sent in parcels to be collected. Films, books, maps, toilet paper, scourers, spare poly bags, matches and other essentials were also sent in the parcels, along with a few favourite foods: Shippam's *Chicken Supreme*, Caugant *Pâté de Campagne*, Grant's *Haggis*, Moroccan *Spiced Sardines*, and John West *Kipper Fillets*. Fresh baking, vegetables and fruit were picked up whenever available, along with chocolate, nuts, biscuits, eggs, conserves, tins of meat, cheese or other lunch-time snacks. Storm stuck to his daily handful of biscuits, which he had when I picnicked, and his *Frolic* which he had when I ate at night. *Frolic* is a semi-moist complete food, in packets, a great help, the product of Pedigree Petfoods. He thrived on it. In the course of the walk he ate *my* body weight of it. I usually had tea and muesli for breakfast, sometimes with some bread and jam, but at 6 a.m. there was no great hunger. Two or three times a day I would brew and have snacks, and the main meal was kept for the evening once the tent was pitched and the day's darg done. I seldom bothered to fry or cook other than by boiling. A cube in the vegetable/pasta water made a better soup than any packet. Eggs could be boiled or poached. Tinned meats required little gas. Butter I seldom carried, nor other fats, they are messy luxuries. Simplicity was essential – and nutritious goodness. If you eat well then you can forget calories.

Many years ago, from trial and error, I wrote down a basic food list in my diary and this would be checked each morning and any shopping done.

BASIC FOOD LIST

matches	cubes	biscuits/cake
sugar	meats	tomatoes
tea	vegetables	fruit/apple flakes
coffee and/or	rice/pasta/spuds	cheese/sardines
milk	raisins	salt
bread and/or	eggs	soups
honey or jam	nuts	butter
muesli or oatmeal	chocolate	*Frolic*/dog biscuits

THE MUNROS OF ENGLAND, IRELAND AND WALES

THERE HAS BEEN a great deal of changing over the last few years due to new surveying and metrification. Even the summits may have varying names (e.g. Scafell Pikes on the Ordnance Survey maps) so in these lists common usage of heights, as listed by Bridge or Wall, is followed, and those volumes should be studied for further details. The outlining of what is a *separate mountain* is my own tentative choice but is made after many visits to all these summits and comparing the topography with Scotland's original Munros. Under this study there is no way the Glyders can be two Munros when something like Alligin is only one. Bridge applies a rule of mathematical precision, which is demeaning because it promotes everything. The Reeks in Ireland certainly merit several *separate mountains* by comparison with Scottish ridges like the Mamores or Glen Sheil (Bridge would simply promote them all). Anyone who has done all the Munros and plans to add those "Furth of Scotland" in Maxwell's resonant phrase, is well advised to climb everything to be sure. Subsidiary Tops are indented in the list below. Those marked * are not named in Wall but as someone, some time, has used names, these are given rather than leaving uninspired figures. Willie Docherty in his fabulous volumes and lists was not beyond inventing names.

ENGLAND	ft		ft
Scafell Pike	3210	Brandon Mountain	3127
Broad Crag	3054	Lugnaquillia (Wicklows)	3039
Ill Crag	3025+		
Scafell	3162	Galtymore	3018
Helvellyn	3116		
Lower Man	3033	**WALES**	
Skiddaw	3054	Snowdon (Y Wyddfa)	3560
		Crib-y-ddysgl	3496
		Crib Goch	3026
IRELAND		Glyder Fawr	3279
Carrauntoohil (Reeks)	3414	Glyder Fach	3262
Knockoughter (Tooth)*	c. 3000	Y Garn	3104
Beenkeragh	3314	Elidir Fawr	3030
Caher	3250	Tryfan	3010
N.W. Top	3200	Carnedd Llywelyn	3485
Cumeenhapeasta*	3191	Foel-grach	3196
Knockacullion	3141	Yr Elen	3152
Beerna Rua	3159	Foel-fras	3092
Lackagarrin	c. 3100	Carnedd Dafydd	3424
Cruach Mhor	3062	Penyrolewen	3211

BIBLIOGRAPHY

THIS IS ONLY a brief, selective list of books, concerning areas and themes covered in *The Groats End Walk*, but it should help further reading. Books long out of print are marked OP, and those in paperback are marked pb. Many in print have gone through several editions so I have omitted publication dates. If any book is unobtainable from booksellers, your local library will order a copy if it is in print. There are thousands of books on Lakeland and already dozens on the Pennine Way. I have given what I feel are the best or most easily found.

General (anything covering more than one country or of subject rather than regional interest)

Bartholomew: National Map Series, 1:100,000. Excellent for planning, and carrying for wider views, etc. Marks the Munros, which are covered on sheets 47–52, 54–56, 58–60. Sheets 41, 45 took me to the Borders. The Pennine Way appears on sheets 29, 35, 39, 41, 42, the Lakes on sheets 34, 38. No. 28 took me to Wales, 27, 22, 17, 13 to the Severn, and 7, 3, 1 to Lands' End.

Bell, Bozman and Fairfax-Blakeborough: *British Hills and Mountains*, Batsford, OP.

Burritt, Elihu: *A Walk from London to John o'Groats*, Sampson Low, 1864, OP.

Chadwick, N. K.: *Celtic Britain*, Thames & Hudson.

Clark, R. W. and Pyatt, E. C.: *Mountaineering in Britain*, Phoenix, OP (History).

Climber and Rambler, The, ed. Holmes McDougal (monthly climbing magazine).

Darlington, A.: *Mountains and Moorlands*, Hodder & Stoughton.

Debenham, F.: *Map Making*, Blackie, OP.

Defoe, D.: *A Tour Through the Whole Land of Great Britain*, Penguin, pb.

Docharty, W. M.: *A Selection of Some 900 British and Irish Mountain Tops*, three vols, privately printed (lists and unique panoramas) OP.

Dry Stone Walling, The British Trust for Conservation (the best on the topic).

Fitter, Fitter and Blamey: *Wild Flowers of Britain and Northern Europe*, Collins, pb.

Fox, E. W.: *2,000 Miles on Foot*, Walter Scott, OP.

Great Outdoors, The, ed. Holmes McDougal (monthly covering all aspects of walking).

Hawkes, J. and C.: *Prehistoric Britain*, Penguin, pb.

Heinzel, Fitter and Parslow: *The Birds of Britain and Europe*, Collins, Fontana, pb.

Hillaby, J.: *Journey through Britain*, Constable, Paladin, pb (A Groats End Walk).

Kyme, E. H.: *A Million and More Strides*, Hale (Durness to Dover).

Lang, T.: *Cross Country*, Hodder & Stoughton, OP (A Groats End Walk).

Langmuir, E.: *Mountain Leadership Handbook*, S.C.P.R., pb (practical and useful).

Manley, G.: *Climate and the British Scene*, Collins.

Marples, M.: *Shanks's Pony*, Country Book Club. OP (a history of walking and walkers).

Matthews, H.: *British Mammals*, Collins.

Merrill, J.: *Turn Right at Land's End*, Oxford Illustrated Press.

Millar, T. G.: *Long Distance Footpaths of England and Wales*, David & Charles.

Millward, R. and Robinson, A.: *Upland Britain*, David & Charles.

Naylor, J. and R.: *From John o' Groats to Land's End*. Caxton Publishing, OP.

Pearsall, W. H.: *Mountains and Moorlands*, Collins.

Pyatt, E. C.: *Mountains of Britain*, Batsford, OP.

Raven, J. and Walters, M.: *Mountain Flowers*, Collins.

Rolt, L. T. C.: *Thomas Telford*, Longmans, OP.

Stamp, D.: *Britain's Structure and Scenery*, Collins.

Thom, A. C.: *Megalithic Sites in Britain*, Oxford University Press.

Unwin, D. J.: *Mountain Weather for Climbers*, Cordee, pb.

Walker, A.: *The Big Walk*, Prentice-Hall, OP (the Butlin G. E. W.).

Westacott, H. D.: *The Walker's Handbook*, Penguin, pb (useful addresses, information).

Wilson, K. and Gilbert, R.: *The Big Walks*, Diadem (sumptuous coffee-table book).

Scotland

Aitken, R.: *The West Highland Way*, H.M.S.O. (guide/map-pack).

Andrew, K. M., and Thrippleton, A. A.: *The Southern Uplands*, SMC District Guide.

Bennet, D.: *Scottish Mountain Climbs*, Batsford.

—— : *Southern Highlands*, SMC District Guide (fine pictures).

Borthwick, A.: *Always a Little Further*, McKay/Smith (amusing escapades).

Boyd, E. O.: *Cross Country Walks in the West Highlands*, Oliver & Boyd, OP.

Breadalbane, Marchioness of: *The High Tops of Blackmount*, Blackwood (period piece).

Brown, H. M.: *Hamish's Mountain Walk*, Gollancz, Paladin pb. (describes the Munros).

Brown, P. H.: *Early Travellers in Scotland*, reissued Mercat Press, pb.

Cameron, A. D.: *The Caledonian Canal*, Dalton.

Corson, F. R.: *Beyond the Great Glen*, Oliver & Boyd, OP.

Crockett, W. S.: *The Scott Country*, Black, OP.

Darling, F. F. and Boyd, J. M.: *The Highlands and Islands*, Collins, Fontana pb. (an essential book).

Feacham, R. W.: *A Guide to Prehistoric Scotland*, Batsford.

Fraser, G. Macdonald: *The Steel Bonnets*, Barrie and Jenkins, Penguin pb.

Gilbert, R.: *Memorable Munros*, Cordee, pb.

Gordon, Seton: *Highways and Byways in the West Highlands*, Macmillan, OP.

—— : *Highways and Byways in the Central Highlands*, Macmillan, OP.

Grant, I. F.: *Highland Folkways*, Routledge, pb.

Grant, W.: *Tweeddale*, Oliver & Boyd, OP.

—— : *The Call of the Pentlands*, Grant, OP.

Haldane, A. R. B.: *The Drove Roads of Scotland*, Nelson.

—— : *New Ways through the Glen*, Nelson (military roads, etc.).

Holliday, F.: *The Wildlife of Scotland*, Methuen (essays and sumptuous pictures).

Humble, B. H.: *On Scottish Hills*, Chapman & Hall, OP. (pictorial/ autobiographical).

Johnson and Boswell: *A Journey to the Western Islands of Scotland* and *The Journal of a Tour in the Hebrides* (ed. R. W. Chapman), Oxford Paperbacks.

Kilgour, W. T.: *Twenty Years on Ben Nevis*, Gardner, OP (observatory story).

Lang, J.: *A Land of Romance*, OP (Borders).

Lang, T. (ed.): *The Border Counties*, Hodder & Stoughton.

Lindsay, M.: *The Discovery of Scotland*, Hale (accounts of early travellers, etc.).

—— : *The Eye is Delighted*, Hale (literary travellers' accounts).

Linklater, E.: *The Prince in the Heather*, Hodder & Stoughton, Panther pb.

Lister, J. A.: *The Scottish Highlands*, Bartholomew (illustrated gazetteer).

Lochhead, M.: *Portrait of the Scott Country*, Hale.

MacCulloch, D. G.: *Romantic Lochaber, Arisaig and Morar*, Chambers, OP.

MacInnes, H.: *West Highland Walks* (2 vols), Hodder & Stoughton.

Mackenzie, Osgood: *A Hundred Years in the Highlands*, Bles, OP.

McLaren, M.: *The Shell Guide to Scotland*, Ebury Press (excellent).

MacNally, L.: *The Year of the Red Deer*, Dent.

—— : *Highland Deer Forest*, Dent.

Macrow, B.: *Kintail Scrapbook*, Oliver & Boyd, OP.

Mack, J. L.: *The Border Line*, Oliver & Boyd, OP.

Maxwell, H.: *The Story of the Tweed*, Nisbet, OP.

Moir, D. G.: *Pentland Walks*, Bartholomew, pb.

—— : *Scottish Hill Tracks* (2 vols), Bartholomew, pb.

Mould, D. D. C. P.: *The Roads from the Isles*, Oliver & Boyd, OP.

Munro's Tables – and Tables of Lesser Heights, New Edition 1981, ed. Donaldson and Brown.

Munro, Neil: *The New Road* and *John Splendid*, Blackwood (two historical novels).

Murray, W. H.: *Mountaineering in Scotland*, Diadem (classic).

—— : *Undiscovered Scotland*, Diadem.

—— : *Companion Guide to the West Highlands*, Collins (thorough).

—— : *The Scottish Highlands*, SMC (covers many topics).

Nethersole-Thompson, D.: *Highland Birds*, H.I.D.B., pb.

Nicolaisen, W. F. H.: *Scottish Place Names*, Batsford.
Plumb, C.: *Walking in the Grampians*, Maclehose, OP.
Prebble, J.: *The Highland Clearances*, Penguin, pb.
Price, R. J.: *Highland Landforms*, H.I.D.B., pb.
Simpson, W. D.: *Portrait of the Highlands*, Hale.
Stephen, D.: *Highland Animals*, H.I.D.B., pb.
Steven, C.: *The Story of Scotland's Hills*, Hale (history).
—— *The Central Highlands*, SMC District Guide.
—— : *The Straths and Glens of Scotland*, Hale.
Strang, T.: *The Northern Highlands*, SMC District Guide.
Taylor, W.: *The Military Roads in Scotland*, David & Charles.
Tranter, N.: *Portrait of the Border Country*, Hale (best of recent titles).
Wainwright, A.: *Scottish Mountain Drawings* (6 vols), Westmorland Gazette.
Weir, T.: *Highland Days*, Cassell, OP (his early wanderings).
—— : *The Western Highlands*, Batsford (descriptive).
—— : *Tom Weir's Scotland*, Wright.

England: Borders, Lakes, Pennines

Berry, G.: *Across Northern* [English] *Hills*, Bartholomew (illustrated gazetteer).
Bogg, E.: *A Thousand Miles of Wandering in the Border Country*, OP.
Bonser, K. J.: *The Drovers*, Macmillan.
Bradley, A. G.: *Highways and Byways in the Lake District*, Macmillan, OP.
Breeze, D. J. and Dobson, B.: *Hadrian's Wall*, Pelican, pb.
Bridge, G.: *The Mountains of England and Wales*, Gaston/West Col (tables).
Carruthers, F. J.: *Love of the Lake Country*, Hale.
Collingwood, W. G.: *Lake District History*, Kendal, OP.
Countryside Commission, The: *Lake District National Park*, H.M.S.O., pb.
Duerdon, N.: *Portrait of the Dales*, Hale.
Edwards, K. C.: *The Peak District*, Collins.
Forestry Commission, The: *The Border*, H.M.S.O., pb.
Fraser, M.: *Companion into Lakeland*, Methuen, OP.
Gower, E.: *Exploring the Yorkshire Dales*, Dalesman, pb.
Griffin, A. H.: *Long Days in the Hills*, Hale.
—— : *Freeman of the Hills*, Hale (all the 2,000ers).
—— : *In Mountain Lakeland*, Guardian Press.
Hartley, M. and Ingilby, J.: *The Yorkshire Dales*, Dent, Aldine pb.
Hill, H.: *Freedom to Roam*, Moorland Publishing.
Lefebure, M.: *Cumberland Heritage*, Gollancz.
—— : *The English Lake District*, Batsford.
Mee, A.: *The Lake Counties* (King's England series), Hodder & Stoughton, OP.
Millward, R. and Robinson, A.: *The Lake District*, Eyre & Spottiswoode.
—— : *The Peak District*, Eyre Methuen.

Mitchell, W. R.: *Haworth and the Brontës*, Dalesman, pb.
—— : *Men of Lakeland*, OP.
Nicholson, N.: *The Lakers*, Hale (the poets and early visitors).
—— : *The Lakes*, Hale, pb (descriptive).
—— : *The Lake District*, Penguin, pb (anthology of prose and verse).
Norway, A. H.: *Highways and Byways of Yorkshire*, Macmillan, OP.
Ordnance Survey, The: *The English Lakes*, 1:25,000 Outdoor Leisure Maps, 4 sheets, Nos. 4, 5, 6, 7 also cover parts of the Pennine Way; *The Three Peaks*, No. 2, *Malham and Upper Wharfedale*, No. 10, *South Pennines*, No. 18, *The Dark Peak*, No. 1.
Parker, J.: *Cumbria*, Bartholomew (illustrated gazetteer).
Pearsall, W. E. and Pennington, W.: *The Lake District*, Collins.
Peel, J. H. B.: *Along the Pennine Way*, David & Charles (the best on the subject).
Poucher, W. A.: *The Lakeland Peaks*, Constable.
—— : *The Peak and the Pennines*, Constable.
Raistrick, A.: *Green Roads of the Mid-Pennines*, Moorland, pb.
—— : *The Pennine Walls*, Dalesman, pb.
Ramblers' Cheviot, Ramblers' Association, pb.
Redfern, R. A.: *Portrait of the Pennines*, Hale.
Symond, H. H.: *Walking in the Lake District*, Maclehose, OP.
Unsworth, W.: *The High Fells of Lakeland*, Hale.
Wainwright, A.: *Pennine Way Companion*, Westmorland Gazette.
—— : *A Pictorial Guide to the Lakeland Fells* (7 vols), Westmorland Gazette.
Walton, J. (ed.): *The Border* (Forest Park Guide), H.M.S.O., pb.
Wood, G. B.: *The North Country* (Regions of Britain), Hale.
Wordsworth, Dorothy: *Journals*, many editions, and in pb.
Wright, C. J.: *A Guide to the Pennine Way*, Constable.
Wright, G.: *The Yorkshire Dales*, David & Charles.
Wright, N.: *English Mountain Summits*, Hale.

Ireland

A.A. Illustrated Road Book of Ireland, The, 1966, OP.
Barrington, T. J.: *Discovering Kerry*, Blackwater (comprehensive).
Barrow, L.: *Irish Round Towers*, Academy Press (large, comprehensive – also a Jarrold booklet).
Craig, M. and Knight of Glin: *Ireland Observed*, Mercier (illustrated gazetteer).
Curtis, E.: *A History of Ireland*, Methuen, pb.
de Breffny, B. and Mott, G.: *Castles of Ireland*, Thames & Hudson.
—— : *The Churches and Abbeys of Ireland*. Thames & Hudson.
—— : *The Land of Ireland*, Thames & Hudson (magnificent pictures).

Harbison, P.: *Guide to the National Monuments of Ireland*, Gill & Macmillan, pb (comprehensive).

Hayward, R.: *In the Kingdom of Kerry*, Dundalgan Press.

———: *Munster and the City of Cork*, Phoenix.

———: *Leinster and the City of Dublin*, Barker (all good reading and nice drawings).

Irish Ramblers' Club: *Dublin and Wicklow Mountains* (access routes), pb.

Irish Walk Guides, 6 small vols, general editor J. Lynam, Gill & Macmillan, pb (vols 1, 5, 6 cover the Munros).

Jennett, S.: *Munster*, Faber.

Killanin, Lord and Duignan, M. V.: *Shell Guide to Ireland*, Ebury Press (excellent).

Lehane, B.: *The Companion Guide to Ireland*, Collins.

MacLiammoir, Michael: *Ireland*, Thames & Hudson (superb pictures).

Maxwell, C.: *The Stranger in Ireland*, Cape (travellers).

Mould, D. D. C. P.: *The Mountains of Ireland*, Batsford.

———: *The Monasteries of Ireland*, Batsford.

———: *Ireland From the Air*, David & Charles.

Mulholland, H.: *Guide to Eire's 3000-foot Mountains*, Mulholland, Wigan (new pb guide, very useful).

O'Connor, F.: *Leinster, Munster and Connacht*, Country Books, Hale.

O'Connell,: *The Meaning of Irish Place Names*, Blackstaff Press, pb.

Ordnance Survey (Irish): Half Inch, map nos 16, 18, 20, 22 cover the Munros, and I also used 19 and 21. One Inch: *Wicklow District*; *Killarney District*.

Praeger, R. L.: *The Way That I Went*, various editions (classic).

———: *The Natural History of Ireland*, Collins.

Severin, T.: *The Brendan Voyage*, Hutchinson, Arrow pb.

Wall, W. C.: *Mountaineering in Ireland*, F.M.C.I., pb (survey and lists).

Wallace, M.: *A Short History of Ireland*, David & Charles.

Warner, P.: *A Visitors Guide to the Comeragh Mountains*, Blackstaff, pb.

Whittow, J. B.: *Geology and Scenery in Ireland*, Pelican, pb.

Woodham-Smith, C.: *The Great Hunger*, Hamilton, pb (history of famine years).

Wales

Barber, C.: *Walks in the Brecon Beacons*, Pridgeon (Ross-on-Wye), pb.

Beezley, E., and Howell, P.: *Companion Guide to North Wales*, Collins.

Borrow, G.: *Wild Wales*, many editions.

Bowen, E. G. (ed.): *Wales—A Physical, Historical and Regional Geography*, Methuen.

Bradley, A. G.: *Highways and Byways in North Wales*, Macmillan, OP.

———: *Highways and Byways in South Wales*, Macmillan, OP.

———: *In Praise of North Wales*, Methuen, OP.

Bridge, G.: *The Mountains of England and Wales*, Gaston/West Col (tables).

Carr, H. R. C. and Lister, G. A.: *The Mountains of Snowdonia*, OP (general survey).

Condry, W. M.: *The Snowdonia National Park*, Collins.

——: *Exploring Wales*, Faber, pb.

Countryside Commission, The: *The Brecon Beacons* (National Park guide), H.M.S.O., pb.

——: *Snowdonia National Park*, H.M.S.O., pb (an excellent series).

Davies, D.: *Welsh Place-names and their Meanings*, Cambrian News, pb.

Edwards, G. R.: *Snowdonia National Park*, H.M.S.O., pb.

Edwards, T.: *The Face of Wales*, Batsford, OP.

Firbank, T.: *I Bought a Mountain*, New English Library, pb.

Forestry Commission, The: *The Cambrian Forests*, H.M.S.O., pb.

Godwin, F. and Toulson, S.: *The Drover's Roads of Wales*, Wildwood House, pb.

Hughes, C.: *Portrait of Snowdonia*, Hale.

Jones, R.: *Exploring the Wye Valley and Forest of Dean*, Barton, pb.

Kilvert, F.: *Kilvert's Diary* (ed. W. Plomer), Penguin, pb.

King, D. J. C.: *Castle and Abbeys of Wales*, H.M.S.O., pb.

Mason, E. J.: *Portrait of the Brecon Beacons*, Hale.

Millward, R. and Robinson, A.: *Landscapes of North Wales*, David & Charles.

Ordnance Survey, The: *Snowdonia National Park*, 1:25000 Outdoor Leisure Maps, 5 sheets, Nos. 15, 16, 21, 20, 32 (covers from the north coast down to Machynlleth).

——: Brecon Beacons, 1:25000 Outdoor Leisure Maps, 3 sheets, Nos. 11, 12, 13.

Palmer, W. T.: *The Splendour of Wales*, Harrap, OP.

Poucher, W. A.: *The Welsh Peaks*, Constable.

Ransome-Wallis, P.: *Snowdon Mountain Railway*, Ian Allan, pb.

Red Guide: *The Wye Valley*, Ward Lock.

Reid, A.: *The Castles of Wales*, Letts, pb.

Rowland, E. G.: *Hill Walking in Snowdonia*, Cidron Press, pb (useful).

Senior, M.: *Portrait of North Wales*, Hale.

Styles, S.: *The Mountains of North Wales*, Gollancz (each range described).

Thomas, R.: *South Wales*, Bartholomew.

Vaughan-Thomas, W. and Llewllyn, A.: *Shell Guide to Wales*, Michael Joseph (excellent).

Wales Tourist Board, The: *A Glimpse of the Past*, pb (quarries, mines, mills, museums, etc.).

Wright, C. J.: *Offa's Dyke Path*, Constable.

Young, Sutton and Noyce: *Snowdon Biography*, Dent, OP.

England: South-west

Barton, R. H.: *Cornwall's Structure and Scenery*, Tor Mark Press, pb.

Bates, D.: *The Companion Guide to Devon and Cornwall*, Collins.

Berry, C.: *Portrait of Cornwall*, Hale.

Bradley, A. G.: *Exmoor Memories*, Methuen, OP.

Countryside Commission, The: *Exmoor National Park*, H.M.S.O., pb.

du Maurier, D.: *Vanishing Cornwall*, Gollancz, Penguin pb.

Delderfield, E. R.: *The Lynmouth Flood Disaster*, E.R.D. Publications, pb.

Elkin, T.: *Mendip Walks*, Mendip Publishing, pb.

Hockin, J. R. A.: *Walking in Cornwall*, Maclehose, OP.

Hutton, E.: *Highways and Byways of Somerset*, Macmillan, OP.

Kay-Robinson, D.: *Devon and Cornwall*, Bartholomew.

Mason, J. H. N.: *West Country Walks and Legends*, Granada, pb.

Meynell, L.: *Exmoor* (Regional Books), Hale, OP.

Millward, R. and Robinson, A.: *The South-West Peninsula*, Macmillan.

Norway, A. H.: *Highways and Byways in Devon and Cornwall*, Macmillan, OP.

Peel, J. H. B.: *Portrait of Exmoor*, Hale.

——: *Portrait of the Severn*, Hale.

Pyatt, E. C.: *Cornwall Coast Path*, H.M.S.O., pb.

Richards, M.: *North Cornwall, Exploring the Coastal Footpath*, Thornhill Press, pb (mainly drawings).

St. Leger-Gordon, D.: *Portrait of Devon*, Hale.

South-West Way Association Complete Guide to the Coastal Path, pb (produced annually).

Turner, M. L.: *Somerset* (County Books), Hale.

Waite, V.: *Portrait of the Quantocks*, Hale.

Williams, H. V.: *Cornwall's Old Mines*, Tor Mark Press, pb.

INDEX OF MAJOR PHYSICAL FEATURES, TOWNS, ETC.